Ancient Pathways
and
Hidden Pursuits

Ancient Pathways
and
Hidden Pursuits

*Religion, Morals, and Magic
in the Ancient World*

GEORG LUCK

Ann Arbor

THE UNIVERSITY OF MICHIGAN PRESS

Copyright © by the University of Michigan 2000
All rights reserved
Published in the United States of America by
The University of Michigan Press
Manufactured in the United States of America
♾ Printed on acid-free paper

2003   2002   2001   2000   4   3   2   1

A CIP catalog record for this book is available from the British Library.

Library of Congress Cataloging-in-Publication Data

Luck, Georg, 1926–
    Ancient pathways and hidden pursuits : religion, morals, and magic
in the ancient world / Georg Luck.
        p.   cm.
    Includes bibliographical references and index.
    ISBN 0-472-10790-9 (cloth : alk. paper)
    1. Occultism—Greece—History—Sources.   2. Occultism—Rome—
History—Sources.   3. Civilization, Classical—Sources.   I. Title.
BF1421.L83   1999
133'.0938—dc21
                                                              99-45162
                                                                   CIP

For Annina, Hans, and Stephanie

Preface

It is impossible to understand Greek and Roman culture without paying attention to its various forms of religious experience and what is usually called "superstition." Magic doctrines and occult practices are endlessly fascinating, because they reveal so much that is human, all-too-human, about people. To ignore these dark sides and only to see the luminous qualities of ancient thought would be a mistake.

To help the general reader understand the extraordinary complexity of occult science in antiquity, I wrote *Arcana Mundi* (Baltimore: Johns Hopkins University Press, 1985), which has since appeared in German, Spanish, and Italian. The most comprehensive edition, published by Mondadori under the auspices of the Fondazione Lorenzo Valla, includes the original texts and offers additional commentaries; volume 1 appeared in 1997, volume 2 in 1999.

This collection of articles and reviews written over the last four decades may be useful as a companion volume to *Arcana Mundi*. Almost all of them have been published before; those that originally appeared in German have been translated into English by the author. Very few changes have been made.

There has been an almost dramatic revival of interest in ancient magic during the last ten or twenty years, largely due, I think, to the English translation of the *Greek Magical Papyri*, with commentaries and an excellent introduction, edited by H.D. Betz (Chicago, 1992; 2d ed.). I hope that at least some of the pieces in *Ancient Pathways and Hidden Pursuits* will be helpful in taking the reader back to the sources where work inevitably must begin.

In recent years, there has also been a good deal of important research on the use of hallucinogenic drugs in magic and religion. Among the many psychotropic substances known today, there are quite a few that could explain magical phenomena, and others that may produce religious experiences if they are applied in an appropriate manner. For the second group, the term *entheogens* has been proposed. Naturally, a sharp distinction between the two is difficult, just as it is difficult to differentiate clearly between religion and magic. A great deal can be learned from *Entheogens and the Future of Religion* (San Francisco, 1997), edited by Robert Forte, with contributions by Albert Hofmann, R. Gordon Wasson, and others.

As I returned once more to the material collected in the following pages, it struck me that hallucinations may very often be at the basis of magical experiences. Another key to occult phenomena may be hypnotism and suggestion, techniques that were almost certainly known to the priests of ancient Egypt and Greece and apparently never quite forgotten in the West. These two explanations were not as evident to me at the time I wrote the following pieces, but I would urge the reader today to keep them in mind.

Sincere thanks are due to the University of Michigan Press, its referees, and its editors, especially Dr. Ellen Bauerle, Christina Milton, and Jill Butler Wilson, for having undertaken the publication of pieces that have been scattered in publications of different countries over many years, and for having done a superb editing job. I am also very grateful to Ludwig Koenen for his help and encouragement. My children to whom this book is dedicated, have helped me with the *Indices*. It is my hope that these pieces, placed next to each other in a more or less logical order, will provide a new focus and a modest, but perhaps not unwelcome, frame of reference.

Baltimore, September 1999   Georg Luck

Acknowledgments

Grateful acknowledgment is made to the following publishers and editors for permission to reprint previously published materials, either in the original version or in translation.

C.H. Becksche Verlagsbuchhandlung, München, and Professor Ernst Vogt. Reviews of E.R. Dodds, *The Greeks and the Irrational, Gnomon* 25 (1953): 361–67 and P. Rabbow, *Seelenführung, Gnomon* 28 (1956): 268–71.

Latomus, Bruxelles, and Professor Jacqueline Dumortier-Bibauw. "König Midas und die Orphischen Mysterien," in *Hommages à Marcel Renard,* vol. 2, Collection Latomus 102 (1969), 470–77.

Johns Hopkins University Press, Baltimore and London. "Virgil and the Mystery Religions," *AJP* 94 (1973): 147–66; "Panaetius and Menander," *AJP* 96 (1975): 256–68; "On Cicero, *De Fato* 5," *AJP* 99 (1978): 155–58.

Universitätsverlag C. Winter, Heidelberg. "Epikur und seine Götter," *Gymnasium* 67 (1960): 308–15.

Professor Aires Augusto Nascimento, Lisboa. "Was Lucretius Really Mad?" *Euphrosyne,* n.s., 16 (1988): 289–94; "Two Predictions of the End of Paganism," *Euphrosyne,* n.s., 14 (1986): 153–56.

Verlag Paul Haupt, Bern. "Die Musen in der römischen Dichtung," in *Horizonte der Humanitas: Festschrift für Walter Wili* (1960), 77–89.

Verlag H. Bouvier & Co., Bonn. "Zur Geschichte des Begriffs *sapientia,*" *Archiv für Begriffsgeschichte* 9 (1964): 203–15.

President and Fellows of Harvard College, Cambridge, Massachusetts. "Studia Divina in Vita Humana," *Harvard Theological Review* 49 (1956): 207–18; "Palladas: Christian or Pagan?" *Studies in Honor of Werner Jaeger,* Harvard Studies in Classical Philology 63 (1958), 455–68.

Patrick Cramer, Editeur, Geneva, and Father H.-D. Saffrey. "A Stoic Cosmogony in Manilius," in *Mémorial André-Jean Festugière,* 29–32 (1984).

Oxford University Press, New York, and Professor J. Neusner. "Theurgy and Forms of Worship in Neoplatonism," in *Religion, Science and Magic,* 185–225 (1989).

Verlag Königshausen & Neumann, Würzburg, and Professor Christian-Friedrich Collatz et al. "The 'Way Out': Philological Notes on the Transfiguration of Jesus," in *Dissertatiunculae criticae, Studies in Honor of Günther-Christian Hansen*, 311–21 (1998).

Franz-Joseph Dölger Institut, Bonn, and Professor Ernst Dassmann. "Die Form der suetonischen Biographie und die frühen Heiligenviten," in *Mullus*, Jahrbuch für Antike und Christentum, Ergänzungsband 1 (1964), 230–41 (Studies in Honor of Theodor Klauser); "Humor," in *Realenzyklopädie für Antike und Christentum*, vol. 16 (1992), cols. 753–73.

Professor Everett Ferguson, Abilene, Texas. "The Doctrine of Salvation in the Hermetic Writings," *Second Century* 8 (1991): 31–41.

Editorial Gredos, S.A., Madrid. "Recent Work on Ancient Magic," in *Arcana Mundi*, by Georg Luck, trans. Elena Gallego Moya and Miguel E. Pérez Molina, 9–28 (1995).

The Philadelphia Patristic Foundation, Cambridge, Massachusetts, and Professor Andreas Spira. "Notes on the *Vita Macrinae* of Gregory of Nyssa," in *The Biographical Works of Gregory of Nyssa*, 21–32 (1984).

Contents

Review of E.R. Dodds, *The Greeks and the Irrational*

For a long time, it was fashionable to consider Greek civilization as essentially rational, until, in the last century, scholars such as J.J. Bachofen and E. Rohde taught us to see certain disturbing phenomena. It is no longer possible to believe in a clear progress from μῦϑος to λόγος. Today, we are able to observe the hidden impulses that shaped religious consciousness, as well as its orgiastic exuberance. Modern scholars have become interested in the manifold expressions of personal religion and the psychological significance of so-called superstitions.

Following the example of A.D. Nock and A.-J. Festugière, E.R. Dodds has written a reliable guidebook through a zone which borders on philosophy, religion, and the occult, the zone in which the "irrational" manifests itself. From a wealth of acute observations, he cautiously deduces some principles. His vast learning extends beyond Greek and Roman sources into the fields of anthropology and psychoanalysis. His sense for the characteristic details never loses touch with real life.

The first chapter is an interpretation of Agamemnon (*Il*.19.86ff.) which is designed to justify his behavior toward Achilles. Homer and his audience clearly believed that all human behavior is controlled by inexplicable powers which are embodied in the concept of ἄτη.

Even if one admits that in many passages (*Il*.19.137ff.; 9.119f.; 1.412; etc.) we find only a poetic façon de parler, we must ask how such expressions became possible. In the *Iliad*, for instance, ἄτη always seems to indicate a sudden clouding over of human consciousness through the intrusion of supernatural powers, even though there is no actual guilt. Liddell and Scott inform us that ἄτη is mostly sent as the punishment of "guilty rashness," but this is not true for the *Iliad*.

Just like ἄτη, μένος may signify the intrusion of a divine power into the human soul, producing an enigmatic intensification of the ϑυμός. It is therefore not a purely physical force but a psychological state. M.P.

Nilsson (*Arch. für Religionswiss.* 1924, pp. 363ff.) has explained this sudden change by an "extraordinary psychic instability" of the Homeric heroes. On the other hand, a careful analysis of the meaning of ψυχή and θυμός in Homer (W. Marg, *Der Charakter in der Sprache der frühgriechischen Dichtung* [1938], 43ff.) has established that the poet, lacking a proper word for "soul" or "personality," objectifies human impulses ("Verdinglichung der Triebe," Dodds 16).

Homer often describes a psychological feature as an intellectual achievement (οἶδεν πολεμήϊα ἔργα, etc.). This may be the reason why certain experiences which do not fit into this rational framework of reference were explained as an extrapersonal influence. An important issue was raised by Werner Jaeger (*Paideia* 1:31ff.). He realized how strongly Homeric heroes are motivated by τιμή. This could mean that ἄτη is the expression of an intolerable tension between an individual's impulse to act in a certain way and the standards of society. Borrowing an anthropological term, Dodds calls the culture reflected in Homer's epics a "shame culture."

In the late archaic and the early classical periods the experience of irrational forces takes on new forms. The painful awareness of human helplessness, ἀμηχανία, finds a peculiar expression in the complaint about the "envy of the gods," as we find it in Solon, Aeschylus, and Herodotus. Sometimes, this φθόνος is interpreted in a moralizing spirit as νέμεσις ("righteous indignation," Dodds 31). If the individual who committed a crime escapes punishment, the curse is transmitted to his descendants. Zeus, as the embodiment of cosmic justice, becomes a blind instrument of vengeance. Thus, the Greeks of the archaic period are burdened by the fear that they might become innocent, unwitting victims of ἄτη (which now takes on the meaning of "punishment" or "doom"). The world is populated by demons which may be ἀλάστορες—tools or executioners of the deity, as described by Aeschylus—or projections of special events such as famine or epidemics; they also may be demons of destiny.[1]

How can the transition from the Homeric "shame culture" to the "guilt culture" of the archaic period be explained? Economic changes may have played a role, but someone familiar with pyschoanalysis may find the main reason in the "discomfort" (Dodds 47) which grew out of the protest against the absolute authority of the "paterfamilias" οἴκοιο ἄναξ in the archaic clan system. The subconscious resistance against family ties

---

1. W. Theiler shows in his notes on Marcus Aurelius 2.13 ([Zurich, 1951], 309f.) how the concept of the ἔνδον δαίμων reappears in late Greek thought.

was transferred to Zeus, the great Olympian father figure, and his whole dynasty. As Dodds himself admits, this theory does not explain everything; it fails to explain, for instance, the grandiose passages in the choral lyric of Attic tragedy which express this feeling of guilt.

Under the heading "The Blessings of Madness," Dodds then discusses a series of abnormal psychological states which have had a profound influence on Greek culture. He uses some passages in Plato's *Phaedrus* (244A–245A, 265B) as a starting point. In these passages, Socrates distinguishes four kinds of "divine madness": the prophetic one sent by Apollo, the "telestic" one stirred up by Dionysus, the poetic one inspired by the Muses, and the erotic madness caused by Aphrodite and Eros.

First, Dodds rejects (conclusively, it would seem) the view, often repeated after Rohde expressed it, that prophetic madness was unknown in Greece before the arrival of Dionysus. The Dionysiac μανία is group-oriented; the Apollonian μανία serves to foretell the future through a medium; both are quite different. Moreover, ecstatic prophecy was practiced at least since the eleventh century in Asia Minor, Apollo's original home (see Wilamowitz, *Glaube der Hellenen*, 1:324ff.). The ἐνθουσιασμός of the Pythia[2] is best described in modern terms as "autosuggestive trance" (Dodds 70ff.). The ritual preceding it has magical meaning; the theory of the mephitic vapors must be abandoned.

Dodds thus revives the discussion of these rather complex and ultimately perhaps insoluble problems. It seems to me that he interprets the Pythia's ἐνθουσιασμός with deeper psychological insight than Amandry (*La mantique apollinienne à Delphes* [1950], 234f.), who maintains that the Pythia entered not a stage of pathological trance but only a state of heightened emotional excitability, and who declared that all other theories were based on a misunderstanding of the passages in Plato. Other scholars such as Ph. E. Legrand (*REG* 1951, pp. 296ff.) and H. Berve (*Gnomon* 1952, pp. 8f.) agreed with Amandry, but the testimonies collected from Plutarch (*Amator.* 18.763A, 16.759A/B) by R. Flacelière (*REA* 1950, pp. 309f.) seem to confirm what Dodds (70ff., 90ff.) suggests; his view is also supported by W.K.C. Guthrie (*Cl. Rev.* 1952, pp. 42f.) with solid arguments.

---

2. In spite of Plut. *De Pyth. or.* 22.405C and Ael. Arist. *Or.* 45 (2:11 Dind.), there were priestesses chosen from aristocratic families even under the emperors; see Amandry, *Mant. Apoll.*, 116 n. 2. This seems to have been the rule in the archaic and classical periods; cf. the beginning of Aesch. *Eum.* and Eur. *Ion* 1323 (H. Berve, *Gnomon* 1952, p. 10).

In his discussion of the Dionysiac μανία, Dodds follows I. Linforth (*Univ. of Calif. Publ. in Class. Philol.* 1946). It is cathartic in a psychological sense; it liberates the soul; it leads from the routine of everyday life into ἔκστασις. The corybantic rites are comparable. We know from Aristides Quintilianus (*De mus.* p. 42 Jahn) that ἐνθουσιασμοί could have a damaging effect (see A.D. Nock, *AJA* 1946, p. 155).

Dodds' interpretation of the poetic μανία is particularly enlightening. The epic poet asks the Muse to teach him things past, just as the seer asks the god to illuminate the future for him. When Pindar (fr. 150 S. = 137 B.) asks the Muse μαντεύεο, Μοῖσα, προφατεύσω δ'ἐγώ, he sees himself as the προφήτης,[3] i.e., the interpreter or translator of the Muse's message. The concept of the "mad" poet is not found before Democritus (frs. 17, 18). In Dodds' opinion (82), this is a secondary development, influenced by the cult of Dionysus. But since Dodds himself points out the analogy between the Delphic oracle and the nature of poetic inspiration, one might also consider the possibility that the Delphic ritual helped shape the whole concept of the poet inspired by a Muse.

Dodds then deals with the ways in which Greeks experienced and interpreted their dreams. He distinguishes different types of dreams, for example, significant ones and indifferent ones (the well-known allegory in *Od.* 19.56off.). Among the significant ones, he pays special attention to the "dream revelation" χρηματισμός which, to him, is the model of a "culture-pattern dream" (108 and passim).

A fairly large number of votive inscriptions from the Hellenistic and the imperial ages confirm the literary testimonies. Several techniques were available to produce revelations in dreams. The most important—and perhaps the oldest—of these techniques seems to be incubation. With admirable psychological insight, Dodds describes the typical scenario of a miraculous cure at Epidaurus, and he shows in what peculiar ways individual dreams and contemporary religious tendencies influence each other. Phenomena related to dreams, such as visions and hallucinations, are illuminated by three classic examples: Hesiod and the Muses;

---

3. The remarks of A.S.F. Gow on Theocr. 22.116f., 16.29 (Cambridge, 1950) are excellent. In the curious poem *Anth. Pal.* 14.1 (see Nock, *AJA* 1946, p. 154; Bousquet, *REG* 1951, pp. 469f.), Pythagoras calls his disciples Πιερίδων ὑποφή-τορας. This includes not only the students of the καλὰ μαθήματα but also the students of physics. Pythagoras himself is addressed as "Heliconian offspring of the Muses." This seems to grow out of the epic tradition described by Dodds (8of.).

Philippides and Pan; Pindar and the Magna Mater. Dodds plausibly suggests that these experiences were due to the solitude and sublimity of Greek landscape. Thus Dodds opens, as it were, a back door to beautiful legends that were often dismissed by "enlightened" scholars.

At the beginning of the classical period a new force modifies the Greek worldview. It is different from the older concepts of the immortality of the soul and its identity with what we call "personality." Now body and soul are seen as an antithesis, emphasized by the belief in occult forces of divine origin located in the human soul and illustrated by a series of miracle workers ἰατρομάντεις, such as Abaris, Aristeas, Hermotimus, Epimenides. In an important article (*Hermes* 1937, pp. 137ff.), K. Meuli had shown the relationship of these new currents to shamanism, as it was practiced among the Thracians and the Scyths and as it is still practiced in Siberia and elsewhere. Dodds confirms the value of this theory by drawing brilliant portraits of Pythagoras, Empedocles, and Orpheus.

As far as Orphism is concerned, he resigns himself, following the example of A.-J. Festugière (*Revue Biblique* 1935, pp. 372ff.; *REG* 1936, pp. 306ff.) and I. Linforth (*The Arts of Orpheus* [1941]) to *docta ignorantia*. His survey (147f. with substantial notes) demonstrates clearly the skepticism of modern scholarship. K. Ziegler, in his article "Orphische Dichtung" in *RE*, is more optimistic.

The shamanistic thesis, however, does not fully explain the religious needs which were satisfied by the doctrine of reincarnation. Therefore, two points the author makes must be considered carefully: (1) reincarnation reconciles the problem of undeserved grief with the late archaic concept of a just deity; (2) it explains the feelings of guilt which Dodds considers the main characteristic of that generation.

Between the lifetimes of Aeschylus and Plato the chasm between popular religion and the beliefs of the educated classes broadened more and more. The "inherited conglomerate," as Dodds, following Gilbert Murray, calls the mass of religious experiences which accumulated from one generation to the next, was exposed to a series of attacks. This did not begin with the Sophists; even before them Hecataeus, Xenophanes, and Heraclitus expressed their doubts with all the vigor of Ionian ἱστορία. Their influence should not be overestimated; the Sophists who introduced the antithesis between νόμος and φύσις into ethics found more resonance. Protagoras' search for an "art of living" in the best sense of the word *living* reminds one of Socrates' principles. They both believe that virtue can be taught; they both would like to dispose of the πάθη by dialectical conjuring tricks. Euripides, on the other hand, expressed in poetry the naked flame of passion and the helplessness of the intellect.[4] His doubts as to whether a rational way of life is possible are formulated incisively in the *Bacchae*, a tragedy which reflects not only an age of enlightenment but the reaction against it. This reaction culminated just then in the attacks on Anaxagoras, Diagoras, Socrates, and possibly Euripides himself (Satyrus *Vit. Eur.* fr. 39, col. 10), who were formally accused of atheism. What brought about this dark cloud of fanaticism hanging over an age that seems so enlightened? Did mystic charlatans who saw their influence fade excite the instincts of the populace? Did a wave of hysteria roll through a country worn out by wars? Or was there a fear that the new rationalism might erode the valuable moral legacy of the inherited conglomerate along with its more primitive layers?

In his own way, Plato (see "Plato, the Irrational Soul, and the Inherited Conglomerate," Dodds 207–35) sought to save the values of the religious tradition. In the course of his life, he changed the Socratic rationalism of his youth by expanding it metaphysically under the influence of Pythagoreans in the West, that is, by identifying the occult, divine self with the rational Socratic ψυχή (Dodds 210). In the *Phaedo* (67A, 66C, 94C; see Festugière, *Rev. Philol.* 1948, p. 101), he explains this identification: only when the soul is freed from the body can it return to its divine existence.

When this answer no longer satisfied Plato's searching mind, he saw the problem of evil as a psychological conflict (στάσις), without abandoning the idea of a transcendent self. In the *Timaeus* he connects it (as the δαίμων) with another, mortal self. His effort to purify the "inherited conglomerate" can be seen most clearly in the *Nomoi*, where he bases the belief in gods, their πρόνοια, and fairness logically, legally, and pedagogically in the constitution ruled by his laws.

In the time period between the foundation of the Lyceum and the end of the third century B.C. Greek rationalism achieves its most brilliant results. This is an age that delights in discoveries and experiments. It no longer recognizes tradition as a legacy, as a commitment; it simply uses it for its own purposes (Dodds 237). Thus, Stoicism is able to tie its psychological constructions to the naïve intellectualism of the fifth century; Posidonius' protest (M. Pohlenz, *Die Stoa*, 1:89ff.) was in vain. In analogy to its rational ethical doctrine which aims at ἀταραξία, there is a kind of

---

4. On Eur. *Hipp.* 375ff. as a criticism of Socrates see B. Snell, *Philologus* 97, pp. 125ff.

rational religion whose skepticism colors in many variations funeral inscriptions and other documents. The religion of the ancient polis has vanished almost completely and is replaced by the ruler cult.[5] And yet the "inherited conglomerate" survived, as a facade or a museum piece until the end of antiquity.

The first century B.C. witnessed a turning point when Posidonius revived the old religious dualism of spirit and matter, god and nature, soul and passions[6] and when, a little later, within the Academy, the transition from skepticism to speculation set in motion a development which was to lead to Neoplatonism. The philosophers became psychiatrists and counselors, handing out advice and encouragement for healing and redemption.

Why did rationalism eventually fail? Why the influx of superstition and occultism in philosophical disguise from the East? The cause is not so much the loss of political freedom but the fear of personal responsibility and of making decisions, the inability to bear the spiritual freedom that had been gained with such difficulty. Book religion and book philosophy (Nock, *Conversion*, 241) now take the place of living speculative experience and point ahead to the Middle Ages.

Here Dodds leaves his main subject. Two appendices follow: one titled "Maenadism," a slightly expanded version of an essay published in the *Harvard Theological Review* (1940); and one titled "Theurgy," a reprint, with a few changes, of an article published in the *Journal of Roman Studies* (1947). Both are exemplary.

Dodds' book is very substantial. Problems that have provoked wild speculations are there discussed with great insight and the resources of superb scholarship. Where our texts fail to give the information we need, Dodds opens up new perspectives through anthropological and psychoanalytical methods.

---

5. See Nilsson, *Gesch. d. griech. Rel.*, vol. 2 (1950), 125ff.; Festugière, *REG* 1951, pp. 317f.

6. See Theiler on Marcus Aurelius 2.2.1 (p. 308), 2.13.1 (pp. 309f.), 5.26.1 (p. 320), 7.16.2f. (pp. 326f.); introd., p. 21. See also O. Luschnat, *Deutsche Literaturzeitung* (1952), 529.

King Midas and the Orphic Mysteries

In book 11 of Ovid's *Metamorphoses*, Dionysus' march from Europe to Asia forms a link between the myth of Orpheus and the story of King Midas. The god has punished severely the Maenads who are in his service for having murdered the poet Orpheus (11.67–84), and he, with all his followers, now leaves Thrace, which has become hateful to him, to go to Lydia, the realm of Midas.[1]

The march of the god is, for Ovid, a convenient transition between two myths. But there is also a more important connection between Orpheus, Midas, and Dionysus. I would like to discuss it in this essay.

We are told, in the introduction (85–105) that Midas had been initiated into the mysteries by Orpheus and Eumolpus.

> regem . . . Midam, cui Thracius Orpheus
> orgia tradiderat cum Cecropio Eumolpo.

What mysteries were those? Since Ovid mentions Eumolpus, the hero of the Eumolpides, an Attic clan, one might think of the Eleusinian mysteries. But Ovid also mentions Orpheus; hence, the Orphic mysteries cannot be excluded. Ovid clearly opposes *Thracius Orpheus* and *Cecropius Eumolpus,* probably because he rejects a story attested since the fifth century, that Eumolpus, too, had been a native of Thrace. But some commentators have observed that, for Ovid, Eumolpus was actually a disciple of Orpheus (*Ex P.* 3.3.41ff.).

> at non Chionides Eumolpus in Orphea talis
>   in Phryga nec Satyrum talis Olympus erat
> praemia nec Chiron ab Achille talia cepit.

From *Hommages à Marcel Renard,* vol. 2, Collection Latomus 102, ed. Jacqueline Bibauw (Brussels, 1969), 470–77.

1. On the context see W. Ludwig, *Struktur und Einheit der Metamorphosen* (1965), 51ff.

It can be shown from Conon (*Narr.* 1 *ap.* Phot. *Cod.* 186) that, in the Hellenistic period, Midas became a disciple of Orpheus.

In Silenus, who is led as a captive before him, Midas recognizes a fellow initiate.

> . . . agnovit socium comitemque sacrorum.

The commentators point out, based on Apollodorus 1.3.2, that Silenus, too, was a follower of Dionysus. Perhaps we can say that Ovid was not too concerned with the distinctions between the different mystery religions. He simply wanted to emphasize how old and venerable these mysteries were. Recent scholarship, incidentally, has plausibly established a close connection between the mysteries of Orpheus and those of Dionysus.[2]

After Midas has duly celebrated this unexpected encounter, he brings back Silenus to the god and is granted a wish. This takes us into the world of fairy tales: a god grants a mortal a wish. But there is something else. We have heard of the mysteries into which Midas had been initiated and of his particular devotion to the god. He is a privileged mortal, but the consecration he has received has not prevented him from committing a sin whose consequences only the god by his grace may cancel. The old fairy-tale theme has been charged with religious and moral connotations.

Midas is a complex human being, not a mere abstraction. He is good and generous but at the same time foolish in his greed for gold, like most people, even though he is a great ruler and a friend of the gods. To use the terminology of the mystery religions, he is not yet τέλειος.[3] He does offer protection and hospitality to a fellow worshiper, but that was a matter of course, an elementary obligation, even in Ovid's time. It is a whim of the god to grant a wish to Midas, but, perhaps, he also wants to test him, and it is clear that Midas is not equal to this test (100ff.).

---

2. See M.P. Nilsson, *Geschichte der griechischen Religion,* 2 vols., 2d ed. (Munich, 1955–61), 2:426. There is also a connection between Orphism and Pythagoreanism, which seems important for our understanding of book 15 of the *Metamorphoses.* See W. Burkert, *Weisheit und Wissenschaft* (Nuremberg, 1962), 105ff.

3. See R. Reitzenstein, *Die hellenistischen Mysterienreligionen,* 2d ed. (Berlin, 1920), 191f.

huic deus optandi gratum, sed inutile fecit
muneris arbitrium . . .
ille male usurus donis . . .
adnuit optatis nocituraque munera solvit
Liber et indoluit quod non meliora petisset.

Within five lines the same idea is presented in no less than four variations: Midas is a devout and loyal follower of the god, but he has not
freed himself from human passions and weaknesses.

This connects him with Orpheus, for Orpheus, too, failed a test. In
his case, it was the overpowering love for a woman that made him fail; in
Midas' case, it was the overpowering love for gold. By the special grace
of the gods, Orpheus was able to conquer death,[4] but, like Midas, he
made the wrong use of this privilege. From the point of view of the gods,
both Midas and Orpheus cling too much to earthly things; that is, they
have not yet reached the highest degree of purification.

According to Orphic doctrine, man has a double nature: he is good
and bad at the same time. Through progressive purifications and more
and more advanced initiations he is able to free himself from the material, evil elements of his nature.[5] He who shows himself unworthy of
divine grace will be punished, unless he obtains forgiveness through
repentance and atonement, like Midas.

What may seem strange is the fact that Orpheus, whose love is
purer than that of Midas, is punished more severely. But his death has
all the characteristics of martyrdom.[6] We also ought to remember the
traditional rivalry between the Orphics and the followers of Dionysus.[7]
A later age has smoothed over these conflicts; in Ovid's poem, Dionysus
mourns the singer.

Midas, as a symbolic figure in the Orphic mysteries, points toward a
secondary motive of the myth, omitted by Ovid, perhaps because he
may not have wished to burden the narrative too much with ideas.
There is a connection between the story of the captured Silenus and the
famous passage on the senselessness of life in Aristotle's lost dialogue

---

4. This is the testimony that Bornkamm ("Μυστήριον," *Theol. Wörterbuch zum Neuen Test.* 4 [1941]: 813) wished to find.

5. See Nilsson 1:698f. Nilsson sees in Orphic theology an attempt to explain the tendency of man to sin.

6. O. Kern, in *Festschrift C. Robert* (1920), 26.

7. Nilsson 2:686f.

Eudemus.[8] Crantor, the Platonist, adopts the same reflexion in his much read essay *On Mourning*. Cicero (*Tusc.* 1.115) and Plutarch (*Consol. ad Apoll.* 115B–E) ultimately depend on Crantor.[9] My translation is based on the text given by W.D. Ross (*Aristotelis Fragmenta Selecta* [Oxford, 1955], 18f.).

> Not only nowadays but already in the past, many wise men, as Crantor says, deplored human life, because they considered it a punishment and the very fact of being born the greatest misfortune. Aristotle says that this was also revealed to Midas by the captured Silenus. But it is better to quote the philosopher's own words. In his book *Eudemus, or concerning the Soul*, he writes: "Therefore, my dear friend, one must altogether think of the dead as being fortunate and also blessed,[10] for they have become better and greater. This idea is so old among us that no one knows when it originated and who established it for the first time, but it seems that people have maintained it since time immemorial. Moreover, you will notice that people for a long time[11] have said and repeated something else." "What is it?" he asked. The answer was, "That it is best not to be born and that death is better than life." This has been declared to many by a deity. According to myth, the great Midas, while hunting, had captured Silenus and asked him (for he wanted to know) what is, of all things, the best and most desirable for human beings. At first, it is said, Silenus, did not want to reply and persisted in stubborn silence for a long time. When he was finally persuaded, by

---

8. Werner Jaeger (*Aristotle*, trans. R. Robinson, 2d ed. [Oxford, 1948], 100) sees a connection: "The young Aristotle had really felt the pains of man's dualistic existence, as Plato and the Orphics had felt it before him."; see also p. 160 (on Περὶ φιλοσοφίας, fr. 15 Ross): "It is not accidental that he formulates this epoch-making discovery in connexion with the mystery-religions." See also O. Kern, *Die Religion der Griechen*, vol. 3 (Berlin, 1938), 29, with a reference to H. Diels, *Abh. Preuss. Akad. d. Wiss.* 7 (1915): 93 n. 4. See also n. 9 following.

9. See W. Nestle, *Neue Jahrbücher* 47 (1911): 81ff.; H. Diels, "Der antike Pessimismus," in *Aus Schule und Leben*, vol. 1 (1921), 1ff., esp. 18. All this is relevant for our understanding of Orphism. See also Diels, "Der antike Pessimismus," 23f. on Aristotle (and see n. 8 preceding). M.P. Nilsson (1:737) calls the story of Silenus "eine recht alte Geschichte."

10. We ought to read πάντως καὶ μακαριστοὺς καί, with Wyttenbach, for if we follow the vulgate, printed by Ross, Eudemus would be μακαριστότατος before his death, which does not make sense.

11. Ross reads πολλῶν ἐτῶν instead of πάλαι, but I prefer Wyttenbach's text.

a variety of strategies, to say something, he answered, giving in to necessity: "Short-lived race, engendered by a malicious deity and an unfortunate fate! Why do you force me to say something which it would be better for you to ignore? If one does not know one's own misfortune, life is at least tolerable. It is altogether impossible for human beings to obtain the best and share in the essence of the best. For it is best for all men not to be born, and the second best and the one main benefit for human beings, once they are born, is to die as soon as possible." Clearly, he meant that time spent in death is better than time spent in life.

For a fourth-century Greek, this was already an ancient truth. But where does it come from? After reading what Werner Jaeger (160) says on the influence of the theology and the language of the mystery religions on Aristotle, one would assume that this insight comes from the Orphic mysteries. Midas appears only at the margin, but he does appear, and we have seen that there is a connection between Midas and Orpheus.

Naturally, this gloomy outlook is not the ultimate answer of the mysteries. On the contrary, they offer to help people bear the burden of life. Suicide would seem to be the only way out, but it is precluded, because life, granted by the gods, is sacred. Therefore, religion must equip and fortify human beings to such an extent that they will remain at their appointed post, until the gods call them away.

This is actually the essence of Plato's doctrine, as presented by Aristotle in his early *Dialogues*. In the δρώμενα of the mystery religions, the advice given by Silenus was put into practice, but, of course, only symbolically. "The new life which grants the initiated bliss in the realm of the dead does not begin with death, but with initiation," says Nilsson.[12] The μύσται cross the threshold of death symbolically, and symbolically they experience new birth. This is the interpretation given by the mysteries to that old gloomy perspective. Thus, it loses its sting. The deep pessimism which is the other side of Hellenic self-confidence and exuberance is overcome, and life has a new meaning. The historic significance of this truly liberating step can hardly be overstated.

The ritual of the *mors voluntaria* is well attested for the Isis mysteries of the imperial period.[13] The passage from Aristotle allows us to extrapo-

---

12. 2:692.
13. Nilsson 2:636f.

late the concept for earlier centuries. The symbolic death and rebirth of the μύστης must have had its firm place in the δρώμενα of all great mysteries. What differentiated the Orphic mysteries from the others was probably a reenactment of Orpheus' κατάβασις and his conquest of death. Midas, on the other hand, was probably an allegorical representation of a mortal overly attached to earthly goods.

There is very little concrete information about the importance of mystery religions in Italy in Ovid's time. The interpretation of the wall paintings in the Villa dei Misterii in Pompeii[14] and the stucco reliefs of the so-called Basilica of Porta Maggiore is still controversial. We may take it for granted that Ovid was interested in mystery cults, and the way in which he presents the story of Midas shows, I think, that he knew something about their message. It is possible that he was initiated into one of these esoteric cults, as were so many Romans before and after him.

The religious color of *Metamorphoses* 11.127–45 is certainly striking. The prayer which Midas addresses to Dionysus resembles very strongly, as R. Pettazzoni has argued,[15] a confession of sins, both in content and form.

"da veniam, Lenaee pater! peccavimus" inquit
"sed miserere, precor, speciosoque eripe damno!"

---

14. The interpretations offered by R. Merkelbach (*Roman und Mysterium in der Antike* [Munich, 1962], 48ff.) are quite remarkable.

15. R. Pettazzoni, *La Confessione dei Peccati*, 3 vols. (Rome, 1929–36). 3:117ff.; "Confession of Sins and the Classics," *Harvard Theological Review* 30 (1937): 2ff. The sin which Midas has committed is only superficially his insatiable greed for gold; according to Pettazzoni, there may be a religious offense underneath it. His *pater peccavi* seems to point to a specific ἁμάρτημα of the kind attested in epigraphic texts. The gesture of the raised hands (*Met.* 5.131) is compared by Pettazzoni (*La Confessione*, 3:118, 120, 124, etc.) with *Met.* 4.238 and *Fast.* 4.315. Concerning the ablutions in the sources of the Pactolus, Pettazzoni has this to say: "l'immersione totale di Mida . . . nelle sorgenti spumeggianti del Pactolo in Lidia, su le pendici del Tmolo, avrà anch'essa . . . un fondamento rituale, e lo trovo infatti in quei riti di abluzione che . . . si praticavano appunte in Lidia ad epoche fisse da fedeli organizzati in apposite associazioni religiose." (*La Confessione*, 3:11; in "Confession," 3 n. 7, he refers to Matthew 3:6); cf. n. 19 following. Pettazzoni does not comment on the possibility that Ovid knew of penitential rites, as practiced in the East, from personal experience, but testimonies such as *Ex Ponto* 1.1.51ff. (see Pettazzoni, *La Confessione*, 1:44–46, on this passage) seem to support this. On the confession of sins in Orphism see Pettazzoni, *La Confessione*, 3:185ff.

Ovid actually seems to paraphrase the term *confessio peccati* (134). That the ritual of the mysteries included a confession of sins cannot be doubted after what has been said by O. Kern[16] and M.P. Nilsson.[17] The god grants forgiveness and carries out a *restitutio* (134), which is exactly the term for the "restoration" of the repentant sinner as it is recognized by the Christian church as well; compare Tertullian *De Pudicitia* 19.6: *sane agat paenitentiam . . . , non tamen et restitutionem consecutura. haec enim erit paenitentia quam et nos deberi quidem agnoscimus multo magis, sed de venia deo reservamus*. In other words, a full *restitutio* is only possible by the grace of the god. But this is exactly what Ovid means when he says (134f.),

> mite deum numen: Bacchus peccasse fatentem
> restituit.

Midas performs an act of repentance which is not described as such by Ovid. He wanders along the Pactolus River until he reaches its origin, which is, of course, sacred, like all springs. There he washes himself. This is nothing else but a pilgrimage to a sacred place, undertaken by a repentant sinner who is purified in the end.

Thus, we can reconstruct, I think, for the Orphic mysteries a ritual of penitence which is comparable to early Christian practices. The confession of sins[18]—*peccasse fateri* is equivalent to ἐξομολογεῖσθαι—is followed by absolution. The repentant sinner has been forgiven and is received once more into the religious community (*venia, restitutio*). In the narrative, the sequence of events which we may assume for the mysteries ritual, is overlayed by fairy-tale motives and aetiology.[19]

---

16. O. Kern, *Die griechischen Mysterien der klassischen Zeit* (Berlin, 1927), 30f.

17. 1:382. According to Plutarch (*Apophth. Lac.* 1, p. 217 C.; 10, p. 229 D.), Antalcidas and Lysandrus were asked by the priests whether they had done anything bad in life.

18. See F. Steinleitner, *Die Beicht im Zusammenhang mit der sakralen Rechtspflege in der Antike* (Leipzig, 1913); R. Pettazzoni, *Harvard Theol. Review* 30 (1937): 1ff.; Nilsson 2:579 n. 1; Merkelbach 169f., 175, 185, and elsewhere (see index s.v. "Beichte"). Ovid knows (*Ex Ponto* 1.1.50ff.; see Merkelbach 169f.) the public confession of sins in the cult of Isis. In Asia Minor, many inscriptions recording guilt and repentance have been found, none of them earlier than the second century B.C., it seems.

19. According to Juvenal 6.522ff., worshipers of Isis had to fetch water from the sources of the Nile; but this could be an exaggeration. H. Emonds (*RAC* 2 [1954]: 804) seems to accept the testimony but believes that paganism did not have the "awareness of sin" (*Sündenbewusstsein*). See Merkelbach 40, 106.

But if the whole narrative were only an oriental fairy tale and nothing more, Ovid would not have accentuated so strongly the religious elements, such as repentance, confession of sins, penitence, divine forgiveness. Wonderful things happen in fairy tales, and the wonders are performed by the gods,

nam vos mutastis et illa,

but here it is more than just an entertainment. Ovid, who, for the first time, introduces Dionysus as a protagonist, has shaped the narrative in such a way that it becomes an allegory for the fate of the repentant sinner who is redeemed by the grace of a god. Did Ovid create this allegory? Probably not. It may have been part of Orphism.

B. Kötting, *Peregrinatio Religiosa* (Muenster, 1950), should also be consulted: Kötting has not found an example of a pilgrimage for the sake of penitence before 500 A.D. (p. 329) but thinks that there may be relatively early examples of pilgrimages to healing sources (p. 197).

Virgil and the Mystery Religions

In his *Divine Legation of Moses Demonstrated on the Principles of a Religious Deist* (2 vols. [1737–1741]) Bishop Warburton proposed an interpretation of the sixth book of Virgil's *Aeneid* which seems to be almost completely forgotten today. None of the handbooks, none of the recent books on Virgil, none of the commentaries (not even Norden) seem to know of it, and yet this theory may provide the key to the understanding of Aeneas' descent into the underworld. One of the reasons for this curious *damnatio memoriae* could be the character of Warburton's book. It is full of bold and controversial ideas which are presented with considerable learning, but also in a dogmatic and sometimes presumptuous manner. This manner obviously annoyed Gibbon, the historian, who published in his youth a scathing review which he did not care to sign with his name.[1] It must have made a certain impression on the scholars of that time, for C.G. Heyne, the well-known editor and commentator of Virgil, praises the anonymous author as *doctus . . . et elegantissimus Britannus*. In later years Gibbon himself admitted that he had treated a man who deserved his esteem with contempt and regretted the "cowardly concealment" of his name in a personal attack.[2]

The time has come for a fresh examination of Warburton's views. It should be said that he seems to have taken most of his material from the *Eleusinia* of Ioannes Meursius (1579–1639), and this was held against him at the time. But the idea which electrified the whole mass of evidence

---

From *American Journal of Philology* 94 (1973): 147–66.

1. Gibbon, *Critical Observations* (1770). In the *Memoirs of My Life* (ed. Georges A. Bonnard [1969], 144f.) he speaks more indulgently of the book but still maintains his basic objection. One of the best classical scholars of the time, John Jortin, also attacked Warburton in his *Six Dissertations on Various Subjects* (1755).

2. W.F. Jackson Knight (see n. 13) seems the only modern scholar who refers to Warburton. R.D. Williams (*Greece and Rome*, 2d ser., 11 [1964]: 48) says that we can only speak "in the most non-technical sense of the word . . . of the 'initiation ritual' of Aeneas." He refers to W.K.C. Guthrie, *Orpheus and Greek Religion* (1952), 154f., and L.-A. Constans, *L'Enéide de Virgile* (1938), 208f.

was his own, and we are concerned with the idea. It is also true that many of his arguments are specious. On the other hand, material which he could not have known seems to support his view.

In the sixth book of the *Aeneid* Virgil's hero, led by the Sibyl of Cumae, descends into the underworld to consult his father, Anchises. The ceremonial of his entrance is elaborate, and as we follow him on his path the geography of Hades with its inhabitants unfolds before our eyes. How is it possible that a book which can be said to embody Virgil's answer to the last questions "Whence do we come?" and "Where do we go?" and "What is the meaning of life?" cannot dispense with the traditional conglomerate of mythology? How much of this was still believed in Virgil's time, by Virgil himself?

The function of the book within the epic corresponds to that of Homer's *Nekyia*—but what a change in mood and orchestration! In six or seven centuries the anticipations of life after death had changed entirely. Homer's Achilles had thought it better to be the hired man of a poor Greek farmer than to be king of the dead. There is none of this mood of hopelessness in Virgil's Hades; only the great sinners are being punished as they were in Greek mythology. But in six or seven centuries Homer's dreary panorama of hell had been brightened.

There were two main sources of light: Platonism and the mystery religions. Both forces are so complex that they cannot be defined here. Even in Virgil's time there was no general agreement as to what Plato said, and the central message as well as the ritual of the various mystery religions was still a well-kept secret, though certain allusions which would mean nothing to ordinary people were apparently tolerated. We find such allusions in Pindar, in Sophocles, in Isocrates, in Cicero, in Apuleius, and though they are deliberately obscure or ambiguous, they all seem to point to a message of hope beyond extinction and a promise of life everlasting. Such a message can also be found in the sixth book of the *Aeneid*.

Pindar, for instance, praises in a famous fragment (137 Snell) the man who has "seen those things" before he descends into the underworld, for he "knows the end of life, and he knows its beginning, given by Zeus."

ὄλβιος ὅστις ἰδὼν κεῖν᾽ εἶσ᾽ ὑπὸ χθόν᾽.
οἶδε μὲν βίου τελευτάν,
οἶδεν δὲ δώσδοτον ἀρχάν.

A passage from one of Sophocles' lost plays (fr. 719 Dindorf = 837 Pearson) provides a parallel and a commentary: "Thrice happy are those mortals who, having seen these rites, go into Hades; for they alone are allowed to live there; to the rest all there is bad."

> ὡς τρισόλβιοι
> κεῖνοι βροτῶν, οἳ ταῦτα δερχθέντες τέλη
> μόλωσ᾽ ἐς Ἅιδου · τοῖσδε γὰρ μόνοις ἐκεῖ
> ζῆν ἔστι, τοῖς δ᾽ἄλλοις πάντ᾽ ἐκεῖ κακά.

The literary source is, of course, *Hymn. Hom. ad Cer.* 480ff. Sophocles is more specific: in one respect he speaks of τέλη, "rites," whereas Pindar speaks of "those things," but there is no question that they both refer to the experience of the μυόμενοι at the mysteries. The act of initiation reveals the meaning of death and gives one hopes of a new and better life after death, while the uninitiated must resign himself to the dreary kind of existence which Homer described. Isocrates (*Paneg.* 28) praises Athens because mankind owes two incomparable gifts to it: our daily bread, and the Eleusinian mysteries, which give those who have been initiated "sweeter hopes about death and about all eternity" (δούσης δωρεὰς διττάς, αἵπερ μέγισται τυγχάνουσιν οὖσαι, τούς τε καρπούς . . . καὶ τὴν τελετήν, ἧς μετασχόντες περί τε τῆς τοῦ βίου τελευτῆς καὶ τοῦ σύμπαντος αἰῶνος ἡδίους τὰς ἐλπίδας ἔχουσιν).

Clearly, the mysteries had replaced Homer's Hades by a much more attractive prospect of life after death. This life, however, was reserved for those who had been initiated, who had "seen those things." So little is known about the doctrine of the mysteries and their initiation rites that the skepticism of the late eighteenth and early nineteenth centuries found it easy to declare, in De Quincey's words, all ancient mystery religions "a gigantic hoax, the great and illustrious humbug of ancient history." No one would doubt today that there was, indeed, a central message of great beauty and simplicity and that the rites were designed to make the initiation an unforgettable experience. But we still do not fully know what was seen and heard, τὰ δρώμενα καὶ τὰ λεγόμενα. At the end of his great book *Eleusis and the Eleusinian Mysteries* (1961), which examines the literary and archaeological evidence, George E. Mylonas writes: *"We cannot know, at least we still do not know, what was the full content and meaning of the Mysteries of Demeter held at Eleusis.* We know details of the ritual but not its meaning. The ancients kept their secret well. And Eleusis still lies under its heavy mantle of mystery" (316). Among the theories of scholars which he calls "unfounded and therefore untenable" he does not mention Warburton's hypothesis, and yet it is important for both the mysteries and the interpretation of *Aeneid* 6. It is not quite true that the ancients kept their secret well: there are allusions in Apuleius, Lucian, and Claudian; there are fairly clear testimonies in ecclesiastical writers and philosophers; and there may be, as we shall see, a very elaborate symbolism in Virgil.

Warburton wrote, "The descent of Virgil's hero into the infernal regions, I presume, was no other than a figurative description of an initiation, and particularly a very exact picture of the spectacles in the Eleusinian mysteries, where everything was done in show and machinery, and where a representation of the history of Ceres afforded opportunity to bring in the scenes of heaven, hell, purgatory and whatever related to the future state of men and heroes. . ."[3]

Strange as this may seem at first sight, it is a hypothesis that should be reconsidered. Even if it does not supersede all the other philosophical and religious ideas which Norden has identified in book 6, it complements them, and the whole account becomes more meaningful.

Before examining Warburton's main arguments, I should like to say something on religious symbolism in Virgil. Naturally, the Fourth *Eclogue* comes to mind. There we can grasp a historical person, C. Asinius Pollio, and a historical event, the year of his consulship, but as we try to reason from these facts, we get lost in a world of images. One possible interpretation which seems to have escaped Norden, too (at least he does not refer to it in *Die Geburt des Kindes*), is that of Salomon Reinach,[4] who claimed that the Fourth *Eclogue* owes a substantial part of its imagery and its idiom to the Orphic mysteries. The idea was not completely dismissed by W. Warde Fowler,[5] and even H.J. Rose,[6] though calling it exaggerated, pointed out that childbirth was a symbol used in the mystery religions and that Harpocrates, that is, the Horus child, was almost certainly shown in the Isis mysteries.

I shall not list all of Warburton's arguments, only those that seem plausible or significant, but I shall present them in modern terms and

---

3. *Divine Legation*, vol. 1 (1837), 251.

4. Salomon Reinach, *Revue de l'Histoire des Religions*, 1900, 375 (= *Cultes, Mythes et Religions*, vol. 2 [1910], 66 ff.). The study is well worth reading.

5. W. Warde Fowler, in *Virgil's Messianic Eclogue* (with contributions by J.B.E. Mayor and J. Conway [1907]), 63f.

6. H.J. Rose, *The Eclogues of Virgil*, Sather Classical Lectures 16 (1942), 219.

support them with new evidence, wherever possible. In doing this it would have been awkward to separate his thoughts from my own in every single instance. I have therefore decided to state his case as he might do it today, with all the tools of modern scholarship and the research of two hundred years at his disposal. At the same time I should like to refer readers to Warburton's book, which, for all its eccentricities and prolixity, still makes excellent reading.

We know that many distinguished Romans who visited Athens were initiated into the Eleusinian mysteries. Cicero is a good example, and Augustus—who took this seriously—is another. We know that, in principle, every Greek-speaking person, whether Athenian or foreigner, freeborn or slave, could be initiated, if he had committed no crime, paid the fees, and was properly introduced. One might assume that many Romans underwent this experience out of sheer curiosity, and perhaps this is true. But Cicero, echoing Isocrates, says (*De leg.* 2.14.36) that Athens has given to mankind nothing more excellent or divine than the Eleusinian mysteries. When Virgil read book 6 to him, Augustus probably understood the allusions to a marvelously impressive and deeply symbolical ritual, and he may have found in the music of Virgil's poetry a very special appeal because it brought back to him a profound religious experience.

A hero descending to the underworld and returning from it seems to be a popular theme of mythology and literature: witness Theseus, Heracles, Orpheus, Dionysus, the Dioscuri, and now Aeneas. But at least two of these heroes are also connected with the mysteries. A little-known tradition, preserved in the pseudo-Platonic *Axiochus* (371e1), records that both Heracles and Dionysus had been initiated into the Eleusinian mysteries before they went down to Hades, in order to be fortified for the ordeals which they were about to face. This anachronism suggests that part of the ritual at Eleusis somehow included a κατάβασις. The testimonies of Pindar and Sophocles would allow us to see in the initiation rites a symbolic death as a preparation for real death. The initiation of Heracles, by the way, is attested on Greek vases.[7] Perhaps all the heroes of Aeneas' list (119ff.) had some connection with mystery religions.

> si potuit manis accersere coniugis Orpheus
> Threicia fretus cithara fidibusque canoris,

---

7. Cf. H. Lloyd-Jones, *Maia*, n.s., 19 (1967): 206ff., an important article which deals with *Aeneid* 6, too.

si fratrem Pollux alterna morte redemit
itque reditque viam totiens. quid Thesea, magnum
quid memorem Alciden? et mi genus ab Iove summo.

If initiation consisted, at least partly, in a symbolic experience of Hades, the memory of those heroes who descended to hell and returned safely to the upper world might well have been invoked at the beginning of the ceremonies to encourage the *mystai*. Perhaps some of them were shown *in effigie*; for Heracles, at any rate, we have the valuable testimony of the Lovatelli Urn, discussed by Mylonas (205ff.). The so-called Orphic *katabasis* which Virgil may have used[8] would be a literary equivalent; it must have been much more of a religious document than the sixth book, but then so much of Greek archaic and classical poetry had a deep religious meaning and represented a form of worship. But perhaps it is more than coincidence that the legendary initiates, Dionysus and Heracles, are represented on a hydria from Cumae (Mylonas 213 and n. 71).

Virgil represents the sanctuary of the Sibyl of Cumae as a huge cave, *antrum immane* (11), but he also gives the impression of high, elaborate buildings, *arces* (9), *aurea tecta* (13), *immania templa* (19), *alta templa* (41), with an ornate entrance (20ff.) and a grove of Hecate (ibid.). In other words, Aeneas enters a sacred precinct with various buildings, a grove, and a cave. The main temple had been constructed by Daedalus, and on the doors he wrought scenes from Cretan mythology, including the Minotaur and possibly a map of the labyrinth (24ff.).

hic crudelis amor tauri suppostaque furto
Pasiphae mixtumque genus prolesque biformis
Minotaurus inest, Veneris monimenta nefandae,
hic labor ille domus et inextricabilis error;
magnum reginae sed enim miseratus amorem
Daedalus ipse dolos tecti ambagesque resolvit,
caeca regens filo vestigia.

The cave might be reminiscent of the "cave with the temple of Plouton above which tower the rocks of the eastern extremity of the Eleusinian hill . . . ," a deep cavern which "could give to the spectator the impression of a χάσμα γῆς, a chasm in the earth, and even suggest to him the

---

8. Cf. Norden, *Aen.* VI, 3d ed. (1926), 156f. Lloyd-Jones 224ff.

'gates of Hades'. . ." (Mylonas 100f.). Orphic tradition refers to "the cave at the deme of Eleusis where are the gates of Hades" (*Hymn. Orph.* 19.12ff.; cf. Mylonas 149). Cumae and Eleusis have this in common: they both guard the entrance to the underworld.

The Minoan scenes on the huge temple doors (for they must have been huge if one considers the whole architectural complex suggested by Virgil) may be connected with modern attempts to derive the Eleusinian mysteries from prehistoric Crete. This was the bold and imaginative hypothesis of Axel Persson;[9] it was broadly accepted by Martin P. Nilsson and others, and it cannot be dismissed as easily as Mylonas (16ff.) seems to think; the archaeological evidence is ambiguous, to say the least, and Mylonas (283) is quite willing to admit that the Eleusinian mysteries were established in the Mycenaean age, when Cretan civilization had a strong influence on life on the mainland. Was there a tradition that the main temple at Eleusis had been built by Daedalus? And did the doors of the temple depict scenes from Minoan mythology?

The unexpected role which the Cumaean Sibyl plays may give us another clue. It has often been observed (e.g., by Lloyd-Jones, p. 225) that Virgil makes her not only fulfill her usual duties; she is not only a prophetess but a μυσταγωγός. In fact, this is her primary function in the book. True, she has an ecstatic vision (45ff., 77ff.), but, as Aeneas gently remarks (103ff.) she reveals nothing new to him (this is before he learns of Misenus' death), and it is not yet the prophecy he needs.

> non ulla laborum,
> o virgo, nova mi facies inopinave surgit;
> omnia praecepi atque animo mecum ante peregi.

Instead he asks her to throw open the gates to the underworld and "teach" him the way (109).

> doceas iter et sacra ostia pandas.

The "opening of the sacred gate" is nowhere said, as far as I can see, to be one of the duties of the *mystagogos*, but *docere iter* would be a good description of his functions. The Sibyl not only leads Aeneas; she also explains what happens along the way.

---

9. A. Persson, *ARW* 21 (1922): 287–309; cf., e.g., M.P. Nilsson, *Minoan-Mycenaean Religion*, 2d ed. (1950), 452.

In her answer (125ff.) the Sibyl tells him that he must do two things to be admitted: he must bury Misenus and then obtain the Golden Bough. The funeral offerings to his dead companion are described as *piacula* (153), and the Golden Bough is called a gift to Persephone (142).

The first prerequisite could mean, in terms of Warburton's hypothesis, that Aeneas as a μύστης had to be ritually clean. This was announced at Eleusis on the very first day of the mysteries, in a proclamation delivered by the Hierokeryx. As far as we can reconstruct the πρόρρησις, only those who had clean hands, were pure from all pollution, were conscious of no evil, had led a good life, and spoke Greek would be admitted (Mylonas 247). There may have been more restrictions: it is hard to see how anyone who had not fulfilled certain elementary duties, like burying poor relatives and friends at his own expense, would be welcomed. At this moment, Aeneas does not know that Misenus is dead; nevertheless, it is his duty to look for the corpse and bury it properly, before he can proceed.

The second prerequisite, the Golden Bough,[10] is like a passport, a token which guarantees safe-conduct through Hades. Volumes have been written on this. The simple truth may be that Virgil chose this token because it resembles the wreath of myrtle that the initiates wore on their heads or the βάκχος made up of branches of myrtle which they carried in their hands (Mylonas 252). Golden branches were carried in the πομπή of the Isis mysteries, and Apuleius records (*Met.* 11.102) that one of the new initiates *(turbae sacris divinis initiatae)* carried a golden palm branch and the staff of Hermes *(ibat . . . attollens palmam auro subtiliter foliatam nec non Mercurialem etiam caduceum)* in his hands. Hermes *psychopompos* could be the archetype of an Eleusinian *mystagogos* or a *mystes* of Isis.[11]

---

10. Sir James Frazer's monumental work offers enough material to prove or disprove any conceivable hypothesis.

11. Apuleius' *Metamorphoses* is more than an exciting and entertaining story. It starts out as a picaresque novel, but it culminates in the elaborate description of the hero's initiation into the Isis mysteries. Reinhold Merkelbach (*Roman und Mysterium* [1956]) interprets the novel as a kind of pilgrim's progress, the partly autobiographical story of a man who looks for adventure and excitement, intellectual and otherwise, gets into trouble, and in the end finds peace and fulfillment in the Isis religion. This makes excellent sense, I think, but when Merkelbach applies it to other ancient novels he seems to go too far. Light fiction existed in antiquity as it exists today, and then as now readers wanted to be amused without looking for a deeper meaning. We hardly need the testimony of some

At the entrance to the underworld, Aeneas and the Sibyl offer sacrifices to Hecate, Persephone, and other chthonic divinities. We know that at the Eleusinian mysteries the main sacrifice was to Demeter and Persephone, but other divinities apparently were not forgotten, and Virgil's list (Hecate, Erebus, Night, Earth, and Pluto) does not seem unlikely.

The sacrifice is followed by an epiphany of Hecate (255ff.).

> ecce autem primi sub limina solis et ortus
> sub pedibus mugire solum et iuga coepta moveri
> silvarum, visaeque canes ululare per umbram
> adventante dea.

The archaeological evidence connecting Hecate and Demeter at Eleusis is scanty (cf. Mylonas 193f.), but there is a striking passage in Claudian's *De raptu Proserpinae* (1.1ff.), quoted by Warburton, but overlooked by modern scholars. There can be little doubt that Claudian alludes to the celebration of the mysteries at Eleusis; in fact, he may give a very realistic picture. He is more outspoken than Virgil; perhaps the secrets were not kept as carefully in the fourth century A.D. as they were in the first century B.C.

Claudian is possessed by his theme, and the frenzy of inspiration brings back the ecstasy of initiation. Only the images, the idiom of the Eleusinian mysteries, can convey what he feels.

> Inferni raptoris equos adflataque curru
> sidera Taenario caligantesque profundae
> Iunonis thalamos audaci promere cantu
> mens congesta iubet. gressus removete, profani!
> iam furor humanos nostro de pectore sensus
> expulit et totum spirant praecordia Phoebum;
> iam mihi cernuntur trepidis delubra moveri
> sedibus et claram dispergere limina lucem
> adventum testata dei; iam magnus ab imis
> auditur fremitus terris templumque remugit
> Cecropium sanctasque faces extollit Eleusis.
> angues Triptolemi strident et squamea curvis

---

recently discovered papyrus scraps to realize this; but apparently even the Mother Goose tales yield astonishing insights when they are interpreted from a psychoanalytical point of view.

> colla levant attrita iugis lapsuque sereno
> erecti roseas tendunt ad carmina cristas.
> ecce procul ternis Hecate variata figuris
> exoritur levisque simul procedit Iacchus
> crinali florens hedera, quem Parthica velat
> tigris et auratos in nodum colligit ungues;
> ebria Maeonius firmat vestigia thyrsus.

He then asks the divinities of Hades to reveal to him the story he is about to tell: how Dis fell in love, how he stole Proserpina away, how Ceres searched the world for her daughter, and how finally corn was given to mankind.

> vos mihi sacrarum penetralia pandite rerum
> et vestri secreta poli.

This passage (20–31) reflects Virgil's brief address to the infernal gods (264–67); he needs their permission to tell his story.

> di, quibus imperium est animarum, umbraeque silentes
> et Chaos et Phlegethon, loca nocte tacentia late,
> sit mihi fas audita loqui, sit numine vestro
> pandere res alta terra et caligine mersas.

Since these passages correspond to each other, it can be assumed that Claudian's epiphanies of Triptolemus, Hecate, and Iacchus correspond to Virgil's epiphany of Hecate. We know that Triptolemus and Iacchus were among the chief divinities connected with the initiation at Eleusis (Mylonas 237f.). Perhaps we may add Hecate and say that all three were shown to the initiates at the beginning of the ceremony.

The analogy to the Pourtales Vase in the British Museum leaves little doubt that Claudian talks of the actual initiation rites. I quote Mylonas' description (212) of that vase painting: "The figures of the composition are disposed on two levels. In the front and lower level Demeter is seated apparently on the ground and next to her is a throne or seat which remains unoccupied. She turns her head to Triptolemos, seated on his winged chariot drawn by dragons, who talks with animation. Between the two we have the standing figure of Persephone holding a lighted torch. . . . To the seated Goddess are brought by two mystagogoi, actually Iacchos painted twice, Herakles . . . and the Dioskouroi. . . . All three youths hold bacchoi and are crowned with myrtle. There can be little doubt that here the legendary heroes are presented for initiation . . ."

A similar scene occurs on the pelike from Pantikapaion in the Crimea, now in the Hermitage (Mylonas 210ff.). Again we find Demeter, Persephone, Triptolemus, and Iacchus in a characteristic setting. Neither of the two scenes is absolutely identical to Claudian's description. Hecate, for instance, does not seem to appear on the two vases. But we have to remember that the pelike is six or seven hundred years older than the *De raptu Proserpinae*. Some changes in the ritual are likely to have taken place in such a long period of time. That Hecate was one of the Eleusinian deities can hardly be doubted. It is clear, I think, that the painter as well as the poet have in mind a scene which must have been familiar to anyone who had been initiated. Once Claudian's scene has been authenticated, it helps us to interpret Virgil, for Claudian freely borrows from Virgil, showing, perhaps, that he already understood what is, according to Warburton, the deeper meaning of *Aeneid* 6.

But Claudian does refer to actual initiation as well, and I think we may take his description quite literally. This could be the order of events: after the noninitiates had been turned away (*gressus removete, profani* corresponds of course to Virgil's *procul o procul este, profani*), a subterranean thunder which seemed to shake the very foundations of the temple was heard, and at the same time torches were lit throughout the temple, revealing Triptolemus, Hecate, and Iacchus, each in a characteristic pose or motion: Triptolemus in his chariot, Hecate ascending, Iacchus ambling tipsily. The important thing about Claudian's description is the very strong suggestion that these figures actually *moved*. Triptolemus' chariot seems to have been a mechanical contraption, and the dragons yoked to it must have hissed, their rosy crests bobbing in rhythm to the music that apparently now was heard. Hecate seems to have risen up from the ground, and Iacchus was seen walking with uncertain steps. I think we can take it for granted that all this was actually shown, with color, light, and in motion, with music from above and thunder from below. It must have been a superb show, a total experience. No doubt, Greek actors and engineers, directed by the priests, were capable of performing such minor miracles. The Athenians had centuries of stage experience, and the fantastic spectacles offered by Hellenistic kings are well known.

Claudian seems to combine actual knowledge (whether firsthand or not) with reminiscences from Virgil. He is much more outspoken than Virgil, who omits any direct reference to Athens or Eleusis. Both Virgil and Claudian give their readers a ἱερὸς λόγος; but only Claudian's account may be related to the Eleusinian λεγόμενα.

We are told that the initiation was preceded by strange and wonderful sights. In one of his speeches (12.33), Dio Chrysostomus wishes to illustrate the idea that, thanks to the loving care of the gods, all mankind is, in a sense, initiated into the wonders of nature: "It is very much the same as if one were to place a Greek or a barbarian into a mystic sanctuary of extraordinary beauty and size, in order to be initiated. He would see many mystic sights and hear many mystic voices; light and darkness would alternate around him, and a thousand other things would happen." Dio describes the initiation rites in terms of a total experience which was obviously designed to stir the soul and leave a lifelong impression. This is what Aristotle (quoted by Synes., *Or.* 48) meant when he said that the initiates did not have to *learn* anything; they had to undergo an experience.

The Sibyl's cry *procul o procul este, profani* in Virgil (258) has already been compared with Claudian's version. We know that the warning was invariably uttered at the beginning of the real τελετή in Eleusis, but in Virgil's context it seems strangely out of place. Who was there to be turned away? I think this is an important clue. Any ancient reader would immediately think of the ἑκάς ἑκάς ἐστε, βέβηλοι (Serv. ad loc.) of the mysteries; only in such a celebration would the cry have a meaning.

Before Virgil goes on he stops for a moment to apologize to the powers of the underworld for telling some of their secrets (264ff.).

> di, quibus imperium est animarum, umbraeque silentes
> et Chaos et Phlegethon, loca nocte tacentia late,
> sit mihi fas audita loqui, sit numine vestro
> pandere res alta terra et caligine mersas.

We have seen that this corresponds to Claudian's verses 20–31. Virgil requests permission of the chthonic deities to tell about their world. Now if this were a simple κατάβασις no such permission would be needed, for the theme had been treated before, and the topography of hell was known. But Virgil seems to indicate that he is touching on a much more delicate matter. To reveal any of the δρώμενα or λεγόμενα of the mysteries in so many words or to discuss them in public was a crime for anyone who had "seen those things," that is, who had been initiated. Certain details were commonly known in the fifth century B.C. (cf. Mylonas 227), but Aeschylus almost lost his life because he was accused of having divulged in at least four of his plays Eleusinian ἀπόρρητα. His defense was (Aristotle *Nic. Eth.* 3.1.1111a10) that he did not know they were ἀπόρρητα. The answer seems to have become almost proverbial, and though the charge against Aeschylus was dismissed, it is not likely that the Athenians believed him.

Virgil insists that he speaks of "those things" only from hearsay.

sit mihi fas audita loqui.

To him they are *audita*, not *visa*. If we remember the Greek expression "to have seen those things" for "to have been initiated," we are perhaps justified in taking this as an admission that he was never actually initiated but had *heard* about "those things." What little we know of Virgil's life tends to confirm this. We are told of only one trip to Greece, and his final illness must have made it impossible for him to take part in any religious ceremonies, even assuming that the mysteries were celebrated in Athens at that time. If, unlike Augustus, he had never been admitted to the mysteries, he was free to speak of things commonly known, and since he carefully avoids any direct reference to Eleusis, no one could blame him.

The attitude of a true initiate and convert, the hero of Apuleius' novel, is revealing. The story culminates in his taking part in the Isis mysteries, and Apuleius is quite willing to reveal some details, but only up to a certain point. Of course the reader will be anxious to learn what was said and done (τὰ λεγόμενα καὶ τὰ δρώμενα) after Lucius had been led into the innermost sanctuary, and Apuleius would be glad to tell him if it were right. On the other hand, he does not want to leave his reader utterly frustrated, for he might have a genuine interest in religious matters (*Met.* 11.23): *quaeras forsitan satis anxie, studiose lector, quid deinde dictum, quid factum; dicerem, si dicere liceret; cognosceres, si liceret audire. sed parem noxam contraherent et aures et linguae illae temerariae curiositatis. nec te tamen desiderio forsitan religioso suspensum angore diutino cruciabor.* "All right," Apuleius continues, "listen, but believe that which is true. I have reached the border of death, I have stepped on the threshold of Proserpine, I have traversed all the elements, and I have returned. At midnight I have seen the sun shining with dazzling light; I have approached the gods of the underworld and the heavenly gods, and I have worshiped them from close distance. Look, I have told you what you cannot possibly understand, though you have just heard it. So I will tell you only what may be brought to the understanding of the uninitiated without committing a sin" *(ecce tibi rettuli quae quamvis audita ignores tamen necesse est. Ego quod solum potest sine piaculo ad profanorum intellegentias enuntiari, referam).*

This remarkable passage shows that it was permissible for one who had been initiated and took his initiation as seriously as Lucius did to tell certain details, because they would make no sense to those who had never "seen those things." He who only *heard* about them and did not know the whole truth would commit no crime by talking about them. Hence Virgil's plea

sit mihi fas audita loqui.

Apuleius is more communicative than Virgil, and Claudian (especially if we take his epic as a poetic version of the ἱερὸς λόγος) is even more communicative than Apuleius. All this would tend to confirm our assumption that Virgil was not initiated and was therefore free to hint very cautiously at certain mystic experiences that were deeply meaningful only to initiates.

Hence Gibbon's most formidable argument is really immaterial. He said in his review: Either Virgil was initiated, then he would not tell; or he was not initiated, then he could not tell. The truth was probably not all that simple. Arthur Nock has drawn attention to a third possibility: "We know from Apuleius that an initiate could count upon other initiates to recognize an allusion to things which they held sacred."[12] He had in mind *Apologia* 55 rather than the passage from the *Metamorphoses* quoted earlier, which illustrates yet another possibility: an initiate telling a mixed audience as much as he thought safe to tell. Virgil may well represent yet another variation: a noninitiate telling certain things that were, perhaps, commonly known, but using heavily symbolic language. Readers who had "seen those things" would understand at once, and for all the others there was enough to enjoy and to admire in Aeneas' κατάβασις.

The only Virgilian scholar of our time who comments on Warburton, W.F. Jackson Knight, says in his posthumous book *Elysion*:[13] "There is truth in this, though probably nothing in Virgil can be called 'nothing

---

12. A.D. Nock, *Mnemosyne* 5 (1952): 183 (= *Essays on Religion in the Ancient World*, ed. Zeph Stewart (1972–), 2:796).

13. W.F. Jackson Knight, *Elysion: Ancient Greek and Roman Beliefs concerning Life After Death* (1970), 135f.

but anything': there are always different layers of meaning. But if there is a strong reference to the Eleusinian Mysteries, which were always kept very secret, in Virgil's Sixth Book, it would not be surprising if Virgil subtly indicated, at the end, that, whatever the secret truth of life and death might be, he himself had not revealed it in any guilty sense, or to any guilty degree. He prefaced his description of the Descent with—for him a rarity—a personal prayer:

> sit mihi fas audita loqui."

The marvelous lines that follow (268ff.)—

> ibant obscuri sola sub nocte per umbram
> perque domos Ditis vacuas et inania regna, etc.

—might suggest the march of the *mystai* through dark labyrinthine halls. Lucian's *Cataplus sive Tyrannus*, definitely in a lighter vein than *Aeneid 6*, offers a valuable parallel. There, a rather mixed group of people travels through the underworld. It is very dark, and at one point, one of them, Micyllus, cries out (22): "Lord! how dark it is! . . . Everything the same and of the same color . . . [to Cyniscus:] Give me your hand. Tell me. You have been initiated into the Eleusinian mysteries, haven't you? Doesn't this remind you of those things? [οὐχ ὅμοια τοῖς ἐκεῖ τὰ ἐνθάδε σοι δοκεῖ;]." Cyniscus replies: "You are right. Well, look, there comes a woman holding a torch and staring at us in a fierce and threatening manner. Could this be a Fury?" To this, Micyllus says, "Yes, I think so; that's the way she looks."

Micyllus, though not initiated himself, knows that the *mystai* had to walk through darkness and were suddenly confronted with terrifying figures, such as Furies brandishing torches at them.[14] Virgil's list of the horrors of the underworld (273ff.) includes sorrows, pangs of conscience, diseases, old age, poverty, death, and tribulation, but Virgil also mentions the *ferrei . . . Eumenidum thalami* (280), the Gorgons, the Harpies, and other mythological monsters. When Aeneas actually sees them, they are so real that he draws his sword, and the Sibyl has to reassure him (292f.).

---

14. Cf. Norden on *Aen.* 6.260f.

tenuis sine corpore vitas
. . . volitare cava sub imagine formae.

There is good evidence that during initiation rites the *mystai* had to face terrible visions: Virgil's list may give us an idea of their forms and their associations. Cerberus, for instance, is such a frightening reality that Aeneas has to appease him with a drugged cake (417ff.). We know from Philostratus (*Vita Apollon. Tyan.* 8.15ff.) that sometimes, at the beginning of initiation, the *mystai* were handed such cakes to appease any monsters they might encounter on their way. Celsus (Origenes *C. Cels.* 4, p. 167 Koetschau) speaks of the φάσματα καὶ δείματα that were produced in the Dionysiac mysteries, and Themistius (*Or.* 20, p. 235a Dind.) describes the feeling of total helplessness which the candidate was apt to experience. Proclus (*Theol. Plat.* 3.18)[15] describes the emotional experience of the candidate as ἔκπληξις, "shock," and θαῦμα, "amazement." We may assume that the candidates were deliberately put into a state of shock, fear, and bewilderment, before they were allowed to hear the ἱερὸς λόγος which gave them new hope.

Aeneas' *subita formido* (290) corresponds, I think, to the ἔκπληξις which the *mystai* at Eleusis felt. On an inscription discussed by P. Roussel[16] the Dadouchos Themistokles is specially commended for his valuable contribution, ἐξ ὧν τὸ περὶ τὰ μυστήρια μεγαλοπρεπὲς περιττοτέρας ἐκπλήξεως ὑπὸ παντὸς ἀνθρώπου καὶ τοῦ προσήκοντος ἀξιοῦται κόσμου . . . Roussel compares this testimony to Aristides, *Eleusin.* (*Or.* 22.2 = 2:28K.) τὰ δρώμενα μεῖζον᾽ ἔσχε τὴν ἔκπληξιν and other testimonies.

There is a very beautiful and unusual Greek text which describes the candidate's feelings at this stage. It is quoted anonymously by Stobaeus (*Anth.* 3:1089 Hense) and has been attributed to various authors, Themistius among others, but Wyttenbach[17] seems to have discovered the true source: it is probably from Plutarch's lost essay *On the Soul.* I am quoting C.J. Herington's translation:[18] "At its time of dying the soul's

---

15. W. Beierwaltes, *Proklos* (1965), 358f.

16. P. Roussel, *Mélanges Bidez*, vol. 2 (1934), 833f. I owe this reference to Professor James Oliver who also pointed out to me that Professor Kevin Clinton of Cornell University is publishing the Eleusinian inscriptions.

17. Daniel Wyttenbach, *Plut. lib. de num. vind.* (1772), 129f.; cf. Bernardakis, ed., *Plutarchi Moralia*, vol. 7 (1896): 21ff.; Ziegler, *RE* 21 (1951): 752.

18. C.J. Herington, *Arion* 7 (1968):392.

feelings are like those of the initiates into the Great Mysteries; that is why our words for 'dying' (τελευτᾶν) and 'to be initiated' (τελεῖσθαι) are alike, because they mean almost the same thing. Lost at first. Exhaustion. Whirling race. Frightening, aimless ways in darkness. Just before the end itself all terror; cold shuddering, trembling, sweat, bewilderment (θάμβος). After that there is astounding light. The soul is welcomed by clear places. Here are deep fields, in them voices and dancing, majesty of pure sounds and holy sights which enfold the dead man and make his initiation perfect. He is free, there are no more chains. Part of the Mystery now, he wears his garland under his feet: the mass of men who were not initiated, not cleaned during life. These were afraid of death, not believing what happens here, and so took the evil side. They are trampled and compacted under him in a blur of mud and mist.—Friend, this might help you to see that the soul's entanglement, its imprisonment in the body, is no true part of nature."[19]

This extraordinary passage describes vividly the state of shock produced in the μύστης. Perhaps some individuals experienced this more profoundly than others, but the average Athenian was neither naive nor unsophisticated, and on the whole he seems to have felt the shock deeply. We can only wonder at the psychological and technical knowhow of the priests; it would certainly be wrong to belittle the effect. No doubt the long and careful preparation of the μύσται, the fasting, and the prayers, contributed to it. The Plutarch fragment (if it is, indeed, from his lost treatise Π. ψυχῆς) also dramatizes the transition from a state of shock to a state of bliss, as the *mystai* are allowed to see Elysium. This, if Warburton is right, would be the culmination of the Eleusinian rites. After all the grim and horrifying sights, lovely images now present themselves, and in the soul of the *myomenos* shock and fear yield to enchantment and hope. Themistius (*Or.* 20, p. 235b Dindorf) speaks of the transition from frightful visions to a marvelous luminous experience: καὶ ἐξεφαίνετο ὁ νοῦς ἐκ τοῦ βάθους, φέγγους ἀνάπλεως καὶ ἀγλαΐας ἀντὶ τοῦ προτέρου σκότου. At this point, presumably, the μύστης is told the ἱερὸς λόγος.

---

19. The translation of πλάναι and περιδρομαί is not quite accurate, and the "dead man" is an interpolation (Plutarch clearly speaks of ὁ παντελὴς ἤδη καὶ μεμυημένος, i.e., the man who has reached the highest degree of initiation). The ὅσιοι καὶ καθαροὶ ἄνδρες apparently correspond to the heroes Aeneas sees. Finally, Plutarch speaks of ὀργιάζειν as part of the τελετή; this does not become clear in the translation.

After Aeneas has passed through the various regions of the underworld and seen the place of the damned, he approaches Elysium, a lovely landscape bathed in light where the blessed spirits dwell (638ff.).

> devenere locos laetos et amoena virecta
> fortunatorum nemorum sedesque beatas.
> largior hic campos aether et lumine vestit
> purpureo, solemque suum, sua sidera norunt.

This could be the radiant light which is often mentioned in the testimonies of the mystic rites, the φῶς μυστικόν of Aristophanes' *Frogs* (342ff., 454ff.),[20] the sun shining at midnight of Apuleius' initiation scene (*Met.* 11.23.8), the radiance remembered by Themistius (*Or.* 20, p. 235b Dindorf), which, to him, seems to symbolize the rebirth of the soul from the night of death.

Among the blessed, Aeneas finds not only his father and the mythical kings of Troy but heroes, priests, poets,

> inventas aut qui vitam excoluere per artis
> quique sui memores alios fecere merendo,

and Orpheus (645ff.) and Musaeus (666ff.), both mentioned prominently. According to Diodorus Siculus (4.25.1) Orpheus had been a hierophant at Eleusis, and other sources see in him a direct descendant of Eumolpus, the instigator and first celebrant of the mysteries. These myths no doubt reflect a historic truth: the Orphic elements which had become assimilated by the Eleusinian religion. Musaios, too, one of the mythical founders of Orphism, may have had a subordinate place at Eleusis; it is he who shows Aeneas the way to Anchises.[21]

From his father Aeneas learns the doctrine of *metempsychosis* (703ff.) which may be called the ἱερὸς λόγος of *Aeneid* 6. Was this doctrine also part of the λεγόμενα at Eleusis? Mylonas (282) assumes that the fortunes of Demeter and Persephone, dramatized during the rites, symbolized the vegetation cycle—life, death, and life again. Hence, life is eternal, not only for the world of vegetation, but for men, at least for those who had been initiated. The idea of *metempsychosis* would, in a sense, give a very attractive philosophical explanation to the central myth, and it would

---

20. Cf. Norden 39f.; *Agnostos Theos* (1913), 299 n. 1, 396.
21. On Musaios cf. Lloyd-Jones 223.

certainly agree with the presumable rites which we have discussed. The initiation might have been conceived as a spiritual rebirth, possibly the first in a long series. The μύστης died symbolically and experienced symbolically the horrors of hell, probably as a punishment for the sins he had committed before his initiation. Under the impact of the frightening visions (the monsters, the sinners being tortured in Tartarus), he may have confessed his sins (the practice seems to be established for some mystery religions), and the voice which pierces the darkness (620)—

discite iustitiam moniti et non temnere divos

—may very well mark this point. The μύστης would now declare his repentance and then was allowed to see Elysium and hear the message of rebirth. Having been through hell symbolically, he will no longer be afraid of death, because his initiation exempts him from the punishments he has seen, and he is assured reincarnation or Elysium.

All this, of course, remains hypothetical, though the picture that has emerged seems plausible enough. Warburton's hypothesis, even if tested critically in the light of fresh evidence, is attractive, not only because it gives us a key to the Eleusinian mysteries, but also because it illustrates the richness and complexity of Virgil's art.

Review of Paul Rabbow, *Seelenführung: Methodik der Exerzitien in der Antike*

During the last century B.C. we notice a new trend in the philosophical schools. Instead of devoting themselves mainly to research and speculations, they now pay close attention to the problems of everyday life. The great legacy of classical and postclassical thought becomes the small change for an art of living. The philosopher creates for himself a new role as psychotherapist. This emphasis on the emotional needs of the individual is quite different from the Socratic θεραπεία τῆς ψυχῆς. It is related to Epicurus' rejection of all higher education and all research that does not lead toward ἀταραξία. But during the imperial age the image of the philosopher as priest and servant of the deity, as tutor and adviser, takes shape.[1]

Rabbow believes that there was a definite "system of pedagogy," a "technology" designed to control life through practical ethics (16) during the imperial age. He states clearly (20f., 132) that we have no books on spiritual exercises from antiquity. Strangely enough, he concludes from this lack of evidence an "extraordinarily intense activity" (21, 25, 56). But he is forced to use the *Exercitia* of Ignatius of Loyola, which he sees as the culminating point of this development, as a basis for his observations. The criteria which he abstracts he then applies to texts of Epicurus, Seneca, Plutarch, Epictetus, and Marcus Aurelius.

The continuous analogies between ancient texts and Christian traditions make Rabbow's work look somehow iridescent and vacillating. One might say that Rabbow's thesis, original as it is, would best be presented in a long article but is not solid enough to sustain a whole book. He often introduces Christian terms, such as "Betrachtung und Bedenkung" (23, 131) and "retraite spirituelle" and "bonnes pensées"

From *Gnomon* 28 (1956): 268–71.

1. On the historic reasons for this development see E.D. Dodds, *The Greeks and the Irrational* (1951), 248 ff.; see also A.D. Nock, *Conversion* (1933), chap. 11, on the social role of Hellenistic and later philosophers.

(91), and that does not always help us understand these pagan authors. What is just and enlightening in these comparisons gets lost when analogy is used as a method. Wherever a text is not easily accessible to interpretation, Rabbow speaks of "virtuose Vernebelung" (22), which is eo ipso clear evidence for what he considers a common usage.

One of the most important techniques for training willpower is the meditation which he describes as "sittlich gerichtetes Betrachten und Erwägen" (23; cf. 55). This spiritual exercise is often referred to metaphorically in Epictetus and others, for example, as "chewing," "digesting," or "drilling into the soul" (see the passages collected on Rabbow 325f.). Images such as "Griffbereitschaft" (112ff.) are interpreted by Rabbow as "ideograms" for psychosomatic processes, and by claiming that they are meant quite seriously (326), he practically elevates them to the rank of thought patterns. It is impossible to discuss how strongly the image was felt as such in each case.

In Aeschylus or Pindar, philosophical statements are made through images, but in Seneca or Plutarch, such faded metaphors are used as a stylistic device in popular discourse. It is not clear why Rabbow considers them as a characteristic of "streng methodisch geformte Meditation" (23).

He discusses examples taken from Epictetus, Marcus Aurelius, and other authors. Their themes are how to resign oneself in the face of death, how to accept the world as it is, the idea that everything is transitory. These passages are presented in no discernible order, in translation, and with attempts at an interpretation. Often, we find rather elementary information in the text, while we must look in the notes and in the appendices for the material that would enable us to interpret the crucial passages. Sometimes, essential arguments are hidden in the appendices or the notes (e.g., p. 306 on "Prämeditation" or pp. 333f. and 337 on "Beherzigung"). The book would be easier to read if the author had chosen a few characteristic passages and interpreted them thoroughly.

An example may show how the author reads things into his texts. In Marcus Aurelius 7.1 he sees a "streng geformte Meditation" (51f.; cf. 24, 92, 95, 117, 124f.), mainly because the terms πρόχειρον and συνήθης are used. But is it possible to find in Marcus Aurelius a "technique of making things familiar"? Γνωρίζειν simply means "to recognize," as in 4.29 or 4.33. Theiler's notes in his edition (1954) are useful. On the other hand, passages such as 10.31a which would really support Rabbow's thesis are not discussed. What these *exercitia* have in common with those of Ignatius is essentially only the rhetorical presentation. Stylistic devices such as *amplificatio* through comparison (58f., 63), ascending series of thoughts

(59f., 63f.), dissection of a situation (60f., 64), effective contrast (69f.), concrete description (71 ff.), and, in general, the power with which sensual reality is evoked, often with a tendency toward coarseness—all this derives ultimately from ancient rhetoric and does not touch the essence of meditation; therefore, it should not be considered proof of the survival of meditation in the Christian world. Rabbow is right when he finds the origin of this type of self-persuasion—one might almost say, self-deception—in rhetoric. He could have mentioned that μελέτη, "meditation," also means "declamation." This explains the effective pointedness, the colorful language, and a certain coolness which seems to create a distance. One of the valid results of the book seems to be that the method of contemplation in the West is rhetorical in origin and that meditating, in antiquity, proceeds in a way of talking that may be well-tempered or passionate but always is structured.

Certain recurrent themes (Rabbow calls them "Gedankenhilfen") are striking, for example, the invitation to ἀναχώρησις (Rabbow 91–100; see A.-J. Festugière, *Personal Religion among the Greeks* (1954), 53ff.). This does not always have to be a flight from people; the wise man finds even in the midst of a crowd the way to a self-sufficient contemplation (Sen. *Epist.* 104.7). But the mood, the direction of Christian *exercitia* is totally different from that of ancient texts. A Christian such as Francis of Sales (*Introduction à la vie dévote* 2:12) experiences his own smallness and weakness, while Christ, Mount Calvary, the Cross seem to grow high into another dimension. The meditating self gets lost in the deity from which alone it hopes for salvation. The Stoic seeks salvation in himself: a god is in him; he is the god. The Christian, in his meditation, feels the burden of sin, the message of mercy, while the Stoic gets enraptured with the certainty of participating in the divine by his *ratio*. For him, the aim of moral perfection is in himself; he owes it to himself to give a heroic dimension to his ἦθος (Rabbow 168–70, 176–79, 317). The point of departure is often the same (an anecdote, a quotation, something seen or experienced), but the destinations are far and wide apart.

Rabbow then discusses various methods and forms of "Seelenführung" (e.g., "Beherzigungsakte," pp. 113, 333f.; free meditation, pp. 140–50; premeditation, pp. 160–79; self-examination, pp. 180–88; soliloquy, pp. 189–20; "confession," pp. 276–79) and their specific techniques. What he has to say about articulating, reading aloud, memorizing, taking notes (200–215) is enlightening. He should not emphasize the importance of memorizing in Epicureanism (Epicur. *Epist.* 3.135) without adding that this exercise was recommended by Plato (*Epist.*

6.323C7; on the authenticity see W. Jaeger, *Aristoteles*, 2d ed. [1948], 112ff.; A.-J. Festugière, *Contemplation et vie contemplative selon Platon* [1936], 360 n. 3). Since Rabbow concentrates mainly on the training of willpower, he selects his texts, as well he might, primarily from Stoic and Epicurean sources. But there is, in ancient philosophy, a form of intellectual ἄσκησις which is a means to an end, namely, pure contemplation. It is described by Socrates (Aristoph. *Clouds* 694ff.; cf. Festugière, *Contemplation*, 70ff.) and in the *Phaedo*.

What seems new in the "Seelenführung" of the imperial age lies in the form. Once free speculation was abandoned, the philosophers limited themselves to preserving and interpreting the school tradition and to organizing the curriculum within the school. Epictetus insists on *meditari mortem;* but this is anticipated by Plato (*Phaedo* 64A, 67E, 80E). Now the death experience is described with great intensity, with a wealth of colorful details. This is new. The "Seelenführung" of this period employs an almost breathless self-persuasion, an autosuggestive hyperactivity which cannot hide now and then a certain lack of substance. The author may have overestimated the significance of these new stylistic techniques.[2]

---

2. Something might have been said about Ovid's *Remedia amoris*. Love is here treated as a kind of sickness or delusion, certainly an obstacle to the happy life, and Ovid gives advice on how to remove this obstacle. The whole work is a good example for the philosophic methods of *Seelenführung,* as applied to a specific problem. There are connections between the *Remedia* and Cic. *Tusc.* 4.74f. (derived from Chrysippus' *Therapeutikos,* according to M. Pohlenz, *Hermes* 1906, pp. 321ff.) and Lucretius 4.1141ff. (see K. Prinz, *Wiener Studien* [1914], 57 ff.).

Panaetius and Menander

In one of his letters to Lucilius (*Ep.* 116.5) Seneca tells a charming anecdote of the Stoic philosopher Panaetius of Rhodes.

> eleganter mihi videtur Panaetius respondisse adulescentulo cuidam quaerenti an sapiens amaturus esset. "de sapiente" inquit "videbimus: mihi et tibi, qui adhuc a sapiente longe absumus, non est committendum ut incidamus in rem commotam, impotentem, alteri emancupatam, vilem sibi. sive enim nos respicit, humanitate eius irritamur, sive contempsit, superbia accendimur. aeque facilitas amoris quam difficultas nocet: facilitate capimur, cum difficultate certamus. itaque conscii nobis imbecillitatis nostrae quiescamus; nec vino infirmum animum committamus nec formae nec adulationi nec ullis rebus blande trahentibus." quod Panaetius de amore quaerenti respondit, hoc ego de omnibus affectibus dico: quantum possumus nos a lubrico recedamus; in sicco quoque parum fortiter stamus.

The story reflects the way in which Hellenistic philosophers sometimes dealt with an ethical or psychological problem. A student would ask a question, and the master would answer it briefly, often with logical arguments, sometimes with a joke, but usually in a quaint or colorful way. In that period the philosopher had become a kind of spiritual guide, a father-confessor figure. He kept in touch with his disciples even after they had left the school, counseling and admonishing them by letters.[1] The epistles of Epicurus and those of Seneca are good examples for this continuing philosophical conversation, this soul-searching dialogue that never ends. But the teaching by question and answer, perhaps at the end

---

From *American Journal of Philology* 96 (1975): 256–68.

1. Cf. A.D. Nock, *Conversion* (1933), chap. 11; E.R. Dodds, *The Greeks and the Irrational* (1951), 265ff.; P. Rabbow, *Seelenführung* (1954), passim; G. Luck, *Gnomon* 25 (1953): 367; 28 (1956): 268–71 (in this volume, pp. 35–38).

of a formal lecture, remained popular, as Epictetus' *Diatribes*, recorded by
Arrian, show.[2]

We should note the form of the question. In Greek it would have
been ἆρ' ἐρασθήσεται ὁ σοφός; in analogy to such questions as ἆρα
πολιτεύσεται ὁ σοφός; Panaetius avoids the issue and takes the problem
down to the level of his student, politely including himself.[3]

The young man in the story is obviously a little naive, for the question
had been answered in the affirmative by Zeno and Chrysippus.[4] Yes,
according to the early Stoics, the wise man may love. Of course Panaetius
knew this, and since his doctrine of ethics is in general much less rigid
than that of the early Stoics, he would certainly not have denied the wise
man the right to fall in love. After all, Panaetius even recognized a natural
kind of pleasure, ἡδονὴ κατὰ φύσιν,[5] and he rejected the Stoic orthodoxy
even when it came to ἀναλγησία and ἀπάθεια.[6] But Panaetius clearly
distinguishes between the σοφός and ordinary men who have not yet
reached that stage or will never reach it. For the σοφός alone it is safe to
love; for anyone else love is a danger to be avoided at all costs, like wine,
like flattery, like temptations *(res blande trahentes)* in general.[7]

Love, from the Stoic viewpoint, is a form of disease, and the four
symptoms which Panaetius describes so vividly can be observed in every-

---

2. Cf. Emile Bréhier, *Histoire de la philosophie*, 8th ed., vol. 1 (1967), 373: "Le
maitre (ou un élève) vient de faire une leçon technique; il donne la permission de
l'interroger, et commence alors une improvisation, libérée de toutes formes techniques, dans un style souvent brillant et imagé, plein d'anecdotes, ayant recours
à l'indignation ou à l'ironie." Cf. Aulus Gellius 1.26 on the philosopher Taurus
and Arrian *Epict. diss.* 2.1.1–7, where we seem to have a summary of the lecture
of the day, followed by a diatribe (Bréhier, n. 2).

3. Cf. Fritz-Arthur Steinmetz, *Die Freundschaftslehre des Panaitios* (= Pal-
ingenesia 3 [1967], 10, on Panaetius' concept of the σπουδαῖος. Steinmetz quotes
Cic. *Laelius* 18: *negant enim* [sc. *Stoici veteres*] *quemquam esse virum bonum nisi
sapientem. sit ita sane, sed eam sapientiam interpretantur quam adhuc mortalis nemo est
consecutus; Tusc.* 2.51: *in quo vero erit perfecta sapientia, quem adhuc nos quidem
vidimus neminem, sed philosophorum sententiis qualis hic futurus sit, si modo aliquando
fuerit, exponitur.*

4. *SVF* III 65off., 716ff. v. A.

5. Sext. Emp. *Adv. dogm.* 5.73 = fr. 112 van Straaten. He may have been
influenced by Aristotle (cf. *NE* 10.1–5, pp. 1172a16ff.). Seneca (*De ira* 2.20.4)
recognizes that *modica voluptas . . . laxat animos et temperat.* In the same context
Seneca warns against *noctes sollicitae et desideria amoresque et quidquid aliud aut
corpori nocuit aut animo, aegram mentem in querelas parat.*

6. Gellius 12.5 = fr. 111 van Straaten.

7. Professor Siegfried Jäkel has pointed this out to me. I am grateful to him
for several other comments.

day life. Yet it occurred to me that the philosopher may have in mind a literary work or genre which traditionally represented the four conditions he names. It might be the Hellenistic love elegy—but we know too little about it; it might be the erotic epigram as we know it from Meleager's *Garland*—but there the theme of the love-slave is neglected. Perhaps Panaetius was thinking of the typical lover in Menander's plays; perhaps he was thinking of one comedy in particular. I think it can be shown that all four symptoms listed by Panaetius were dramatized by Menander in a famous play, the *Misumenos*. This play is much better known today than it was about twenty years ago, thanks to recently discovered and edited papyri. We now see that from this one play, all four aspects of love can be illustrated: (1) love as a deep emotional disturbance; (2) love as a paralysis of one's willpower; (3) love as a form of voluntary enslavement; (4) love as a loss of self-respect. Here we have the typical themes of romantic love which Menander brought onto the comic stage in so many variations; but he combined them all most strikingly, I think, in the *Misumenos*.

First of all, the phrase *incidere in rem commotam* seems to suggest Greek expressions for "falling in love" which Menander uses: for example, at *Georgos* fragment 4, εἰς ἔρωθ᾽ ἥκων, and, perhaps, at *Kitharistes* 94, with Sandbach's plausible restoration, ἔπεσον [γὰρ εἰς ἔρωτ᾽ ἐγώ.[8]

My second point is that all the symptoms occur in New Comedy. Let us consider them one by one.

(1) Love as *res commota* (probably χρῆμα ταραχῶδες) is described by Terence at *Andria* 26off. (after Menander): *tot me impediunt curae quae meum animum divorsae trahunt: / amor, misericordia huius, nuptiarum sollicitatio, / tum patris pudor.* And Terence again describes it at *Eunuchus* 59ff. (again after Menander): *in amore haec omnia insunt vitia: iniuriae, / suspiciones, inimicitiae, indutiae, / bellum, pax rursum.* There is also a fragment of the comic poet Caecilius, quoted in a Stoic context by Cicero (*Tusc.* 4.68 = p. 259ff. R.): *deum qui non summum putet, / aut stultum aut rerum esse imperitum existimem, / cui in manu sit quem esse dementem velit, / quem sapere, quem insanire, quem in morbum inici, / quem contra amari, quem expeti, quem arcessier.* This is probably also an adaptation from Menander. In the same context (*Tusc.* 4.68–76) Cicero deals with the passion of love and quotes this passage as well as *Eunuchus* 59ff. (just cited) to illustrate

---

8. Cf. Peter Flury, *Liebe und Liebessprache bei Menander, Plautus und Terenz* (1968), 19 n. 25. He also compares Antiph. fr. 235.3 K., εἰς ἔρωτα τ᾽ ἐμπεσών, and Aesch. *PV* 473f., ἐς νόσον πεσεῖν. On the merits of Flury's book cf. G. Luck, *Gnomon* 43 (1971): 211ff.

the common Stoic doctrine (72): *Stoici vero et sapientem amaturum esse dicunt et amorem ipsum conatum amicitiae faciendae ex pulchritudinis specie definiunt. qui si quis est in rerum natura sine sollicitudine, sine desiderio, sine cura, sine suspirio, sit sane: vacat enim omni libidine, haec autem de libidine oratio est. sin autem est aliquis amor, ut est certe, qui nihil absit aut non multum ab insania* . . . The first sentence is an almost literal translation of a Stoic fragment (261) which I will discuss shortly: Cicero distinguishes between *amor* as a form of *amicitia* and *amor* as *libido*. The wise man—if he really exists—is by definition free from *libido* and therefore free from all the torments of sexual desire (*sollicitudo* is close to *res commota*), but the love we can observe in real life (or in comedy, the mirror of life) is a form of madness, a mental disease. Like Panaetius, whom he may follow in this whole context,[9] Cicero distinguishes between the σοφός and the ordinary human being (58): *sed quoniam suspicor te non tam de sapiente* [sc. *quaerere*] *quam de te ipso—illum enim putas omni perturbatione esse liberum, te vis* . . . This is exactly the situation of our anecdote.

(2) Love as *res impotens* (probably χρῆμα ἀκρατές) can be illustrated from the *Andria* (879ff.) again: *adeo impotenti esse animo ut praeter civium / morem atque legem et sui voluntatem patris / tamen hanc habere studeat cum summo probro.*[10]

(3) The one Menander play which presents love as a form of voluntary slavery perhaps most memorably (as well as the other aspects of love, of course) is the *Misumenos.*[11] The plot was roughly known from Arrian *Epicteti Dissertationes* 4.1.19 (= fr. 2 Sandb.), but the new papyri give us a much better idea (though much remains puzzling) of a play which was clearly one of Menander's greatest. Thrasonides, a professional soldier (we would say, an officer) of the *miles gloriosus* type has come into possession of a young woman, Krateia. He falls in love with her, but she rejects him (hence the title), and though she is his property, he does not take her by force, because he wants to be loved. Epictetus mentions the play and

---

9. It is generally recognized, I think, that Cicero borrows from Panaetius in the *Tusc.* The numerous quotations from Greek and Roman plays are characteristic for this work. One should remember that, according to Zeno's definition (Diog. Laert. 7.110 = *SVF* I 205), any πάθος is ἄλογος καὶ παρὰ φύσιν ψυχῆς κίνησις.

10. Aristotle, for whom Panaetius had great admiration, deals with ἀκράτεια at *NE* 7.2, pp. 1145b11ff. There he quotes Socrates as saying that the ἀκρατής is the slave of the temptations to which he yields.

11. I use Sandbach's Oxford text (1972) and the commentary of Gomme and Sandbach (1973).

quotes two lines from it in his lecture on true freedom. He makes the point
that the owner of the slave girl actually becomes her voluntary slave. To
Epictetus this is the worst form of slavery, worse than the form he had
known himself. The lines he quotes must come from the beginning of the
play, though they cannot be joined to A1–16, the first important piece of
text preserved on a papyrus. When the play begins the officer comes out
of his house in the middle of the night (when most normal Greeks are
asleep or make love) and confesses his wretched, shameful love. The
irony of the situation is stressed by the two lines preserved in Arrian:
παιδισκάριόν με καταδεδούλωκ᾽ εὐτελές, / ὃν οὐδὲ εἷς τῶν πολεμίων ⟨οὐ⟩
πώποτε. Thrasonides, the great military hero, has become the prisoner of
love.[12] The woman he possesses (or thinks to possess) legally possesses
him emotionally. She is in his power, and yet he refuses to touch her. This
unexpected delicacy of feeling must have amused an Athenian audience.
The slave image can be paralleled from other plays (e.g., Men. Samia 624f.:
ὅρκος, πόθος / χρόνος, συνήθει᾽, οἷς ἐδουλούμην ἐγώ; Plaut. Bacch. 92f.:
mulier, tibi me emancupo: / tuos sum, tibi dedo operam), but the Misumenos
offers the most striking, the most paradoxical instance.

(4) The lover tends to cheapen himself and is ready to throw his life
away.[13] Epictetus (loc. cit.) tells us that Thrasonides later on (i.e., still at
the beginning of the play and probably in the same scene) demands a
sword to kill himself, but someone (most likely his slave, Getas) has
taken the precaution of collecting all the swords within reach and depos-
iting them with a neighbor. Thrasonides is furious at that person who
only meant well. Again, suicide threats are not uncommon in New Comedy (c.f., e.g., Alcesimarchus in Plaut. Cist. 639ff.), but by now it has
become almost certain, I think, that Panaetius thought of the beginning
of the Misumenos.

I shall consider some additional evidence later on; so far I have established, I believe, that all the aberrations to which love may lead can be
found right at the beginning of the Misumenos and—this is important—in
the exact order in which Panaetius lists them. First is the theme of emotional disturbance and suffering; then, the theme of helplessness;[14] then,

---

12. Flury (op. cit.) has well observed this.

13. The interpretation of Max Pohlenz (Stoa und Stoiker [1950]: 218), "der die
eigene Person vergisst," is inaccurate.

14. By falling in love so helplessly, Thrasonides also violates τὸ πρέπον, an
important concept in Panaetius' ethics. Cf. R. Reitzenstein, Werden und Wesen der
Humanität (1907), 11, 28; M. van Straaten, Panétius: Sa vie, ses écrits et sa doctrine
avec une édition des fragments (1946), 160ff.

the slave image; finally, the suicide threat. Thus, the anecdote confirms the order in which the fragments are printed in Sandbach's new Oxoniensis and the reconstruction of Gomme and Sandbach (commentary pp. 438ff.). We have seen that four hundred years after Menander's death a Stoic philosopher, Epictetus, still quotes from the *Misumenos* to document the madness of love. We shall see that the same play was already used in the early Stoa for the same purpose. No doubt Panaetius, who represents the so-called Middle Stoa, remembered the same play when he answered the young man's question.

There is only a short section on love in von Arnim's *Stoicorum veterum fragmenta* (III 716–22), but the first fragment (716) from Diogenes Laertius 7.129, shows that both Zeno and Chrysippus[15] thought it was right for the σοφός to love "the young men who by their looks show a natural talent for ἀρετή." To the early Stoics love is an "attempt toward being friends because of physical beauty; its end is not sex but friendship. Thrasonides certainly, though he had the woman he loved in his power, stayed away from her because she hated him. Thus love is for the sake of φιλία as Chrysippus, too, writes in his book *On Love*, and it is not to be blamed. Beauty they describe as the bloom (or shine) of ἀρετή."

> καὶ ἐρασθήσεσθαι δὲ τὸν σοφὸν τῶν νέων τῶν ἐμφαινόντων διὰ τοῦ εἴδους τὴν πρὸς ἀρετὴν εὐφυΐαν, ὥς φησι Ζήνων ἐν τῇ Πολιτείᾳ καὶ Χρύσιππος ἐν τῷ πρώτῳ Περὶ βίων καὶ Ἀπολλόδωρος ἐν τῇ Ἠθικῇ.
> 130   Εἶναι δὲ τὸν ἔρωτα ἐπιβολὴν φιλοποιΐας διὰ κάλλος ἐμφαινόμενον· καὶ μὴ εἶναι συνουσίας, ἀλλὰ φιλίας. τὸν γοῦν Θρασωνίδην καίπερ ἐν ἐξουσίᾳ ἔχοντα τὴν ἐρωμένην, διὰ τὸ μισεῖσθαι ἀπέχεσθαι αὐτῆς. εἶναι οὖν τὸν ἔρωτα φιλίας, ὡς καὶ Χρύσιππος ἐν τῷ Περὶ ἔρωτός φησι· καὶ μὴ εἶναι ἐπίμεμπτον αὐτόν. εἶναι δὲ καὶ τὴν ὥραν ἄνθος ἀρετῆς.

Part of this important testimony has been translated by Cicero (*Tusc.* 4.72), almost word by word. He renders φιλία by *amicitia*, and I suppose

---

15. There is an anecdote about Chrysippus, preserved by Stob. *Flor.* 63.31 Mein. (= *SVF* III 720), which shows that this philosopher was not always very scrupulous about both his logic and his language: Χρυσίππου· εἰπόντος τινός ʽοὐκ ἐρασθήσεται ὁ σοφός· μαρτυρεῖ γοῦν Μενέδημος, Ἐπίκουρος, Ἀλεξῖνόʼ. ʽταύτῃʼ ἔφη ʽχρήσομαι ἀποδείξει· εἰ γὰρ Ἀλεξῖνος ὁ ἀνάγωγος καὶ Ἐπίκουρος ὁ ἀναίσθητος καὶ Μενέδημος ὁ ——— οὔ φησιν, ἐρασθήσεται ἄρα. This might be called arguing with a club. One wonders what shocking epithet was in the textual gap.

we have to translate both terms by "friendship," since there seems to be no other word; but we should remember that φιλέω also means "to kiss" and that *amicus* is derived from *amare*.[16] For the Stoics this "friendship" which does not involve sex (it is contrasted to συνουσία) is the true, the highest form of love.[17] The σοφός may love someone because he or she is beautiful, but only because physical beauty indicates a natural talent for ἀρετή; hence it is called the "bloom" of ἀρετή.

The most important part of the testimony is the clear reference to the *Misumenos*, even though neither author nor title is mentioned. But the play was so famous that the name of the main character, Thrasonides, was sufficient. Hence this is a valid *testimonium* for the play, and it should definitely be included in critical editions,[18] along with the Epictetus passage and the other texts. We see that Zeno, the founder of the school, a younger contemporary of Menander, realized the value of the play, which he may have seen performed, for his theory of love. Even a man like Thrasonides does not just want sex (which he could have had); he wants love, and without love the mere physical act means nothing to him. This is the point which the play makes, and it makes it as it opens; the early Stoics as well as Epictetus paraphrase the famous first scene.

It can be shown, I think, that Panaetius' ethics were deeply influenced by Menander. The extant fragments do not reflect this adequately.

---

16. Cf. Steinmetz 46ff. He quotes Cic. *Laelius* 26: *amor enim, ex quo amicitia nominata est princeps est ad benevolentiam coniungendam.* Later on he writes (27), *deinde cum similis sensus exstitit amoris, si aliquem nacti sumus, cuius cum natura et moribus congruamus, quod in eo quasi lumen aliquod probitatis et virtutis perspicere videamur.* Steinmetz (50 n. 186) compares *Tusc.* 2.58: *sumus enim natura . . . studiosissimi appetentissimique honestatis: cuius si quasi lumen aliquod aspeximus, nihil est quod, ut eo potiamur, non parati simus et ferre et perpeti.* Cicero is probably following Panaetius in both contexts (Steinmetz loc. cit.), but it should be added that this is Panaetius' variation of the early Stoic concept that beauty leads to φιλία, because it is ἄνθος ἀρετῆς. Cicero translates ἄνθος by *lumen* which is perfectly legitimate (cf. Theog. 452). Steinmetz should have said more about the emotional character of φιλία in antiquity: the translation "friendship" is rather misleading.

17. This may be true of Aristotle's concept of φιλία in *NE* 8 and 9. Steinmetz, p. 59 n. 186, suggests that Panaetius owes much to Aristotle and Menander. On Peripatetic ideas in Menander cf. now F. Wehrli, *Entretiens Fondation Hardt* 16 (1970): 147ff. Steinmetz (148ff.) also notes that Panaetius warned his disciples against the "flatterer," κόλαξ, a well-known type of the New Comedy.

18. It is missing in the recent editions which I compared, but Gomme and Sandbach quote it in their note on *Misum.* A12 without any comment.

We have to look at the first two books of Cicero's *De officiis*, which are based on Panaetius' treatise Π. καθήκοντος, to see how passages from the New Comedy are used by the philosopher to illustrate some of his ideas. It has been suggested[19] that each time Cicero quotes Terence, his Greek original had a quote from Menander. I think this is true, because all the Terentian comedies quoted are derived from plays by Menander. To give an example, at *De officiis* 1.30 Cicero quotes *Heautontimorumenos* 77 with the following comment: *est enim difficilis cura rerum alienarum, quamquam Terentianus ille Chremes "humani nihil a se alienum putat."* The line has been discussed many times,[20] but there seems to be no general agreement about its original Greek form. Fragment 475 Koerte-Thierfelder (= 602 Kock) is, perhaps, the likeliest candidate, if one accepts Headlam's restoration: ⟨ἄνθρωπος εἰμ', ἄνθρωπος⟩ οὐδείς ἐστί μοι ἀλλότριος, ἂν ᾖ χρηστός. But there can be little doubt that in Panaetius' treatise the original Greek line from Menander's *Heautontimorumenos*, whatever it looked like, was quoted.

Menander's influence on Panaetius can also be seen in his use of the term *humanitas* in our anecdote. It may seem a strange term in this context—the *humanitas* of the beloved toward the lover? But it is contrasted with *superbia* (ὕβρις), and it implies *facilitas amoris*. This may give us a clue to the Greek.

Broadly speaking, *humanitas* corresponds either to φιλανθρωπία or παιδεία or to a combination of both. As times changed, one aspect could be emphasized more than the other, and the aspects themselves could be interpreted differently. In certain contexts, for instance, φιλανθρωπία as well as *humanitas* means nothing more than "good manners." Isocrates (*Antidosis* 132) gives the following piece of advice: "if you wish to succeed in politics you must be pleasant and polite in your manner, your way of speaking"; the adverb he uses is φιλανθρώπως. And the rhetor Porcius Latro, quoted by the Elder Seneca (*Controv.* 2.7.3), speaks about the way in which a Roman *matrona* should behave in the street: "let her go about with her eyes on the ground. In the face of overzealous greeting (by a gentleman) let her be impolite rather than immodest" *[ferat iacentis in terram oculos; adversus officiosum salutatorem inhumana potius quam inverecunda sit]*. It would have been a sign of *humanitas* to respond

---

19. Steinmetz 149ff.

20. E.g., by A. Koerte, *Hermes* 77 (1942): 101ff.; M. Pohlenz, *Hermes* 78 (1943): 270ff.

to the effusive greeting of the man with a smile or a few kind words. Not to return the greeting at all—because it might encourage him—is definitely *inhumanum*, ἀπάνθρωπον.[21]

It has often been said that it was Panaetius' concept of *humanitas* that influenced the Scipionic circle. This view has been disputed,[22] and again it must be said that the extant fragments of Panaetius' teaching are not very helpful. Still, I think it can be shown indirectly how important Menander's concept of *humanitas* was for Panaetius and, through him, for the Scipionic Circle and for Cicero.

For Menander, φιλάνθρωπος and related terms seem to have a variety of meanings. In passages such as *Aspis* 395, *Samia* 35, *Papyrus Didot* 1.41, and *Dyskolos* 105 and 573 it means "kind," "friendly," "generous," "courteous";[23] it comes close to the "well mannered," and it includes politeness, understanding, sympathy. In Cicero, too, *humanitas* is associated with *suavitas* (social grace), *mansuetudo* (gentleness), *facilitas* (pleasantness), *liberalitas* (generosity).

But the terms ἄνθρωπος and ἀνθρώπινος also have a special value in Menander. A famous line (fr. 484 K.-Th. = 761 Kock) is very significant for Menander's *humanitas*:

ὡς χαρίεν ἔστ᾽ ἄνθρωπος, ἂν ἄνθρωπος ᾖ.

Gomme and Sandbach (547) compare it to *Samia* 17, δι᾽ ἐκεῖνον ἦν ἄνθρωπος, and it is worthwhile to quote their comment: " 'Through him I was a human being.' The idea that man is by nature admirable, pride in being human, and the belief that to be human means to be humane are concepts more than once expressed by Menander's characters. They lie behind the use of the adverb ἀνθρωπίνως, *Aspis* 260, *Mis.* 302, and the line frag. 484 . . ."

It can be shown that Panaetius embodied this value of Menander's *humanitas* in his ethics. Again, we must turn to Cicero. We have already said that in *De officiis* 1 and 2 he follows Panaetius. It is very likely that most of *De republica*, especially book 1, is based on Panaetius' II.

---

21. In Seneca *humanitas* is almost always equal to φιλανθρωπία and is often associated with *clementia* or *misericordia*. Cf. *Ep.* 88.30, 99.20; *Clem.* 1.2. etc.; Reitzenstein 6, 25.

22. E.g., by R. Harder, *Hermes* 69 (1934): 68ff.

23. Gomme and Sandbach (95) on *Aspis* 395.

πολιτείας.[24] The idea that a truly human being, *homo vere humanus*, represents a superior breed, a social ideal, can be found at *De officiis* 1.105 *(sunt enim quidam homines non re sed nomine;* cf. 3.26: *quid cum eo disseras qui hominem ex homine tollat?)* and at *De republica* 1.17.18 *(quod autem imperium, qui magistratus, quod regnum potest esse quam despicientem omnia humana et inferiora sapientia ducentem nihil umquam nisi sempiternum et divinum animo volutare? cui persuasum sit appellari ceteros homines, esse solos eos qui essent politi propriis humanitatis artibus).* Both passages are very close to each other and to Menander fragment 484, but the second one introduces a new definition of the *homo vere humanus:* (1) he looks down on all human things; (2) he is well educated. If Cicero did follow Panaetius in *De republica* 1, we can claim for the Stoic philosopher the idea that παιδεία is part of *humanitas*.

I think it has become probable that Panaetius' view of love and his concept of *humanitas* as part of his ethics owe a great deal to Menander. From what we know about him, Menander himself embodied the culture, the lifestyle, the charm and ease of a great Athenian gentleman;[25] he shows us in his plays the good society of Athens in the late fourth century, as he knew it, perhaps the most civilized society that ever existed. These plays, written to entertain, tell us a great deal about human nature and human relations, and since this is the subject of ethics, Panaetius must have realized how valuable they were to illustrate problems and conflicts in everyday life. Much of his ethical doctrine, as we can reconstruct it, may be considered an interpretation of the world of Menander, the incomparable world of Athens in the late classical period.

Not only the Stoics but other philosophers of the Hellenistic and the imperial periods are fond of quoting Menander when they discuss the

---

24. Philippson, *RE* 13 (1939): 1116; Pohlenz, *RE* 18, no. 2 (1949): 437. In book 2 he seems to follow Polybius, another member of the Scipionic circle and himself influenced by Panaetius' thought, it would appear.

25. There is a miniature bronze portrait of Menander in the J. Paul Getty Museum in Malibu, California, published and discussed by Bernard Ashmole in *AJA* 77 (1973): 60, plates 11–12. It authenticates the more than fifty replicas of a well-known type, because the base, which has never been separated from the bust, clearly bears the name "Menandros." The little bust alone among all the replicas, as Bernard Ashmole observes, conveys the impression that the poet squinted, as the *Suda* says he did (ed. A. Adler [1933], 361, 589). The poet is not idealized at all: one has the feeling of looking at a real person—charming, perceptive, and with a great sense of humor. It is altogether an unusual portrait.

phenomenon of love. Plutarch, in a fragment from his essay *De amore* preserved by Stobaeus (*Ecl.* 4.20.34), calls love the πνεῦμα κοινόν which animates all of Menander's plays, and he describes the playwright himself as an "enthusiastic worshiper," θιασώτην . . . καὶ ὀργιαστήν, of the god Eros.[26] In the same fragment Plutarch says that Menander deals with the theme of love "in a rather philosophical manner," and he then quotes fragment 568 Koerte-Thierfelder (= 541 Kock).

> τίνι δεδούλωνταί ποτε;
> ὄψει; φλύαρος· τῆς γὰρ αὐτῆς πάντες ἄν
> ἤρων· κρίσιν γὰρ τὸ βλέπειν ἴσην ἔχει.
> ἀλλ᾽ ἡδονή τις τοὺς ἐρῶντας ἐπάγεται
> συνουσίας; πῶς οὖν ἕτερος ταύτην ἔχων
> οὐδὲν πέπονθεν, ἀλλ᾽ ἀπῆλθε καταγελῶν,
> ἕτερος⟨δ᾽⟩ ἀπόλωλε; καιρός ἐστιν ἡ νόσος
> ψυχῆς· ὁ πληγεὶς δ᾽ εἰσβολῇ[27] τιτρώσκεται.

It would be tempting to think that this passage is from the *Misumenos;* Plutarch was familiar with this play and quotes (*De cup. div.* 525a) the lines A4–5.

What positive attitude did Panaetius recommend against the dangers and temptations and worries of life? I think it can be summed up by the term εὐθυμία. We know that he wrote a treatise titled Π. εὐθυμίας, and it has been suggested that Plutarch's essay with the same title is based on it.[28] There are certainly Stoic ideas in this essay, and Menander is quoted in it no less than five times. At least the conclusion should be presented here for its beauty and quiet dignity.

> 20. Ἄγαμαι δὲ τὸ τοῦ Διογένους, ὃς τὸν ἐν Λακεδαίμονι ξένον
> ὁρῶν παρασκευαζόμενον εἰς ἑορτήν τινα καὶ φιλοτιμούμενον,
> "ἀνὴρ δ᾽," εἶπεν, "ἀγαθὸς οὐ πᾶσαν ἡμέραν ἑορτὴν ἡγεῖται;" καὶ

26. The terms are borrowed from the language of the mystery religions, as in Xenophon (*Symp.* 8.1), who calls the worshipers of Eros θιασῶται τοῦ θεοῦ. For some parallels in Latin love poetry cf. G. Luck, in *Antike Lyrik* (Wissensch. Buchgesellsch. Darmstadt [1970]), 472 n. 15.

27. In the last line I prefer Bentley's εἰσβολῇ to Sandbach's recent suggestion, εἰς ἀκμήν. The unmetrical †εἴσω δή† of Stobaeus cannot be corrected from *Amat.* 763 because of a lacuna, coextensive with these letters, in the MSS.

28. G. Siefert, *Plutarchs Schrift* π. εὐθυμίας (1908), accepted by Pohlenz, Ziegler, and others.

πάνυ γε λαμπράν, εἰ σωφρονοῦμεν. ἱερὸν μὲν γὰρ ἁγιώτατον ὁ
κόσμος ἐστὶ καὶ θεοπρεπέστατον· εἰς δὲ τοῦτον ὁ ἄνθρωπος
εἰσάγεται διὰ τῆς γενέσεως οὐ χειροκμήτων οὐδ᾽ ἀκινήτων
ἀγαλμάτων θεατής, ἀλλ᾽ οἷα νοῦς θεῖος αἰσθητὰ μιμήματα νοητῶν,
φησὶν ὁ Πλάτων, ἔμφυτον ἀρχὴν ζωῆς ἔχοντα καὶ

D   κινήσεως ἔφηνεν, ἥλιον καὶ σελήνην καὶ ἄστρα καὶ ποταμοὺς νέον
ὕδωρ ἐξιέντας ἀεὶ καὶ γῆν φυτοῖς τε καὶ ζῴοις τροφὰς
ἀναπέμπουσαν. ὧν τὸν βίον μύησιν ὄντα καὶ τελετὴν τελειοτάτην
εὐθυμίας δεῖ μεστὸν εἶναι καὶ γήθους· οὐχ ὥσπερ οἱ πολλοὶ
Κρόνια καὶ Διάσια καὶ Παναθήναια καὶ τοιαύτας ἄλλας ἡμέρας
περιμένουσιν, ἵν᾽ ἡσθῶσι καὶ ἀναπνεύσωσιν, ὠνητοῦ γέλωτος
μίμοις καὶ ὀρχησταῖς μισθοὺς τελέσαντες. εἶτ᾽ ἐκεῖ μὲν εὔφημοι

(477) καθήμεθα κοσμίως· οὐδεὶς γὰρ ὀδύρεται μυούμενος οὐδὲ θρηνεῖ
Πύθια θεώμενος ἢ πίνων ἐν Κρονίοις· ἃς δ᾽ ὁ θεὸς ἡμῖν ἑορτὰς

E   χορηγεῖ καὶ μυσταγωγεῖ καταισχύνουσιν, ἐν ὀδυρμοῖς τὰ πολλὰ
καὶ βαρυθυμίαις καὶ μερίμναις ἐπιπόνοις διατρίβοντες. καὶ τῶν
μὲν ὀργάνων χαίρουσι τοῖς ἐπιτερπὲς ἠχοῦσι καὶ τῶν ὀρνέων τοῖς
ᾄδουσι, καὶ τὰ παίζοντα καὶ σκιρτῶντα τῶν ζῴων ἡδέως ὁρῶσι,
καὶ τοὐναντίον ὠρυομένοις καὶ βρυχωμένοις καὶ σκυθρωπάζουσιν
ἀνιῶνται· τὸν δ᾽ ἑαυτῶν βίον ἀμειδῆ καὶ κατηφῆ καὶ τοῖς
ἀτερπεστάτοις πάθεσι καὶ πράγμασι κἀκ φροντίσι μηδὲν πέρας

F   ἐχούσαις πιεζόμενον ἀεὶ καὶ συνθλιβόμενον ὁρῶντες, οὐχ ὅπως
αὐτοὶ μὲν ἑαυτοῖς ἀναπνοήν τινα καὶ ῥᾳστώνην πορίζουσιν·
πόθεν; ἀλλ᾽ οὐδ᾽ ἑτέρων παρακαλούντων προσδέχονται λόγον ᾧ
χρώμενοι καὶ τοῖς παροῦσιν ἀμέμπτως συνοίσονται καὶ τῶν
γεγονότων εὐχαρίστως μνημονεύσουσι καὶ πρὸς τὸ λοιπὸν ἵλεω
τὴν ἐλπίδα καὶ φαιδρὰν ἔχοντες ἀδεῶς καὶ ἀνυπόπτως
προσάξουσιν.

For him who has peace of mind, every day is a holy day and the whole
world a sanctuary. He overlooks the worries and conflicts of daily life
with supreme indifference, and he will naturally avoid all the temptations against which Panaetius warns.

Epicurus and His Gods

"The world lives in pain, because for this it has the greatest aptitude." This was said in the third century B.C. by a Greek whose complex personality still defies any simplistic approach. Epicurus, like Pythagoras or Heraclitus, cannot be placed into a neatly labeled drawer by scholars. He was a believing skeptic, a rationalist endowed with imagination, a rebel aware of tradition, an ascetic hedonist—and more than that, for it would be easy to add a whole string of paradoxical pairs of concepts. Epicurus understood the paradoxes of life. He designed a system, gave it a scientific basis, and—most important—lived it.

The sentence just quoted is, in a sense, the key to Epicurus' philosophy. At one point, he must have realized that all human beings live in fear and are trying to escape from it. As a young man, Epicurus must have known this feeling of fear, confusion, and helplessness.

The gods of the ancient city-state were not dead but no longer played their role in protecting the individual and the community. The old questions—to what extent are divine powers active in this world? what is the relationship between religion and ethics? what is the meaning of human life?—were still being discussed, but the traditional answers found in myth and poetry were no longer acceptable to philosophical minds.

In the battle between tradition and philosophical thought, tradition was still a formidable opponent. In 399 B.C., Socrates was accused of having introduced new deities and corrupted the youth of Athens. He was sentenced to death and died in prison. But for the forces of tradition, this was not a real victory. In Socrates' disciples, especially in Plato, the new faith of free thought spoke forth. Plato's theology included a cosmic god, a divine principle of the visible order within the universe.

Pythagoras already had understood the nature of the universe as

From *Gymnasium* 67 (1960): 308–15.
This essay owes a great deal to the book of a man who was my teacher and friend, A.-J. Festugière's *Epicure et ses dieux* (Paris, 1946).

κόσμος, that is, an order, a harmony. Democritus, the father of atomism, had postulated that human beings can actually understand the universe and, to a certain extent, control it. But for Plato, there is something beyond the world of familiar phenomena: it is the realm of ideas, the true reality, as he claims, because only the ideas are not subject to the law of coming into being and passing away.

Now there are within the visible order things whose changes take place in regular movements. These are the heavenly bodies. Since their movements presuppose a moving force endowed with a mind, a divine spirit, Plato's cosmic god, must be posited as the ultimate mover of the heavenly spheres.

Thus, Plato created a religion for the "sage" or the "wise man"— perhaps we should say, "the intellectual"—but not to destroy the old religion of the city-state. As citizens, the intellectuals—or most of them—still respected the ancient gods. Little had changed, as far as we can tell: the cults, the liturgies, the conservative elements of religion— they were still the same. The sacred ship on wheels, the peplos flowing from its mast, was still dragged up to the Acropolis in a solemn procession. But the essential meaning of religion was changing. Convention was taking the place of spontaneous emotion.

When Alexander the Great, in 324 B.C., ordered the allied Greek city-states to worship him as a god, Demosthenes proposed to the Assembly of the Athenians to recognize the king as the son of Zeus or even as Poseidon himself, if this would make him happy. The Athenians, who no longer had much use for polytheism, did not take such issues very seriously. Menander, the great playwright who represents Attic humanism in its most elegant form, introduced in his *Arbitration* an intelligent slave. Onesimus, who tosses up, in an ironic mood, ideas about the gods and divine providence: "Just think of the many cities on earth and the many human beings in these cities. Do you really believe that the gods are concerned about the problems of all these people? Do you want to burden the gods with worries? That's no existence worthy of gods!"

This is not necessarily an echo of Epicurean ideas. Epicurus acknowledges the existence of the gods, and he knows that they consist of the very finest substance and belong to the highest order of beings. But they live a life of purest pleasure, and they are totally unconcerned about the well-being of mankind. Menander must have known Epicurus personally, and he probably knew about his teaching, but in the passage just quoted he seems to express a general feeling of resignation.

Menander's plays could be represented on any stage of the Greek-speaking world, because they are free of traditions and conventions. An Athenian audience could identify more easily with the dramatis personae, of course, but the citizens of any of the new major cities which flourished in Egypt, Syria, and Asia Minor could understand and enjoy these comedies. In Alexandria, Antiochia, or Ephesus, the individual was no longer protected by inherited social and religious systems. He had to find a new orientation in a new world. There was certainly no lack of old and new gods, religions, and cults, but the choice was difficult. Were not all gods ultimately representatives of one and the same supreme deity, identical with the cosmic principle, the world soul, *anima mundi*? The Pantheon, a grandiose creation of the Augustan Age, symbolizes this Hellenistic worldview by uniting under one cupola, an image of the heavenly sphere, all the gods.

Into this world Epicurus was born, in 341 B.C., on the island of Samos, a territory settled by Athenian colonists. At the age of fourteen, the boy was sent to the school of Nausiphanes on the island of Teos. This was a kind of boarding school for the children of the upper crust of the islands. Among the subjects he studied were mathematics, rhetoric, and philosophy. Nausiphanes was a follower of Democritus, and from him, Epicurus must have heard, for the first time, about atomism.

As an Athenian citizen, he was obliged to serve in the army. He underwent basic training and performed garrison duties in Attica. During these two years, he met Menander, the playwright, but we do not know of any other important contacts.

After his discharge at the age of twenty, Epicurus must have felt uprooted, homeless, for his father, like all Athenian colonists, had been driven from the island of Samos. Years of poverty in exile followed. These must have been the years in which his character was formed and his philosophy shaped. It was a period of learning through hardship, characteristic, perhaps, of a new era. Plato and Aristotle had grown, so to speak, into the kind of education that was appropriate for them. The academic life as we know it from Plato's dialogues seems easy, beautiful, almost playful. Epicurus, on the other hand, had to fight for his education.

After ten years of traveling, Epicurus opened his first school in Mytilene on Lesbos. Soon, affluent students came and contributed to his livelihood. Five years later, the philosopher, accompanied by his students, moved to Athens, where he bought a plot of land, the "Garden." From now on, this would be the background of his life and that of his congregation. In 270 B.C., not quite seventy years old, he died, suffering great pain, but peaceful and serene. "This is the happiest day of my life," he wrote to friends, "the last one. The pain in my bladder and my stomach is as bad as always; it goes on and does not abate. But when I think of our conversations, I balance this with inner joy. Friends, you have been faithful to me and to philosophy since your youth; take care of the children of Metrodorus."

What we hear is the voice of a man who is about to depart from a life of suffering, and it is his acceptance of suffering and sorrow that lends weight to his words. In his will he remembered his closest friends and students and made arrangements for the continuation of the school. Festive days in memory of the founder, celebrations of friendship, were instituted in order to preserve the warmth, the joy, and the spirit of freedom characteristic of his message.

A philosophical school in ancient Greece was not at all like a modern university. Plato's Academy, Zeno's Stoa, and Epicurus' Garden were not academic institutions in our sense. To a certain extent, Plato's Academy and Aristotle's Lyceum could be considered prototypes of an *universitas litterarum,* but the Stoa and the Garden are not really comparable. Like the Pythagorean societies of Magna Graecia, they were communities of friends who share the same interests and ideas. Teaching and research were often done in the form of discussions, and the disciples were expected not just to learn but to live a certain doctrine.

For Epicurus, friendship is an end in itself, not just the path to wisdom, but part of wisdom. True education, as he saw it, is not the result of hard work and intensive study but should be a gift of leisure. Too much knowledge and education is superfluous or even, in a sense, damaging, for such studies and pursuits may divert the disciple from the supreme goal, tranquillity of mind. Epicurus nevertheless recommended science as a study of nature, because it may dispel certain prejudices and superstitious notions. Scientific knowledge, however, is not enough: it needs an ethical orientation, and this lies within the free will, the personal responsibility, of the individual.

Secure in the circle of his friends, Epicurus looked up to his gods. To judge from their names, they were still the gods of the old city-state. But much had happened in Epicurus' lifetime. There was a new religious mood, a new understanding of religion. Of course there had been skeptics, even thinkers accused of atheism before. And there were still devout supporters of the traditional cults. But skepticism and agnosticism now appeared in new forms. There was also a variety of new religions and cults, mostly imported from the Near East. To be on the safe side, many sought initiation into the mystery religions. These rituals, kept secret, provided a passport to eternal bliss in the next world.

Fear of the gods and fear of the terrors of life after death in Hades are two essential factors in Greek religion. Epicurus must have been aware of the tremendous power of religion and superstition in the daily life of his fellow citizens. If he, personally, had found the way from fear and doubt to serenity and peace of mind, it must have been his desire to share this experience with others and show them the path to "freedom from emotion," ἀταραξία, a state of mind equally remote from hope as from fear. He wished to communicate to his disciples his own detachment, his particular way of contemplating the world, its creatures, and the gods.

By limiting his ambitions and desires, the wise man achieves freedom from anxiety and, ultimately, true contentment in this life. The gods, by their very nature, enjoy this privilege forever. They are immortal, and they know perfect bliss. For human beings, happiness consists in freedom from cares and anxieties. He who leads a simple life, who despises success, wealth, and fame, has conquered his passions and desires and will achieve ἀταραξία.

But what is true for human beings must also be true of the gods. It would be absurd to imagine gods who are constantly worrying about the functioning of the universe and the well-being of every single individual. In one of his letters, Epicurus writes: "We must not believe that the motions of the heavenly bodies, their displacement from one point to another, their eclipses, their rising and setting, and other phenomena such as these are caused by a being that controls them and will always control them—a being that enjoys, at the same time, perfect bliss and immortal life—for the disturbances caused by activities, duties, emotions such as anger or benevolence are not compatible with bliss; all this is found only in areas ruled by weakness, fear, and dependence on others."

Epicurus was neither a skeptic nor an atheist. He believed in the reality of the gods and did not deny the validity of traditional religion. Personally, he obeyed the religious ordinances and obligations. His piety could almost be called old-fashioned, but not in a superficial sense. He imagined the gods as living an idyllic life of euphoria and utter contentment. Ideally, Homer's gods could have enjoyed this kind of existence, but, as we know from the *Iliad* and the *Odyssey,* they fought among themselves and were dragged into the affairs of mere humans, just like their royal counterparts on earth. Obviously, this kind of theology did not satisfy Epicurus, nor did other philosophers feel comfortable with it.

To put it in modern terms: Was it possible to salvage the old religion in view of modern doubts? Some sort of compromise had to be found. Epicurus insisted on prayers, on active participation in the festivals of the city-state. This was the proper way to approach the gods and to share, somehow, in their blessed state. There is a mystic element in this, not usually associated with Epicureanism. Give the wise man a piece of barley cake and a drink of water, and his happiness will be equal to that of the gods.

Epicurus' doctrine of ἀταραξία does not undermine religion: it purifies it. From now on, the faithful no longer will have to approach their gods in order to pacify them or persuade them to be benevolent; they will be able to feel united to the gods and enjoy a share of their bliss even in this world. An Epicurean text found on an Egyptian papyrus preserves these words: "Do you prefer to believe that your sacrifice of thousands of oxen will reconcile god, when you have committed a crime? Can you imagine that he will accept your offering and postpone, as if he were a human being, your guilt indefinitely?"

What Epicurus has created is a very serene, human image of the gods. His gods are not malevolent, and they do not constantly observe human behavior in order to punish sins at once with thunder and lightning or—even worse—make a note that the evildoer will have to be punished severely in the next world.

The theology of Epicurus is not the only attempt to give to the "wise man," that is, the intellectual, a faith that satisfies his religious needs as well as his scientific curiosity. The doctrine of the cosmic deity, as it was developed in Plato's Academy and in Aristotle's Peripatos, has more or less the same function. According to this doctrine, the cosmic order, as it is reflected in the movements of the heavenly bodies, is eternal and unchangeable. The stars themselves are living beings with a soul, endowed with sense perceptions and reason. In other words, they are divine. Man cannot possibly interfere with this order or change the workings of the cosmic clock, as it has been set from the beginning of the world.

The faithful could speak to Homer's gods and offer sacrifice to them, and they would listen to him or reject his wishes according to their mood of the moment. But fate, εἱμαρμένη, cannot be influenced by offerings and prayers and takes its course, determined by ironclad laws. And yet it would not be true to say that the heavenly bodies, conceived as divine beings and identified with the ancient gods (Zeus, Aphrodite, etc.) are beyond the appeal of the faithful. There is astrology—an attempt to predict the future, based on the movements of the star—but there is also astral religion—an attempt to influence powers that, by definition, cannot be influenced at all. Religion is never quite logical. Needless to say, there is no room for either astrology or astral religion in the system of Epicurus.

The foundations of Stoic ethics, on the other hand, are cosmological. According to their doctrine, the movements of the heavenly bodies reflect a divine mind which governs everything that happens on earth according to rigid laws. Even though the Stoic also strives to achieve the ideal of ἀταραξία, he knows that he will find it not in denying fate but in accepting fate.

For Epicurus, cosmic religion is a real threat to happiness. In his Letter to Pythocles, he writes: "The regular order of the heavenly bodies must be seen in the same way as events on earth. Under no condition should you drag the essence of the deity into this discussion: in the abundance of its bliss, it must be kept free from public service. Otherwise, the whole study of the causes of celestial phenomena becomes mere futile talk. This has happened already to those who did not follow the path of the possible but fell into that mania which declares that things can only happen in a certain way. . ."

Epicurus' philosophy is a doctrine of salvation, and Lucretius, in his great poem *On Nature,* celebrates Epicurus as a savior figure. Epicurus himself seems to have been more modest: he saw his function more as that of a psychiatrist. In his letters—and perhaps even more in the personal conversations which are lost to us—he asked about the everyday problems and conflicts of his disciples and friends. Apparently, he even encouraged them to confess openly the mistakes they made, and the master responded with comforting words and good advice. Short, pregnant sentences were compiled from the major works of the master, and they were read aloud, often repeated, commented on, and committed to memory, as a catechism of Epicurean ethics.

Thus, Epicurus seems to have initiated a new and very fruitful development within the history of ancient thought. By rejecting all higher education, all scientific research that had not ἀταραξία as its goal, he endowed his doctrine with unity and self-sufficiency, and these became its main weapons in the continuous controversies between the various philosophical schools. His method of ψυχαγωγία, that is, of winning people's souls, leading them toward higher goals, was adopted by Stoics and Platonists alike. The ambition of the philosopher was no longer to formulate new ideas, develop new systems, but to deal with the problems of everyday life. This is certainly true of Seneca, Plutarch, Epictetus, and Marcus Aurelius. Teaching the inherited doctrine, making it applicable and palatable to the needs of their disciples and friends, became the vocation of the true philosopher. Thus, the large inheritance of classical and Hellenistic thought is transformed into what might be called the "small change" of practical wisdom, the art of living, of adapting oneself to circumstances. Through his knowledge and self-discipline—which often has ascetic features—the philosopher becomes a priestlike figure, an educator of mankind.

Far from our island home in this universe, totally unconcerned about our lives, are the gods. They are the perfect Epicureans. The peace of mind which the wise man acquires only through asceticism and purification is their natural property. They are anthropomorphous, of human shape, and endowed with human virtues in their highest degree of perfection. Through their very existence—a remarkable theological concept—they are, for us, the incentive, the motivation, to become perfect ourselves. But they do not offer a helping hand. If a reflection of their bliss falls on the toiling apprentice, it is not thanks to their goodness and mercy—another remarkable concept.

Essentially, these are still the Homeric gods in that they "live the easy life," but they are without the limitations and weaknesses they have in the archaic epics. According to the ancient poets, they live in the serene light of Olympus; from there, Epicurus removes them into the universe and settles them in the interspaces between the worlds, the μετακόσμια. Homer's deities sometimes walk among men, but Epicurus separates his gods carefully from the earth and from any human intercourse. Only their images, εἴδωλα, breathlike projections of their appearance which emanate from their surfaces, travel through space with incredible speed and reach our terrestrial abode. That these images, detached from the gods as they are, may produce good or bad effects on earth is acknowledged reluctantly by Epicurus. Obviously, he had to find a compromise between the traditional religion and his own theology.

Since the gods do not interfere with the whole cosmic order, they cannot have created it, at one point in time, out of nothing. The universe is not arranged for the convenience of mankind, and even if it were, the gods would not have felt the need for doing this. Of course they could have created the world if they had wanted to, but there was no reason for them to actually do anything of the kind. Or did they create the world in a capricious mood? To amuse themselves? This would contradict their very nature.

The historical impact of Epicurus' teaching was celebrated by his disciples and successors for centuries, and the memory of the great man was kept alive in many ways. Like all seminal ideas, his theology was able to undergo various transformations or adaptations, but its nucleus hardly changed; as a school, Epicureanism was rather conservative. It was the image of the master himself, his life "full of herbs, fruits, and abstinences," his humanity, and his deep religious feeling which motivated and encouraged his faithful followers in the battle of doctrines.

Was Lucretius Really Mad?

Almost everything we seem to know about the life and death of T. Lucretius Carus comes from St. Jerome who notes as an important event of the year 94 B.C., *Titus Lucretius Carus nascitur qui postea amatorio poculo in furorem versus, cum aliquot libros per intervalla insaniae conscripsisset quos postea Cicero emendavit, propria se manu interfecit anno aetatis XLIV.*

Scholars are divided in their acceptance of these pieces of information. First of all, there are chronological difficulties. According to another tradition, Lucretius died in 54 B.C., not in 50. Jerome could be wrong either about the year of the poet's birth or about the age at which he died. There may be a simple explanation of this discrepancy, but I propose to deal here only with the question of whether the story of Lucretius' mental illness can be traced to earlier sources or whether it is likely to have been circulated by the Christians.

In a curiously impassioned piece, Konrat Ziegler[1] tried to destroy what he called a legend. He rejected—rightly, I believed—Postgate's attempt[2] to prove that there are symptoms of the author's madness in certain parts of *De natura rerum*. Ziegler also refused to believe in the authenticity of the so-called *Vita Borgiana* of Lucretius,[3] after Woltjers

---

From *Euphrosyne*, n.s., 16 (1988): 289–94.

I owe this title to an apocryphal paper invented by my colleague Diskin Clay. He has read my piece and made a few comments, for which I am grateful: "The passage from Persius was seen to refer to Epicurus by J.W. Spaeth, 'Persius and Epicurus: A Note on *Satires* 3.83–84,' *TAPA* 73 (1942): 119–22. One apparent problem with your identifying the sickly old man with Lucretius is the fact that we know very well that Epicurus grew to a (comparatively) old age and that he was ill for many of his last years. Also the figures the centurion cannot tolerate are Greeks. . . . If you recognize this possible objection then you can counter with your . . . argument about *aegrotus*. . . . Your note on *vetus* is essential, too. (I touch on this passage in *Lucretius and Epicurus* [1983], p. 179 and n. 29)."

1. *Hermes* 71 (1936): 421–40.

2. *Bulletin of the John Rylands Library* 10 (1926): 134ff.

3. This vita appears in a humanist hand on separate sheets before the *Editio Veneta* of 1492 which once belonged to Girolamo Borgia and is now in the British

and Hermann Diels had already argued against it. That *Vita* gives the following version: *vixit annos IIII et XL et noxio tandem improbae feminae poculo in furias actus sibi necem conscivit reste gulam frangens vel, ut alii opinantur, gladio incubuit, matre natus diutius sterili.*

To this extent I am able to follow Ziegler, but the rest of his article seems nothing else but an elaborate *argumentum ex silentio*, as he reluctantly acknowledges himself (427). Why did Cornelius Nepos, Ovid, Pliny the Elder, and others say nothing about Lucretius' alleged madness and suicide? Clearly, Ziegler says, because they did not know a story which, for various reasons, they would have told with great relish had they known it. This, of course, does not prove anything, and Ziegler's article, even though it has impressed many scholars, represents, as I have said, a classical case of an *argumentum ex silentio* and deserves to be read for that reason alone.

Ziegler knows, of course, the testimony of Statius (*Silv.* 2.7.75–76),

et docti furor arduus Lucreti,

and it is very instructive to see how he disposes of it: "Uebrigens das feinste antike Wort über unsern Dichter. Aber wäre es nicht äusserste Geschmacklosigkeit, ja eine Schnödigkeit gewesen, das Wort *furor* in bezug auf die Kunst eines Dichters zu brauchen, den sein Geschick mit *furor* im medizinischen Sinn geschlagen hatte? Ganz gewiss: Statius hat nichts vom Wahnsinn des Lukrez gewusst." To this line of reasoning one might object: (1) The ancients did not distinguish clearly between poetic μανία and μανία in the "medical sense." (2) The ancients were not squeamish in referring to people's physical and mental abnormalities; in fact,

---

Library. It was published by J. Masson, *Journal of Philology* 32 (1895): 220–37; *Academy* no. 1155 (1894): 519; it is also found, with useful notes, in H. Diels' edition of *De natura rerum*, vol. 1 (Berlin, 1923), xli–xlii. Masson thought that this was an extract from the vita in Suetonius' lost work *De viris illustribus*, and F. Leo (*Plautinische Forschungen*, 2d ed. [Berlin, 1912], 40 n. 3) accepted this, but Woltjer (*Mnemosyne* 23 [1895]: 222ff.), followed by Diels, argued convincingly that it must be the work of a humanist, perhaps Pontanus, to whom Girolamo Borgia refers. What makes this vita suspicious is the fact that it takes Lucretius and Lucilius as one and the same person. The list of Roman Epicureans could be compiled from Cicero's works and letters, though it does not exist in this form anywhere and actually represents scholarly research of some kind. There are some details for which we have no source, and they may be authentic. "Polidemus" as teacher of L. Calpurnius Piso Frugi could be Philodemus, as Diels suggests (the same corruption occurs in the ms tradition at Cicero *De fin.* 2.119).

they could be rather coarse and cruel. (3) Statius has, indeed, used a very delicate and beautiful phrase: if Lucretius was stricken by madness, it was sublime madness!

Lactantius attacks the Epicureans in general, calling them "blind," "stupid," "mad," "insane," "deranged"; at the same time he admires Lucretius and quotes him more than sixty times.[4] But there is no contradiction: the vocabulary Lactantius uses is the normal vocabulary of philosophical and theological debate in antiquity. In these terms the rival schools insulted each other, and Ziegler himself suggests that Lactantius did not necessarily hate the Epicureans because he had become a Christian but because, before his conversion, he had been a Stoic. There is no allusion to the fate of Lucretius in all of Lactantius, although an excellent opportunity would have offered itself at least once (*Inst. Div.* 3.18.5f.) where Democritus' suicide is reported in the words of Lucretius (3.1041) and suicide in general is condemned.

Lactantius' silence can be explained in different ways. One may assume[5] that Lactantius had not read Suetonius' *De viris illustribus*, but that seems very unlikely, considering the popularity of the work.[6] Of course there is no certainty. Classicists have a tendency to assume that an ancient reader remembered almost everything he had ever read and that he, if he happened to be an author himself, was eager to quote anything he remembered on any suitable or unsuitable occasion.

Following Brieger,[7] Ziegler claims that Jerome must have disliked Lucretius because he was an atheist (though he is obliged to redefine the term *atheism* almost at once), just as Lactantius detested the *persecutores* (although he is obliged to add, at once, that Lucretius could hardly be called a persecutor of Christians).

But Ziegler's last argument is the most bizarre of all. He postulates that Jerome found the last part of Lucretius' book 4 (vv. 1037–1287) particularly repulsive, because "in no other work composed by an ancient poet the essence and the effect of the sexual urge are described as forcefully" as here. Unfortunately, Ziegler forgets that Lucretius' treatment was meant to serve as a warning, not an encouragement; the poet describes the dangers of erotic passion, not its delights. In this context Ziegler also revives the extravagant idea of Fr. Marx[8] that the whole story

---

4. S. Brandt, *Jahrbücher für Klass. Philol.* 143 (1891): 225ff.
5. Ibid.
6. Ziegler 431ff., following A. Brieger, *Bursians Jahresberichte* 89 (1896): 96.
7. *Bursians Jahresberichte* 105 (1900): 48f.
8. *Rhein. Mus.* 34 (1891): 136.

of Lucretius' madness and the *lucida intervalla* during which he wrote his work was concocted by someone who had misunderstood two lines of *De natura rerum* (3.828f.):

> adde furorem animi proprium atque oblivia rerum,
> adde quod in nigras lethargi mergitur undas.

Ziegler comments: "It does not at all appear implausible that a 4th century scholar would take *furorem animi proprium* as 'periods of (my own) madness,' and *oblivia rerum* as 'periods of (my own) loss of memory,' and the second line as a paraphrase of suicide." I can only apply to Ziegler's interpretation the words he uses to describe Jerome's supposed understanding of the two lines: "Mit ernster Wissenschaft hätte diese Interpretation ja nichts mehr zu tun." Of course not, but let us not forget, that this is just a supposition. One would imagine that Jerome was a better Latinist than Professor Ziegler and that he could hardly have become the victim of such a bizarre misunderstanding. If Jerome was malicious enough to invent or circulate the story of Lucretius' madness on the basis of this passage, he surely was not naive enough to read it as a prediction of the poet's own suicide. "Ernste Wissenschaft"? No, "Fröhliche Wissenschaft," I think.

But there is a testimony which has been overlooked or at least not properly recognized in this whole discussion, as far as I can tell. It is Persius' *Satire* 3.77–84.

In the section preceding this particular passage of *Satire* 3, the tutor or companion of the young poet delivers a short *protreptikos* on the theme.

> discite et, o miseri, causas cognoscite rerum (66)

Then the satirist introduces a typical representative of the Roman middle class who rejects philosophical studies altogether[9] as useless and ridiculous.

---

9. But it should be also said that upper-class Romans such as Lucilius and Varro (*Sat. Men.* 57, 105, 122, 243, 245 Bue.) in their satires attack philosophers, regardless of their school. Horace, like Persius, acknowledges the need for philosophy but introduces enemies of philosophical pursuits; cf. M. Coffey, *Roman Satire* (London, 1976), 140, 157, 160f., 250 n. 132.

hic aliquis de gente hircosa centurionum
dicat "quod sapio, satis est mihi. non ego curo
esse quod Arcesilas aerumnosique Solones
obstipo capite et figentes lumine terram
murmura cum secum et rabiosa silentia rodunt
atque exporrecto trutinantur verba labello,
aegroti veteris meditantes somnia, gigni
de nihilo nihilum, in nihilum nil posse reverti.
hoc est quod palles? cur quis non prandeat hoc est?"

Persius' "smelly" centurion makes fun of the philosophers in general, but he singles out two names—Arcesilas, a Platonist, and Solon, one of the Seven Wise Men—and he has also heard of a "sick man of old"[10] who taught such delusions as "nothing can come from nothing; nothing can revert to nothing." That *aegrotus* in this context means "insane" is clear from Cicero (*Tusc.* 3.8: *nomen insaniae significat mentis aegrotationem et morbum, id est insanitatem et aegrotum animum*), and *vetus* means, among other things, "belonging to a past age," as in Cicero (*Brut.* 69: *cum ita sit* [sc. Cato] *ad nostrorum temporum rationem vetus*). This madman who lived in a bygone age had *somnia,* that is, delusions. It is clear, I think, that the centurion who despises all philosophers aims his contemptuous remarks specifically at Lucretius, of whose work he must have heard; the allusions to *De natura rerum* 1.150, 237, and 248 are unmistakable.[11]

We have to look at Persius' passage against the background of philosophical controversy. To the centurion, all philosophers are mad, but the philosophers of rival schools themselves accused each other of being insane. *Somnia* is the very word an Epicurean uses in Cicero (*De Nat. Deor.* 1.42) to denounce some (mainly Stoic) theories that he considers utterly bizarre: *exposui . . . non philosophorum iudicia sed delirantium somnia.* The same Epicurean attacks Plato and the Stoics in similar terms (Cicero *De*

---

10. *Aegrotus vetus* must mean just this, not "a sick old man" or "a man who has been sick for a long time," as Villeneuve (Paris, 1918) and other commentators preferred to explain it.

11. Niall Rudd, in the notes to his excellent translation in *The Satires of Horace and Persius* (Penguin Classics, 1973) lists the relevant passages in Lucretius but adds "In that case Persius had Epicurus chiefly in mind" (179). It would seem more plausible to me that Persius' centurion is thinking of Lucretius, not of Epicurus or Epicureans in general, because it is Lucretius he quotes in a compendiary manner, almost as if referring to a handbook.

Nat. Deor. 1.18): *portenta et miracula non disserentium philosophorum sed somniantium.*[12] A general attack on philosophy is found in Cicero (*De Div.* 2.119): *sed nescio quo modo nihil tam absurde dici potest quod non dicatur ab aliquo philosophorum.*

This last passage almost certainly reflects two lines in one of Varro's *Menippean Satires* (122 Bue.), which Persius must have had in mind:

postremo nemo aegrotus quicquam somniat
tam infandum quod non aliquis dicat philosophus.

[finally, no sick man talks so wildly about monstrous things that some philosopher might not say it.]

Here, *somniare* could refer to the feverish talk of a patient who is very ill but not a lunatic, although the phenomenon itself would have been more or less the same to an ancient observer.

Both Persius in his third *Satire* and Statius[13] in the passage mentioned earlier seem to reflect a Stoic line of attack against the Epicureans, especially their most brilliant Roman exponent, Lucretius. It is virtually the same polemic which the Epicureans used against the Stoics and other schools, as the testimonies from Cicero show. These insults were hurled back and forth in Rome in the first century B.C. as they were, no doubt, in the Greek world before.

But there is a difference. Both Persius and Statius are poets as well as Stoics, and they direct an attack on the Roman poet they admire. Persius puts the criticism of Lucretius into the mouth of an uncouth but not totally illiterate centurion, and Statius praises the "sublime" madness of Lucretius. Both endorse, in a way, the ideology of their school but distance themselves from it. This is the attitude of Seneca, who often quotes Epicurus with approval, although he sometimes seems to feel a little uncomfortable when he does it.

To sum up: The story of Lucretius' madness, whether it be true or false, originated long before the time of Jerome as part of the polemic between Stoics and Epicureans.

---

12. Cf. A. St. Pease (1955–58), ad loc. and on 1.39: *Chrysippus qui Stoicorum somniorum habetur vaferrimus interpres. . . .*

13. On Statius' Stoic creed see now Margarethe Billerbeck, "Aspects of Stoicism in Flavian Epic," *Papers of the Liverpool Latin Seminar* 5 (1985): 352f.; "Stoizismus in der römischen Epik," *ANRW* 32 (1986): 3143ff.

The Muses in Roman Poetry

Cum Musis, id est, cum humanitate et doctrina

—Cicero *Tusc.* 5.66

In the loneliness of woods and mountains a Greek or Roman could meet the gods. A grove, a cave, a spring, a mountaintop crowned with clouds were places where the presence of a numen was felt. Here was a dreamworld which had no boundaries of time or space. Among the deities of nature are the nymphs and the Muses, who are closely related.

Odysseus has fallen asleep on the shore of the island of the Phaeacians. The voices of girls at play wake him up, and at first he imagines to hear the nymphs who dance through nature, as they sing.

> iam Cytherea choros ducit Venus imminente luna,
>   iunctaeque Nymphis Gratiae decentes
> alterno terram quatiunt pede . . .
> (Horace Carm. 1.4.5–7)

The beauty of the nymphs reveals itself in the half-conscious movements of the landscape, even though the deities themselves remain hidden. Now they are here; now they are gone—only a breath that emanates from the secrets of all-surrounding nature.

The harmony of all terrestrial elements is too awesome to be discussed. It is reflected in a feeling that loses itself in the distance and does cling to real objects. Plato has experienced this. He calls this harmony ἔρως, and at the beginning of the *Phaedrus*, the dialogue which explores the nature of ἔρως, he creates a magical mood to which the shade of a tall plane tree, the cool breeze coming from a spring, the song of the cicadas, and the delicate smell of the flowers contribute. Here, near the Ilissus, Socrates senses the presence of the nymphs; an enthusiasm inspired by the Muses fills him, and nature and reflection join to form an image.

From *Horizonte der Humanitas: Festschrift für Walter Wili* (Bern, 1960), 77–89.

Originally, the Muses dwelled on mountaintops (the Latin word *mons* is probably related to Greek μοῦσα), and their sanctuaries were in natural grottos. Shepherds, farmers, and wanderers placed there their humble offerings, testimonies of an ancient popular cult which predates literary evidence.

The nymphs also dwell in the humid chasms of the earth; where there is water and earth, there is life. In front of the grotto of Calypso, nature unfolds such a wealth of beauty that even Hermes, the messenger of the gods, is charmed. The darkness of a grotto hides mysteries. Pythagoras is said to have withdrawn into a cave to lead a life of pure contemplation; there he found quiet and concentration; there the nymphs shared their knowledge with him. In a hymn to Apollo quoted by Porphyry in his treatise "On the Cave of the Nymphs," we read, "For you they have hollowed out the sources of waters endowed with reason, dwelling in grottos, nourishing with their breath the earth, accompanied by the sacred voice of song."

In his excellent book *Die Musen*, Walter F. Otto has made plausible the close relationship of the nymphs with the Muses. Both sing and are teachers of song. Both are originally nature spirits, powers that reveal themselves to naive, unsophisticated people who are open to the charm of a landscape. There is another clue: the Roman Camenae whom Ennius invokes at the beginning of the *Annales* and whom he associates with the Greek Muses were originally nymphs living near springs.

If history, according to Ranke, tells us "what really happened," the nature spirits tell us "what always was there," the prehistory of that which came into being. Their knowledge goes back to a primeval age which has left no written records, not even myths. In his ninth *Paean*, Pindar affirms that the Muses know the remote past—the Muses know everything—and that they impart their knowledge, which ordinary mortals cannot share, to the poets. The poet himself is the custodian of the lore that comes from the Muses.

We use the term *natural history*, which is misleading, for *history* still has its original meaning of "exploration" or "research" (ἱστορία). The Greeks and Romans were able to see in nature the sum of everything that had come into being. In every simple object, they sensed the mysteries of the universe. Trees, rocks, rivers had always been there. They had witnessed the early centuries of the earth. The hamadryad of the tree, the oread of the rocky mountaintop, the Nereid of the stream—all knew something of the ultimate truth. The worship of the Muses comes from a desire to lend a voice to speechless things. The Muses are, in fact, the sounding organ of nature, and the poet who listens to them is the true scientist who has the privilege to speak about all areas of life. But without the favor of the Muses, he will achieve nothing.

The Muses are the daughters of Zeus and Memory. According to Hesiod, there are nine sisters, and Homer, too, knows more than one, even though he invokes only "the Muse" at the beginning of the *Iliad*. The Muses are ancient Hellenic deities, for their name, like that of their mother, Mnemosyne, is Greek. As Memory's daughters, they represent an intellectual gift, and a vague recollection of the past becomes knowledge.

> et meministis enim, divae, et memorare potestis.
> (Virgil *Aen.* 7.465)

It is exciting to think that we are surrounded by hidden knowledge, that we live in a world full of "songs that have never been sung." In his ninth *Paean*, Pindar says, "I have been consecrated and chosen by the gods . . . to create a noble song to the sound of the flute, with the whole power of my talent." Just as the harmony of the spheres is, according to Pythagoras, always there even though we do not hear it, so there are sounds all around us that only the poet hears.

It should be said that this knowledge of things past is solid, accurate, and concrete. The poet may approach it with a vague notion, but he has to take a firm hold of it.

Thanks to the Muses, nature in its infinity thinks itself, expresses itself, and transforms its dreams into music. In ancient Greece, according to Jacob Burckhardt, "the deities of nature became noble personalities, full of life, conscious agents of the universal order." We shall see how the greatest among the Roman poets have faithfully recorded this experience.

Originally, the Muses were not at all a poetic device, a mere ornament; this is the role they play in later poetry. Ovid (*Amores* 3.1) walks through a sacred grove, thinking about a new subject for his "Muse," and sees elegy and tragedy personified. Tragedy strides in her buskin, while one of Elegy's feet is a little longer than the other, which is not unattractive, as Ovid says.

In one of his last poems (*Ex Ponto* 4.8.77–80), addressed to an amateur poet, Ovid ventures a phrase which weakens the powerful symbolism of the Muses and turns it into an abstraction.

sic tibi nec docti desunt nec principis artes,
  mixta sed est animo cum Iove Musa tuo:
quae . . . nec nos unda summovit ab illa
  ungula Gorgonei quam cava fecit equi.

The Greeks worshiped the Muses on Helicon and on Olympus. On Mount Helicon, the Hippocrene, the spring that had been created by Pegasus' hoof, gushed forth. There Hesiod met the Muses; and later poets, such as Callimachus, Ennius, and Propertius, saw them there at least in their dreams.

visus eram molli recubans Heliconis in umbra,
  Bellerophontei qua fluit umor equi . . .
                    (Propertius 3.1.1ff.)

First Apollo appears to Propertius and shows him the way to the grotto of the Muses, where he finds the nine sisters as they gather flowers and make music. Elsewhere, the poet says that they also sing and dance under the direction of Dionysus (*Ex Ponto* 2.30.25ff.). In his youth, the poet danced with them (3.5.19–20), and he wants his mistress to follow him to their sacred precinct.

Drinking from the Hippocrene is synonymous to becoming a poet. This idea reflects the religious symbolism propagated by the great oracles of the ancient world. In certain sanctuaries where oracles were delivered, the priest first drank from a sacred spring and then uttered his prophecies. A spring sacred to the Muses played an important role in the worship of Apollo at Delphi. The seer is a servant of Apollo; the poet is also a servant of the god as well as a messenger of the Muses. "Tell me the truth, Muse," Pindar says, "and I will be your prophet." Originally, a προφήτης is a person who speaks for someone else.

Hesiod's experience on Helicon is often called "the consecration of the poet." Virgil certainly saw it as such, for he places Cornelius Gallus, the elegiac poet, near the Permessus, as if he were a successor of Hesiod.

tum canit errantem Permessi ad flumina Gallum
Aonas in montis ut duxerit una sororum,
utque viro Phoebi chorus adsurrexerit omnis;
ut Linus haec illi divino carmine pastor

floribus atque apio crinis ornatus amaro
dixerit "hos tibi dant calamos, en accipe, Musae,
Ascraeo quos ante seni, quibus ille solebat
cantando rigidas deducere montibus ornos."

(Ecl. 6.64–71)

And yet the phrase "consecration of the poet" has an intellectual connotation and does not quite capture the original character of the event.
Hesiod is personally involved in this miraculous occurrence. The Muses
are his Muses; he wants to know something, and they answer him. He
hears how they angrily shout at the shepherds, calling them "worthless
fellows, nothing but bellies." The shepherds do not wish to know the
truth, although it is there, all around them. Finally, the Muses begin to
speak.

In early Greek poetry, such an encounter is a true religious experience. The deepest insights are granted to mortals only as a gift from a
deity. Horace ends his prayer of thanks to "the Muse" (*Carm.* 4.3) as
follows:

totum muneris hoc tui est . . .
quod spiro et placeo, si placeo, tuum est.

Neither Homer nor Hesiod nor Pindar use the word ποιητής,
"maker," to designate the poet. This word, the origin of the English
word *poet*, is very common in later times. Of course, these early poets
are "makers" or "craftsmen," but when Hesiod speaks of the "divinely
speaking voice" which he receives as an "inspiration" from the Muses,
he wants to say that they now speak out of him and through him. He
now may announce "what will be and what was."

Now we understand the poet's invocation of the Muses at the beginning of a new work or a particularly difficult or important part of his
work. *Musae quae pedibus magnum pulsatis Olimpum* is the beginning of
Ennius' *Annals,* and soon after the famous first line of the Aeneid, *Arma
virumque cano,* Virgil addresses himself to "the Muse": *Musa, mihi causas
memora.*

The epic poet always deals with concrete knowledge, with facts.
Hesiod calls on the Muses before he unravels the complicated genealogy
of the gods, as does Homer at the beginning of book 2 of the *Iliad*, before
he names all the Greek ships and heroes that assailed Troy. Within his
epic, Virgil calls on the Muses when he needs specific details.

Quis deus, o Musae, tam saeva incendia Teucris
avertit? tantos ratibus quis depulit ignis?
dicite.

(*Aen.* 9.77–79)

The Greek lyric poets of the archaic period prayed to the Muses whenever they were in need of specific facts and appropriate words. There is a significant relationship between facts and words. Without words—that is, without poetry—facts are insubstantial. A victory in a great athletic event, for instance, is no victory, if it is not celebrated in a song. To celebrate extraordinary events, the poet needs the assistance of the Muses. We see this in Horace, too.

Descende caelo et dic age tibia
regina longum Calliope melos,
seu voce nunc mavis acuta,
seu fidibus citharaque Phoebi.

(*Carm.* 3.4.1 ff.)

Walter Wili (*Horaz und die augusteische Kultur* [1948], 146) was right when he called this poem "the most Pindaric" of Horace's songs; he added, "It begins as a personal statement and preserves later on the concrete feeling of being chosen which the Muses bestowed on the poet as their favor."

Hesiod's cult of the Muses became a rather playful convention in later poets. Callimachus has already been mentioned: in a dream, he found himself on Mount Helicon, where the Muses talked to him on subjects both literary and antiquarian. Propertius, the Roman Callimachus, boldly calls his mistress his true Muse.

Quaeritis, unde mihi totiens scribantur amores,
unde meus veniat mollis in ora liber?
non haec Calliope, non haec mihi cantat Apollo,
ingenium nobis ipsa puella facit

(2.1.1–4)

He also invokes the divine spirits of his Greek predecessors.

Callimachi Manes et Coi sacra Philetae,
in vestrum, quaeso, me sinite ire nemus.

(3.1.1–2)

The beginning of a new book of poems is traditionally reserved to an invocation of the Muses, but Propertius has replaced them by a living woman, Cynthia, and by two dead poets, Callimachus of Cyrene and Philetas of Cos. But they are not dead for Propertius: their Manes, that is, their divine spirits, are alive and can take over the function of the Muses.

Not only poets and musicians invoked the Muses. Philosophers, scientists, statesmen have felt that the Muses have something to say to them. Shortly before his death, Socrates said that he always considered philosophy as an occupation inspired by the Muses. Plato, his disciple, founded his school, the Academy, as a θίασος, that is, an organization devoted to the cult of the Muses. Horace carries on the same tradition when he praises the gifts of the Muses to Caesar Augustus.

> vos Caesarem altum, militia simul
>   fessas cohortes abdidit oppidis,
>   finire quaerentem labores
>   Pierio recreatis antro,
>
> vos lene consilium et datis et dato
>   gaudetis almae . . .
>   (*Carm.* 3.4.37ff.)

The Muses lend their assistance wherever we need to think and speak and preserve the spiritual values of the past. Art and science are impossible without tradition, even though every creative act represents a new beginning. Historians, orators, sculptors, physicians, even statesmen are dependent on the Muses. Virgil wrote four books on agriculture, but thanks to the Muses, he transcended the limits of a technical treatise and achieved an interpretation of human existence. He admits his debt to the Muses, his love for them, in the famous lines

> me vero primum dulces ante omnia Musae
> quarum sacra fero ingenti percussus amore
> accipiant . . .
>   (*Georg.* 2.475ff.)

The "life devoted to the Muses" is described by the Roman poets in a variety of images. Horace calls himself *Musis amicus* (*Carm.* 1.26.1) or *Musarum sacerdos* (*Carm.* 3.1.3), and the Muses are always his companions. Once he praises "the Muse" as the "kind star" of his birth (*Carm.* 4.3.1ff.).

Even in a tragic situation, the Muses do not abandon their favorite. Ovid testifies to this in a moving prayer of thanks written in exile.

> ergo quod vivo durisque laboribus obsto,
>   nec me sollicitae taedia lucis habent,
> gratia, Musa, tibi: nam tu solacia praebes,
>   tu curae requies, tu medicina venis.
> tu dux et comes es, tu nos abducis ab Histro
>   in medioque mihi das Helicone locum;
> tu mihi, quod rarum est, vivo sublime dedisti
>   nomen, ab exequiis quod dare fama solet.
>
> <div align="right">(<i>Trist.</i> 4.10.115ff.)</div>

Both Apollo and Dionysus were the patrons of poetry and music; therefore the Muses are regularly associated with both gods. Their participation in both worlds, the realm of the Apollinian and the realm of the Dionysiac, shows that one should not emphasize the separation between the two as strongly as Nietzsche did.

The Muses are not always the elegant, luminous, benevolent deities that we meet in handbooks of mythology. They are, of course, related to the Graces, and Euripides praises, in a choral ode, the "loveliest alliance" between the Graces and the Muses. But sometimes the Muses show a dark, threatening face. A Muse fell in love with Demodocus, took away his eyesight, and bestowed on him the gift of poetic vision as a compensation. There seems to be an affinity between the Muses and the capricious nymphs as well as the sinister Sirens. As Odysseus sails by, the Sirens offer him their knowledge, which embraces all the secrets on earth, but he knows that he will become their victim if he surrenders to the magic of their song. The demoniac power of the Muses, their *amabilis insania*, as Horace (*Carm.* 3.4.5f.) calls it, releases forces that could be destructive. He who loves the Muses without restraint may be stunned by them as if he had been struck by thunder.

We know from mythology that the favorites of the Muses—Linus, Thamyris, Orpheus—all died a tragic death. Linus, the beautiful singer, perished in his youth; his name lived on in a melancholy folk tune. Thamyris competed with the Muses in the art which he had learned from them: they struck him with blindness and took his gift away from him. Orpheus, who was able to charm trees and animals with his music, lost his beloved Euridyce and was torn to pieces by a horde of women when he refused to marry again. Ovid, the last great poet of the Augustan Age, saw himself as the darling of the Muses: they made him famous. They also caused his exile.

> nisi peccassem, nisi me mea Musa fugasset.
> (*Ex Ponto* 3.5.21)

But at least they comforted him in the desolate place at the end of the civilized world where he was forced to live.

The cult of the Muses was originally—as strange as it may seem—restricted to peasants and shepherds, and we do not know why they became the deities of poetry and music. There was a theory (accepted by Tibullus [2.1]) that poetry, music, and dancing had their origin in the country, among the rural population.

Persius, a satirist of the first century A.D., presided over the retreat of the Muses from Roman poetry. He ridiculed what has become a cliché, and soon no one wanted to hear about the Muses and their haunts: Hippocrene, Parnassus, and Helicon.

The nine sisters found a last refuge on the magnificent sarcophagi of the late Roman Empire, but their symbolism was probably no longer understood by the pagans, while their survival was odious to some Christians.

Notes on the History of Lat. *Sapientia*

The word *sapientia* appears for the first time in the third century B.C., at a time when Greek philosophy already colors the Latin vocabulary. We have no literary testimonies for *sapientia* that are not influenced by Greek σοφία. To find out something about the etymology of the word, we have to appeal to linguistics. It will become clear why the Latin word partly corresponds to σοφία, without ever being identical with it. Moreover, the etymology will show what *sapientia* signified originally, before Greek ideas and terms spread in Italy.

It is well known that *sapientia* derives from *sapio, sapere* and that *sapio* means "I taste, I have a sense of taste." By a process of assimilation documented in other languages as well, it can also mean "I smell." Thus it appears that *sapio* at first served to express the function of two separate senses (smell and taste) and later the function of all five senses (*sapio* meaning "I am normal") and the intellectual evaluation of the data furnished by the senses. At an early date, *sapio* can also mean "I judge correctly." The dictionaries tell us that *sapio* means "I am wise." True, no doubt, but this meaning already reflects Greek σοφία; we want to explore the original, "pre-Greek" period.

Only through its close association with σοφία does *sapientia* begin to play a significant role in the history of European thought. And yet even in Augustine the concept does not deny its roots but can be used for a variety of linguistic games. Therefore, we should, at least for the time being, not pay too much attention to equivalents such as "wisdom" or "insight" offered by the dictionaries. Let us use "I judge correctly" as a starting point. The normal functioning of one sense organ is extended to the functioning of all sense organs, to which is added the intellectual organ.

From *Archiv für Begriffsgeschichte* 9 (1964): 203–15.

This essay is a shortened version of a lecture delivered at the "Arbeitstagung der Senatskommission der Deutschen Forschungsgemeinschaft für begriffsgeschichtliche Forschung" which took place in Heidelberg on 5–7 March 1962. I am very grateful to Prof. Wolfgang Schmid, Bonn, and Prof. Viktor Pöschl, Heidelberg, for valuable suggestions.

A similar development took place in other Indo-European languages. German *weise, Weisheit, Weistum, weissagen, wissen,* and *Witz* have their root in Indo-European *u̯eid-* which is present in Greek εἶδον, "I saw," and οἶδα, "I know" (originally "I have seen"), and in Latin *video,* "I see" (the perfect, *vidi,* sometimes means "I have experienced").

An early testimony confirms that *sapere,* "to taste," is not merely something that happens to us. It implies a deliberate intellectual effort to determine an unknown taste, possibly in order to decide whether something is edible or poisonous. Thus Accius, the dramatist, says (fr. 296 R.), *sapimus animo, fruimur anima;* and Nonius comments on this phrase, *animus est, quo sapimus, anima qua vivimus.* Thus, *animus* is the organ of *sapientia,* the ability to taste; it is being distinguished from *anima* (ψυχή), the vital principle. To recognize a familiar taste is also an intellectual achievement.

The root *sap-* has produced a number of words in Latin, but only *sapientia* seems to have freed itself completely from its origin in sense perception. In Apuleius, *sapidulus* means "wise" as well as "tasty." *Insipidus,* "tasteless, watered down," appears in Christian authors practically only in a transferred sense, although the original meaning shines through. The same may be said of *insipiens,* "feebleminded, foolish, unreasonable." In his commentary on *Ev. Joh.* 8:3 Augustine restores to *insipiens* its original sense, which it never quite lost: *quia et nos aqua eramus, et vinum nos fecit, sapientes nos fecit; sapimus . . . fidem ipsius, qui prius insipientes eramus.* Obviously, "he/she who knows" is a person who is endowed with good taste and who "tastes good" as well. There is a transference of qualities, just as in the case of *salsus/insulsus:* he who spices his speech with *sal* ("salt, wit") is "salty" himself, whereas *insulsus,* "saltless," designates one who is "tasteless, witless." Those who have faith are "knowledgeable," according to Augustine, not because they have tasted of faith but because they "taste of faith." The Spanish verb *saber* means both "to taste" and "to know."

In colloquial Latin, *sapiens* never seems to have lost the meaning "to be (mentally) normal." If your five senses and your mind function normally, you are *sapiens.* In Plautus, *sapio* often means "I am responsible, in command of my mental faculties," and in legal language *sapiens* is the opposite of *mente captus* or *furiosus,* "insane." *Sapere* in its highest sense is a rare quality, but in everyday Latin and in some technical texts it is a sort of minimum requirement. Even today we use the term *homo sapiens,* to distinguish human beings, who are able to think, from animals, who presumably are not. In the testimonies we have, it is often said that only a human being, not an animal, may be called *sapiens*. Wherever this idea appears—for example, in Accius (as quoted in Cicero's *Brutus*) or in Lactantius (*Institutiones* 7.4.13, following Cicero)—we may assume a Stoic source. In a bold image, Naevius calls the mulberry tree *sapientissima arborum*. The Latin title of one of Plutarch's philosophical essays is *de sollertia animalium*, not *de sapientia animalium*, and the Greek title uses the word φϱόνησις, not σοφία.

There is evidence that, in colloquial Latin, the terms *sapere, sapiens*, and, to a limited extent, *sapientia* were devaluated. Literary Latin, however, offers a different picture, and it seems that this difference has not been pointed out sufficiently so far. But it is important. Literary Latin has made a deliberate attempt to restore to these words their original rank and value. We know from other languages and literatures that poets, and writers in general, deliberately give back its old status to a word that vanished from the spoken language or was devaluated for some reason. An example comes from Middle High German. It annoyed Walter von der Vogelweide that it was no longer correct to call a woman *wîp*. In his opinion, *wîp* was not only no degradation but, in fact, high praise. In the paraphrase of P. Wapnewski, the poet said: " 'Woman' will always be the highest designation of the female sex and bestows, in my opinion, more honor than 'lady.' "

Where *sapiens* and *sapientia* are first attested in literary Latin, in the epitaphs of the Scipio family and in Ennius, we may observe the tendency to assimilate them to Greek σοφός, σοφία, on the one hand, and to φϱόνιμος, φϱόνησις, on the other. The epitaph of Scipio Barbatus, consul in 289 B.C., may serve as an example: he is called *fortis vir sapiensque*, "a brave and intelligent man." Here, *sapiens* corresponds not to σοφός but to φϱόνιμος. The influence of Greek is evident, even in this early period. The epitaphs are the work of a poet who knew Greek, just as the artwork on the sarcophagi would be unthinkable without Greek models.

What is true for early Latin poetry is also true for early Latin oratory. One of the oldest monuments of Latin prose is the funeral oration delivered in 221 B.C. by Q. Caecilius Metellus for his father, L. Caecilius Metellus, the general who had defeated Hasdrubal. He says of his father that he had achieved the ten most important goals in life: *voluisse enim primarium bellatorem esse, optimum oratorem, fortissimum imperatorem, auspicio suo maximas res geri, maximo honore uti, summa sapientia esse, summum senatorem haberi, pecuniam magnam bono modo invenire, multos liberos relinquere et clarissimum in civitate esse*. According to the elder Pliny (*Nat. Hist.* 7.43), who has preserved this summary, the son then argued that his father had realized these ideals to a higher degree than anyone else since the foundation of Rome. In this long list, *sapientia* is probably not only a practical virtue; a Roman statesman of this distinction was expected to have his share of Greek σοφία.

We find *sapientia* more than once in Ennius, the "father of Roman poetry." Ennius (239–169 B.C.) was born in Calabria, where, at the time, three different cultures were in contact with each other: Greek, Latin, and Oscan. Ennius spoke all three languages and said of himself that he had three "hearts," that is, three intellectual centers. This is an important testimony for the early insight that speaking and thinking depend on each other mutually.

Even in Ennius, whose works have survived only in fragments, *sapientia* already has a wealth of meanings comparable only to the range it has in Cicero and Augustine. In a fragment from an unknown tragedy (320 R.), it means "medical knowledge" and corresponds to Greek τέχνη or perhaps to σοφία in its original meaning, "skill." At any rate, it designates some kind of special knowledge or expertise.

Sapientia means something else in a fragment from Ennius' tragedy *Alcmeo.* The protagonist, terrorized by the Furies, says that his *sapientia* had fallen from his heart (21 R.). The heart (actually the breast, *pectus*) is the seat of reason, and the loss of *sapientia* indicates the madness that takes hold of Alcmeo when the Furies approach.

Ennius' fragment 240 R. is from a tragedy whose title is lost, and it forms a *sententia:*

qui ipse sibi sapiens prodesse non quit, nequiquam sapit.

It so happens that we have the Euripidean line (fr. 905 N.²) which seems to have influenced Ennius:

μισῶ σοφιστήν, ὅστις οὐχ αὑτῷ σοφός.

Ennius says, in fact: "He who claims knowledge and is unable to help himself knows in vain." The play on words—*sapiens* and *sapit, quit* and *nequiquam*—cannot be imitated in translation. In Latin, *sapiens* corresponds to Greek σοφιστής, which means not "sophist, quibbler, cheat" but rather "authority, expert."

In his *Annals* (7.218 V.), Ennius says that we must learn *sapientia;* it does not come in dreams. Scholars have assumed that Ennius here speaks of himself and wants to say that it has been hard work for him to study Greek literature and acquire σοφία or τέχνη, "poetic technique"—that even though Homer appeared to him in a dream and consecrated him as a poet, so to speak, the technical skills he mastered were the result of great efforts. This interpretation was first suggested in the sixteenth century. It seems to be relevant in the sense that *sapientia* here means ποιητικὴ τέχνη, but Ennius is probably not talking about himself (H. Fränkel, *Hermes* 1932, pp. 309ff.; 1935, p. 65, n. 2).

In another passage of the *Annales* (8.268), *sapientia* is the opposite of *vis*. The same antithesis occurs in Tacitus. In a famous line, anticipating Virgil (*Aen.* 6.847ff.), Ennius (v. 180) calls the

> stolidum genus Aeacidarum
> bellipotentes . . . magis quam sapientipotentes.

A scene from Pacuvius' *Antiope* is even more significant. The brothers Amphion and Zethus symbolize in Euripides' *Antiope* (known to us only from fragments) the antithesis of the life of action and the intellectual life. Euripides reflects contemporary philosophy, thoughts that we find also in Plato and Aristotle. As he adapted the Greek play to the Roman stage, Pacuvius also debated the question whether the life of action should be valued more highly than the life dedicated to art, music, literature, philosophy, or science. The same debate goes on throughout Cicero's philosophical writings, and in the final myth of his *Republic* he reconciles the opposite points of view on a higher level. Of course he knew Pacuvius' play—and probably the Greek original as well.

One of the great scenes of the *Antiope* was an emotional discussion between the brothers. They argued about the value of σοφία, that is, the sum of all things that one "can know" or "should know." This scene must have made a powerful impression on the audience and the readers; unfortunately, we only know it from fragments.

The author of *Rhetorica ad Herennium* (2.27.43) tells us that the brothers Amphion and Zethus quarreled about the value of music in human life. The debate arose out of Amphion's profession: he is a musician, an artist. Music stands for all the arts, for a life devoted to the Muses in general. Thus the debate began with music but soon touched on *sapientiae ratio et virtutis utilitas*, as the author of *Rhetorica ad Herennium* says. We further know from Cicero's early treatise *De inventione* that in the great debate of the drama, music was belittled—by Zethus, the man of action, of course. Thereupon Amphion, according to Cicero, praised *sapientia*, which here almost certainly corresponds to Greek σοφία, for φρόνησις could not cover arts, sciences, and intellectual endeavor in general. If Amphion had no better defense of music than the praise of σοφία, this must have included music and the other arts and also φιλοσοφία, "love of or search for σοφία."

I have discussed this famous scene in such detail because it helps us, in spite of its fragmentary state of preservation, to reconstruct an important phase in the history of the concept of *sapientia*. Without this play, the concept—as used by Cicero and, later, following Cicero, by the church fathers—could not have developed as it did. Cicero still lives in the world of the Republican tragedy, and to his writings we owe substantial fragments.

In Roman comedy we meet a more limited concept of *sapientia*. From a play on words (*Truculentus*, v. 78) based on the name "Phronesium," we know that, for Plautus, *sapientia* is the equivalent of φρόνησις. This seems to be contradicted by Plautus' reference to the *sapientia* of Thales of Miletus (*Capt.* 274ff.; cf. *Bacch.* 122). Since Thales is one of the "Seven Sages," *sapientia* apparently renders σοφία. But the correspondence is not certain. There was a debate in antiquity whether the "Seven Wise Men" really deserved to be called "wise." They all had demonstrated that they were not just speculative philosophers but practical men. Thales' correct prognosis of the olive harvest made him wealthy, according to the anecdote. This means that we should not postulate for Plautus the exalted concept of *sapientia* that we find in Pacuvius. For Plautus, as F. Leo (*Plautin. Forschungen,* 2d ed. [1912], 107 n. 2) has shown, *sapientia* seems to be the equivalent more of φρόνησις than of σοφία. This is also true for Cicero, but not always. A good example is *De finibus* 5.58, where Cicero refers to Plato (*Sympos.* 202A). If we compare the Greek text, we find that Cicero's *sapientia* translates φρόνησις. In another passage of the same work, *De finibus* 1.42, Cicero understands *sapientia* as *ars vivendi* (see Madvig's note ad loc.).

Terence uses *sapientia* in the same sense as Plautus, but in *Adelphi* (427) he also plays with the etymology. A slave tastes the food in the kitchen and says: "This has too much salt, this has not been washed sufficiently . . ." and adds that he gives his instructions *pro mea sapientia*, that is, "according to my taste," but also "according to my expertise."

"The Greeks call me 'Σοφία,' you [i.e., the Roman audience] 'Sapientia.' " This is a line from the prologue of a lost play by Afranius. Σοφία personified recites the prologue. She appears on the stage, introduces herself, and gives an outline of the plot. In other comedies, Tyche or

Pronoia takes over this role, and Sophia or Sapientia seems to be a deity, too, at least as far as the poet and this particular play are concerned. She never seems to have been a real deity, like Mens Bona, "Common Sense," for example. Augustine (*Civ. Dei* 4.20) wonders why she never had any cult in Rome. Apparently, people did not pray to Sapientia or present her with votive offerings. Therefore her apotheosis in this play might be a joke. Afranius even gives her a fancy pedigree: her father is *Usus*, Ἐμπειρία, "Experience"; and her mother is *Memoria*, Μνημοσύνη, "Memory." These are abstractions, but they tell us something. Experience and memory are, indeed, two sources of insight or knowledge.

The Republican period is important for the history of the concept, but it would be difficult to isolate a specific aspect of *sapientia* in Cicero, for example, or to identify any specific aspect as typically Greek. There is an excellent study by Helene Homeyer (*L'Antiquité classique* 1956, pp. 301ff.) which attempts to do this. The author has observed that the *sapientia* of Roman statesmen is praised quite often, and she interprets this particular virtue in its practical consequences as "Leistungstugend." This is doubtful.

Incidentally, Greek σοφός was not at all unusual in colloquial Latin. A distinguished statesman who belonged to the family of the Sempronii had the surname *Sophus*. In the *Digesta* (12.2.37), Pomponius writes, *fuit . . . maximae scientiae Sempronius, quem populus Romanus "sophon" appellavit*. He refers to the Roman people, not just the members of his own social class. A distinguished lawyer is called σοφός by the people not because he is "wise" but because he wins his cases in court. If this happens once, he may have been lucky; if it happens several times, he may have *prudentia*; if it happens again and again during a long life, he has *sapientia*. Another virtue, *constantia*, as we will see later, contributes to such a success.

The passage from the *Digesta* shows that, in the late fourth century B.C., σοφία could also be interpreted as *scientia*. This agrees with the testimony from Ennius where he uses the word *sapientia* to designate medical science. Both physicians and lawyers need *sapientia*, "expertise, special knowledge," to be successful. This is not the same as "wisdom." Seneca (*Epist.* 89.7) says, in fact, that there is no difference between *scientia* and *sapientia*. When a Roman audience applauded a singer or an actor, they cried, σοφῶς! σοφῶς!

In Cicero's works, *sapientia* displays the widest range of meanings. They are the great reservoir from which Greek philosophy was transmitted to the church fathers of the West. Through reading Cicero, the humanists later felt the urge to study Greek philosophy in the original language. For Cicero we have good lexica and a few monographs. A thorough study of his use of *sapientia* would be useful.

Instead of presenting as many passages as possible, I would prefer to characterize briefly what seems to me a significant tendency in Cicero's philosophical works. This tendency manifests itself clearly in the six books of *De republica*, which is, in some respects, his most important treatise. Cicero tries to reconcile the two points of view which Euripides, in his *Antiope*, had opposed to each other so sharply. This attempt to build a bridge between two opposites is magnificent. Cicero breaks a pattern of thought which had been recognized as valid for centuries, by showing that *vita activa* and *vita contemplativa* do not exclude each other. He is convinced that it is possible to be a great Roman statesman and a highly educated human being. The examples he cites are his personal heroes, Laelius and Scipio Africanus, but he almost certainly thinks of himself as well.

Wherever the concept of *sapientia* occurs in such a context, it is associated with παιδεία, "culture" or "higher education." Not very many Romans lived up to this ideal, and Cicero himself, who was firmly convinced that he had realized it, has not been treated kindly by posterity. But no matter how we judge him, his effort to establish a compromise between two completely different ideals of life is worthy of our admiration. His *Dream of Scipio*, the eschatological myth that concludes and crowns *De republica*, owes its appeal to this.

Cicero likes to think that *sapientia* is not really Greek but agrees with the Roman *mos maiorum*—that you do not have to be a scholar, a philosopher, or a scientist to be qualified as *sapiens*. Cicero says (*De republ.* 1.7.12) that the so-called Seven Sages of Greece, *septem quos Graeci sapientes nominaverunt*, were not academics but men who had acquired a good deal of practical experience. Thus, the Greeks also had a practical σοφία. It is a view that Cicero borrows from Dicaearchus, the Peripatetic, in order to support his opinion that there were σοφοί among the Romans of the past who had never read any Greek philosopher.

We find the same ideas in an important passage in the *Laelius* (2.6–7) which we ought to read carefully. Cicero distinguishes clearly the various meanings connected with *sapientia* and documents them: (*a*) L. Acilius was called *sapiens* because he was *prudens in iure civili*; this will remind us of Sempronius, called *Sophus*. Hence *sapientia = prudentia =* σοφία in the sense of practical reason. (*b*) Cato was called *sapiens* because he had a great deal of experience, *quia multarum rerum usum habebat*. This is a paraphrase of Greek ἐμπειρία, which we already encountered in a comedy (Usus as the father of Sapientia). Cato also had all of the following qualities: *providentia, constantia, acumen*. It might be said that the sum of them is *sapientia*. (c) Cicero's third example is Laelius, whom he admired all his life. In the dialogue, Cicero writes that Laelius was *sapiens* in two respects: (1) *natura et moribus* (which would be Greek φύσει); (2) *studio et doctrina* (which would be Greek παιδεία). Cicero pursues this

ginning of book 3 of *De republica*, where he says
dy *leges et instituta maiorum*, but that it is desir-
παιδεία. Only then does one reach the kind of
mire in Laelius and Scipio Africanus.
dividuals existed and left their imprint on Ro-
challenge for Cicero. From something that is,
itable, he deduced certain norms, and one has
root of his definitions there is always some
reality. If there had been no such men as
definition of *sapientia* would have been differ-
ple, was *sapientissimus*, but not really more so

on to transplant Greek philosophy to Rome.
many of his fellow citizens saw no need for it.
an introduction to philosophy, his *Protrep-*
enians that philosophy, that is, intellectual
was a worthwhile activity. For Aristotle,

φιλοσοφία included science, and that must be true for Cicero's concept of *sapientia*, too. Taking the *Protreptikos* as a model, Cicero wrote his *Hortensius*, which is, unfortunately also lost as a whole, though O. Plasberg's reconstruction gives a good idea of its content and structure. It must have been a magnificent piece of work; Augustine testifies that it was a turning point in his life when he read the *Hortensius*.

The main issue of such "introductions" was whether one should devote oneself to philosophy. We must keep in mind that "philosophy" in Aristotle's sense includes the kind of scientific research that is documented by his preserved treatises on psychology, zoology, and so on. The problem of whether such pursuits were valuable or even necessary is solved by Aristotle—and by Cicero after him—in an elegant manner. If you carefully consider the problem and then answer yes or no, you are thinking like a philosopher, even if you reject philosophy. In his *Protreptikos*, Aristotle calls philosophical insight φρόνησις in the sense that Plato used this word. In his later writings, he strips φρόνησις of any philosophical meaning and distinguishes it from σοφία (W. Jaeger, *Aristoteles,* 2d ed. [1955], 83–84). For Cicero, there was no reason for such a distinction.

The public that Cicero wrote for was not as open-minded, flexible, and intellectually curious as Aristotle's public in Athens. Cicero had to move much more cautiously if he wanted to convince his readers of the value of philosophical research. In the prologue to book 3 of *De republica* which we know in part from Lactantius, Augustine, and a few barely legible pages of the famous palimpsest, Cicero deals once more with *sapientia.* He distinguishes those who live the βίος πρακτικός from those who live the βίος θεωρητικός, and he adds that no matter to which group you belong, you may achieve great things, as long as you have *sapientia.* Here he seems to criticize the Greek philosophers who define σοφία so narrowly that it covers only their own special knowledge. It is well known to what degree the Stoics idealized σοφία. It could practically not be realized in this world. The true "wise man" in the Stoic sense was alone happy, alone rich, alone powerful; he had everything and was everything. Cicero studied this sublime concept of *sapientia* in his *Paradoxa Stoicorum.* In the *Laelius* he seems to speak of philosophy in general, but he has in mind the Stoics: *eam sapientiam interpretantur quam adhuc mortalis nemo est consecutus.* He uses similar terms in *De natura deorum* 3.79, where Pease, in his commentary, lists a number of parallels. *Sapientia* here becomes a divine principle, almost inaccessible to mere human beings; and the "wise man" becomes a θεῖος ἀνήρ, in anticipation of the Neoplatonists. Of course there were no "wise men" in this exalted sense in Cicero's Rome, but Seneca claims to have known one or two.

The beginning of another important passage in *De republica* is lost in the palimpsest; a few pages are missing. When the text reappears, we read, "nevertheless there was this difference between the two kinds of *sapientia* [i.e., the theoretical and the practical], that they [i.e., the teachers of theory] helped develop natural gifts through doctrine, while others did it through constitutions and laws." Cicero continues, "Our commonwealth has produced a fairly large number of men who were not *sapientes,* since those [i.e., the Greek philosophers, especially the Stoics] defined this concept so narrowly, but who are nevertheless worthy of the highest praise, because they appreciated the doctrines and the theories of the *sapientes*" [*tamen hoc in ratione utriusque generis interfuit, quod illi verbis et artibus aluerunt naturae principia* [= τὰ πρῶτα κατὰ φύσιν], *hi autem institutis et legibus. Pluris vero haec tulit una civitas, si minus sapientis, quoniam id nomen illi tam restricte tenent, at certe summa laude dignos, quoniam sapientium praecepta et inventa coluerunt*]. These are the men who distinguished themselves as thinkers and as men of action. As Cicero writes in the same book (3.25.37), *sapientia* is the outstanding part of the mind, *optima pars animi.*

Cicero, following Plato, draws a portrait of an ideal statesman who has *sapientia* in the highest degree. Naturally, Cicero also knows the ideal of the *vir prudens;* he compares him to an African or Indian driver of elephants (*De republ.* 2.40.67). Apparently, it impressed the Romans to see that a man sitting on top of an elephant was able to control easily, either through sounds or light touches, a huge animal. It is easy to associate a man who controls a large animal with the man who controls the *belua centiceps,* the people. This man needs a large measure of *prudentia* in its original sense of *providentia.* But this is a part of *sapientia,* and Cicero must have dealt with it in the following pages of the palimpsest, which are missing.

It seems remarkable that, for Cicero, *sapientia* could also mean "good taste," as we see from a passage in the *Orator* (70) which has not yet been evaluated sufficiently: *sed est eloquentiae sicut reliquarum rerum fundamentum sapientia, ut enim in vita, sic in oratione nihil est difficilius quam quid deceat videre;* πρέπον *appellant hoc Graeci, nos dicamus sane decorum.* The "appropriate" is, indeed, a criterion which played an important role in later Greek thought, especially in Panaetius. His ethics as well as his esthetics are guided by this particular term. But one may assume that Cicero made the decisive step and declared *sapientia* the highest judge of the "appropriate," for only in Latin could "taste," "good taste," "prudence," and "wisdom" be covered by one and the same word. If we compare Cicero with Horace (*Ars p.* 309: *scribendi recte sapere est et principium et fons;* cf. also Quintil. *Inst. or.* 12.2.6), we will see how typically Roman this way of thinking is.

Let me conclude this survey with Cicero. Augustan poetry (Horace above all) and the philosophy of the imperial age (Seneca above all) depend on him.

Studia Divina in Vita Humana:
On Cicero's *Dream of Scipio* and Its Place
in Graeco-Roman Philosophy

In the first book of the *Tusculanae,* and in the last book of *De republica,* Cicero has left us two notable documents in the development toward later views of the soul and the hereafter. Both works are among his best; both are composed with care; neither is a random compilation of doxographical material. In the *Somnium Scipionis,* the language of the dream reflects with particular persuasiveness the impulse of the soul to take wings and fly away into the ever-calling unknown. But the essential doctrines of both works are the same: the hereafter in its reality, as a return to the beginning of things, as the true life; and the death of kings and philosophers as a robing, a sacred investiture.

Many of the secondary themes[1] found in both works were obviously quite commonplace in Cicero's time; yet their tendency and certain more or less explicitly stated assumptions are, if not completely new in themselves, at least presented in a new light. Since the scarcity of firsthand Greek texts makes our knowledge of Hellenistic philosophy so inadequate, it seems desirable to identify the main themes of the *Somnium* and *Tusculanae* 1, to transform, as it were, anonymous ideas into a new chapter in the history of late Greek thought. In this essay, I shall limit myself to the *Somnium;* it is needless to say that a similar method, yielding similar results, can be applied to *Tusculanae* 1.[2]

From *Harvard Theological Review* 49 (1956): 207–18.

I am deeply grateful to Arthur Darby Nock, my teacher, colleague, and friend, for his criticism and kind encouragement.

1. Death is a *peregrinatio* (*Somn.* 9f., 15)—the Platonic *poreia* (see *Apol.* 40E)—a return to our real home (*Somn.* 20.29; cf. *Tusc.* 1.72, 5.9), whereas what we call life is actually death (*Somn.* 14), an imprisonment of the soul in the body (Plato *Phd.* 67D; Arist. *Protr.* fr. 10b W.). These concepts appear quite frequently in Hellenistic popular philosophy; cf. the pseudo-Platonic *Axioch.* 365E; Virg. *Aen.* 6.734; and in general P. Boyancé, *Etudes sur le Songe de Scipion* (1936), 126f.

2. K. Reinhardt ("Poseidonios," Pauly-Wissowa 22 [1953]: 575–86) in a detailed discussion of *Tusc.* 1, stressing its parallels to the *Somnium,* has maintained

Strictly speaking, the themes of the *Somnium* are neither Platonic, nor Aristotelian, nor Stoic, but rather they are common to all three schools, without being—and this is important—characteristic of one of them in particular.[3] Its general tendency is to minimize the differences between the great philosophical schools in favor of a broad imaginative synthesis that might appeal to the educated Roman who refused to be bothered by the finespun theorizing of controversial Greek dogmas.

First of all, it is clear that Cicero has transformed a Platonic theme into something new. Like the myth of Er that crowns Plato's *Republic,* the *Somnium* is a vision of afterlife. The central idea in both texts is the great statesman's just claim to immortality. There are, however, considerable differences in the manner in which this idea is presented. Cicero has transformed Plato's straight narrative into a dialogue. He does not state as explicitly as Plato did that kings must be philosophers and philosophers kings. For Cicero, the great statesman is the living embodiment of the universe as a natural order, thus fulfilling on earth the function of the Cosmic God. On the other hand, Plato does not place the ultimate destiny of the soul in the celestial spheres.[4] Cicero's description of these spheres suggests familiarity with the research of Hellenistic astronomers.[5]

In a text which was meant to rival a famous Platonic work, these changes are surprising. We may wonder whether they are due to Cicero personally[6] or, perhaps, to his adaptation of an unknown Greek treatise.

---

that this book reflects the thought of Antiochus of Ascalon. Independently and almost simultaneously, H. Strohm (*Museum Helveticum* 1952, p. 137ff.) and G. Luck (*Der Akademiker Antiochos* [1953], 36ff.) have come to the same conclusion.

3. For details see H. Usener, *Rhein. Mus.* 1873, p. 397f.; R. Harder, "Ueber Ciceros Somnium Scipionis," *Schr. Königsb. Gel. Ges.* 6, no. 3 (1929): 15; R. Philippson, *Philol. Wochenschr.* 1930, p. 1209; O. Seel, *Philol. Wochenschr.* 1938, p. 489f.; M. Pohlenz, *Die Stoa* (1949), 2:132.

4. But see, e.g., the pseudo-Platonic *Axioch.* 366A. Its close relationship to the *Somnium* deserves a special study; some points of view are in M. Meister "De Axiocho dialogo" (Diss. Breslau, 1915).

5. This last point, taken by itself, would not justify our hypothesis that the *Somnium* is based on the (lost) work of a Hellenistic philosopher. A.D. Nock, (*AJA* 50 [1946]: 163f.) has shown that, in Cicero's time, there was a great familiarity with astronomy. The subject was taught at schools. Aratus' poem was widely read and translated into Latin. A man like Galen was thoroughly at home in astronomy (*Scripta minora* 1.32 Marquardt). Cf. also G.M.A. Hanfmann, *The Season Sarcophagus in Dumbarton Oaks,* vol. 1 (1951), 124.

6. It is the concept of the *ratio quasi deus* (where *ratio* stands for the cosmic *Nus;* W. Theiler, *Die Vorbereitung des Neuplatonismus* [1930], 44) that underlies the

I shall suggest here that the second solution is more plausible. It would be unfair, of course, to deny that Cicero had a mind, a personality, and a style of his own. He was not, and did not claim to be, an original philosopher, but when he writes on the good statesman, we should expect a little more from him than a mere reproduction of the thought of the Greek philosophers he had heard or read.[7] For the time being, let us only say that the *Somnium* as a whole reveals an unusually broad knowledge of classical and postclassical Greek thought. Unlike the majority of Cicero's philosophical treatises, it is *not* doxographical in character; that is, it does not, like *De finibus* or *De natura deorum*, confront and compare the tenets of various schools. In a manner that reminds readers of Cicero's smaller treatises (e.g., *De amicitia* or *De senectute*), it approaches an important subject imaginatively, or even poetically. Wilamowitz called it "eine schöne Dichtung," meaning that it is essentially a literary work of art. For this very reason, an investigation of its "background" or its "sources" is particularly difficult.

The concept of the statesman in the *Somnium* is characteristic for the skillful blend of various philosophical doctrines which I have already noted. It would have been unrealistic in Cicero's time to identify the philosopher and the statesman. More than that, it was unnecessary, since the Stoics had maintained that the life of action, βίος πρακτικός, was the best. This view, attractive enough to a Roman reader, embodied into a cosmic myth, would have been perfectly acceptable at the conclusion of *De republica*, especially since the whole work shows a strong Stoic influence. If Cicero, in writing the *Somnium*, had followed a Stoic philosopher, he would have simply glorified the life of action.

Instead, he praises the practical *and* the theoretical life as equally valuable. He declares that not only statesmen and military leaders but philosophers and poets as well are rewarded by an eternal life of happiness in heaven. In raising the life of pure speculation, βίος θεωρητικός, to the highest place, he follows Plato[8] and Aristotle,[9] perhaps also Posi-

---

Somnium. If Cicero had intended the *Somnium* as a summary of his own political thought, he would have stressed more strongly the individual *ratio* as the agent responsible for the highest human achievements (H. Leisegang, *Philol. Wochenschr.* 1938, p. 1310); he does this only in the books of *De rep.* and *De off.* which are influenced by Panaetius (Philippson 1175), but not in the *Somnium* and not in *De leg.* I, where the influence of Antiochus is reasonably certain (Luck 69ff.).

7. See the remarks of A.H. Armstrong, *Gnomon* 1954, p. 485.

8. Plato *Apol.* 40f. and—already taken for granted—in the *Axioch.* 371C.

9. Arist. *Protr.* fr. 12 W., quoted in Cicero's *Hortensius* and in later eclectic literature, e.g., Cicero *Tusc.* 1.43ff., 62, 73; *De fin.* 2.51, 4.12, 5.48ff.

donius.[10] Although he abandoned the Platonic ideal of the statesman-philosopher, he refused to make a choice between the two ways of life but coordinated them instead, "and this was bold enough an adventure in those days."[11] In a very significant passage of the *Somnium,* the connection between the theoretical and the practical way of life is clarified (16). How will Scipio be able to follow his ancestors on the road to heaven? The answer is: By observing *iustitia* and *pietas.* But how will he realize the meaning of these two virtues? By the contemplation of the heavenly bodies!

This singular concept has a close parallel in *De finibus* 4.12, in a book which is strongly influenced by Antiochus of Ascalon.[12] There we are told that the contemplation of the universe is the foundation of μεγαλοψυχία and δικαιοσύνη. In other words, the good conduct of life is inseparable from physical research or metaphysical speculation. Therefore, all men who have led a life of the intellect on earth will be rewarded, after their physical death (which is a spiritual rebirth), by celestial immortality.

Among these men, whose life on earth is a "life of gods" (*Tusc.* 1.72), we find the inventor of the alphabet, the first astronomers, those who first taught their fellowmen to build houses and to cultivate the fields (*Tusc.* 1.62), as well as the great poets and musicians, in short, all those who *praestantibus ingeniis in vita humana divina studia coluerunt* (*Somn.* 18). Their role on earth is thus comparable to that of the statesman and general;[13] and their achievements on earth, reflecting the divine origin of their soul, mark them as representatives of the cosmic principles of order and justice.

In coordinating the statesman and the philosopher, and in mediating between the Stoic ideal of action and the Platonic-Peripatetic ideal of pure knowledge, Cicero clearly honors the philosophy of the Scipionic circle, whose members play such a prominent role in the whole of *De*

---

10. On the background of Sen. *Epist.* 90 and Manil. *Astr.* 1.66ff. see F. Boll, *Jahrb. f. Philol. Supp.* 21 (1894): 221ff.

11. L. Edelstein, *AJP* 1938, p. 363. He is the first scholar who has without qualification ascribed the *Somnium* to Antiochus.

12. R. Hirzel, *Unters. z. Cic. philos. Schr.* 2:657ff.; R. Philippson, "Tullius," Pauly-Wissowa 7A (1939): 1137ff., 57ff.

13. The promise of eternal rewards to those who served their country is a well-known Platonic theme (*Phd.* 82A/B; *Rep.* 615B). It may seem tempting, for a moment, to connect it with the cult of the ruler as benefactor and savior, but A.D. Nock ("Soter and Euergetes," in *The Joy of Study,* ed. S.E. Johnson [1951], 122ff.) has shown that the word *soter,* when applied to a man, did not necessarily suggest that he belonged or even approximated to the category of the gods.

republica. This philosophy had been formulated by Panaetius of Rhodes, the founder of what is known as Middle Stoicism and a close friend of Scipio Aemilianus.[14] His brilliant student Posidonius of Apamea, whose glory in later days overshadowed that of his master, taught that the first philosophers were the first kings and lawgivers.[15] This doctrine of Posidonius, as well as many others, marks a decisive return of Stoicism to Platonism.

It is fairly certain that Panaetius had written a book on political science. Cicero knew this treatise when he was working on *De republica* and borrowed a few important concepts from it.[16] But when it came to the definition of the best way of life, Panaetius was not so much φιλοπλάτων and φιλαριστοτέλης as a Stoic of the old school. For him, the life of pure speculation was justified in an individual who showed exceptional gifts and interests; but since man is a "political animal," the best life is a life of action in a concrete political community.[17] For Panaetius, the beauty of the world is a reality, something that can be experienced here and now and every day, not, as the *Somnium* would have it, only after the ascension of the soul to the celestial spheres. There is no room in his philosophy for the pessimism of the *Somnium*.[18]

If we proceed by way of elimination, Posidonius presents himself as the next likeliest candidate. The influence of this last great encyclopedic mind of paganism is tangible in the works of such different authors as Cicero, Manilius, Seneca, Marcus Aurelius, Plutarch, and Philo. Some of the more common themes of the *Somnium*, and, above all, its mood of pessimism and mystic expectation, could be traced back to Posidonius. But since the *Somnium* is an organic whole, not a compilation of commonplaces and doxographical notes, it ought to be consistent with Posidonius'

---

14. Latest competent discussion by M. Pohlenz, "Panaitios," Pauly-Wissowa 18 (1949): 418ff.

15. Sen. *Epist.* 90.5f.; Manil. *Astr.* 1.762ff. See F. Boll, loc. cit.; A.J. Festugière, *La Révélation d'Hermès Trismégiste*, vol. 2, (1948), 443 n. 2; F. Cumont, *Lux Perpetua* (1949), 174, 182.

16. R. Reitzenstein, *Nachr. Gött. Ges.* (1917), 399ff.; M. Pohlenz, *Gött. Gel. Anz.* (1938), 134; idem, "Panaitios," Pauly-Wissowa, (1949), 437. The definition of the state in *De rep.* 1.39 (cf. 40f., 49, 2.34, 3.43) which determines to a large extent the structure of the whole work, corresponds to Panaetius' in *De off.* 2.73.

17. Cf. *De off.* 1.69ff., based on Panaetius' work περὶ τοῦ καθήκοντος, and the discussion of this passage by Pohlenz, "Panaitios," Pauly-Wissowa, (1949), 435f.

18. He was, as Pohlenz ("Panaitios," 433) puts it, "gefühlsmässig . . . reiner Diesseitsmensch."

doctrine in every detail, except, perhaps, for obvious misunderstandings or mistranslations of Cicero. There is nowhere any direct criticism of Posidonius, but some of his tenets are ignored, and some are modified.[19]

The eschatology of the *Somnium* is characteristic for its relationship to Posidonius.[20] According to both Posidonius and the *Somnium*, the soul consists of fire and air and thus is able to ascend to the upper regions of the cosmos after leaving the body at the time of physical death. As soon as it reaches the sphere of the moon,[21] it establishes a kind of dynamic equilibrium, because it has penetrated into a substance identical to its own. It has, therefore, according to both the *Somnium* and *Tusculanae* 1, reached its natural home *(naturalis sedes)*. For Posidonius, however, the soul does not come to a rest in the aetherial region around the moon but starts out from there on a new circular movement back to earth.[22]

To sum up the results we have reached so far: The *Somnium* represents the point of view of a Hellenistic thinker other than Panaetius and Posidonius but familiar with the work of both and, above all, anxious to interpret Platonism in "modern" terms. We wonder whether such an eclectic synthesis of Platonism and Middle Stoicism is conceivable in Cicero's time. We should inquire, in other words, whether Cicero was familiar with a philosopher to whom the various levels and phases of both Platonism and Stoicism had become a unity, because he was willing

---

19. Both Panaetius (fr. 33 Fowler) and Posidonius (R.M. Jones, *Class. Philol.* 1923, p. 211ff.) maintained that the tropical and arctic zones of the earth are inhabitable; this theory is implicitly rejected (*Somn.* 16; cf. *Tusc.* 1.45, 68f.).

20. Both Posidonius and Panaetius denied the immortality of the individual soul; for Panaetius, this deviation from Plato is attested by Cicero (*Tusc.* 1.79; cf. Cumont, *Lux Perp.*, 115); for Posidonius, by Hermias (*In Plat. Phaedr.* [ed. Couvreur (1901)] 102). *Somn.* 27f. (= *Tusc.* 1.53f.) preserves the Platonic tradition.

21. The *Somnium* specifies (19) that the Milky Way is the ultimate destination of the soul and is its natural home; but in a parallel text (*Tusc.* 1.43), the soul is said to ascend to the sphere of the moon. It is not quite clear whether Cicero, in the *Somnium*, visualizes the Milky Way at an infinite distance from the earth (moon and earth appear quite small, the former *ultima a caelo*). There is some evidence, however, that Aristotle and Heraclides of Pontus did not locate the Milky Way in the sphere of the fixed stars, at the outer limits of the universe, but closer to the earth, at the *confinium* of air and aether (P. Boyancé, *Rev. Et. Gr.* 1952, 335; M.P. Nilsson, *Numen* [1954], 108f.), and this *confinium*, according to both *Tusc.* 1 and the *Somnium*, coincides with the lunar sphere.

22. On Posidonius' eschatology, reflected in such texts as Sext. Emp. *Adv. math.* 9.73 and Plut., *De fac. in orb. lun.* p. 928, see Reinhardt, "Poseidonios," Pauly-Wissowa 22 (1953), 574.

to sacrifice the subtler points of difference—a philosopher who coordinated the ideals of θεωρία and πρᾶξις by postulating a metaphysical foundation for the life of action, thus defining the "good life" in terms appealing to any Roman schooled in classical Greek thought.

There is, in Cicero's philosophical writings, an important passage which reads like a summary of the *Somnium*.[23] In *De finibus* 5.57, man's role in life is defined in these terms: *itaque ut quisque optime natus institutusque est, esse omnino nolit in vita, si gerendis negotiis orbatus possit paratissimis vesci voluptatibus*. After this summary of the rejection of Epicureanism which took up the whole of *De finibus* 2,[24] Cicero continues: *nam aut privatim aliquid gerere malunt aut, qui altiore animo sunt, capessunt rem publicam honoribus imperiisque adipiscendis aut totos se ad studia doctrinae conferunt*. Here, the active life, no matter whether it takes place in the private sphere or in the service of the community, is presented as an alternative to the life of θεωρία. Then, Cicero contrasts both ways of life once more with the βίος ἀπολαυστικός of the Epicureans: *qua in vita tantum abest, ut voluptates consectentur, etiam curas, sollicitudines, vigilias perferunt optimaque parte hominis, quae in nobis divina ducenda est, ingenii et mentis acie fruuntur nec voluptatem requirentes nec fugientes laborem*.

In both the *Somnium* and *De finibus* 5, the statesman and the philosopher are coordinated. In both texts, this coordination is based on two reasons: (*a*) the divine nature of the soul, and (*b*) the worthlessness of a life of pleasure. In the same characteristic manner, both texts arrive from two rather commonplace (by that time) concepts to a startling new conclusion. Following Plato, Aristotle, and the later Stoics, the *Somnium* asserts that man is not *quem forma ista declarat, sed mens cuiusque, is est quisque* (26) and that man, since the soul is of divine origin, is divine, *deum te igitur scito esse*.[25] That it is man's duty to use the best part of himself (*optima parte hominis . . . fruuntur*) is also put forward in the *Somnium* (29), only more urgently and directly: Scipio's soul will ascend to the heavenly regions if he puts it to work (*exercere*) in the highest

---

23. This correspondence between the main theme of the *Somnium* and *De fin.* 5.57 has been pointed out by L. Edelstein (loc. cit.).

24. *De fin.* 2 follows very closely a text of Antiochus directed against the Epicureans, probably part of the same work on which books 4 and 5 depend (R. Philippson, Pauly-Wissowa 7A [1939]:1137ff.; Luck 56f.).

25. The body is only the vessel of the soul (on this topos see F. Husner, *Philologus Supp.* 17, no. 3 [1924]: 77ff.; W. Theiler, *Marc Aurel* [1951], 312); the real man is identical with his soul (Plato *Leg.* 959B; Arist. *NE* 1178a7; Stoic testimonies collected by Husner [141]; Boyancé, *Etudes*, 124; Theiler 340) and therefore divine.

possible activities (*optimis in rebus*). And the *Somnium* closes with a threat to those who prefer a life of pleasure to either θεωρία or πρᾶξις, which are precisely the two highest possible goals of life according to both the *Somnium* and *De finibus* 5.[26]

If we now ask whose philosophy the fifth book of *De finibus* reflects, the answer is: Antiochus' of Ascalon. Cicero says so himself in several places (*De fin.* 5.8, 14, 16, 75, 81).[27] There are few books in the whole of Cicero's philosophical *corpus* whose relationship to a Greek "original" can be more clearly defined. It reflects Antiochus' favorite theory that Academy, Peripatos, and Stoa are essentially the same school, trying to say the same thing, disagreeing only *in verbis*, not *in rebus*.[28] This is certainly the unspoken assumption on which the *Somnium* is based, an assumption which seemed quite plausible to Cicero at that time (although he abandoned it later), for in his other political treatise, *De legibus*, written soon after *De republica*, he maintains it personally (*De leg.* 1.53f.).

Antiochus of Ascalon was the head of the so-called Fifth Academy. He was born around 120 B.C., went to Athens to study at the Academy under Philo of Larissa, and became his successor after his teacher's death. It seems probable that at an earlier period of his life, he had come in contact with Stoic philosophers who introduced him to the works of Panaetius. But for a number of years, Antiochus wrote and lectured in the tradition of the New Academy; that is, he maintained the skepticism of Carneades, Clitomachus, and Philo. Then, suddenly, for reasons we do not know, he radically changed his position from skepticism to dogmaticism, claiming that he had finally revived the old Platonic Academy. This claim he substantiated by asserting that both Aristotle and Zeno

---

26. Those who obey the passions and pleasures of the body will find it very difficult to fly through the universe (*Somn.* 29). If they have violated the laws of gods and men, they will be imprisoned in the atmosphere of the earth for many centuries (cf. *Tusc.* 1.27 on the afterlife of the undistinguished, and on the *topos peri palingenesias* in general see E. Norden on Virg. *Aen.* 6.733ff.).

27. The fact has been established conclusively by Madvig in his annotated edition of Cic. *De fin.* (1876) and by Hirzel (3:691ff.); see Luck 55ff.

28. Cic. *De fin.* 5.7, 14; *Luc.* 131. *De leg.* 1.53f.; Sext. Emp. *Pyrrh. Hyp.* 1.235, etc. O. Gigon (*Deutsche Lit. Zeit.* [1955], 171) has pointed out that this tendency to integrate earlier philosophies is not completely new; it is tangible already in Arist. *Met.* 983b6ff. and *De An.* 403b24ff. and in the fragments of Theophrastus' *Physikon Doxai*. Antiochus, however, carried it to an extreme and based his whole interpretation of Platonism on it.

had understood Plato better and followed him more closely than Carneades and his successors. Antiochus' philosophical adversaries at once replied that he had always been a Stoic at heart.[29]

Antiochus had experienced this conversion a few years before Cicero came to Athens, in 79 B.C., and heard him lecture in the Ptolemaeum. Several decades later, Cicero recalls Antiochus as *politissimus et acutissimus omnium nostrae memoriae philosophorum* (*Luc.* 113), a man whom he not only admired as a teacher and thinker but also—he repeats it time and again—loved as a friend. He mentions Antiochus more than fifty times in his philosophical writings and in his private correspondence: We know from a number of references that large parts of the *Academica* and of *De finibus* reflect the thought of Antiochus. Unfortunately, Cicero is less explicit about the kind of research he did for *De republica*,[30]—unfortunately because here, if anywhere, in a work whose scope and title were determined by the great example of Plato's *Republic*, he had to clarify his own position in regard to the old Academy, that is, to its official representative Antiochus.

There was an astonishing number of distinguished Roman statesmen among Antiochus' students: Cicero himself, Varro, Lucullus, Brutus, M. Pupius Piso Calpurnianus—all of whom were fascinated and stimulated by his lectures.[31] Since he claimed to be the true interpreter of Plato, it is more than likely that they looked at Plato's political theory—which was certainly not the least of their interests—through the eyes of Antiochus. As the head of the Platonic Academy in Athens, he was no doubt familiar with Plato's dialogues. On the other hand, it is hard to reconcile the doctrine of the dialogues with Antiochus' Platonism. If his eclectic interpretation of Plato's thought appealed so much to Cicero, it could hardly fail to impress a Brutus or a Piso. His bold compromise between Platonic idealism and Stoic rationalism must have satisfied the

---

29. The testimonies for this tentative reconstruction of Antiochus' biography are collected and discussed by Luck (13ff., 73ff.).

30. N. Wilsing, "Aufbau und Quellen von Ciceros Schrift de re publica" (Diss. Leipz., 1929) has presented the evidence. On Pohlenz' theory of Panaetius as chief "source" see n. 16.

31. His relationship to Lucullus was very close. He accompanied Lucullus on a trip to Alexandria in 87/6 B.C. and was later, during the Second Mithridatic War, his constant companion. It is hard to believe that, in such a case, the fascination was purely one-sided. Whoever lives, for so many years, close to a *grand-seigneur* of Lucullus' class is bound to become a different person (W. Wili, *Horaz und die Augusteische Kultur* [1948], 25).

more practical demands of his Roman students and added to the prestige of the Platonic school in Athens. Antiochus' claim that the Stoa was essentially derived from Platonism took the wind out of the sails of the Stoic competition, and many Roman students who might have been attracted by the Stoa flocked to the Academy instead.

Among all the thinkers who influenced Cicero at one time or another, Antiochus is the only one who could have combined, in the manner of the *Somnium*, discordant concepts. We have seen that he coordinated the statesman and the philosopher. But the *Somnium* goes beyond that. It also compromises between, on the one hand, the concepts that life is death,[32] glory vain,[33] and the earth but a small island in the universe[34] and, on the other, the concepts that life is valuable in itself,[35] as far as it is in accordance with virtue, and that glory follows virtue automatically.

Both Plato and the young Aristotle had declared the worthlessness of τὰ ἀνθρώπινα.[36] But in later years (e.g., in the *Nicomachean Ethics*), Aristotle had become more realistic. Friendship, wealth, a good reputation, he specified, are the necessary ingredients of perfect happiness. If the author of the *Somnium* had been a strict Platonist, or a strict Stoicist, he would have disregarded Aristotle. Actually, the *Somnium* takes great care to work in the conciliatory position of the later Aristotle. Glory, it says, is not worthless by definition; on the contrary, we must interpret the desire for glory that stimulates the great statesmen, poets, and philosophers, in the most favorable light. They all think of posterity; therefore they implicitly believe in immortality.[37] Moreover, virtue without glory is inconceivable; for glory follows virtue like a shadow. Glory, to be sure, should not be desired for its own sake, but whoever lifts his eyes

---

32. See n. 1. Following Empedocles and Plato (E. Norden, *Jahrb. Philol. Supp.* 18 [1892]: 330ff.), the *Somnium* (17) identifies the underworld with the atmosphere of the earth; cf. Xenocrates fr. 15 H.; Cic. *Tusc.* 1.92. See in general F. Cumont, *Le Symbolisme funéraire des Romains* (1942), 124; *Lux Perp.*, 208.

33. On this concept see Boyancé, *Etudes*, 147ff.; Cumont, *Lux Perp.*, 135.

34. A theme frequent in post-Aristotelian philosophy. See A.J. Festugière, *Eranos* 44 (1946): 379ff.; Cumont, *Lux Perp.*, 6 (on Posidonius).

35. Suicide is forbidden, for the universe, including our earth, is a temple of God (Boyancé, *Etudes*, 115ff.; Festugière, *Révélation*, 233ff.), and man fulfills an essential function in this life (*Somn.* 15).

36. Plato *Rep.* 486; *Tht.* 173E. Arist. *Protr.* fr. 10a W.

37. Another Platonic concept (e.g., *Symp.* 208C/E), popularized by Cicero in one of his speeches (*Pro Arch.* 26); see Cumont, *Lux Perp.*, 133f.

up to heaven and leads a life of virtue will find glory at the same time: *quid de te alii loquantur, ipsi videant, sed loquentur tamen* (*Somn.* 25).

This is a very important point. The *Somnium* proclaims that both philosopher and statesman represent the highest ways of life. But how can they be coordinated, when the philosopher, contemplating the universe and comparing its vastness to the smallness of the earth, must come to the conclusion that ambition and glory mean nothing, whereas the statesman—not the ideal statesman whom Plato had in mind, but Scipio, who, although idealized, is nevertheless a real person—needs the assurance that his deeds are known to the world and to posterity?[38]

According to the *Somnium*, there is no contradiction. We have already seen that the life of action is actually based on the contemplation of the universe (*Somn.* 16). We have also seen that this is the position of Antiochus (*De fin.* 4.12). Why is it necessary to assure Scipio that glory will be among the rewards of a life of virtue (*Somn.* 25)? Could this be a qualification due to Cicero himself? But Cicero, as he states himself in *Tusculanae* 5.21ff., sees no compromise between the Stoic concept of the *vita beata*, which consists of virtue alone, and the Aristotelian definition, which includes a number of necessary ingredients, such as wealth, friends, good repute, and so on. On this point, he says, he had to disagree with Antiochus, who distinguished a *vita beata* (consisting of virtue alone) from a *vita beatissima* (adding to virtue the Aristotelian ingredients).[39] Thus, it is Antiochus' cumulative concept of the *vita beatissima* which underlies *Somnium*. Glory is not absolutely necessary for the happy life, but if Scipio has it, he must be called perfectly happy—and he will have it: *sed loquentur tamen!*

I have tried to suggest, in this essay, that the *Somnium* is eclectic in character without reflecting Cicero's own selective skepticism or the uncritical method of a doxographical compiler. Its unity, the equilibrium of its central thoughts, and its method of careful compromise indicate that it is based on the lost work of a Hellenistic philosopher who was thoroughly familiar with the philosophies of the Academy, the Peripatos, and the Stoa. He tried to reconcile them with each other and to endow them with the permanence of a cosmic myth. I have also

---

38. When Scipio has learned to measure the Roman Empire with cosmic standards, he is ashamed of its small size, *ut me imperii nostri . . . paeniteret* (*Somn.* 16).

39. On Cicero's personal attitude toward glory see U. Knoche, *Philologus* 1934, p. 102ff.

suggested that this Hellenistic thinker was in all probability Antiochus of Ascalon. The theme of the *Somnium*—the dignity of man as a creative personality, no matter whether he is creative in the theoretical or the practical sphere—this theme which coordinates the Roman with the Greek ideal of life, seems characteristic for a philosopher whose most enthusiastic students were Roman statesmen.

On Cicero *De fato* 5 and Related Passages

In the gap near the beginning of our text of *De fato*, Cicero must have presented Chrysippus' and Posidonius' doctrines of fate and their base, the idea of συμπάθεια. When the text begins again, Cicero seems to have disposed of most of Posidonius' arguments, though he is ready to admit that, in some cases, the principle of συμπάθεια works. After the gap, we read, *quorum in aliis, ut in Antipatro poeta, ut in brumali die natis, ut in simul aegrotantibus fratribus, ut in urina, ut in unguibus, ut in reliquis eiusmodi, naturae contagio valet, quam ego non tollo, vis est nulla fatalis.* The key term of the whole discussion is συμπάθεια, but this cannot be expressed by *contagio*. Read *cognatio*. It is a spoonerism of the type *suscipit/suspicit* (Martin L. West, *Textual Criticism and Editorial Technique* (1973), 21),[1] perhaps not surprising in a context which deals partly with medical examples.

The same corruption occurs, later on, in *De fato* 7, where an important transition is marked. So far, Cicero has dealt with Posidonius; he now turns to Chrysippus: *sed Posidonium, sicut aequum est, cum bona gratia dimittamus; ad Chrysippi laqueos revertamur. cui quidem primum de ipsa cognatione* [codd. nonn. Turnebi, Bremi ex coni.: *contagione* vel *cogitatione* vel sim. plerique] *rerum respondeamus, reliqua postea persequemur.* The more recent editions, as far as I can see, all keep *contagione* in the text, but it is essential for the concept of συμπάθεια that the thing affected does not have to "touch" the thing that affects it; cf. Marcus Aurelius 9.9.9: ἡ ἐπὶ τὸ κρεῖττον ἐπανάβασις συμπάθειαν καὶ ἐν διεστῶσιν ἐργάσασθαι δύναται.

In Cicero, *cognatio naturae* or *cognatio rerum* or similar expressions

---

From *American Journal of Philology* 99 (1978): 155–58.

I am grateful to Wendell Clausen and to David Marwede for their help.

1. Such transpositions of letters (sometimes called anagrams) are very frequent. Cf., e.g., Lucretius 3.170: *vis horrida leti* for *v. h. teli* (em. Marullus); Lucan 4.595: *typhon* (most MSS) becomes *python* in V; 740: *limite* in most MSS appears as *milite* in some. Many examples are listed by Housman, *Manilius*, vol. 1 (1937), livff.: cf. James Willis, *Latin Textual Criticism* (1972), 81ff.

regularly translate συμπάθεια; cf. *De natura Deorum* 2.19: *quid vero tanta rerum consentiens conspirans continuata*[2] *cognatio quem non coget ea quae dicuntur a me comprobare?* (see Pease ad loc.); 3.28: *itaque illa mihi placebat oratio de convenientia consensuque naturae quam quasi cognatione continuata* [Davies ex codd., ut videtur: *continuatam* A V B alii] *conspirare dicebas . . . illa vero cohaeret et permanet naturae viribus, non deorum, estque in ea iste quasi consensus quam* συμπάθειαν *Graeci vocant.*

In an important passage of *De divinatione* (2.33), Cicero describes the Stoic συμπάθεια τῶν ὅλων; as in *De fato*, he does not reject it outright, but he denies that it proves anything for divination. After having listed briefly some of the principles of the *Etrusca disciplina*, he adds that its claims are founded on συμπάθεια: *cum rerum autem natura quam cognationem habent? quae ut uno consensu iuncta sit et continens, quod video placuisse physicis eisque maxime qui omne quod esset unum esse dixerunt, quid habere mundus potest cum thesauri inventione? si enim extis pecuniae mihi amplificatio ostenditur idque fit natura, primum exta sunt coniuncta mundo, deinde meum lucrum natura rerum continetur. nonne pudet physicos id dicere? ut enim iam sit aliqua in natura rerum cognatio* [Orelli ex codd., A ante ras., ut videtur: *contagio* vulgo], *quam esse concedo; multa enim Stoici colligunt* [many examples follow] . . . *ut distantium rerum cognatio naturalis appareat—demus hoc . . .* [and now he returns to the *Etrusca disciplina*] *num etiam, si fissum cuiusdam modi fuerit in iecore, lucrum ostenditur? qua ex cognatione* [Orelli ex codd.: *coniunctione* AB alii: *contagione* Klotz 'coniectura mea ex librorum vestigiis'] *naturae et quasi concentu atque consensu*[3] *quam* συμπάθειαν *Graeci appellant, convenire potest aut fissum iecoris cum lucello meo aut meus quaesticulus cum caelo terra rerumque natura?* Without rejecting the Stoic notion of συμπάθεια, Cicero reduces the conclusions that the Stoics based on it *ad absurdum,* by using two arguments: (a) there is no συμπάθεια between the entrails of an animal and the hidden treasure which I am to find; (b) there is no συμπάθεια between my sudden increase in wealth and the rest of the universe. In a later context of *De divinatione* (2.152), Cicero deals with "prophetic" dreams. Again, he denies that they work through συμπάθεια, though he does not reject that idea in itself: *etenim . . . quae est continuatio coniunctioque naturae quam, ut dixi, vocant* συμπάθειαν, *eius modi ut thesaurus ex ovo intellegi debeat?* He admits the possibility of medical diagnosis and prognosis but sees no

---

2. *Continuatio* translates συνέχεια: cf. Cic. *Nat. D.* 2.84, 3.32; Seneca *QNat.* 2.2.2; Zeller, *Philos. d. Gr.* III 1⁵ (1923), 186 n. 1.

3. Later (*Div.* 2.144) he paraphrases συμπάθεια by *vis consensusque naturae.*

"natural relationship" between dreams and treasures, dreams and inheritances or victories, and so on.

In all these passages, *rerum cognatio* or *naturae cognatio* or *naturalis cognatio* is the Latin equivalent of συμπάθεια. Sometimes Cicero adds a few synonyms or a paraphrase, such as *consensus naturae* or *convenientia naturae* or *concentus ac consensus naturae* or *continuatio coniunctioque naturae* (hence no change is necessary in *Div.* 2.34). All these terms seem to exclude the notion of *contagio,* which, in Cicero, often has a negative meaning (*Div.* 1.63, 2.58). It is neutral in *De divinatione* 2.92: *quae potest igitur contagio ex infinito paene intervallo pertinere ad lunam vel potius ad terram?* The astrologers whom Cicero attacks here do not operate with the concept of συμπάθεια; they postulate a direct influence of the stars on every form of life on our planet, but the enormous distances between the planets make this improbable, Cicero says. Here, *contagio* is the correct reading, and it stands alone, without *naturae* or *rerum* or *naturalis*.

Since the article *cognatio* in the *Thesaurus* presents the material in hopeless confusion, I briefly list some other testimonies for *cognatio* = συμπάθεια: Plin. *Nat. hist.* 2.96, 6.211; Rufinus' translation of Origenes *Ad Levit.* 5.1: *cognationem sui ad invicem gerunt visibilia et invisibilia, terra et caelum, anima et caro.* But *cognatio* in itself can also express another important Stoic idea, the idea of συγγένεια; cf. Cic. *Div.* 1.64: *quod provideat animus ipse per sese, quippe qui deorum cognatione teneatur;*[4] Seneca *QNat.* 7.30.4 (in a beautiful, hymnlike passage); Marc. Aur. 12.26; Zeller, *Die Philosophie der Griechen*, III 1[5] (1923), 204.

---

4. *Div.* 1.110 should be added here, for Cicero clearly refes to the συγγένεια between gods and men: *necesse est cognatione divinorum animorum animos humanos commoveri.* The older MSS have *cognitione,* but what the sense requires is, once more, *cognatione* (Marsus, Orelli ex codd.). The recent editors (but not Pease) print *contagione,* a poor conjecture made by Davies and defended by W. Theiler (*Vorbereitung des Neuplatonismus* [1930], 136 n. 1); but Theiler's references to Epictetus *Diss.* 1.14.6 and K. Reinhardt (*Kosmos und Sympathie* [1926], 227) are inconclusive: in Epictetus συνέχεια serves to explain συμπάθεια (in paragraph 5), and Reinhardt only says that Cicero is arguing against Posidonius, because the main topic is συμπάθεια, which I doubt.

A Stoic Cosmogony in Manilius
(1.149–72)

    ignis in aetherias volucer se sustulit oras
150 summaque complexus stellantis culmina caeli
    flammarum vallo naturae moenia fecit.
    proximus in tenuis descendit spiritus auras
    aeraque extendit medium per inania mundi.
155 tertia sors undas stravit fluctusque natantis,
    aequoraque effudit toto nascentia ponto,
    ut liquor exhalet tenuis atque evomat auras
    aeraque ex ipso ducentem semina pascat,
154 ignem flatus alat vicinis subditus astris.
159 ultima subsedit glomerato pondere tellus,
    convenitque vagis permixtus limus harenis
    paulatim ad summum tenui fugiente liquore;
    quoque magis puras umor secessit in undas
    et saccata magis struxerunt aequora terram
    adiacuitque cavis fluidum convallibus aequor,
165 emersere fretis montes, orbisque per undas
    exsiliit, vasto clausus tamen undique ponto.
168 idcircoque manet stabilis, quia totus ab illo
    tantundem refugit mundus fecitque cadendo
170 undique, ne caderet medium totius et imum.
    [ictaque contractis consistunt corpora plagis
    et concurrendo prohibentur longius ire.]

[Flying fire soared upward to the aetherial zones, spread along the very top of the starry sky, and made from panels of flames the walls of the world. Spirit, next, sank down and became light

From *Mémorial André-Jean Festugière: Antiquité Païenne et Chrétienne, Vingt-cinq études réunies et publiées par E. Lucchesi et H.D. Saffrey*, ed. Patrick Cramer (Geneva, 1984), 27–32.

breezes and spread out air through the middle of the empty space of the world. The third element expanded (in the form of) water and floating waves and poured out the ocean born from the whole sea. This happened so that water might breathe out and exhale the light breezes and feed the air which draws its seeds from it [i.e., the water]; also, that the wind might nourish the fire which is placed directly under the stars. Finally, earth drifted to the bottom, ball-shaped because of its weight: slime, mixed with drifting sand, took shape as the light liquid gradually evaporated. More moisture withdrew and became pure water, and so the oceans were filtered, and land built up, and flat expanses of water came to lie next to hollow valleys. Mountains emerged from the earth, though still locked on all sides by the ocean, leapt through the waves, and it remains stable because the firmament keeps at every point the same distance from it, and by falling from all sides preserved the middle and lowest part from falling. [For bodies hit by blows coming from inside remain as they were, and because of the centripetal force, they cannot move very far.]]

Before commenting on some details, I should like to point out that Manilius' cosmogony, though it represents the common Stoic doctrine, is quite unique and that it deserves a place in any treatment of Stoic physics. As far as I can see, it has been neglected so far; but now that Manilius is accessible in G.P. Goold's excellent Loeb edition, with its fine translation and helpful introduction, one would expect its importance to be more widely recognized. It is so brief and—in parts—enigmatic that it reads like a much abbreviated poetic version of a more fully developed Greek prose text. There are also certain gaps and omissions,[1] but on the whole it shows a good grasp of the school theory.[2]

It could be pointed out in detail how close Manilius is to the relevant chapter (17) of Cornutus' *Theologia Graeca*,[3] but this would take up too

---

1. Manilius does not discuss the "primary state" and the "primary principle," a discussion that one might expect in a Stoic text; cf. J. Duchesne-Guillemin, *RE* suppl. 9 (1962): 1546. The transition from water to air is discussed (157), also the transition from air to fire (153f.) and the transition from earth to water (159ff.). The opposite sequence, attested by Seneca (*Nat. quaest.* 3.10.1ff.) is not developed.

2. The doxography seems to be characteristic of Posidonius; cf. Diels, *Doxographi Graeci* (1929) 229ff.

3. Cf. also *SVF* I 98ff., 102, 497; II 579–584.

much space. Slight differences can be explained by Cornutus' tendency to harmonize Stoic doctrine with Hesiod's cosmogony, for he quotes Hesiod with approval, it seems, and interprets him, while Manilius only mentions him briefly (1.125–27).

Manilius' account is also close to several passages in Seneca's *Naturales quaestiones* (e.g., the *praefatio*, 5.16.1, and 6.16.2). Either Seneca and Manilius followed the same source or Seneca had read Manilius; compare, for example, Seneca's phrase (*Nat. quaest.* 6.16.2) *totum hoc caelum quod igneus aether, mundi summa pars claudit* with Manilius 149–51: Seneca's *igneus aether* clearly corresponds to Manilius' *ignis in aetherias . . . oras*, and Seneca's *summa pars* corresponds to Manilius' *summa . . . culmina*.

Perhaps I should first give a summary of the Stoic doctrine of cosmogony. It would be difficult to improve on the admirable account given by E.V. Arnold (*Roman Stoicism* [1911], 196), partly based, as he acknowledges, on notes by A.C. Pearson:

> At the beginning of each world-period, expansion and tension is supreme, and only the world-soul exists. Next, the fiery breath begins to cool, the opposing principle of contraction asserts itself, the universe settles down and shrinks; the aether passes into air, and air in its turn to water. All this while tension is slackening. . . . The fire, still unextinguished within, works upon the watery mass or chaos, until it evolves from it the four elements as we know them. On its outer edge, where it meets the expansive aether, the water rarefies, until the belt of air is formed. All the while . . . particles of fire still pass into air and thence into water and earth. Earth still in turns yields to water, water to air, and air to fire. . . . Thus by the interaction of conflicting tendencies an equilibrium (ἰσονομία) is established, and the result is the apparent permanence of the phenomenal world.

This account, based on sources other than Manilius, confirms that he simplifies somewhat (see n. 1). He leaves out one whole phase, the κάτω ὁδός. The early Stoics had borrowed from Heraclitus (fr. 76 D.-K.) the concept of the "downward" as well as the "upward" motion of the elements, as they emanate from the primary fire: fire into earth, earth into water. Cicero, *De natura Deorum* 2.84 (cf. 2.33, 3.12) is more explicit: *et cum quattuor sint genera corporum, uicissitudine eorum mundi continuata*

natura est. nam ex terra aqua, ex aqua oritur aer, ex aere aether, deinde
*retrorsum uicissim ex aethere aer, inde aqua, ex aqua terra infima.*4

But while Manilius does not seem to present the Stoic position fully,
he also transcends it in some ways. His Stoicism is, as might be expected
from an author of that time, more eclectic than that of Chrysippus; it is the
kind of eclecticism that one finds in Virgil (*Aen.* 6.724ff.) and Ovid (*Met.*
1.26ff., 15.237ff.), even though it is definitely Stoic in character. At the
same time Manilius is clearly familiar with the Epicurean διακόσμησις, as
it is, for example, presented by Lucretius 1.782ff. and 5.416ff.5 Manilius
certainly does not reject the Epicurean theory where he has a chance to do
so, in 1.128ff. That his eclecticism could go so far is, perhaps, less surprising when one considers how carefully Seneca had studied Epicurean
thought and how some of it clearly appealed to him.

What is remarkable, too, is the mystic,6 almost apocalyptic, style of
the passage. There is a sense of the dramatic and spectacular, especially
at the beginning (149–54) and later on (247–54). Manilius has been no
less successful in transforming Greek philosophical ideas into Latin poetry than was Lucretius, who was clearly one of his models.7

This religious mood can be felt in other parts of Manilius' work, for
example, in 2.99–104:

> denique sic pecudes et muta animalia terris,
> cum maneant ignara sui legisque per aeuum,
> natura tamen ad mundum reuocante parentem
> attollunt animos caelumque et sidera seruant
> corporaque ad lunae nascentis cornua lustrant
> uenturasque uident hiemes, reditura serena.

To show that the stars affect life on earth, Manilius mentions, in a
series of arguments, the "dumb animals," who are unaware of their

---

4. Cf. Marc. Aur. 4.46, 6.17, 9.28; Diog. Laert. 7.136.

5. Cf. also Manilius 4.488ff.; Villoison and Osann, in their edition of Cornutus (1844), pp. 230, 412.

6. *Tacita ratione* (251) is probably μυστικῶς; cf. Seneca *Tro.* 843: *sacris tacitis*
gaudens Eleusis.

7. The Stoic distinguished two types of "elements," ἀρχαί and στοιχεῖα, a
distinction which is often obscured: only the supreme god and matter could,
ultimately, be ἀρχαί, whereas fire, air, etc. were στοιχεῖα. The ἀρχαί are eternal,
but the στοιχεῖα will be dissolved in the ἐκπύρωσις. They have a shape, whereas
the ἀρχαί do not; cf. Villoison and Osann, 451f.

identity and are not ruled by the laws of human society and yet have an obscure knowledge of celestial phenomena and can tell when the weather is about to change, because the voice of nature reminds them that they are related to the sky.[8]

Let us now look at the details.

149–51. There is a textual problem in verse 149: the manuscripts have *auras*, but Bentley's *oras* is necessary, as Seneca *Naturales quaestiones* 2.13.4 shows: *expurgatus ignis in custodia mundi summa sortitus oras operis pulcherrimi circumit.* This parallel, incidentally, has a problem of its own, though it does not affect *oras*; here the manuscripts have *pulcherrime*, but Madvig's change supplies the epithet for *opus* ("universe") which it needs; compare *Dialogi* 1.1.2: *non sine aliquo custode tantum opus stare.*

Manilius' description of the cosmic fire is very close to Lucretius 5.457–59: *ideo, per rara foramina, terrae / partibus erumpens primus se sustulit aether / ignifer et multos secum leuis abstulit ignis.* Even the expression *flammarum uallo* (Manilius 1.151; cf. 2.118: *mundi flammea tecta*) is reminiscent of Lucretius 1.73: *flammantia moenia mundi.*

152f. Housman rightly transposed verse 154 after verse 158 (see later discussion); we therefore have a period which consists of two lines. Manilius seems to differentiate between *spiritus, aurae, aer* and *inane* (*inania mundi*). *Aer* could be the air which we breathe; *aurae,* the air in motion (the winds); and *inane,* "empty space," an abstraction and therefore not identical with "air." But what is *spiritus*? If it is equal to πνεῦμα, then it comes close to the meaning "wind" and cannot be separated from *aurae.* There is also the difficulty that according to the Stoics there was, strictly speaking, no empty space (Diog. Laert. 7.140). Either Manilius uses *inane* loosely or he is influenced, through Lucretius, by Epicurus. In a parallel passage, *Naturales quaestiones* 3.10.2, Seneca combines *uenti, aer, spiritus, spatium,* and this may give us the key to understanding Manilius, for if we substitute *uenti* to *auras* and *spatium* to *inania mundi* we

---

8. *Aetna* 224ff. and Seneca *Nat. quaest.* 7.1.1 are not exact parallels, though there are some similarities. The author of *Aetna* speaks of *pecudes* in a derogatory sense (224f.): they do see *miranda,* but they do not understand them or care about them: *non oculis solum pecudum miranda tueri/more nec effusos in humum graue pascere corpus.* Seneca, on the other hand, says that no creature (and that seems to include animals) can possibly be so dim-witted as not to get excited and enthusiastic about the divine, the wonderful: *nemo usque adeo tardus est et hebes et demissus in terram est, ut ad diuina non erigatur ac tota mente consurgat, utique ubi nouum aliquod e caelo miraculum fulsit.* Seneca seems closer to Manilius than to the *Aetna* poem.

have an exact analogy: *quid si mireris quod, cum uenti totum aera impellant, non deficit spiritus, sed per dies noctesque aequaliter fluit? nec, ut flumina, certo alueo fertur, sed per uastum caeli spatium lato impetu uadit.* This reads almost like a paraphrase of John 3:8: τὸ πνεῦμα ὅπου θέλει πνεῖ. Seneca affirms the presence, the permanence, the constant motion of the πνεῦμα in the world. Similarly, to Manilius, the air and the winds are manifestations of the πνεῦμα, and the term *inania mundi* is probably not meant as an exact philosophical term. But Manilius may also have in mind the distinction between ἀήρ and αἰθήρ, *spiritus* being almost equivalent to the latter; compare Macrobius *Commentarii in Somnium Scipionis* 1.22.5: *quidquid ex omni materia . . . purissimum ac liquidissimum fuit, id tenuit summitatem et aether uocatus est; pars illa cui minor puritas et inerat aliquid leuis ponderis, aer extitit et in secunda* [fort. leg. *secundas*, sc. *partes*] *delapsus est.* On the other hand, the winds (i.e., ἀήρ in motion) also nourish the αἰθήρ (Manilius 2.74). It is also possible that Manilius thinks of πνεῦμα in terms of the "surrounding air," like Marcus Aurelius (9.2).

155, 156, 157, 158, 154. The five lines, arranged in this sequence, form a single period. It was Housman who first placed verse 154 after verse 158, where it makes good sense. The line apparently had lost its place when the eye of a scribe traveled from *aeraque* (153) to *aeraque* (154), a mechanical error sometimes called "saut du même au même." But the line, in order to fit smoothly between verses 158 and 159, as the last clause of the period, needs a connection; read, therefore, *ignem <et> flatus alat uicinis subditus astris; et* could easily drop out between *ignem* and *flatus* by double haplography in a script in which *t* and *f* looked alike.

After fire and air, Manilius discusses water (the poetic color is borrowed from Lucr. 5.48off., it seems), an element which exhales air (e.g., in the form of steam) and therefore adds to the air above ("feeds" it), just as the air "feeds" the heavenly fire, which is even higher above. Manilius here describes the ἄνω ὁδός. The two phases distinguished by Manilius are separated and then combined into one movement by Cornutus (chap. 17)—ὁ ἀὴρ . . . κατὰ ἀνάδοσιν [sc. γέγονεν]· τὸ δὲ λεπτομερὲς τοῦ ἀέρος γέγονε πῦρ . . . ὁ γὰρ πρῶτος ἀρθεὶς ἀπὸ τοῦ ἀρχεγόνου ὑγροῦ ἀὴρ ζοφώδης καὶ σκοτεινὸς ἦν, εἶτα λεπτυνόμενος εἰς αἰθέρα καὶ φῶς μετέβαλεν . . .—indicating that the process is a continuous one, though it can be divided by the mind. The air itself is not homogeneous, but from a dark and cloudy element it gets transformed into a bright and shiny one. In this sense the earth can be said to have "created" heaven, that is, air (Cornutus loc. cit.). The air is transformed from a dark and cloudy element into a bright and shiny one. Earth and water, too, undergo this sort of refinement, as Ovid *Metamorphoses* 15.244ff. says.

omnia fiunt

ex ipsis et in ipsa cadunt resolutaque tellus
in liquidas rarescit aquas, tenuatus in auras
aeraque umor abit dempto quoque pondere rursus
in superos aer tenuissimus emicat ignes . . .

This process of refinement can be partly explained by the enormous distance (*longum interuallum*) between the surface of the earth and the *culmina caeli* (cf. Cicero *Nat. Deor.* 2.43). Seneca *Naturales quaestiones* 6.16.2f. lists all the parts of the universe which are nourished by the *halitus terrarum:* they are *igneus aether; stellae; caelestium coetus; sol.* All of those share *alimentum ex terreno.* But the earth could not provide this nourishment for the upper regions if it were not full of *spiritus* (Manilius 1.247ff.). Cf. Seneca *Naturales quaestiones* 6.16.1: *non esse terram sine spiritu palam est.* We know from Aetius *Placita* 2.17.4 that, before the Stoics, Heraclitus taught that sun, moon, the heavenly bodies in general, feed on exhalations from the earth: Ἡράκλειτος καὶ οἱ Στωϊκοὶ τρέφεσθαι τοὺς ἀστέρας ἐκ τῆς ἐπιγείου ἀναθυμιάσεως. The exhalations rise from the surface of the earth as well as from rivers, lakes, and seas, as Cicero *De Natura Deorum* 2.83 says: *terra . . . ipsa . . . [alitur] uicissim a superis externisque naturis* [i.e., *elementis*] *eiusdemque expirationibus et aer alitur et aether et omnia supera.*[9] The very term *exhalare* which Manilius (157) uses is a translation of ἀναθυμιάω; a near synonym seems to be ἐξατμίζω (Stobaeus *Eclogues* 1.21 [pp. 184f. W.]).

159–66. The earth takes on the shape of a ball because of its weight, but earth is mixed with water, and water is mixed with earth. In a river or a lake the water nearer the surface tends to be pure; near the bottom, muddy. (Cf. Lucr. 5.496f.: *omnis mundi quasi limus in imum/confluxit gravis et subsedit funditus ut faex.*) The same process of refinement described earlier is at work; compare Seneca *Naturales quaestiones* 2.54.1: *nunc ad opinionem Posidonii reuertar. e terra terrenisque omnibus pars umida efflatur, pars sicca et fumida* [*remanet* add. pars codd.]: *haec fulminibus alimentum est, illa imbribus. quicquid in aera sicci fumosique peruenit, id includi se nubibus non*

---

9. Cf. Cicero *Nat. Deor.* 2.43: *(sidera aluntur) marinis terrenisque umoribus longo interuallo extenuatis;* ibid. 3.37; Cleanthes, *SVF* I 501; Macrob. *Sat.* 1.23.1; Reinhardt, *Kosmos und Sympathie* (1926), 108.

fert sed rumpit claudentia . . . This passage is difficult in several ways. First, a doctrine attributed to Aristotle (*Meterol.* 1.3, 2.4, 2.9) in *Naturales quaestiones* 2.12.4ff. is here attributed to Posidonius. One may assume, as Gercke (ad loc.) did, that Posidonius reported Aristotle's doctrine (perhaps with approval, perhaps with certain reservations). But the parallelism clearly shows that the addition *remanet* in some witnesses misses the sense, and this is also true for Schultess' conjecture *remeat.* When Seneca writes *e terra terrenisque omnibus,* he includes water, but with *pars . . . pars* he distinguishes the exhalation of water from the exhalation of air.

To a Stoic this chain of transitions from one element to another was so natural that Seneca could ask the question (*Nat. Quaest.* 3.10.1ff.) *quare . . . non ex terra fiat aqua?*

168–72. There are two textual problems in this passage. First, verse 167, *imaque de cunctis mediam tenet undique sedem,* has been transposed after verse 214 by Housman. Second, verses 171f. have been deleted by Bentley. Both proposals are accepted by the latest editor, G.P. Goold. It is easy to see that verse 167 does not belong after verse 166. On the other hand, it does not seem plausible that it traveled over a distance of forty-eight lines, and the archetype, as Goold has plausibly reconstructed it (pp. cvif of his Loeb edition), offers no clues. The reason why the line seems to fit so well into the other context (194–214) is fairly evident: that context is very similar to the one we have here; compare, for example, verse 159, *ultima subsedit glomerato pondere tellus,* with verse 214, *sic tellus glomerata manet mundumque figurat.* In fact, the stray line would fit quite well after verse 159, because the conclusion of the whole passage, verses 169f., makes it clear that the earth is, at the same time, *medium et imum.* Then the problem of transposition may be connected with the other one, discussed earlier (29); and we should probably arrange the verses in the following order: 153, 155, 156, 157, 158, 154, 159, 167, 160, etc. The problem of verses 171f. will be discussed shortly.

The planet earth keeps its stability, because every point of the universe is equidistant from it, and because the earth is at the center as well as the bottom. This last statement sounds like a Stoic paradox, and perhaps it is meant as one; it is certainly Stoic doctrine, as we know from Cicero *De natura Deorum* 2.84, *medium locum mundi qui est infimus;* cf. 115, *ita stabilis est mundus itaque cohaeret, ad permanendum ut nihil ne excogitari quidem possit aptius.*[10]

---

10. Villoison and Osann (338) collect testimonies for the concept that the earth is in the center of the universe; according to Stoic doctrine it is at the center and at the bottom.

The last two lines of this passage, verses 171f., have been brack-eted, as mentioned earlier, by G.P. Goold, who follows Bentley. I admit that they pose a problem, but not so much as far as the doctrine is concerned. It is more a question of poetic style and form; they seem unfinished. Perhaps Manilius left them in a rough form, hoping to revise them later. They could hardly be an "interpolation" by a later hand, for who would have had the knowledge and the gift of versifica-tion? The lines are unsatisfactory as they stand, but perhaps we have to admit that Manilius—like Lucretius, like Virgil, like Ovid, like Lucan—did not have an opportunity to apply the *labor limae* to his work. Such a hypothesis would explain a number of textual problems in Manilius, as it does in Ovid's *Metamorphoses.*

The doctrine itself seems to be a Stoic modification (through Posi-donius?) of an Aristotelian theory, as I have noted already. First, I pro-vide the Aristotelian context (*De Caelo* 2.14.8): ἕκαστον . . . τῶν μορίων (sc. τῆς γῆς) βάρος ἔχει μέχρι πρὸς τὸ μέσον, καὶ τὸ ἔλαττον ὑπὸ τοῦ μείζονος ὠθούμενον οὐχ οἷόν τε κυμαίνειν ἀλλὰ συμπιέζεσθαι μᾶλλον καὶ συγχωρεῖν ἕτερον ἑτέρῳ, ἕως ἂν ἔλθῃ ἐπὶ τὸ μέσον. Second, I present the Stoic adaptation, from the anonymous source quoted in Achilles, *Isagoge* 9 (on the universe) πάντα αὐτοῦ τὰ μέρη ἐπὶ τὸ μέσον νένευκεν; cf. 4 τὴν γῆν πανταχόθεν ὑπὸ τοῦ ἀέρος ὠθουμένην ἰσορρόπως ἐν τῷ μέσῳ εἶναι καὶ ἑστάναι.

I hope that I have been able to show that Manilius' "cosmogony in a nutshell" preserves in a poetic form genuine Stoic doctrine.

Theurgy and Forms of Worship
in Neoplatonism

The murmur of spirits that sleep in the shadow of gods from afar . . .
—Algernon Charles Swinburne

The need of pagan believers to enter into direct contact with their gods led to the development of a certain technique or a set of techniques codified during the reign of Marcus Aurelius, it seems, and given the name "theurgy."[1] It was the subject of philosophical discussions within the Neoplatonist schools, and many followers of Plotinus accepted it

From *Religion, Science and Magic,* ed. J. Neusner, E.S. Frerichs, and P.V. McCracken Flesher (Oxford, 1989), 185–225.

1. A brief bibliography:

Armstrong, A.H., ed. *The Cambridge History of Later Greek and Early Medieval Philosophy.* Cambridge, 1970.

Bidez, J. *La vie de l'empereur Julien.* Paris, 1930.

Boyancé, P. "Théurgie et télestique néoplatonicienne." *Rev. Hist. Rel.* 147 (1955): 189ff.

des Places, E. *La religion grecque.* Paris, 1969.

Dodds, E.R. *The Greeks and the Irrational.* Berkeley, 1951.

Eitrem, S. "Die *systasis* und der Lichtzauber in der Magie." *SO* 8 (1929): 49ff.

———. "La théurgie chez les Néoplatoniciens et dans les papyrus magiques." *SO* 22 (1942): 49ff.

Ganschinietz, R. *Hippolytus' Kapitel über die Magier.* TUGAL 39 (1913).

Hopfner, Th. *Griechisch-ägyptischer Offenbarungszauber.* 2 vols. Leipzig, 1921.

Lewy, H. *Chaldaean Oracles and Theurgy.* Cairo, 1940.

Pfister, Fr. "Ekstase." *RAC* 4 (1959): 944ff.

Prächter, K. "Zur theoretischen Bergründung der Magie im Neuplatonismus." *ARW* 25 (1927): 209ff.

Sicherl, M. "M. Psellos und Jamblichos, *De Mysteriis.*" *BZ* 53 (1960): 8ff.

Svoboda, K. *La démonologie de Michel Psellos.* Brno, 1927.

Wallis, R.T. *Neoplatonism.* London, 1972.

Wavell, St., A. Butt, and Nina Epton, eds. *Trances.* New York, 1967. This book is full of fascinating analogies to theurgical rituals as referred to in our Greek texts.

West, D.J. *Psychical Research Today.* 1962.

Zintzen, C. "Die Wertung von Mystik und Magie in der neuplatonischen Philosophie." *RhM* 108 (1965): 71ff.

enthusiastically, almost as a way of life. The man who wrote the code in the second century A.D. is known as Julian the Theurgist, to distinguish him from his father, Julian the Chaldaean. The code itself is known as the *Oracula Chaldaica,* a collection of logia, or sayings, in Greek hexameters, of which fragments have survived.[2] In its original form, the collection might be called the "Bible" of theurgy, although its enigmatic style and its use of exuberant imagery would have made it difficult to use even then without the help of a spiritual guide or mentor. It seems to address itself to readers who knew already what the theurgical experience is like. Of its style E.R. Dodds has said that it "is so bizarre and bombastic, [the] thought so obscure and incoherent, as to suggest . . . the trance utterances of modern 'spirit guides.' "

Julian the Theurgist was a kind of spiritual adviser to the emperor Marcus Aurelius, whom he accompanied on his campaign against the Dacians. He modeled a human face from clay and turned it toward the enemy. When they approached and were about to attack the Roman legions, unbearable flashes of lightning came out of the face and drove the barbarians away in a panic.[3]

Although the *Oracula* were known to the Neoplatonists as the ultimate source of theurgical lore, some of them—for example, Proclus[4]—saw in Plato the true founder of theurgy, whereas others—for example, Plotinus himself[5]—apparently considered Orphism as the origin of one branch of theurgy, the part that dealt with the animation of statutes, which has been called τελεστική.

The term *theurgia* can be explained in contrast to *theologia.* It is an activity, an operation, a technique, dealing with the gods, not just a theory, a discussion, an act of contemplation. As such it was considered a form of worship, possibly the best kind of worship, and it clearly had its own rewards for those who practiced it. In his work *On the Mysteries of Egypt,* an elaborate defense of theurgy against skeptics and unbelievers, Iamblichus says (2.11):

> It is not thought that links the theurgist to the gods; else what should hinder the theoretical philosopher from enjoying theurgic

---

2. *Oracles chaldaïques,* ed. E. des Places (Paris, 1971), with a French translation and notes.

3. *Oracles* pp. 221f. des Places, from Psellus.

4. *In Timaeum* 2.255.26f.

5. *Enn.* 4.9.11; P. Boyancé, "Théurgie et télestique néoplatonicienne," *Rev. Hist. Rel.* 147 [1955]: 195ff.

union with them? The case is not so. Theurgic union is attained only by the perfective operation of unspeakable acts correctly performed, acts which are beyond all understanding, and by the power of the unutterable symbols intelligible only to the gods.[6]

To understand the whole concept and the ideology behind it, we ought to look at some synonyms and paraphrases as they were more or less commonly used. It is not my ambition to give a complete list, only a few analogies.

Another name for theurgy is ἱερατικὴ τέχνη, "priestly art," suggesting that the theurgist saw himself as a priest.[7] Θεαγωγία, another name, means literally "evocation of a god"; similarly, φωταγωγία means "evocation of light"; the terms are synonymous, because god is light. A more general term, ἔργα εὐσεβείας (in Latin this would be *opera pietatis* or *pia opera*), shows that theurgy was considered a part of religion, a religious duty, in fact, by some.[8] Iamblichus (*Myst.* 3.19) speaks of the "execution of eternal actions" when he clearly has in mind theurgical operations. The term "fire" appears in several terms—for instance, "actions of eternal fire," πυρὸς ἀφθίτου ἔργα, and the knowledge of the theurgist is called "understanding heated by fire."[9] A closely related group of synonyms—ὄργια, μυστήρια, τελεταί, μυσταγωγία—indicates that, in later paganism, theurgy had acquired the status of the old mystery religions; in fact, theurgy can be considered the ultimate development of the mysteries, because it represents an initiation into the highest mystery of all, the union of man and god.[10] Other names are "theosophy," "service," "ritual," "divine knowledge."[11]

Philosophy and Theurgy

The basic doctrine of theurgy could be found, as I have said, in the *Oracles,* but it was greatly expanded and interpreted by the Neo-

---

6. Cf. Proclus, *Elements of Theology,* edited, with a commentary, by E.R. Dodds (Oxford, 1933), xx.

7. *Oracles* p. 219 des Places. The term θεαγωγὸς λόγος is also found in the Magical Papyri.

8. *Oracles* p. 177 des Places.

9. *Oracles* frs. 6, 133, 139.

10. J. Bidez, "Notes sur les mystères néoplatoniciens," *RBPh* 7 (1928): 1477–81.

11. Iambl. *Myst.* 5.22; cf. des Places, *Oracles,* p. 45, n. 2.

platonists—not all of them, but quite a few. The philosophers who belonged to the various schools of Neoplatonism can be divided into those who placed theurgy above thought, those who did not, and those who were undecided.

Let us look at the basic doctrine first. An excellent account has been given by Franz Cumont.

> Following Plato, the Chaldean theurgists clearly opposed the intelligible world of the ideas to the world of appearances which are perceptible by the senses. They had a dualist concept of the universe. At the top of their pantheon they placed the intellect whom they also called the Father (Νοῦς πατρικός). This transcendent god who wraps himself in silence is called impenetrable and yet is sometimes represented as an immaterial Fire from which everything has originated. Below him are, on various levels, the triads of the intelligible world, then the gods who reside beyond the celestial spheres (ἄζωνοι) or who preside over them (ζωναῖοι). . . . The human soul is of divine substance, a spark of the original Fire, has of its own will descended the rungs of the ladder of beings and has become imprisoned in the body. . . . When it is freed of all the material wraps by which it is burdened, the blessed soul will be received in the fatherly embrace of the highest God.[12]

Using this doctrine as a starting point, the Chaldeans perfected a technique that could apparently be learned, at least up to a certain point, and more or less guaranteed a manifestation of the divine in a variety of forms on this earth and a union with it in this life as well as salvation in the next.

Obviously, we know only a part, perhaps only a very small part, of the whole procedure, and we can only guess at how and why it worked. No introduction to theurgical operations has survived. We know that Iamblichus, Proclus, and others practiced a kind of theosophy, which, by ascetic exercises, special rites, and certain material objects could bring the deity down to earth or make the soul ascend to the higher regions.[13] Even if we had Iamblichus' voluminous work on the *Oracles*, which the

---

12. *Lux Perpetua* (Paris, 1949), 363f., 367. See also *Religions orientales dans le paganisme romain* (Paris, 1928), 282 n. 69; des Places, intro. to *Oracles*, pp. 1ff.

13. J. Bidez, *La vie de l'empereur Julien* (Paris, 1930), 73ff.

emperor Julian was so anxious to read in a good edition,[14] we would probably not understand much more, and we could hardly expect to be able to reproduce these procedures and obtain the same effects, even if we wanted to. I have collected as many specific details as possible and tried to piece together a picture, but much of it remains a puzzle. One clearly had to be initiated, as Julian was himself, by a master. Part of the technique appears to have been a closely guarded secret handed down in certain families, but also in the philosophical schools—they were, after all, like families.

From the way in which these experiences are referred to—the seriousness, the warmth of the tone, the enthusiasm—one may conclude that the technique usually worked, though failures occurred, it seems, and had to be explained. There also seems to have been a certain amount of fraud; at least this is alleged by outsiders and adversaries, such as the Christians; and even within Neoplatonism there were critics and skeptics. Some theurgists must have been better than others.

But assuming that something truly extraordinary happened, we must look for a plausible explanation in modern terms, and this I shall try to do at the end of my discussion, though I cannot claim to have found the solution; in this area all research must remain more or less tentative.

It has been said that theurgy was essentially a higher form of magic, merely a respectable cousin of what the Greeks called γοητεία.[15] Γόης can designate not only a "sorcerer" but also a "juggler" and quite often a "swindler."[16] That theurgy was nothing else but magic and closely allied with fraud was the opinion of Christian authors.[17] Believers, on the other hand, distinguished their art carefully from γοητεία. Iamblichus (*Myst.* 3.28–290) attacks the "makers of images," and he seems to have in mind magicians who can produce false apparitions of the gods.[18] These practitioners apparently claimed the status of theurgists, but for

---

14. Cf. A.-J. Festugière, *Trois dévots paiens*, vol. 3, *Sallustius* (Paris, 1944), 8; *Révélation d'Hermès Trismégiste*, vol. 3 (Paris, 1953), 48.

15. H. Lewy, *Chaldaean Oracles and Theurgy* (Cairo, 1940), 190ff., 238; cf. S. Eitrem, "La théurgie chez les Néoplationiciens et dans les papyrus magiques," *SO* 22 (1942): 47ff.

16. W. Bauer, W.F. Arndt, and F.W. Gingrich, *A Greek-English Lexicon of the New Testament* (Chicago, 1979), s.v.

17. Gregory of Nazianzus *Or.* 4.55f.; cf. C.A. Lobeck, *Aglaophamus*, vol. 1 (1829), 113ff.

18. N.P. Nilsson, *Geschichte der griechischen Religion*, vol. 2 (1961), 434.

Iamblichus they are nothing else but γόητες.[19] It is not quite clear in what sense the apparitions they produced were false. Perhaps they used the kind of magical apparatus described by Hippolytus in his chapter on magicians; perhaps there were certain signs that their trance was fake; in antiquity even an ordinary person was able to distinguish a real trance from a fake one.

A similar distinction is made by Porphyry. Although he is not always sure—unlike Iamblichus—that theurgy is the highest form of religious worship, he strictly rejects the lower forms of magic. In book 2 of *De abstinentia*, which deals with the gods and the ways in which they are worshiped, one chapter (43) discusses the kind of magic performed through evil powers—that is, the powers which evil magicians worship and use, especially their leader (τὸν προεστῶτα αὐτῶν). Demons may send deceptive images and fool persons by "miracle working" (τερατουργία), here used in a negative sense; there are actually wretched creatures who prepare potions and love charms with their help. All this has nothing to do with theurgy.

The aim of all theurgical operations is clearly described in fragment 97 of the *Oracles* (though a few words in the text are hypothetical); it is, in one word, to embrace God and be embraced by God: "Having flown upward, the human soul will embrace God vigorously. Free of any mortal element, she[20] will be wholly intoxicated by God." The theurgist aims at "unification with the unparticipated One,"[21] and it is the willingness of the gods to descend that makes theurgy possible.

Through the mystical union with the One and the release from the bonds of fate, humans become actually equal to the gods,[22] at least

19. *Myst.* 4.2; cf. Porphyry *De regr. anim.* fr. 2 Bidez (quoted at Augustine *Civ. Dei* 10.9); Proclus *Theol. Platon.* 2.9. The distinction is made elsewhere—e.g., in Apul. *Apol.* 26; Apollonius of Tyana *Epist.* 16; Heliodorus *Aethiop.* 3.16. Cf. Zintzen, "Die Wertung von Mystik und Magie in der neuplatonischen Philosophie," *RhM* 108 (1965): 92 n. 75.

20. The word for God is masculine in Greek, that for the soul is feminine. One wonders whether there were sexual undertones to the image of the mystical union.

21. A.C. Lloyd, "The Later Neoplatonists," in *Cambridge History of Later Greek Philosophy,* ed. A.H. Armstrong (Cambridge, 1970), 321. He refers to Proclus *Elem. Theol.* 140; *In Platon. Remp.* 2.232ff.; *In Platon. Tim.* 1.209.

22. A.D. Nock, ed., *Sallustius: Concerning the Gods and the Universe* (Cambridge, 1926) liv, xcviii. The distinction between σύστασις (encounter) and ἕνωσις (union) is made by S. Eitrem, "Die *systasis* und der Lichtzauber in der Magie," *SO* 8 (1929): 49ff.

for a short time; afterward they assume their human condition again. Theurgists rank higher than theologians, because they not only think and talk about the gods; they know how to act on them.[23]

Theurgy is also the path to salvation, another blessing that connects it with the mystery religions. It saves the soul and can even save the body, according to the *Oracles* (fr. 128). It will help the soul to leave the "flock" (of ordinary human beings), subject to fate (frs. 102 and 103), and it will wash the soul from its terrestrial pollution (fr. 196). How is all this possible? The human soul is fiery by nature and related to the cosmic fire; therefore it has a natural tendency to return to it and rejoin it.[24]

These beliefs are based on four main principles: (1) the principle of power (δύναμις); (2) the principle of cosmic sympathy (συμπάθεια τῶν ὅλων); (3) the principle of sameness (ὁμοιότης); (4) the idea of the soul-vehicle (ὄχημα).[25]

I should like to discuss these principles briefly. First, there is power, which is used not as a philosophical term but as a general concept, not unlike *mana*. There is power available in the universe to those who know how to plug into it, so to say. Magic, of course, is also based on this concept, and it, too, operates with the principle of cosmic sympathy. This second principle involves certain hidden relationships in the universe that cannot be explained by the sequence of cause and effect, or in terms of time and space. A force located thousands of miles from where I am may nevertheless affect me and my whole life. The universe is a huge living organism in which nothing happens without influencing some other part. Even if the connection is not obvious, the result is clear, and philosophy or occult science has to find an explanation. Plotinus says (*Enn.* 4.4. [28] 32.13), "The universe is one and affected by common feelings and like a living being, and what is far is near."[26] And Porphyry (*Letter to Anebo* fr. 24 Parthey) writes that sympathy exists, as those can attest who "call the gods, carry stones and herbs, tie sacred ties, open what is closed, and produce valid apparitions of the gods"—that is, theurgists.

The third principle, sameness, connects the subject with the object—

---

23. J. Bidez, *Vie de l'empereur Julien,* 369 n. 8; Lloyd, "Later Neoplatonists," 277.

24. F. Cumont, "Le mysticisme astral," *Bull. Acad. Belge* 1909, pp. 256ff.; Nilsson, *Geschichte,* 470.

25. Only three principles (the ὄχημα is not considered) in Nilsson, *Geschichte,* 679.

26. Zintzen, "Die Wertung," n. 83; G. Luck, *Arcana Mundi* (Baltimore, 1985), 147ff.

those who see and understand with those who are seen and understood.[27] There is a definite "family relationship"[28] between us and the
gods; for if we did not share, in some way, in the nature of the divine, how
could we know the divine? If the human eye did not share somehow in the
nature of the sun, how could it see the sun?

The fourth principle underlying theurgy is the vehicle of the soul
(ὄχημα), a kind of astral body that we have; the gods have one, too. The
"evocation of the Light" (φωταγωγία; the word is also used as a synonym for theurgy, as we have seen already) illuminates the ὄχημα of the
theurgist with a divine light, and so divine apparitions (φαντασίαι)
move our "active imagining perception" (ἡ ἐν ἡμῖν φανταστικὴ δύναμις),
according to Iamblichus (Myst. 3.14). The shiny vehicles of the gods can
actually be made apparent by means of theurgy.[29] In a modified form the
doctrine of the ὄχημα seems to survive in modern spiritualism; but there
are other indications, as we shall see, that in ancient theurgy medium-
ship played a role.[30]

Many Neoplatonists between the third and the sixth centuries were
practicing theurgists and tried to accommodate their philosophy to the
mystic experiences they had. Some did not practice it, although they
may have found it interesting, but there is no general agreement within
the school as to the comparative merits of philosophical discussion in the
traditional Platonic sense versus theurgy. The Chaldean doctrine may
have had roots in Platonism, but it is really a new development. According to Olympiodorus (In Platon. Phaed. 123.3–5 Norvin), Plotinus and
Porphyry put philosophy first; Iamblichus, Syrianus, and Proclus put
theurgy first. This may be an oversimplification. Porphyry was certainly
attracted by theurgy, although he hesitated to place it above theology.
Moreover, Olympiodorus' list is incomplete: many other philosophers
named in Damascius' Vita Isidori and in Eunapius' Vitae Sophistarum
were either practicing theurgists or devotees of some kind—for example,
Aedesius, Antoninus the Anchorite,[31] Asclepiodotus,[32] Chrysanthius,

27. Psellus (following Proclus) "On Greek Theurgy," CMAG 6 (1928): 148; cf.
Iambl. Myst. 3.14.

28. Cf. E. des Places, "Syngeneia: La parenté de l'homme avec dieu," Etudes
et Commentaires 51 (1964): 164ff.

29. J. Trouillard, L'un et l'âme selon Proclus (Paris, 1972), 186ff.

30. E.R. Dodds, in his edition (with commentary) of Proclus' Elements of
Theology, pp. 313ff.

31. On Antoninus "the Anchorite" see G. Luck, "Two Predictions of the End
of Paganism," Euphrosyne, n.s., 14 (1986): 153ff. (in this volume, pp. 257–61).

32. Cf. Zintzen, "Die Wertung," 93 n. 31.

Eunapius, Eustathius, Heraiscus, Isidorus, Julian the Emperor, Marinus, Maximus, Nestorius, Plutarch of Athens, Sallustius, Sopater, Sosipatra, Syrianus, and Theosebius.

The career of Sosipatra, a celebrated philosopher and psychic, as we would say, is told by Eunapius (*Vit. Soph.* pp. 466–70 Boiss.).[33] As a little girl she was educated by blessed demons or heroes who appeared one day on her father's estate, recognized her talents, and took her away; her father knew better than to object. Later she was brought back, and it turned out that she had developed her psychic gifts to an astonishing degree. Eventually, she became a great teacher and thinker in Pergamon. A relative of hers by the name of Philometor, "overcome by her beauty and eloquence," as Eunapius says, fell in love with her and cast a love spell on Sosipatra, but his magic was defeated by an even more powerful performance by Maximus, the pupil of Aedesius and teacher of the emperor Julian. The frustrated lover felt trapped and ashamed of himself, which impressed Sosipatra; she "looked at him with different eyes and admired him because he had admired her so much."

The story is fascinating, because it tells us something about the intellectual elite of paganism at the time of the emperor Julian. Magic was everywhere, but it could be defeated, and—most important of all— theurgy worked. It looks like the pagan elite's last stand in the battle against the Christians. To prove that they were on the right side, the pagans claimed to have inherited not only the best of Hellenic culture— Platonism and rhetoric—but also direct contact with the ancient gods at any time they desired. Add to this the beauty and charm of Sosipatra and her psychic gifts, and you have an irresistible argument that paganism is better. The emperor Julian, by returning to it, accepted this kind of thinking and endorsed it.

As we try to define the nature of theurgy, we face the question: Does it involve compulsion? Can theurgists actually force the gods to appear, to communicate with mortals? The issue is controversial, but it seems to me that inasmuch as theurgy is a kind of higher magic and all magic recruits demons and gods, presses them into service, as it were, sometimes against their will, it is reasonable to suppose that even theurgy is a form of pressure. There is evidence of this in the *Oracles,* fragment 220: "Listen to me, though I am unwilling to speak, for you have bound me by compulsion [ἀνάγκη]." Similarly, fragment 223 states: "Drawing some

---

33. A summary is given by Lloyd, "Later Neoplatonists," 278.

of them [gods] by unspeakable [?] charms [ἴυγγες] from the air, you made them descend easily on this earth, even though they did not want to; those in the middle,[34] riding on the winds of the middle, far from the divine fire, you send to the mortals like prophetic dreams, treating demons disgracefully [ἀεικέα δαίμονας ἔρδων]."

The Techniques of Theurgy

What actually happened? What did you have to do to make the gods appear or have their statues smile at you or to have wonderful visions of light? We have certain clues but no authentic step-by-step description of the whole procedure, and it is unclear in what order or sequence the ritual was performed. Perhaps every practitioner had an individual technique that worked well for him or her but not so well for anyone else.

Roughly speaking there seem to have been two types of operation. One depended on the use of "symbols" and "tokens" (σύμβολα, συνθή-ματα) to consecrate and animate the statues of the gods. The other one depended mainly on mediumistic trance. This distinction has been made by E.R. Dodds[35] in his fundamental essay on theurgy, and it has been accepted by the scholars with whose work I am familiar. The second type of operation, involving a medium in a state of trance, has been experienced and described in modern times; but the first, the animation of statues, is not something we can deal with easily, though it may also have required trance or some similar state of mind.

Any attempt at reconstructing the whole ritual must be tentative, as I have said. There are some elements that can be identified; here I partly follow Edouard des Places,[36] the learned editor of the Oracles, who based his distinction on fragments 132, 139, 208, and other texts.

1. Long periods of silence (fr. 132). This is an ascetic discipline,[37] like fasting, forcing oneself to stay awake, praying for long periods of time. It means depriving oneself of a natural activity like eating, sleeping, or talking. I shall discuss this as well as other elements later on.

2. The "understanding warmed by fire" (fr. 139), an enigmatic

---

34. Probably the demons of the air as intermediaries between ether and earth; cf. Lobeck, *Aglaophamus*, 730 (c).

35. Dodds, *The Greeks and the Irrational* (Berkeley, 1951), 283ff.

36. *Oracles* pp. 17f. des Places.

37. Cf. O. Casel, "De Philosophorum Graecorum Silentio Mystico," *RGVV* 16, no. 2 (1919).

phrase that also occurs as a synonym for the whole art of theurgy. The divine fire that theurgists hope to see at some point will help them understand all of theurgy in a flash. It will teach them to pray properly and give them knowledge of all classes of gods (fr. 139). The ability to distinguish higher from lower gods, heroes from demons, and elevated souls from common ones plays a great role in pagan demonology[38] and in the theurgical operations based on it.

3. Material things, such as herbs and stones, but also words uttered or written down, because words were considered just as real as any material things. These are included in the category of "symbols" and "tokens" (σύμβολα, συνθήματα), and they really could be anything—an object, a magical formula, from the stone *mnizouris* to a *vox mystica*—anything that would establish a contact between a human being and a god. It looks as though the "symbols" and "tokens" were passwords or guarantees that everything was all right: the god would recognize the theurgist as a legitimate petitioner, and the theurgist would recognize the god as a real god, not just a demon or a hero. But the whole doctrine is not clear on this particular point, and I will have to return to it.

4. Specific magical tools, such as the "bull-roarer" (ῥόμβος or στροφάλος) and similar objects that may look like simple magical toys to us but apparently produced the desired effects under certain conditions. Again, I will have to say more about these devices at a later point.

5. In some cases, perhaps, use of drugs which were similar in their effects to mescaline or LSD. Very little is said in our sources about the ingestion of mind-altering substances, but there are allusions to heavy perfumes and aromatic vapors. This is another problem that will have to be dealt with more fully at a later point.[39]

There can be little doubt that silence, fasting,[40] praying, and lack of sleep over long periods of time may induce a state of consciousness quite different from what we call normal. Add to these techniques the art of concentration described in *Oracles* fragment 2, which stresses the importance of walking "through the channels of fire not by dispersing

---

38. Perhaps also in the early church; see Paul's 1 Cor. 12:10 διακρίσεις πνευμάτων.

39. Dodds (*Greeks and the Irrational,* 296) briefly mentions the steps leading to trance.

40. On the discipline of fasting in various religions and cultures see R. Arbesmann, "Das Fasten (*RVV* 21 [1929]); Felicitas D. Goodman et al., *Trance, Healing, and Hallucination: Three Field Studies in Religious Experience* (New York, 1974); Judith H. Dobrzynski, *Fasting* (New York, 1979).

oneself but with full concentration [μὴ . . . σποράδην, ἀλλὰ στιβαρόν]." These "channels of fire" lead toward the "intelligible fire" (fr. 66), which Iamblichus (*Myst.* 3.31) calls the "end of every theurgical operation." Remaining in total darkness for a long time is a related technique; by not seeing or hearing or saying anything, our senses are being manipulated in a certain way. Monotonous, endlessly repeated prayers, incantations, formulas, litanies, and names have a hypnotic effect. The Tibetan mantra, *om mani padme hum,* may be compared. Let us not forget that firm belief that the gods would eventually manifest themselves and previous discussions with persons who had had such experiences, or having watched them in the midst of one, would create a climate in which miracles not only seemed possible but actually occurred. This, at least, is what Iamblichus seems to suggest (*Myst.* 1.15; 3.11, 17; 5.26). Music and dancing, rhythmic sounds, and motions of different kinds also may lead to trance. There is a more dramatic form of ecstasy that expresses itself in shouting and wild gestures.[41] These ecstatic and visionary experiences result from a psychic disposition but can be developed and activated, as we have seen, by ascetic disciplines, specific rituals, and physical resources.

To understand the experiences of the theurgists, we have to study the phenomenon of ecstasy. What the Greeks called ἔκστασις we would call "trance" today, but not every trance is ἔκστασις in the Greek sense of the word; it is the religious context that counts.

The two best discussions of ecstasy published in more recent years are, in my opinion, an article by F. Pfister in the *Reallexikon für Antike und Christentum*[42] and a chapter in E. des Places' book *La religion grecque.*[43] I will summarize the results of their research as far as it is of interest to us. Pfister (who does not deal with theurgy) begins with a standard definition of ecstasy, as he found it in a modern dictionary of psychology: "ecstasy . . . is an exalted state in which, as if in a dream, visions are seen, truths understood, voices heard."[44] It is interesting to compare this definition to the definition of trance, as it is given in the *Shorter Oxford English Dictionary:* "a state characterized by a more or less prolonged suspension of consciousness and inertness to stimulus, a cataleptic or

---

41. Iambl. *Myst.* 3.5, 25; Nilsson, *Geschichte,* 686; F. Pfister, "Ekstase," *RAC* 4 (1959): 944ff.

42. Pfister, "Ekstase"; cf. W.R. Inge, "Ecstasy," *ERE* 5 (1910): 157ff.

43. E. des Places, *La religion grecque* (Paris, 1969), 308ff.

44. Fr. Giese, *Psychologisches Wörterbuch,* revised by F. Dorsch, 8th ed. (1968).

hypnotic condition." Ecstatic experiences are found in many different cultures,[45] and they are mainly explored today by anthropologists and parapsychologists.

The very word *ecstasy* implies that those who have this experience step outside themselves, step outside, as Plato says (*Phaedrus* 249d: ἐκ τῶν ἀνθρωπίνων σπουδασμάτων), normal human occupations; he calls this state a "divine madness" (θεία μανία). Another synonym or near synonym for ecstasy is "movement," κίνησις, implying a change in psychological structure. Thus the so-called Dionysius Areopagita, a Christian Neoplatonist,[46] speaks of the "special power of theologians when they are moved by the spirit." He says "theologians," but he clearly means "theurgists." Other synonyms, as collected by Father des Places, are ἐνθουσιασμός, ἔκπληξις, θάμβος.

In his speech *Apologia sive de magia,* Apuleius speaks of ecstasy as follows: the human mind can be drugged by incantations and heavy aromatic smoke until it gets completely out of control (he uses the verb *externare,* a Latin equivalent of ἐξίστασθαι); then it forgets everything, but afterward it returns to its own nature (chap. 43).

According to Proclus (*In Platon. Alcibiad.* 1.92.3ff.; cf. Plotin. *Enn.* 6.4f.), ἔκστασις involves ἔκτασις, "expansion." This is probably a play on words; even though they are not related—ἔκστασις is derived from ἐξίστασθαι, whereas ἔκτασις is derived from ἐκτείνειν—the two words sound alike, and by means of the weird logic of false etymologies, a relationship between them suggested itself to Proclus: "the soul expands in order to get closer to god, and god expands to meet the soul, without ever stepping outside, for he always remains inside himself," he explains.

The Greeks believed that a certain psychic disposition was a necessary requirement; "only individuals who tend by their nature toward ecstasy will become possessed," says Plutarch (*Quaest. Roman.* 112). Not all so-called philosophers will experience this state, but a human being who is "beloved by the gods" and whose soul is "god-loving" (θεοφιλής can mean both) will be privileged to experience visions and enjoy theophanies.[47]

Plotinus was one of these privileged individuals, as it appears from Porphyry's *Vita Plotini* (23): four times during the years of Porphyry's discipleship the master succeeded in rising to the highest god. Plotinus

---

45. H. Findeisen, *Schamanentum* (Berlin, 1957), 162ff.
46. *De divin. nom.* 1 (PG 3.585).
47. F. Pfister, *RE* 11:218; suppl. 4:319f.

himself defined ecstasy as an awakening of the soul from its physical nature (*Enn.* 4.8.[6] 1.1).[48] Proclus, too, had such experiences (Marinus *Vita Procli* 7.30). The gift itself, not just technical knowledge, was passed on in certain families, and it could be transmitted from teacher to disciple by the laying on of hands. A devout visitor might catch it, by osmosis, as it were, from a holy place.[49]

Wine and other intoxicating substances were apt to bring about a trance, and Iamblichus (*Myst.* 3.25) compares trance to a state of drunkenness. I will consider later the possibility that the ancients used drugs comparable to hashish (used in Sufism), mescaline, or LSD. Strong perfumes and burning incense had a powerful effect, as a medical writer notes (Ps.-Galen *Defin.* 487 = 19.462 Kühn): some persons are filled by the god, get into trance when they inhale the smells during the ritual. Music and dancing, as I have said already, must have played an important role, but the dancing, just as the screaming and the violent gestures mentioned before, can also be considered an effect of trance, not only a cause.

Pfister touches on prayers and incantations and refers to earlier research. The person who serves as medium in these rites will get into trance as a result of being exposed to words uttered in a certain way over a long period of time, and in trance this person will be in touch with supernatural powers that will enable him or her, among other things, to prophesy.[50]

A recently published book on trance, as observed in so-called primitive societies[51]—and I emphasize *so-called*, because who are we to judge what is primitive and what is advanced?—dwells on most of the points we have considered already—fasting, music, dancing, smells, drugs—but mentions, in addition to all this, (1) the personal magnetic power of a shaman; (2) breath control; (3) masks, costumes, and tattoos. Our ancient sources say nothing about breath control, as far as I can tell, and very little about costumes and the like, although one assumes that theurgists would dress up for the ritual—even wear a mask that would identify them with the god they were about to conjure up. The practice

---

48. H.-R. Schwyzer, *RE* 21:571; Pfister, "Ekstase," 980.

49. Heliodorus *Aethiopica* 2.11.

50. A. Abt, *Apuleius' Apologie* (*RVV* 4, no. 2 [1908]), 232ff.; Fr. Heiler, *Das Gebet* (Munich, 1923), 252ff.

51. Trance can be induced "by a cleverly-dosed combination of music, song, incense and the personal magnetic power of the [shaman]" (Nina Epton, "Trance in the Shadows," *Trances*, ed. S. Wavell, Audrey Butt, and Nina Epton [New York, 1967], 128).

of having magical spells tattooed on the body of a miracle worker is attested. Can you think of a handier reference? But what is perhaps the most important factor—the magnetic power of theurgists, their personal charisma—is also the most elusive factor, and we can only guess its impact from the enthusiastic allusions to successful experiments.

In the book on trance I just mentioned, there are photographs of women and men in so-called primitive societies who seem to be getting ready to go into trance. It is impossible not to notice the look of deep concentration and seriousness on their faces: there can be no doubt, I think, that they are about to experience something very important, something wonderful in their lives. It may be an escape; they know that they will be in another world, at least for a short time.

How did a witness recognize true ecstasy? I have said already that there was such a thing as a fake trance and that in antiquity it could be detected without too much trouble. Real trance was indicated by some or all of the following signs: shouts, spasms, foam at the mouth, wildly kicking feet, jumping around, being insensitive to pain. Some of these symptoms could probably be faked, but not all of them, and not convincingly.

The highest experience granted to a person in ecstasy is a vision of the deity, the ultimate knowledge of what the nature of the deity is, and mystical union with the Highest, the Unthinkable.[52]

What were the experiences of theurgists like? That is the main question, but there is no clear answer to it.

The testimonies we have often deal with fire and light. In fragment 147 of the *Oracles* the goddess Hecate addresses the theurgist as follows:

> After this invocation you will see either a fire which, like a child, leaps in the direction of the flow of the air, or a shapeless fire from which a voice rushes forth, or an abundant light which encircles, as it whirrs, the earth, or a horse which flashes more brightly than light, or a child riding on the swift back of the horse, on fire, or covered with gold, or else naked, or holding a bow and standing on the [horse's] back.

These are different types of light visions, nine altogether, some shapeless, some in the shape of a horse or a child on a horse.

In other fragments of the *Oracles* (147, 148) we are told of the sacred

---

52. Nilsson, *Geschichte*, 415.

fire that shines without a shape[53] and speaks to the theurgist; but sometimes the theurgist sees everything in the shape of a lion, and everything is lit by flashes of lightning. I would guess that these were utterances of one or several mediums in trance recorded over a period of time and put into verse by the compiler of the *Oracles.*

The theurgist spoke of αὐτοψία when the person who had been initiated "saw the divine light" (Marinus *Vita Procli* 28). Another type of vision was called ἐποπτεία; it describes a vision seen by the theurgist in charge of an initiation. It could also happen that a great teacher or priestlike figure would radiate light. This is reported to have happened during Proclus' lectures; he himself communicated with luminous apparitions of Hecate during theurgic rites.[54] It was the theurgists' ambition to see the gods themselves, their αὐτοφανῆ ἀγάλματα.[55]

There is a remarkable anecdote in the *Apophthegmata Patrum* (PG 65.314c/d).[56]

The abbot Olympius told the following story: A pagan priest once came down to Scetis [the name, or the location, of the monastery], entered my cell, and spent the night there. When he observed the lifestyle of the monks, he said to me, "Leading this kind of life, do you see anything of your God?" I said to him, "No." Then the priest said to me: "When we perform the sacred rites for our God,[57] he hides nothing from us but reveals his mysteries to us. But you, after so many labors, vigils, periods of silence, ascetic exercises say, 'We see nothing'? Altogether it would seem that, if you see nothing, you keep evil thoughts in your hearts which separate you from your God and that because of this he does not reveal his mysteries to you." I went away and reported the words of the priest to the

---

53. A.D. Nock, *Sallustius,* xcix; Dodds, *Greeks and the Irrational,* 251. According to Psellus' commentary on *Oracles* fr. 148 (p. 173 des Places), many see the divine light, but it must be shapeless; if it has a shape, a form, one should not consider true the voice that comes from it.

54. Nilsson, *Geschichte,* 415, 440.

55. Iambl. *Myst.* 2.4; cf. 1.12, 2.5, 3.6; Nilsson, *Geschichte,* 686 n. 2.

56. Quoted by Reitzenstein, *Poimandres* (Leipzig, 1904), 34; cf. Nilsson, *Geschichte,* 686 n. 2.

57. He uses the verb ἱερουργέω, which seems equivalent to θεουργέω; cf. Porphyry *Ad Marcellam* 18; Iambl. *Vita Pythag.* 3.14. Paul uses the verb (Rom. 15:16), but with εὐαγγέλιον as an object, perhaps "serve the gospel as a priest" (Bauer, Arndt, and Gingrich, *Lexicon,* s.v.).

elders, and they marveled and said that it was so; for unclean thoughts separate God from humans.

Reitzenstein points out the naive character of the story and the almost cozy relationship between Christians and pagans in Egypt during the period of transition which it seems to attest. It must be said, however, that the theurgist comes out on top.

That the theurgists were granted bodily visions of the gods is declared in *Oracles* fragment 142: "For your sake, bodies have been attached to our autophanies [αὐτόπτοις φάσμασιν]." By their nature the gods are incorporeal, but for the sake of humankind, or rather, for the sake of a chosen few, the θεοφιλεῖς, they assume a physical shape and become αὐτόπτοι. Such a vision is called αὐτοφάνεια or αὐτοπτικὸν θέαμα.[58] But not only gods appear; visions of lesser spirits—angels, demons—are also possible; hence it becomes very important for the theurgist to distinguish between the various categories.[59] According to Psellus (commentary on *Oracles* fr. 88 [p. 175, des Places]), the *parousia* of Nature, when she is invoked by the theurgist, is preceded by a whole "choir" of demons in various shapes, her precursors; they appear to be gracious and kind, and they feign goodwill toward the person who has been initiated. By implication this probably means that these demons are not really kind, and the person who has just been initiated presumably lacks experience and may easily be fooled by them (Iambl. *Myst.* 2.4; 7).

Generally speaking, good demons have round bodies; bad demons are recognizable by their square shapes. Unfortunately, all demons can change their shapes and appearances very quickly.[60]

Real danger may be involved in theurgical practices. If a terrestrial demon approaches, the theurgist must immediately sacrifice the stone *mnizouris*, whatever it is, and invoke him.[61] The sacrifice of the stone

---

58. Cf. *Oracles* fr. 101; Iambl. *Myst.* 5.23. Both the *Oracles* and Iamblichus seem to prefer φάσμα to φάντασμα, the latter, perhaps, implying a less authentic experience (des Places, *Oracles*, pp. 101, 144).

59. Paul's διάκρισις πνευμάτων (1 Cor. 12:10) may be compared, but cf. also E. Lerle, "Diakrisis Pneumaton" (Diss., Heidelberg, 1946).

60. K. Svoboda, *La démonologie de Michel Psellos* (Brno, 1927), 7, 20.

61. Audrey Butt ("Training to be a Shaman," in *Trances,* ed. Wavell, Butt, and Epton, 155) writes about the Akowaio Amerindians of Guyana:

The possession of spirit stones, *wata,* as we have learned, is a major weapon of both defence and attack in the control of a skillful shaman.

makes another demon appear, a greater demon than the terrestrial one, a demon who will tell the truth (Psellus on *Oracles* fr. 149 [p. 184 des Places]). From Porphyry's account of Plotinus' experience in the temple of Isis (see later discussion), we know that sometimes an assistant had to hold chickens as a safety measure and strangle them when something went wrong. Apparently one did not always get the visions one wanted, and certain precautions were considered indispensable. Behind this particular fear lies the magical concept that mischievous demons are always lurking around, ready to interfere, perhaps just out of boredom, to do something rather than nothing at all, but sometimes because they are evil. It was also possible that a hostile theurgist, jealous of another's success, would try to interfere with a ritual; Psellus[62] says that the theurgists "make the gods descend to them by enchanting songs, and they fetter and release them, as Apuleius did, who by oaths forced the 'god with the seven rays' [Heptaktis, but another reading seems to be Epaktos] not to communicate with the theurgist [i.e., Julian the theurgist]." Because Julian the theurgist and Apuleius were contemporaries, the story implies that Apuleius, who was taken for a magician by his enemies, although he protested his innocence and was acquitted by a court, actually practiced theurgy and was a rival of the formidable author of the *Chaldean Oracles*.

The spirit, or spirits, in each stone are helpers who can intercept and catch the spirit of sickness which is being sent. If the shaman wishes to be aggressive he may use the following method: when *Imawali*, the forest spirit, has stolen the spirit, *akwalu*, of a living person and so renders him ill and in danger of death through the deprivation, then the shaman will in turn steal that *Imawali*'s baby and will place it on one of the spirit stones in his collection. This act will make the spirit baby, the little *Imawali*, ill. *Imawali*'s father will then, to save his child, quickly give back the human spirit he has stolen. In this way the shaman is believed to be able to perform one of his main tasks, the restoration of stolen spirits.

Apart from this method, the shaman can use his spirit stones as projectiles with war heads, that is, with a built-in spirit aggressor. A spirit battle, utilizing spirit stones, may occur between two enemy shamans, as a contest to prove which of the two is superior as well as a means of releasing a patient from spirits under the control of the enemy shaman.

The Greek *mnizouris* seems to be such a "spirit stone."

62. In the treatise entitled "For Those Who Asked How Many Kinds of Philosophical Investigations There Are," in *Oracles* pp. 221f. des Places and in *Scripta minora* 1.446 K.-D.

The story, which may well be apocryphal, does not seem to be known to the scholars who have worked on Apuleius.

There are other dangers. When a medium—the Greek term is δοχεύς, literally, a "recipient"—is employed, he or she may be too weak to bear the full impact of the divine presence. In *Oracles* fragment 211, Hecate seems to complain (the context is not clear) about this, for she says, "The wretched heart of the medium is too weak to bear me."[63]

Still other possible dangers are foreshadowed in *Oracles* fragment 141: "A careless mortal with a tendency toward these things [i.e., earthly passions] is a liberation of the god." This must mean that in such a case the theurgist loses his hold on the god and sets him free prematurely. The theurgist has to put his whole faith into his prayers and his rites, or else the god will slip out of the temporary compulsion (ἀνάγκη) that binds him. This possibility would support the older doctrine, rejected by more recent scholars, that theurgy was a form of compulsion. It seems that the gods were not always in a mood to be conjured up or evoked; they sometimes resented being called.[64] Porphyry (*De philos. ex oracul. haur.* pp. 162ff. Wolff) describes a certain theurgical ritual during which a statue of Apollo was bound with wreaths and linen straps, surrounded by bright lights, and assaulted by prayers and chants to force the god to descend and reveal the truth to his insistent worshipers. Finally the god—through the voice of a medium, no doubt—begs them to leave him alone.[65]

Material Resources Used in Theurgical Practices

Some of these resources seem to be very old, but the Neoplatonists justified their use philosophically by saying, as Iamblichus (*Myst.* 5.23) does, that matter is not necessarily evil. On the contrary, there is a kind of matter that is pure and divine and does not prevent our communicating with the gods; in fact, it may become a receptacle for their manifestations on earth. The statue of a god is, after all, a material object. Matter

---

63. Psellus *Accusation of Michael Cerularius* 1.249 K.-D.: "Sometimes, along with the advent of divine powers, earth spirits are moved whose approach and motion when they happen with some force the weaker mediums cannot bear." For the Stoic doctrine see Lucan *Pharsalia* 5.144–20.

64. Cf. Damascius *In Platon. Parmen.* 2.95.1a; E. Chaignet, *Comm. Procl. Parm.,* vol. 2 (Paris, 1900), 306 n.5.

65. Cf. Nilsson, *Geschichte,* 418.

(ὕλη) is offered by the gods, and it is "congenial" (συμφυής) to them, says Iamblichus (ibid.).[66]

Psellus confirms this when he writes (*Expos. Chald.* p. 191 des Places), "They [the theurgists] . . . say that there exists a sympathy between the upper world, especially the one beneath the moon, and the lower world." And elsewhere (*Comment.* p. 169 des Places) he claims: "We can only ascend toward God by strengthening the vehicle of the soul by material rites; he [i.e., the theurgist] thinks that the soul must be purified by stones, herbs, and incantations." This is in accordance with Iamblichus, who writes (*Myst.* 5.22–23) that a single stone or a single herb can put us in touch with some divine activity.[67]

To make and consecrate statues of deities in the proper way seems to have been an important branch of theurgy. It was recognized as such by Plotinus, who attributed the art to the "sages of old," probably the Orphics. It is embodied in the *Oracles* (fr. 224, of doubtful authenticity): "Create a statue, purified in the manner I shall teach you. Make the body of Mountain rue [πήγανον ἄγριον = *Ruta halepensis*, according to Dioscorides 3.45, who identifies it in 3.46 with the magical Homeric herb *moly*] and adorn it with little animals, with domestic lizards, and when you have crushed a mixture of myrrh, gum [στύραξ], and frankincense, blend it with these creatures, go out into the open air under a waxing moon and perform the rite by saying this prayer." This sounds very much like a recipe from the magical papyri.[68] Porphyry (*De philosoph. ex oracul. haur.* pp. 130f. Wolff) prescribes a similar process: "You consecrate a statue of Hecate in the following way: Produce a certain kind of fillet; grind lizards together with fragrant essences and burn all that; say a certain prayer in the open air under a waxing moon; do all this to consecrate the statue of Hecate. Then she will appear to you in your sleep." The two prescriptions are remarkably similar. One notices that certain steps are outlined very clearly but others are left open, so to speak, to be filled in by the theurgist—for instance, the prayer whose text is not quoted; the theurgist probably learned it from a mentor, along with the proper way of

---

66. Cf. Trouillard, *L'un et l'âme*, 184f.

67. Cf. also Proclus *Elem. Theol.* p. 276 Dodds. Dodds notes that this doctrine is borrowed from Egyptian magic and that lists of symbolic animals, plants, and stones are frequent in the Magical Papyri. Elsewhere (*CMAG* 6 [1928]: 129) Proclus says that stones, plants, animals, perfumes, and other "sacred, godlike things" can share in the nature of the divine.

68. See G. Wolff, *De philosophia ex oraculis haurienda* (1856), App. III, pp. 195ff.

reciting it. The written word was incapable of teaching this. The "sleep" in which Hecate will appear is probably more like a trance or a state of hypnosis.

Some of the tools used in theurgy are clearly of a magical nature. There is the so-called *rhombus* of Hecate, described by Psellus (on *Oracles* fr. 206 [p. 170 des Places]) as a golden ball enclosing a sapphire and covered with magical characters; it was rotated at the end of a strap made of bull's hide.[69] Originally this was a rhombus-shaped object, made of wood, bone, or metal; the spheric shape and the precious materials seem to be a later development. The *rhombus* is mentioned in descriptions of magical rites, notably in Theocritus (2.30).[70] It is the "bull-roarer" of the Australian aborigines. Another name for this tool is στροφάλος or Ἑκατικὸς στροφάλος (*Oracles* fr. 206), which des Places translates as *tourbillon*—"whirlwind" or "toupie"—that is, "spinning top," but it is almost certainly the magical *rhombus*. When the magician or theurgist rotates it above his head, it produces a whirring or whizzing sound called ῥοῖζος (*Oracles* fr. 107), which apparently was thought to imitate the whirring of the heavenly bodies as they move with incredible speed through space.[71] The rotation of the tool was thought to affect the ritual through its unspeakable force. As the theurgist rotates the *rhombos*, he makes his invocation to the gods (ἐπίκλησις), but sometimes he laughs or produces indistinct yells or imitates animal sounds as he whips the air. All this sounds more like a ritual performed by the shaman of some primitive tribe, and it is hard to picture a Neoplatonist like Iamblichus or Proclus uttering inarticulate sounds or imitating an animal or laughing insanely as he rotated his bull-roarer.[72] Perhaps they let someone else do this for them and simply watched and listened.

The magical wheel, or ἴυγξ, should be distinguished from the rhombus. It is also mentioned by Theocritus in the poem just mentioned.[73] Originally, the ἴυγξ was a bird, the wryneck, *Iynx torquilla,* a kind of woodpecker; for magical purposes, it was tied or nailed onto a wooden wheel. Later, the wheel itself, with no bird attached, could be called ἴυγξ; it is often represented on Greek vases.

---

69. Bidez, *Vie de l'empereur Julien,* 78.

70. Gow's note gives all the necessary information, and his commentary even has a photograph of a reconstructed model, on pl. V.

71. See des Places, in his introduction to Iambl. *Myst.,* p. 18.

72. Clapping, whistling, or hissing—imitating various animals—is attested in the Magical Papyri; see Eitrem, "La théurgie," 70.

73. See Gow, pp. 39 and 41, of his commentary (vol. 2, Cambridge 1952).

For A.S.F. Gow, who had a model reconstructed and photographed for his commentary on Theocritus, it is a "spoked wheel, or a disk, with two holes on either side of the centre." He continues:

> A cord is passed through one hole and back through the other; if the loop on one side of the instrument is held in one hand, the two ends . . . in the other, and the tension alternately increased and relaxed, the twisting and untwisting of the cords will cause the instrument to revolve rapidly first in one direction and then in the other.

Once more, we are considering a very simple, probably very ancient, magical tool adapted by the theurgists for their purposes and loaded by the Neoplatonists with philosophical ideas. I disagree with Gow on one point only. He underlines the facts that the ἴυγξ is never mentioned in the numerous love spells of the Magical Papyri and that there is no clear Latin equivalent of it (the *turbo* of Horace *Epodes* 17.7 is either this or a *rhombus*), and he concludes that it may have passed out of use.[74] The opposite is true, as the testimony of the theurgists shows. Marinus reports (*Vita Procli* 28) that Proclus used the "divine wheels" to communicate with the gods. There may be a connection with the "magical wheels" hanging from the ceiling of a palatial hall in Babylon, according to Philostratus (*Vita Apollonii* 1.25.6). They are also seen on Apulian vases. The Babylonian magi called them the "tongues of the gods."[75]

I have already mentioned the "symbols" and "conventions," σύμβολα and συνθήματα, that link every material thing here with spiritual principles "there." Their exact nature is still controversial. They were known to the theurgists and used by them to achieve union with the gods.[76] They are scattered throughout the universe through the kindness of the gods, says Iamblichus (*Myst.* 5.23) and work without our knowledge (ibid. 2.11). Some of them are spoken, others are unspeakable, according to Proclus (*Theol. Platon.* 1.5C = p. 24.4 S.-W.).[77] Some were concealed inside the statues of the gods, Proclus attests (*In Platon. Timaeum* 1, p. 273 Diehl); they ensure the presence and intervention of the gods and are known only to the τελεσταί.[78]

---

74. See Gow's article "Iynx, Rhombos, etc." *JHS* 54 (1934): 9.
75. Eitrem, "La théurgie," pp. 78f.
76. Proclus *Elem. Theol.* p. 223 Dodds.
77. *Oracles* fr. 109, with the note of des Places.
78. See Dodds, *Greeks and the Irrational*, 292; P. Boyancé, "Théurgie," 196 n. 2.

We have seen that the theurgists, during their rituals, uttered inarticulate sounds. Like the sorcerers of the Magical Papyri, they also used
foreign names and words, preferably not in Greek "translation" (we
would probably say, "transliteration"); otherwise they would lose their
power. This is what Psellus (on *Oracles* pp. 169f. des Places) says, and he
cites as examples *Serapheim, Cherubeim, Michael, Gabriel*—all Hebrew
names. In the case of *Cherubeim* the ending in Greek transliteration could
also be *-bin* or *-bim,* but a thoroughly Greek ending, *-eis,* is found in
Josephus (*Antiqu.* 7.378). This is presumably the form one should not
use; it was important to stay as close as possible to the Hebrew. Similarly,
Daniel would have been fine, but not *Danielos,* a hellenized form also
found in Josephus (*Antiqu.* 10.193).

I have said before that φωταγωγία, "evocation of light," is another
term for theurgy. It seems to refer to a specific technique that may have
been just one part of a more complex ritual. The theurgist stares at a
lamp, then closes his eyes, then opens them again, then prays, and so
continues. If he repeats this for a long time, he will no longer see a lamp
but an overwhelming radiance. There is a variation of this technique: the
theurgist stares for a long time at a white wall covered with magical
symbols; the wall was probably illuminated.[79]

Whether any animals were sacrificed during theurgical rites is not
clear. Porphyry condemns the practice (*Letter to Anebo* fr. 29; cf. Theodoretus, bishop of Cyrrhus, *Curatio* 3.66). He argues that it makes no
sense to kill animals and use them for ritual purposes when the demons
and deities themselves declare it taboo to touch any dead body.[80] It
seems that the theurgists were divided on this particular issue. One
might say that part of their doctrine was dictated by the various deities
and spirits who manifested themselves: one spirit might say, "I abhor
animal sacrifices," but another one insisted on it. This is purely speculative, but it could explain, at least in part, the obscurities and apparent
contradictions we find in our texts. We have seen already how the doctrine itself accounted for failures.

Let us assume now that twelve Neoplatonists conducted twelve different theurgical practices within the space of a month and then met to
discuss their results. It seems very unlikely that anything like a uniform
picture or a consensus would emerge. It then became the duty, I would

---

79. See Iambl. *Myst.* 3.14; Eitrem, "Die *systasis,*" 49ff.; Nilsson, *Geschichte,*
508f.

80. Nilsson, *Geschichte,* 422.

imagine, of the senior theurgist or the most distinguished teacher to present a theory that would account for the analogies as well as the anomalies. A work like Iamblichus' *De mysteriis,* with its labyrinthian, sometimes erratic, train of thought, may reflect a number of experiences and represent an attempt to account for their exasperating variety. If the doctrine was partly based on mystical revelations and parapsychological experiments, we should not be surprised that everything was in constant flux.

On the basis of fragmentary testimonies that survive, Joseph Bidez, in his well-known work *La vie de l'empereur Julien* ([Paris, 1930], 79), has reconstructed Julian's own initiation into the rites of theurgy. It is a remarkable piece of historical fiction, and very plausible at that. Bidez speaks of voices and noises and appeals, disturbing music, heady perfumes, doors that open by themselves, luminous fountains, moving shadows, fog, sooty vapors, statues that seem to be animated and look at the candidate kindly and threateningly in turn, as they are surrounded by radiance, thunder and lightning, earthquakes to announce the arrival of the supreme god, the inexpressible Fire itself.

How can we explain these happenings? Julian's enemies accused his teacher, Maximus, of being a sophist and a fraud, but they did not completely discount the participation of real demons.[81]

There is a story behind the story. A Neoplatonist of the school of Pergamon, Eusebius of Myndus, who was critical of theurgy, described to the future emperor Julian, when he was a student of his, a scene in the temple of Hecate orchestrated by Maximus. Eusebius clearly tried to warn the prince against this sort of thing, but—in sublime irony—his warning had exactly the opposite effect: Julian had been waiting to find a man like this, and he at once bid farewell to Eusebius and went to study with Maximus, who then introduced him to theurgy.

Eunapius (*Vit. Soph.* p. 475 Boiss.), who was a wholehearted believer, tells another story. After Maximus had assembled a large number of friends in the temple of Hecate, he burned a grain of incense, recited "to himself" the whole text of a hymn, and made the statue first smile, then apparently laugh; finally the torches she held in her hands burst into a blaze of light.[82] Even Eusebius, the skeptic, was impressed at first,

---

81. Bidez (*Vie de l'empereur Julien,* 79f.), quotes from Gregory of Nazianzus *Or.* 4.55; this, of course, is hearsay, too, but very imaginative and dramatic.

82. The animation of a doll during a graveyard ritual in a country town sixty miles west of Djakarta is reported by Nina Epton, "Trance in the Shadows," *Trances,* pp. 117ff.).

but later—perhaps after he had figured out how it could have been done—he called Maximus a "miracle worker for show," θεατρικός θαυματοποιός.

Psellus describes a theurgical ceremony that took place in 1059 A.D.[83] He had been asked to investigate—he was, after all, an expert on the subject—and his efforts led to a formal accusation of the patriarch, Michael Cerularius, and his protégés, the monks of Chios. It is a fascinating document, which shows how pagan theurgy survived in a Christian context. So far, it has not been analyzed properly, as far as I know,[84] but what it tells us agrees with the information the pagan writers preserve. We hear about singing, monotonous movements of the limbs, blinking of eyelids, ingesting narcotics or hallucinogenics, and rubbing them in and inhaling them as well. After a while the prophetess Dosithea (the medium) began to speak softly; then she trembled; then she levitated. She spoke of cosmic subjects. Soon some Christian prophets, martyrs, and saints and also the Virgin Mary and the Holy Trinity "appeared" (i.e., spoke through the medium), but they had only trivial things to say, such as "Hello" or "Blow twice into your cup" or "I am glad to see you after having seen the moon."[85]

These trivial messages from a higher world must have been disappointing for the patriarch and the monks, but the levitation of the prophetess was an event. Levitation apparently occurred when the medium was in trance, and Iamblichus (*Myst.* 3.5)[86] seems to have observed the phenomenon. It has also been reported in modern times.[87]

Plotinus, Porphyry, Iamblichus, and Proclus

I should like to examine the attitude toward theurgy on the part of these four Neoplatonist philosophers. We have seen already that the school, as a whole, was divided on this issue. Some philosophers were deeply involved in theurgical rites; others were opposed to them; still others seem to have been interested but not committed. The school doctrine,

---

83. *Scripta minora* 1.232ff. K.-D.

84. There is a useful résumé in Svoboda, *La démonologie,* 50f.

85. Ibid.

86. Cf. Nilsson, *Geschichte,* 688.

87. Proclus *Elem. Theol.* pp. 163ff. Dodds; on the famous medium David Dunglas Home see C. Wilson, *The Occult* (New York, 1973), 463ff.

which, in itself, combined "aims that appear divergent, if not incompatible,"[88] did not require any commitment one way or the other. Those who did believe were naturally anxious to convert those who did not, perhaps recruiting candidates for initiation among their more promising students. If Julian left one teacher because he rejected theurgy and went on to study with a renowned theurgist, many others may have done the same.

There was room for theurgy within the school doctrine, and the system provided explanations for how and why it worked, but theurgy was by no means a building block on which other building blocks rested. You could put it in or take it out and the structure as a whole did not change very much. It was more a matter of personal faith and religious belief. Neoplatonism was not a monolith: it counted seven schools in the course of four centuries, and within the schools we find a wide range of differing personalities.

Plotinus dealt with the problem of magic more than once in his lectures (e.g., *Enn.* 2.9.14, 4.4.40–44).[89] He was also credited with supernatural gifts by his biographer, Porphyry. Plotinus clearly believed in the effectiveness of magic up to a certain degree, but this does not make him a practicing magician or a theurgist himself.[90] Because magic existed in the world, Plotinus had to find a place for it in his system and explain it somehow. He did this by borrowing the concepts of sympathy and antipathy—that is, concepts on which magicians and theurgists depended. There are forces in the universe that are freely available, and magic simply reinforces them. Plotinus compared magic to music because both affect the irrational part of the soul.

Some magicians are evil, to be sure, and yet their sorcery works, for the forces are available to them too; but those who use magic for evil purposes will be punished sooner or later. Whatever harm magicians may be able to do to human beings, they cannot affect the universe, and even on earth their powers are limited, for the mind of the wise is safe from magical practices.

According to Plotinus, the magicians use certain substances (φύσεις) and certain gestures or positions (σχήματα) as well as incantations (ἐπῳδὲς τὸ μέλος). Does he have in mind the "symbols" and "tokens" of

---

88. See R.T. Wallis, *Neoplatonism* (London, 1972), 4.

89. See ibid., 7off.; Luck, *Arcana Mundi*, 117ff.

90. A.H. Armstrong, "Was Plotinus a Magician?" *Phronesis* 1 (1955): 73ff., a reply to Ph. Merlan, "Plotinus and Magic," *Isis* 44 (1953): 341ff.

the theurgists? The problem has been discussed at great length, and no agreement has been reached so far.[91]

Plotinus admits the power of magic over the irrational part of the soul, not over reason and free will. Human beings in general are affected by cosmic influences, as they are directed against them by magic, only insofar as they are part of the cosmic organism that is a living being itself. Taking into account the nature of cosmic sympathy, magic can be understood as a perfectly natural phenomenon.[92]

In his well-known chapter on theurgy in *The Greeks and the Irrational*, E.R. Dodds came to the conclusion that Plotinus was neither a magician nor a theurgist. This view was attacked by Merlan but reaffirmed in an admirable article by A.H. Armstrong,[93] and the whole controversy can now be considered closed. But it still is a fascinating problem.

Porphyry, in the biography of his teacher, tells an anecdote (*Vita Plotini* chap. 10, in Armstrong's translation).

> One of those claiming to be philosophers, Olympius of Alexandria, who had been for a short time a pupil of Ammonius, adopted a superior attitude toward Plotinus out of rivalry. The man's attacks on him went to the point of trying to bring a star-stroke on him by magic [ἀστροβολῆσαι μαγεύσας]. But when he found his attempt recoiling upon himself, he told his intimates that the soul of Plotinus had such great power as to be able to throw back attacks directed at him on those who were seeking to do him harm. Plotinus was aware of the attempt and said that his limbs on that occasion were squeezed together and his body contracted like a moneybag pulled tight. Olympius, since he was often rather in danger of suffering something himself than likely to injure Plotinus, ceased his attacks.

It seems fairly clear that Plotinus was complaining of one of the attacks of colic to which, as his biographer writes (chap. 2), he was subject. These attacks must have been real, not imagined, and Plotinus, in a more or less humorous manner (there is a reference to a not very serious passage in Plato's *Banquet*, as Armstrong has shown), explains it

---

91. See Th. Hopfner, *Ueber die Geheimlehren des Iamblichos* (Leipzig, 1922), 204 n. 36; E.R. Dodds, *CO* 28 (1934): 52f.; Fr. Pfeffer, *Studien zur Mantik in der Philosophie der Antike*, Beitr. z. Klass. Philol. 64 (Meisenheim am Glan, 1976), 121.

92. See Pfeffer, *Studien zur Mantik*.

93. See n. 90.

by the black magic of Olympius. What Plotinus meant to say, as Armstrong (74) suggests, is something like: "My colic is very bad this morning; I feel like one of those bisected creatures in Aristophanes' speech when Apollo was sewing him up. Olympius must be at it again." Obviously, Plotinus believed in the ability of his enemy to hurt him by magical means, just as the enemy believed in Plotinus' ability to defend himself against such attacks and send the evil powers right back to where they came from. This, however, does not mean that Plotinus wished to hurt his enemy; the man was indirectly hurting himself, and Plotinus, his target, acted only like a kind of mirror or refractor.

Armstrong then discusses a passage from the fourth *Ennead* (4.4.43), which he translates as follows (75):

> How can the good man [ὁ σπουδαῖος] be affected by magic and drugs? In his soul he cannot be affected by magic; his rational part will not be affected; it will not change his opinions; but as regards that much of the whole in him which is irrational, he will be affected in this, or rather this will be affected. He will not, however, fall in love as the result of philtres [i.e., love potions], for love only occurs when one soul [the higher] assents to the affection of the other [the lower]. Just as his irrational part is affected by spells, so he himself by counterspells disintegrates the powers working there: but he may suffer death from such enchantments, or sickness, or other things that affect the body. Part of the All [in him] may suffer from another part or from the All [itself], but he himself remains unharmed.[94]

This does not mean—I am following Armstrong's interpretation— that the "good man" (the philosopher) is able to practice magic or should, in fact, do so, to protect himself. Plotinus merely admits that magic can affect the philosopher's lower, irrational self, even to the extent of making him sick and killing him; at the same time, he considers this completely unimportant. What the philosopher *can* prevent is the affection of the rational self, which would make him fall in love, among other things. To prevent this, the philosopher uses his own "counterspells" (ἀντεπῳδαί), but those are not real spells: they are philosophical arguments and salutary exhortations.

_____

94. Was Plotinus thinking of Lucretius, the philosopher-poet, who, according to Jerome (*Ann. Abr.*) had become insane after having drunk a love potion? Cf. G. Luck, "Was Lucretius Really Mad," *Euphrosyne*, n.s., 16 (1988): 289–94 (in this volume, pp. 60–65).

Another episode recorded by Porphyry (*Vita Plotini* chap. 10) is the conjuration of Plotinus' tutelary spirit by an Egyptian priest in a temple of Isis. Such a conjuration is without any doubt a theurgical act, but not an act of black magic. The story is told to prove that Plotinus was a very unusual human being and had supernatural abilities.

> An Egyptian priest who came to Rome and wanted to give a display of his *sophia* [Armstrong takes this to mean "occult wisdom"; it is probably *theosophia*, a synonym of *theurgia*, as we have seen] asked Plotinus to come and see a visible manifestation of his own companion spirit. Plotinus readily agreed, and the evocation took place in the temple of Isis: the Egyptian said it was the only pure spot he could find in Rome. When the spirit was summoned [κληθείς] to appear [εἰς αὐτοψίαν], a god came and not a being of the spirit order, and the Egyptian said: "Blessed are you who have a god for a spirit and not a companion of the subordinate order!" It was not, however, possible to ask any questions of the god or even to see him there any longer, for the friend who witnessed the manifestation strangled the chickens [Armstrong translates "birds"] he was holding as a protection, either because of jealousy or because he was afraid.[95]

The implication is that the so-called friend should not have strangled the chickens at this crucial moment; there was no need: the god was benign, not threatening. And yet he disappeared as obediently as if he had been a minor demon, once the chickens' heads were twisted. All this may be a piece of school gossip, as Dodds and Armstrong suspect, but it certainly tells us something about the school's intellectual climate.

It is also noteworthy that Plotinus was perfectly willing to participate in this ritual, chickens and all, and that he had no problem with the distinction made by the Egyptian between a major god and a minor tutelary spirit. When Armstrong says, "No true god could ever be conjured in Plotinus's universe," he reads something into the story that is not there. Why should the philosopher reject a divine manifestation that proved him to be above ordinary mortals? It is the kind of story he might dismiss with a smile or a shrug, but that smile could mean anything.

A third story told by Porphyry in his biography of the master (chap.

---

95. See Eitrem, "La théurgie," 62ff.; Dodds, *Greeks and the Irrational*, 289ff.

10) describes Plotinus' attitude toward ritual and worship. Porphyry writes:

> When Amelius [another disciple of Plotinus] grew ritualistic [Armstrong's translation of φιλοθύτης, which means something like "happy to offer sacrifices"] and took to going round to visiting the temples at the New Moon and the Feasts of the Gods and once asked if he could take Plotinus along, Plotinus said: "They ought to come to me, not I to them." What exactly he meant by this sublime utterance we could not understand, nor did we dare to ask.

The story confirms that there was a certain broadness within Neoplatonism. A disciple of Plotinus might feel the urge of making the round of all the temples on certain holy days to perform the appropriate rites; and he might invite his teacher to come along with him, "church-crawling," as Armstrong calls it. The teacher, on the other hand, might not be in the mood and might give a half-serious answer like "I am not going to visit them: let them visit me," but the disciple could take this seriously and tell it to others. Does it really mean that Plotinus thought that he could *force* the gods to come and see him, as the theurgists claimed they could? Probably not. It *may* mean that Plotinus did not expect to find any of the higher gods waiting for him in their temples and that he himself felt superior to the crowd of lower gods who might be expected to hover around in places of worship at the time when sacrifices were being offered: they were of no use to him. Elsewhere (*De abstinentia* 2.37–43) Porphyry discusses demons who attend such sacrifices: they are sublunary spirits of the lowest order, and those of them who delight in blood sacrifices are definitely evil. The philosopher, who—like Plotinus—lives on the level of the intellect, must regard them as his inferiors, and it is their duty to attend on him, if they care. If they do not, Plotinus obviously does not consider it a great loss. But Plotinus also acknowledged higher deities in the universe, and we have no evidence that he felt superior to them.

Porphyry, the disciple and biographer of Plotinus, was interested in theurgy, acknowledged it as a phenomenon, studied it, and experimented with it, as it appears, but came to no clear conclusion. He may have been a little naive, he may have been eager to believe, as Bidez says,[96] but he was not dishonest. Some of his experiments may have

---

96. *Vie de Porphyre* (Ghent, 1913), 19.

convinced him that theurgy worked, some may have been inconclusive; much depended on the circumstances.[97]

At one point, Porphyry felt that the practice of theurgy was dangerous and deceitful. He told the story of a jealous theurgist who interfered with the practice of a rival and succeeded in tying up the powers that had been conjured up.[98] According to Theodoretus, bishop of Cyrrhus (*Curatio*, 3.59–70), Porphyry was angry at those who deified evil demons and worshiped them in "mysteries and rituals" (τελεταὶ καὶ θυσίαι), because they learned magical incantations from them. Such persons, Porphyry says, are γόητες, not θεουργοί: they specialize in love charms; promise their customers wealth, success, and prestige; and "want to be gods."[99]

It makes no sense, according to Porphyry (*Letter to Anebo* fr. 30), that a human being who is subject to fate threatens not only the soul of a deceased, not only some minor demon, but even the sun, the moon, and the stars, all divine beings, to force them to manifest themselves and tell the truth. On the other hand, Porphyry does not completely reject theurgy; he just keeps wondering whether it is really essential and whether it achieves what its supporters claim.

Porphyry's work *De philosophia ex oraculis haurienda* has been called a "handbook of magic,"[100] and his treatise *De regressu animae* a "blend of Plotinian mysticism and Chaldaean theurgy."[101] But the latter work seems less positive on the subject of theurgy than the former. It is possible that Porphyry, in the meantime, came under the influence of Plotinus and revised some of his views. But he clearly intended to continue his research.

On the one hand, Porphyry seems to believe (*De regr. anim.* frs. 6 and 7 Bidez, quoted at Augustine *Civ. Dei* 10.26–28) that angels come down to teach theurgists knowledge of divine things. On the other hand, he makes a pun and accuses the theurgists of being excessively curious; they should be called "busybodies," περίεργοι, not θεουργοί (*De regr. anim.* fr. 13 Bidez). The Latin equivalent of περιεργία is *curiositas*, and this is almost

---

97. Porphyry *De philosophia ex oraculis hauriendis* pp. 154ff. Wolff; Nilsson, *Geschichte*, 418.

98. Porphyry *De regr. anim.* fr. 2 Bidez.

99. Ibid.

100. Bidez, *Vie de Porphyre*, 18.

101. J.H. Waszink, "Porphyrios und Numenios," *Entretiens sur l'antiquité classique* 12 (1965): 45 and n. 2.

a commonplace in condemnations of the magical arts.[102] Theurgy is, indeed, an example of insatiable human curiosity, but for the theurgists it is a virtue. The human being is a "product of audacious nature," as *Oracles* fragment 106, proclaims; and Psellus, in his commentary on this particular logion, actually uses the verb περιεργάζομαι.

There are certain things that theurgy can do, according to Porphyry, but others it cannot. It does achieve purification of the soul, but it does not enable the soul to return to the deity (*De regr. anim.* fr. 2 Bidez).[103] And even this purification of the "spiritual part" of the soul is not always possible, for envious powers try to prevent it. For this and other reasons, complete salvation through theurgic rites is not possible (ibid., frs. 3 and 7 Bidez).

In conclusion, Porphyry states that theurgy is not essential for the philosopher; it does certain things, but there are other approaches to mystical union with God that achieve the same goal (*De regr. anim.* frs. 7 and 11 Bidez). The crowd, the masses, may need theurgical mysteries, but the true sage achieves happiness without it, and he can return to the Father, purified of all evil, traveling another road.

Porphyry, like Plotinus, was certainly interested in the phenomena of magic and theurgy, without feeling a deep commitment to it as the way to salvation, but Iamblichus was a true believer. He wrote his treatise *On the Mysteries of Egypt* in reply to Porphyry's *Letter to Anebo,* as a defense of the theory and practices of theurgy.

According to Iamblichus (*Myst.* 2.11), theurgy definitely has its place in Platonism; in another sense, it replaces and supersedes all philosophy and theology: "The apparition of the gods gives us physical health and virtue of the soul, purity of mind, in short, an ascent of our whole inner existence toward its proper beginning" (ibid. 2.6). The aim of the theurgist is union, ἕνωσις, with higher beings (ibid. 1.11f., 15, 21; 2.11), and the sacred names of the gods and other divine symbols make the ascent possible. What is required are "hieratic supplications" and a "ritual which involves . . . admirable signs . . . , [for] the ineffable expresses itself in unutterable symbols."[104]

---

102. See H.J. Mette, *Festschrift Snell* (Munich, 1956), 227ff.; A. Labhardt, *MH* 16 (1960): 206ff.; H. Blumenberg, *Revue des Etudes Augustiniennes* 7 (1961): 35ff.

103. Cf. Zintzen, "Die Wertung," 89f.

104. He probably refers to the "symbols" or "seals" that were placed in the hollow statues of the gods and animated them at the right moment; see Dodds, *Greeks and the Irrational,* 292; des Places, intro. to *Oracles,* p. 29.

What were Iamblichus' own specific contributions to theurgy? The question is difficult to answer; because his work is unique in its way and cannot be compared to any other treatment. A large part of it is based on the *Oracles*—for instance, his claim that the theurgist does not belong to the "human herd" and is exempt from fate (*Oracles* frs. 153, 154).

But there are two more technical points that seem to be an elaboration or an adaptation of doctrines outlined in the *Oracles*. Iamblichus distinguishes three kinds of ritual prayer (*Myst.* 5.26): "the one that brings together" (συναγωγόν), "the one that ties together" (συνδετικόν), and "the union" (ἕνωσις). This division seems to have become part of theurgical doctrine, for it appears in a slightly different form in Proclus (*In Timaeum* 1.207f.).[105] I should also like to point out Iamblichus' description of a supernatural experience that persons sometimes have in a state between waking and sleeping and sometimes when they are fully awake (*Myst.* 3.2): an intangible and incorporeal spirit surrounds, as if in a circle, the persons who are stretched out; it cannot be perceived or registered, and it swishes as it enters and spreads out without touching anything. This peculiar noise, ῥοῖζος, is the sound of a whistling arrow, but Iamblichus uses it of the divine spirit approaching the human soul. It is also the technical term for the sound made by the magical *rhombus* (see earlier discussion) and by the stars in their celestial revolutions (*Myst.* 3.9).[106]

Among the lost works of Iamblichus, there was a commentary on the *Oracles* in at least twenty-eight books, known as the *Theologia Chaldaica*. It made a great impression on the emperor Julian, who eagerly sought a reliable copy of the work.[107]

The last of the Neoplatonist theurgists I should like to discuss is Proclus. His vita by Marinus (chap. 28)[108] tells us that Proclus was initiated into the "mysteries of the great Nestorius" by Asclepigeneia, the daughter of the theurgist and miracle worker Plutarchus, son of Nestorius—an important testimony, for it shows that the knowledge and technique of theurgy was handed down in a family from grandfather to son to grand-

---

105. Des Places, *Religion* 305f.

106. Cf. des Places, *Oracles*, p. 109, n. 2; p. 126.

107. Julian *Letters* 1.2, in Bidez' edition of his works (Paris 1924), p. 19; Bidez, *Vie de l'empereur Julien*, 73ff.; *Oracles* p. 44 des Places.

108. Boissonade, ed. (Leipzig, 1814), reprinted in the Didot edition of Diogenes Laertius (Paris, 1849); English translation by L.J. Rosán (New York, 1949), pp. 13ff.

daughter, and by her to a disciple of her father's who seemed to be a worthy recipient.[109] But Proclus was well prepared for the initiation, for, according to Marinus (chap. 26), he had studied "the many works of Porphyry and Iamblichus and the writings of the Chaldaeans which belong to the same order of ideas, and thus, nourished by divine oracles, he rose to the highest level of the . . . theurgical virtues." He knew, of course, De mysteriis, but he had also studied the Sentences of his teacher, Syrianus, and his commentaries on Orpheus. Still according to his biographer, Proclus could influence the weather, heal the sick, conjure up luminous phantoms of Hecate, and had, of course, the supreme experience of seeing the gods themselves (αὐτοψία).

For Proclus, theurgy as a liberation of the soul is a "power higher than all human wisdom [i.e., all of philosophy], embracing the blessings of divination, the purifying powers of initiation, and, in one word, all the operations of divine possession" (Theol. Platon. 1.26.63).[110] He is convinced that the "hieratic art,"[111] as he calls theurgy, leads to the union of the human soul with the One.[112]

For Proclus, theurgy is a process of deification. It crowns the act of contemplation, and only this gives a meaning to the partial advantages that the theurgist may receive, such as divination or healing power. But the theurgist is not supposed to enjoy his privileges in this world; he is called to rise above it and be freed from evil. He must not bother the deity with futile requests, but he should aim at salvation. This is essentially the teaching of Iamblichus.[113] As a theurgist, Proclus is caught in a conflict. He feels the need to be in touch with his gods, to have visible signs of their existence and their goodwill. The gods are happy to oblige

---

109. There are references in the Magical Papyri (e.g., 4.477) to the πατρόθεν παράδοτα μυστήρια); cf. Zintzen, "Die Wertung," 94 n. 79. Sir Francis Galton (Memories of My Life [London, 1908], 273ff.) observes that anomalous powers are hereditary in certain families—e.g., the second sight in Scotland. They are liable to be smothered by modern civilization but can be revived by a "life of solitude."

110. Translated by Dodds, in his edition of Proclus' Elements of Theology, p. xxii; cf. Iambl. Myst. 10.4ff.

111. See Hierocles' commentary on the Aureum Carmen of Pythagoras, 478–82, ed. Mullach; cf. A.-J. Festugière, "Contemplation philosophique et art théurgique chez Proclus," in Studi di storia religiosa della tarda antichità (Messina, 1968), 17f.; P. Courcelles, REA 71 (1969): 509; des Places, intro. to Oracles, pp. 34f.; Trouillard, L'un et l'âme, 34f.

112. See nn. 21 and 22.

113. See nn. 104 and 105.

him. At the same time, he has too much respect for them to "use" or "urge" them in the way the sorcerers summon their gods. He seems to have envisaged a higher form of theurgy, which was essentially a form of worship. It looks, indeed, as if Proclus had made an effort to purify theurgy from its magical elements, but it may also seem to us that, without those elements, it would not have been theurgy anymore.

How does Proclus explain the effects of theurgy? They are possible because a supernatural power is inherent in the world of the phenomena that surround us. This power can be activated, and theurgy is nothing else but the theory and practice of the activation.[114]

How does one become a theurgist? Through a strict vegetarian diet, through prayers to the Sun, through the observance of the rites of the Chaldean initiates, through the observance of the Egyptian holy days.[115]

There are three degrees of initiation, according to Proclus (*Theol. Platon.* 4.16):[116] (1) τελετή, "initiation"; (2) μύησις, "consecration"; (3) ἐποπτεία, "vision." The three steps remind one of Iamblichus' three kinds of prayers, though there is a difference. The first step is effected, for Proclus, by the "gods of initiation" (τελεσιουργοὶ θεοί), who have no place in Iamblichus' division; the second stage is effected by the "gods which give cohesion" (συνεκτικοὶ θεοί); they correspond to the "element which ties together" in Iamblichus where it is the second stage too; but Proclus' third stage, the "vision," is effected by the "gods that bring together," which corresponds to Iamblichus' first step, whereas his third, the "union," has disappeared from Proclus' scheme. This may be a question of terminology, but it might also alert us to the fact that the doctrine was flexible enough to accommodate different kinds of experiences and revelations, which then had to be described and labeled differently by the chief ideologists.

Michael Psellus the Younger (1018–1078 A.D.), a Byzantine Platonist, was fascinated by theurgy, although as a Christian he felt obliged to condemn what was, to him, an old pagan ritual bordering on magic. I have already mentioned his investigation of the séance conducted by the monks of Chios and the accusation of the patriarch, Cerularius, to which it led. To Psellus we owe a number of valuable notes and comments.[117]

---

114. B. Tatakis, *La philosophie byzantine*, in E. Bréhier, *Historie de la philosophie*, fasc. suppl. 2 (Paris, 1959), 20.

115. Lloyd, "Later Neoplatonists," 305.

116. See Trouillard, *L'un et l'âme*, 184.

117. They are conveniently collected by des Places in *Oracles*, passim.

He has summarized lost texts, commented on others; and it is perhaps thanks to his personal interest that Iamblichus' *De mysteriis* has survived at all.[118] As an outsider, he was, in a way, in the situation that we are in, and a number of things obviously made little sense to him; others he rejected out of hand.

In his *Accusation of Michael Cerularius* (*Oracles* pp. 219ff. des Places) he seems to quote extensively from Proclus. He refers to the conditions under which the "invocations" (κλήσεις) take place, the locations where they were performed, those who saw the divine light, women and men alike, the shapes (or gestures) and divine symbols (σχήματα ταῦτα καὶ θεῖα συνθήματα), but without telling us exactly what they were. Some of them appear to be lifeless objects, others living beings, either endowed with reason (ἔμψυχα λογικά) or without reason (ἔμψυχα ἄλογα). According to Proclus, as reported by Psellus, lifeless objects are sometimes filled with divine light, as when statues, inspired by a god or a benevolent spirit, deliver oracles. Human beings receive the divine spirit and are possessed by it (κάτοχοι γίνονται, θεόληπτοι καλοῦνται). Some mediums experience this kind of thing spontaneously, either at certain times or more irregularly, but always "just like that" (ἀορίστως), a point Iamblichus had made (*Myst.* 3.2). But others stimulate themselves (ἀνακίνησις) to enthusiasm by a voluntary action. Some mediums are completely ecstatic and possessed and no longer aware of themselves. Others remain conscious to an astonishing degree, so that they can apply the theurgical experience to themselves; this probably means that the medium, too, benefits from the experience, not just the witnesses. When the medium is in total trance, it is absolutely necessary for someone "sober" (νήφων) to give assistance. Before and during the ritual, one must avoid anything that might interfere with the arrival of the gods and insist on absolute quiet. We are dealing with parapsychological phenomena, I think, which must have been very real to those who participated in them. Something usually happened, it seems, but it was not always what the theurgists desired. If anything went wrong, it could be blamed on the interference of lesser demons or on the inadequacy of the medium, as we have seen.

From Julian the Theurgist to Proclus, and no doubt much later, mystical happenings of the kind referred to were experienced over and over again, and much was written about them; what we have is probably only a small fraction. That there was a technique of inducing them

118. See des Places, *Oracles*, p. 38, n. 1.

cannot be doubted, but knowledge of it is lost, and it seems impossible to reconstruct it from the texts we have.

Analogies in Other Cultures

In order to find an explanation, we have to look for analogies in other cultures. This method has been used with considerable success by E.R. Dodds in his *The Greeks and the Irrational*. A great deal of solid research done by psychologists and anthropologists is available today.

Personally, I found the work of John Raymond Smythies particularly helpful. He wrote, among other things, a book entitled *Analysis of Perception* (New York, 1956), and he edited a volume, *Science and ESP* (London, 1967), to which he contributed an essay, "Is ESP Possible?" Smythies, a physician by training, has carried out an impressive amount of scientific research, including experiments with hallucinogenic drugs, and is recognized as a philosopher. What he has to say about the "reality" of hallucinations was of particular interest to me.

If we think that we only experience physical objects directly and that there is nothing else in the universe but physical objects, then we have to say that hallucinations are not real. At the same time, they can be undistinguishable, from a strictly scientific point of view, from "true" sense experiences.[119] They seem to have their own space, their own time, their specific color; and they occur in a "real" visual field. Persons who are sane, healthy, normal, well educated, even sophisticated, after having been given hallucinogenic agents experimentally, will not admit that their experiences were in any sense unreal. They will just say that they were different. Hallucinations, some of them trivial, may also be induced in susceptible persons by hypnosis.

Visions such as the theurgists claimed to have experienced are rejected instinctively by the modern mind because of our scientific habits of thought, but it seems impossible, considering the evidence we have, to declare all these experiences "unreal" or call them cleverly orchestrated deceit.

Let us assume that some of these visions or happenings were hallucinations induced by drugs or by hypnosis. Even then they could be fully understood only, it seems to me, by those who received them, as they thought, as gifts from the gods, sent to assure privileged human beings

---

119. Smythies, *Analysis of Perception*, 81.

of their favor and goodwill, and thereby affirming the promise of salvation and eternal life.

Smythies (*Analysis of Perception*, 86ff.) quotes at great length from descriptions of visions that persons experimenting with mescaline remembered. This one comes from Havelock Ellis:

> I would see a thick, glorious field of jewelry, solitary or clustered, sometimes brilliant and sparkling, sometimes with a dull, rich glow. Then they would spring up into flowerlike shapes beneath my gaze, and then seem to turn into gorgeous butterfly forms of endless folds of glistening, iridescent, fibrous wings of wonderful insects; while sometimes I seemed to be gazing into a vast hollow revolving vessel, on whose polished mother-of-pearl surface the hues were swiftly changing. I was surprised, not only by the enormous profusion of the imagery presented to my gaze, but still more by its variety.

Another experience described involves vague patches of color that develop into mosaics, flowing arabesques, wonderful tapestries. Then certain objects appear, such as masks, statues, fabulous animals, soaring architecture, and finally human figures acting out coherent stories on some kind of stage. All this is in constant motion and very pleasing.

Again and again the descriptions emphasize the surpassing beauty of the visions and the inadequacy of language to do justice to it. This particular theme—the inadequacy of language to express the ultimate truth—is typical for Neoplatonism.[120] We have seen how often terms like "ineffable" and "inexpressible" occur in theurgical contexts.

It seems to me that an experience that may be primarily esthetic for a twentieth-century subject—though we hear about moving statues, masks, and so on—could very well be a religious one for a second-century person who had been programmed to expect it. The technique of programming was, of course, an essential part of theurgy, just as important as the technique of getting into trance or taking the right drug in the right doses. If anything was done improperly, things could go wrong and the visions were terrifying rather than blissful. It is true that no specific drugs are ever named, but the powers of herbs, stones, aromatic essences, and the like are emphasized many times.

Mescaline is a vegetable alkaloid found in nature in the juices of a small Mexican desert cactus, *Anhalonium lewinii*. The Mexican desert

---

120. Wallis, *Neoplatonism*, 6, 11, 14, 41, 57–59, 88–90, 91, 114–16, etc.

Amerindians make a brew, peyote, from the plant and use it for religious ceremonies. It was discovered for Western science in 1886 by the distinguished pharmacologist Lewin, after whom the cactus is named.[121]

Mescaline also produces changes in other senses. Auditory hallucinations of wonderful music and of voices speaking in strange languages have been reported but are apparently rare (Smythies, *Analysis of Perception*, 90). Fragrant perfumes may be smelled; hard objects may be felt to be soft and malleable. Sometimes synesthesia occurs: sounds are accompanied by appropriate images.

A typical feature of the mescaline phenomena is that the patterns, designs, scenes, and so forth are always changing; they are a continuous kaleidoscope. But it is possible, in certain instances, to predict what vision will follow the one that the subject is having at a given moment. Smythies (*Analysis of Perception*, 92) writes, "If one flash of the stroboscopic lamp is directed at my closed eyes, I will notice that the complex hallucinated pattern will immediately change to be replaced by a more primitive pattern." Therefore it seems entirely possible that the theurgist, working with a medium in trance, could, to a certain extent, influence the kind of hallucination the medium was to have. This may explain the uses of lamps and shiny objects in theurgic rituals.

Smythies refers very briefly and without elaborating to "alleged occult phenomena," such as apparitions of the recently dead, and to precognitive dreams. He is clearly aware of the perspectives that these experiments open up for our understanding of ancient religions: "persons in the early Christian era pursued hallucinatory experiences with . . . passionate intensity believing them to provide a direct method of communication with the supernatural world." Of course this pursuit had been going on for a very long time—think of Delphi and Eleusis—and it continued, as we have seen, to the end of antiquity and beyond.

We have to accept Smythies' conclusion, I believe, that "the decision to call only ordinary sense-experience real is an isolated phenomenon of our more recent type of Western European culture." It is contingent, he

---

121. On the moods produced by mescaline see O.F. Bollnow, *Das Wesen der Stimmungen* (Göttingen, 1943), 160ff. In Sufism trance is achieved by hashish; see J.W. Hauer, *Yoga* (Göttingen, 1598), 29f. In their book *The Road to Eleusis* (New York, 1978), R. Gordon Wasson, Carl A.P. Ruck, and Albert Hofmann argue plausibly that in archaic Greece there was a method to isolate a hallucinogenic drug from ergot, and that this drug was mixed into the κυκεών, the ritual drink served at the initiations. Ergot is related to LSD.

adds, on the biochemical accident that our adrenal glands happen to produce adrenalin and not . . . mescaline. One wonders whether in the course of the history of humankind not only cultures change but also the human brain and the human glands. Perhaps there is even a connection between the two types of change. At any rate Smythies must be right when he says that cultural factors and biochemical accidents are not valid philosophical or scientific criteria when it comes to analyzing sense perceptions.

There is no doubt a kind of sensitivity that, as Gilbert Murray has put it,[122] "is apt to be deadened and disregarded by our all-absorbing material civilization, and if so, disregarded at our peril." Murray maintained, "It is in that region that our great tool, language, fails us and we have most highly developed our ancient pre-linguistic and supra-linguistic sympathy." Gilbert Murray was not only a distinguished scholar; he had himself remarkable psychic gifts. To confirm Murray's fears, Sir Cyril Burtt,[123] a well-known British psychologist, notes that in some remote parts of Wales in the early twentieth century local opinion still took extrasensory phenomena as a matter of course, but half a century later, when he returned to the same villages and spoke to the villagers, he found that these beliefs had practically died out.

Another possible approach to the problem of ancient theurgy seems to me the study of the voodoo cult. At first sight the two worlds appear to be totally unrelated and heterogeneous, but a closer look reveals amazing similarities. In the volume *Science and ESP*, mentioned earlier, there is an excellent essay by Francis Huxley, an Oxford anthropologist, entitled "Anthropology and ESP." It is based on the author's firsthand experiences of the voodoo cult in Haiti today. Huxley states that very little of what he saw in Haiti needed explanations in terms of ESP, although what he witnessed ranged from highly serious religious practices (comparable to theurgy) to vindictive exercises in black magic (goety). He comments briefly on very similar techniques found throughout the world and, one might add, throughout the ages.[124] Incidentally,

---

122. In his presidential address delivered at a meeting of the Society for Psychical Research in 1952, printed in *Science and ESP*, 15ff.

123. "Psychology and Parapsychology," in *Science and ESP*, 97.

124. The following scene was observed by Nina Epton in the slums of Djakarta ("Trance in the Shadows," 115ff.):

The scene I was about to witness was a throwback to a world which is as foreign to progressive, modern Indonesians as it was to me.

the distinction made in Haiti between *un profane* and *un avec connaissance* corresponds to the distinction made in paganism between the uniniti-ated and the one who has already participated in theurgic rites.

A knot of ragged *betjak* boys and a few women with naked babies astride their hips had gathered round an old man and a boy. "There's going to be a *kuda lopeng*" (dance of the human horse), one of the bystanders informed me. "It's been ordered for a birthday *slamentan*," said another.

The old man was thin and bent, with matted hair falling over his shoulders: his face was haggard and his dark eyes sunken, but they shone with an unnatural brilliance. A few feet away from him an emaciated boy crouched shivering as in an epileptic fit. He was astride a hobby-horse, a flat bamboo frame painted in black, with a gaudy fringe tied to the mane. Somebody tossed a bundle of hay into a corner.

Three musicians sat with their backs against a bamboo house, beat-ing drums of various sizes with long, nervous fingers. The old man picked up a whip, stiffened and fixed the boy with his glittering, hypnotic eyes. The drums softened until they came to an imper-ceptible stop. The boy raised his eyes towards the sorcerer and an anguished silence ensued. Nobody in the audience stirred. Whether we wanted to or not we had all been drawn into the magic evil orbit. We were the involuntary prisoners of that loathsome creature with the matted hair and talon-like fingers. We were assisting him with an unrealized force latent in every one of those present.

The old sorcerer gave a bestial snarl accompanied by a crack of the whip; we started and fell back a pace or two. The instant he heard his voice the boy responded with a half-choked sound like a horse's neigh. The sorcerer cracked his whip again and shouted a command in a high, quavering voice. The boy-horse approached the bundle of hay on his hobby-horse. Again he neighed—there was no mistaking the sound—bent forward and began to munch the hay.

After two or three minutes the old man shrieked another command and the boy-horse reared and pranced like a circus pony. Another crack of the whip and he galloped round the sorcerer shaking his long black hair. His muscles appeared to have lengthened; his face had narrowed and looked curiously equine—or were we victims of a collec-tive hallucination?

The performance ended as abruptly as it had begun. The boy-horse suddenly uttered a pitiful cry and rolled over on the ground panting, his body moist with perspiration, his eyes staring skywards with the fixity of the demented. The old man stepped forward and bent over the writhing form, whispering in his ear. Little by little the twitching body of the horse-boy began to relax. The convulsed face became smooth and rounded and the breathing normal.

A state of trance and an overpowering feeling of being possessed by a god are achieved in voodoo mainly through wild dancing and the sound of drums. The possessed often become insensitive to pain or accomplish unusual feats, and afterward they forget the whole experience, although knowledge of it may later come to them in a dream.

Let me quote Huxley's account of a voodoo ritual.

The preparations for a voodoo ceremony are lengthy, consisting of designs drawn in flour or ash upon the ground, libations poured at various points, prayers and songs to Christian saints as well as to the gods of voodoo. When they are accomplished, the drums begin to sound and the choir of men and women attached to the temple sing and dance in praise of the gods. The mounting rhythm of drum and song, and the continual effort of the dance, lead to the first signs of the gods' presence among the dancers: a certain abstraction. It is the drummers who largely provoke dissociation: they are skilful in reading the signs, and by quickening, altering, or breaking their rhythm they can usually force the crisis on those who are ready for it. The dancer thus singled out falters, feeling a heavy weight on neck and in legs, while a darkness invades his sight and mind; he loses his balance and totters with great strides from side to side of the dancing floor, a bewildered or agonized expression on his face. He may collapse among the audience at the sides, who put him back on his feet and send him for another voyage over the floor till the buffets of sound have their full effect. Suddenly a new expression dawns on his face and he draws himself up in an attitude which is often instantly recognizable: the god has possessed him or, as the usual expression goes, he has been mounted by the god as a horse

---

One of the drummers rose and walked round to collect a few rupiahs; the sorcerer continued to bend over the boy who now appeared to be sleeping peacefully. Somebody nudged my arm. It was my *betjak* driver. "Not a bad performance," he remarked casually, "But I have seen better. Anyway it was genuine. Sometimes the boy just pretends he's in a trance. They can't always go into a real one and that makes it awkward for everybody, since they earn their living that way. Of course, the old *dukun* has a few sidelines. He sells medicines—herbal ones—and love potions in the kampong markets. Some poor fools still believe in them."

The use of the whip reminds one of the Greek *rhombos*, but there are other parallels to theurgical operations as well.

by its rider. The god then stalks about the floor, paying his respects to the priest, taking part in the ceremony if necessary, admonishing persons in the audience or giving them his blessing, till he slowly or suddenly absents himself. The dancer comes to himself with a bewildered expression and usually retires for a time to recover. (*Science and ESP,* 286)

In the absence of any explicit, candid, firsthand account from antiquity, I believe that a solution to the problems of theurgy may be found in this direction.[125] As scholars, we should look for explanation in terms of modern psychology, psychic research, and anthropology. What I have to offer are just a few tentative suggestions. A good deal of work remains to be done.

---

125. See R. Ganschinietz, *Hippolytus' Kapitel über die Magier, TUGAL* 39 (1913), passim.

The "Way Out": Philological Notes on the Transfiguration of Jesus

The synoptic Gospels (Mark 9:2–13, Matthew 17:1–13, and Luke 9:28–36) report the transfiguration of Jesus in similar terms, but there are significant differences. As an episode, the Transfiguration is placed in the same context in all three Gospels: it is preceded by the first prediction of the Passion and the Resurrection and followed by the narrative about an exorcism and the second prediction. The debate of Elijah's return, missing in Luke, ought to be interpreted as part of the Transfiguration episode in the two other Gospels.

According to Mark, Jesus takes Peter, James, and John on a high mountain and is "transfigured" (μετεμορφώθη) before their eyes. His clothes assume a dazzling whiteness which no one who bleaches cloth on earth could achieve. Elijah and Moses appear and converse with Jesus. Peter then proposes to build three shelters (σκηνάς, *tabernacula*),[1] one for

From *Dissertatiunculae criticae, Festschrift für Günther-Christian Hansen,* ed. Christian-Friedrich Collatz, Jürgen Dummer, Jutta Kollesch and Marie-Luise Werlitz, Texte und Untersuchungen zur Geschichte der altchristlichen Literatur (Königshausen and Neumann, 1998), 311–21.

I am very grateful to my colleagues, Delbert R. Hillers and P. Kyle McCarter, Jr. (Johns Hopkins University), as well as to Rev. Lance Gifford (Baltimore, MD) and Father Geoffrey Seagraves, O. Cist. (Bregenz, Austria), for having read this essay. They have corrected some errors and contributed a number of valuable comments which I have embodied. Of course this does not mean that they agree with all my views. I also acknowledge the remarks made by an anonymous referee for the *Journal of Biblical Literature.* Instead of listing all the standard commentaries on the New Testament which I have consulted, I should like to refer to the article by Bruce D. Chilton, in the *Anchor Bible Dictionary,* vol. 6 (New York, 1992), 640–44, with a brief but useful bibliography.

1. The tents Peter wants to build are sometimes explained as temporary shelters for distinguished visitors. There is probably no connection with 2 Peter 1:13, where σκήνωμα refers to the human body. (This letter contrasts, in 15–21, the transfiguration of Jesus as a real experience with the "craftily concocted myths" of the gentiles). There may be a connection with σκηνή in Hebr. 9:11 (the

Jesus, one for Moses, and one for Elijah. Like the other two disciples, he is frightened and does not know what to say. A cloud forms and overshadows (ἐπισκιάζουσα)[2] them ("him" is a variant), and a voice comes from the cloud, saying, "This is my beloved Son; listen to him."[3] Suddenly looking around, they can see no one with them except Jesus. As they walk down the mountain, Jesus charges them not to tell anyone of what they had seen, until the Son of Man should rise up from the dead.

The disciples know of a doctrine that Elijah must return first and then the Messiah will come. Since they have just seen Elijah, it would be only natural for them to wonder whether this vision is to be considered the return of Elijah. They ask Jesus: "What do the scribes mean when they say 'Elijah must come'?" Jesus answers: " 'Elijah comes first and restores all things.' How is it written about the Son of Man that he must suffer many things and be set at nought? But I say to you that Elijah has come, and they did to him all the things they wanted, as it is written about him." (Some witnesses have "Pharisees and scribes" in the question asked by the disciples and "will restore all things," the future instead of the present; some have an ambiguous form.)

The Transfiguration, just witnessed by the three disciples, constitutes further proof that Jesus is, indeed, the Messiah. In that case, Elijah must have returned already in some form. Jesus briefly acknowledges the doctrine by a reference to Malachi 3:22–24 (Septuagint; 4:4–6 in the Hebrew text): "Look, I shall send you Elijah the Tishbite before the great, the splendid ["terrifying" is a variant reading] day of the Lord comes. He will restore the heart of the father to the son and the heart of man to his fellow man, lest I come and utterly strike the earth. Remember the Law of my servant Moses, as I gave to him commandments and regulations for all of Israel."[4] In this prophecy, crucial for our understanding of the Transfiguration, both Elijah and Moses are named; another connecting link is the theophany on a mountaintop.

---

greater and more perfect tent of Christ's priesthood) and Rev. 13:6 (God has his tent in heaven).

2. Ἐπισκιάζω is used in Exod. 40:35, where we are told that Moses could not enter the tabernacle "because the cloud overshadowed it." (I owe this reference to Kyle McCarter.) The same verb occurs in Luke 1:35, where the angel says to Mary: "The power of the Most High will overshadow you." (I owe this reference to Father Geoffrey Seagraves.)

3. One witness, perhaps influenced by Luke, adds "whom I have chosen"; several witnesses, perhaps influenced by Matthew, add "with whom I am well pleased."

4. My translation of J. Ziegler's text (1943).

According to Mark, Jesus' clothes become dazzling with a whiteness that "no one who bleaches on earth" could achieve. The reader is probably expected to remember another passage in Malachi (3:2) where the Messenger sent by the Lord is said to be "like a refiner's fire, like fuller's soap . . . ; he will purify the Levites and cleanse them." There may also be a connection with the youth dressed in a white robe, sitting in the empty tomb after the Resurrection (Mark 16:5). According to Mark, only Jesus' clothes, not his face, are shining.

According to Matthew, Jesus' face begins to shine, and his clothes turn "white as light" ("as snow" is a variant reading). Here, the cloud, too, is shiny (φωτεινή). The symbolism is more explicit than in Mark. Clearly, the shiny cloud is a symbol of the Shechinah, the presence of God, or the glory of God, as the author of 2 Peter 1:17 saw it, for according to him, Jesus received on the mountain honor and glory from God the Father, and a voice came to him from the Sublime Presence.

In Matthew's account, the voice from the cloud says, "This is my beloved Son in whom I am well pleased; listen to him." The disciples throw themselves on their faces, full of fear. Jesus touches them and says: "Rise up and be not afraid."[5] They lift up their eyes and see no one except Jesus himself.

In the next section of Matthew's text (17:9–13) there are more details

---

5. There is remarkable parallel in Dio Chrysostomus (*Or.* 36.40–41), as pointed out by D.A. Russell, in his edition, with commentary, of *Or.* 7, 12, and 36 (Cambridge, 1992). Dio, born ca. A.D. 40, was still alive in 110.

40 Τὸ δὲ ἰσχυρὸν καὶ τέλειον ἅρμα τὸ Διὸς σὐδεὶς ἄρα ὕμνησεν ἀξίως τῶν τῆιδε οὔτε Ὅμηρος οὔτε Ἡσίοδος, ἀλλὰ Ζωροάστρης καὶ μάγων παῖδες ἄιδουσι παρ' ἐκείνου μαθόντες· ὃν Πέρσαι λέγουσιν ἔρωτι σοφίας καὶ δικαιοσύνης ἀποχωρήσαντα τῶν ἀνθρώπων καθ' αὑτὸν ἐν ὄρει τινὶ ζῆν· ἔπειτα ἀφθῆναι τὸ ὄρος πυρὸς ἄνωθεν πολλοῦ κατασκήψαντος συνεχῶς τε κάεσθαι. τὸν οὖν βασιλέα σὺν τοῖς ἐλλογιμωτάτοις Περσῶν ἀφικνεῖσθαι πλησίον, βουλό-μενον εὔξασθαι τῶι θεῶι· καὶ τὸν ἄνδρα ἐξελθεῖν ἐκ τοῦ πυρὸς ἀπαθῆ, φανέντα δὲ αὐτοῖς ἵλεων θαρρεῖν κελεῦσαι καὶ θῦσαι θυσίας τινάς, ὡς ἥκοντος εἰς τὸν τόπον τοῦ θεοῦ.

41 συγγίγνεσθαί τε μετὰ ταῦτα οὐχ ἅπασιν, ἀλλὰ τοῖς ἄριστα πρὸς ἀλήθειαν πεφυκόσι καὶ θεοῦ ξυνιέναι δυναμένοις, οὓς Πέρσαι μάγους ἐκάλεσαν, ἐπισταμένους θεραπεύειν τὸ δαιμόνιον, οὐχ ὡς Ἕλληνες ἀγνοίᾳ τοῦ ὀνόματος οὕτως ὀνομάζουσιν ἀνθρώπους γόητας.

Here, the mountain is blazing, struck by a great fire coming from above, and we are explicitly told that "the god" had come to the place. Matthew's μὴ φοβεῖσθε corresponds to Dio's θαρρεῖν κελεῦσαι.

that differ from Mark's account. Jesus calls the experience a "vision" (ὅραμα),[6] a term not used in the other narratives, though by no means uncommon in early Christian literature. He sums up, as in Matthew, the doctrine concerning the return of Elijah, adding that Elijah has already returned, and the disciples—Matthew is explicit—understand that he speaks of John the Baptist.

More strongly than the other two Gospel writers, Matthew emphasizes the supernatural character of the "vision." In addition to Jesus' clothes, his face becomes resplendent, and the cloud shines, too. The disciples fall on their faces, and Jesus has to reassure them.

The account given by Luke has features of its own. Jesus goes up to the mountaintop "to pray," a detail missing in Mark and Matthew. Luke avoids the verb μεταμορφόω, possibly to discourage any connection with the transformation stores of Greek mythology. On the other hand, the phrase ἕτερον γενέσθαι is close to the verb ἑτεροιοῦσθαι, and this could be associated with Ἑτεροιούμενα, practically a synonym of Μεταμορφώσεις as a literary genus.

Luke does not say explicitly that Jesus' face began to shine; he says instead that "while he was praying, the appearance of his face changed" [ἐγένετο . . . τὸ εἶδος [ἡ ἰδέα is a variant] τοῦ προσώπου αὐτοῦ ἕτερον]. To suggest the splendor of his clothes, Luke uses a verb that occurs only here in the New Testament, ἐξαστράπτω, "to gleam like lightning," though the *simplex,* ἀστράπτω, describes, in 24:4, the garments of the two men who were seen after the Resurrection,[7] perhaps another connecting link (see earlier discussion, on Mark).

But what seems most important is this: Luke knows what Moses, Elijah, and Jesus were talking about. They were talking about Jesus' ἔξοδος, his "departure" or "way out," which he was to accomplish in

---

6. For ὅραμα Father Geoffrey Seagraves refers to Acts 7:31 (cf. 16:9) and, in general, to Jacqueline Amat, *Songes et visions: L'au-delà dans la littérature latine* (Paris, 1985), 28, 63, 76; Martine Dulacy, "Songes—Rêves," pt. 2, "Epoque patristique," in *Dict. de Spiritualié,* vol. 15 (Paris, 1989), cc. 1060–66; "Sogni, visioni, profezie nell' antico Cristianesimo" Atti del XVII Incontro di Studiosi dell' Antiquità Cristiana, *Augustinianum* 29 (1989); John S. Hanson, "Dream and Vision in the Graeco-Roman World and Early Christianity," in *Aufstieg und Niedergang der römischen Welt,* vol. 32, no. 2 Halbbd. (Berlin and New York, 1980), 1395–1425, esp. 1421–25 and 1408 n. 51.

7. The verb ἐξαστράπτω occurs in Ezek. 1:5 and 7, in a theophanic context. One should also note the theophanous lightning (ἀστραπή) in Exod. 19:16 and Ezek. 1:13 (Kyle McCarter).

Jerusalem. This information is not found in the other Gospels. In this context, as J.A. Bengel noted (*Gnomon Novi Testamenti* [1746], ad loc.), ἔξοδος does not simply mean "death" but includes Jesus' Passion, resurrection, and ascension. His own predictions, made immediately before and again immediately after the Transfiguration, are thus confirmed by the two visitors from another world; they are dramatized, as it were, by the vision on the mountain.

The word ἔξοδος was chosen by Luke with great care. It could mean "death," and the author of 2 Peter (1:15) uses it in this sense when he refers to his own death, which he describes as "the getting rid of my tent," ἡ ἀπόθεσις τοῦ σκηνώματός μου, where the variant σώματος seems to be a gloss which found its way into the text. But it means more than just "death" when it is applied to Jesus' "way out," and this is true of the verb ἐξέρχομαι, "to go out," as well, for in a speech reported by Luke in Acts 1:16–22 Peter sums up Jesus' life on earth between his baptism and his ascension in the following words: ἐν παντὶ χρόνῳ εἰσῆλθεν καὶ ἐξῆλθεν ἐφ᾽ ἡμᾶς ὁ κύριος Ἰησοῦς. This may be translated as "while we had the Lord Jesus with us, coming and going," as the New English Bible does, but to render it as "while he associated with us" would simplify the meaning and thus obscure a very specific terminology.[8]

Jesus' εἴσοδος is clearly his baptism, and his ἔξοδος is the "way out" which begins with his Passion and ends with his ascension. In the Transfiguration episode, as presented by Luke, there may be an additional nuance to the term ἔξοδος, as will be suggested later in this essay.

In Luke, the disciples do not fall on their faces in fear; they fall asleep. This particular motif anticipates, perhaps, the episode on the Mount of Olives (Luke 22:39–46), but in our passage the disciples are not rebuked. When they wake up, they see Jesus' "glory and the two men standing beside him"—another characteristic feature of Luke's narrative: the "glory" of Moses and Elijah has now been transferred, as it were, to Jesus (v. 32). One has to read and weigh every word to appreciate these nuances.

Luke is also the only one of the synoptic writers to make Moses and Elijah "move away" or "separate themselves" (διαχωρίζομαι) from Jesus, as if to indicate that their mission had now come to an end. But

---

8. "To come and go," as Delbert Hillers points out to me, is a frequent biblical idiom; he refers to Deut. 28:6; Josh. 6:1; 2 Kgs. 11:8. In Acts 1:16–22 the expression refers to the beginning and end of Jesus' public ministry.

what could their mission have been? Were they sent to offer him a "way out" in glory, instead of the one he chose, death on the cross?

At this point in Luke's narrative, Peter proposes to build the three tents, and this is followed, as in the other accounts, by the description of the cloud overshadowing them. But only Luke says that Moses and Elijah "entered" the cloud. This may be a reminiscence of Exodus 24:18 (Moses enters the cloud out of which God has called him). Now the disciples are afraid; before, they had merely fallen asleep, according to Luke, and now, after Moses and Elijah have entered the cloud, the voice comes from it, saying, "This is my Son, the chosen one [variants: "the beloved one"; "in whom I am well pleased"]; listen to him." The term ὁ ἐκλελεγμένος is used of Jesus only here, but ὁ ἐκλεκτός appears frequently as an epithet of the Messiah in the Book of Enoch, and it is this word, together with ὁ χριστός, that the bystanders at the Crucifixion use to mock Jesus (Luke 23:35, not in the other Gospels).

Jesus is now seen by the disciples to be alone; in this point Luke agrees with Mark and Matthew, but he leaves out Jesus' explicit command to the disciples not to tell anyone of what they had seen until the Son of Man had risen up from the dead. Luke only says that the disciples "kept silence" and "in those days" told no one anything of what they had seen. In other words, Luke tells us the result of Jesus' commandment, but not the commandment itself. It seems remarkable that Luke would omit the commandment altogether and replace the clear reference to the Resurrection found in the other accounts (clear to us, that is, but not to the disciples, if we follow Mark) by the vague phrase "in those days." This expression is normally used in the Gospels when the exact time cannot (or is not to be) given; the best-known example is probably Luke 2:1: "In those days a decree was issued by the emperor Augustus . . ." If we had only Luke's account, we could only guess that he was thinking of the time between the Transfiguration and the Resurrection.

Luke also omits the discussion of the return of Elijah which seems to be such an important part of the tradition in the two other Gospels. But the gist of it—Elijah has already returned in the form of John the Baptist—is embodied by Luke elsewhere in his Gospel. In 1:17 the angel announces to Zechariah: "He [i.e., Zechariah's son, the Baptist] will go before him as a forerunner, possessed by the spirit and power of Elijah, to reconcile the hearts of the fathers with the children." Thus, at the very beginning of his Gospel, Luke has found a way of combining the prophecy of Malachi (3:1–4) with the doctrine of Elijah's return, showing how both were fulfilled by the ministry of John the Baptist. This may be the reason why he felt it unnecessary to embody the discussion of Elijah's return in the Transfiguration episode. Anyone who had read his Gospel from the beginning would know or at least be open to the possibility that John was, indeed, Elijah. There were others who denied this—John the Baptist himself, according to the Gospel of John (1:21, 25); it is no coincidence that this Gospel omits the pericope of the Transfiguration altogether and that the Baptist is mentioned only here.

Obviously, even among Jesus' closest followers there was some uncertainty about the return of Elijah. Had he already returned in the form of John the Baptist? Was John the mysterious Messenger of Malachi (3:1), as Mark says at the beginning of his Gospel (1:2) and Matthew (10:11) confirms? Or was he both in one? Or neither, as John implies? The Transfiguration episode settled this question, for who was better qualified to give an answer than Elijah himself? He presumably told it to Jesus, and Jesus, in a veiled, allusive way, shared it with his disciples as they descended. For the author of the fourth Gospel, who seems to have rejected this tradition, the whole Transfiguration episode was best omitted.

There were even some who saw in Jesus himself a kind of reincarnation of Elijah (Mark 6:15, 8:18; Matth. 16:14; Luke 9:8, 19; John is silent on this point), but the synoptic Gospels reject this view, and the Transfiguration episode clearly contradicts it. If Jesus was, indeed, the Messiah, he could not be Elijah, because Elijah's return was supposed to herald the arrival of the Messiah. Another herald or forerunner had to be found to suit the prediction, and that was no one else but John the Baptist.

We have discussed the similarities and the divergences within the synoptic tradition, as far as the transfiguration of Jesus is concerned. One of the motives firmly established in the tradition is the appearance of Moses and Elijah. These two Old Testament figures were obviously chosen for a good reason or for several reasons. The choice of Moses could be explained by the scene and its implications—the mountaintop, the unmistakable presence of God, reminiscent of Moses on Mount Sinai—and predictions found in "Moses and the Prophets," according to the risen Christ (Luke 24:27). The Transfiguration narratives allude to the writings attributed to Moses in various places. Elijah was chosen, it has been suggested already, because he could settle the dispute concerning his return once and for all. But there is another aspect to the problem.

In a recent article,[9] James D. Tabor has discussed the ways in which

---

9. " 'Returning to the Divinity': Josephus's Portrayal of the Disappearances of Enoch, Elijah, and Moses," *Journal of Biblical Literature* 108 (1989): 224–38.

Enoch, Moses, and Elijah disappeared from this world, as narrated in the Old Testament and interpreted by Josephus. The results of his investigation are important in themselves, but they also shed new light on the transfiguration of Jesus. Of the three, only Moses and Elijah appear on the mountaintop, but in a way, Enoch is also present, as will be suggested shortly.

In the line of generations from Adam to Noah (Gen. 5), Enoch is the only patriarch whose death is not clearly recorded as such. His life span of 365 years, however, is recorded, and even though it may seem short in comparison, it is a perfect one, since it corresponds to the number of days of the solar year. The Hebrew text reads, "Enoch walked with God and was not [seen any more], for God took him [away]." The Septuagint has a different version: "Enoch was well pleasing [εὐαρέστησεν] to God and was not found, for God placed him elsewhere [μετέθηκεν]." Both verbs are close in meaning to verbs that occur in the Transfiguration episode, as told by Matthew: εὐδοκέω and μεταμορφόω.

From the Hebrew text of Deuteronomy 34:1–6 we learn that God showed Moses the Promised Land from Mount Nebo, that he died in the land of Moab, and that he was buried there by God. Again, the Septuagint has a different version: not God but "they" buried him.

According to the Hebrew text of 2 Kings 2:11, a chariot of fire and horses of fire separated Elijah and Elisha, as they were talking, and Elijah went up by a whirlwind into heaven. The Septuagint uses "was taken up" (ἀνελήφθη) for "went up." Both ἀναλαμβάνω (see Mark 16:19; Acts 1:11; etc.) and ἀνάλημψις (see Luke 9:51) are used in the New Testament in connection with the Ascension.

In interpreting the Old Testament account of Enoch's disappearance, Josephus (Ant.1.3.4 § 85) uses the concept of ἀναχώρησις πρὸς τὸ θεῖον: "Enoch lived 365 years and then returned [or "went up"] to the divinity; thus it happens that there is no record in the chronicles of his death." Tabor (227) points out that the primary meanings of ἀναχωρέω in Josephus are "to return home," "to go back," "to retreat," "to withdraw." With the phase πρὸς τὸ θεῖον the verb occurs in two other passages in Josephus: both deal with the way in which Moses left this world.

The expression, as used by Josephus, clearly is applied to someone who is allowed to "escape a normal death and burial," as Tabor puts it. It does not occur verbatim in the New Testament, but the concept is essential to our understanding of the Transfiguration episode. What the disciples witnessed on the mountaintop might be called the initial phase of an ἀναχώρησις πρὸς τὸ θεῖον, but the process is interrupted and reversed, as it were, by Jesus' decision to remain on earth to confront the Passion he has already predicted immediately before this episode and which he will predict once more immediately afterward. This may seem a rather bold interpretation, but it is supported by the appearance of Moses and Elijah and by the kind of contemporary speculation documented by Josephus. We may wonder why the Gospels do not use the same term as Josephus. The answer is: They could not, for it is not, properly speaking, an ἀναχώρησις; unlike Moses and Elijah, Jesus remained in this world. But it might be argued that he was offered, at this point, a "way out" or a "return to the divine" and declined. Jesus' warning to his disciples is clear proof that something mysterious had taken place, something that could not be put into words without being misunderstood. Hence it was best not to talk about it. But the Gospel narratives, as we have them, invite us, by their allusive nature, to read between the lines, and if we do this, in the light of Josephus' thought, we may look at Jesus' μεταμόρφωσις as a kind of incomplete ἀναχώρησις.

Josephus comments twice on the end of Moses' earthly life, as recorded in Deuteronomy 34:5–6. In the first passage (*Ant.* 3.5.7 § 96) he writes that the Hebrews were afraid that something had happened to Moses after not having seen him for forty days. The thought that he might have perished was deeply distressing to them; but some (mainly those who were against him) claimed that he had fallen victim to wild beasts. Others said that he had "returned to the divinity." In the second passage (*Ant.* 8.48 § 326), Josephus writes that a cloud descended on Moses as he was talking to Eleazar and Joshua, as he was saying farewell to them, and that he disappeared in a ravine. "But," Josephus continues, "he has written of himself in the sacred books that he died, for fear that any might say he had gone back to the divinity."

In both passages, Josephus introduces the concept of the ἀναχώρησις πρὸς τὸ θεῖον but does not offer it as the only possible explanation of Moses' departure from the earthly scene. He deals with a formidable difficulty, but one that had to be dealt with: the conflict with Moses' own written testimony about his death. There is no conflict, as Tabor seems to suggest, between the idea of ἀφανίζομαι and Moses' disappearance in a cloud or in a ravine. In fact, as Christopher Begg[10]

---

10. "Josephus's Portrayal of the Disappearances of Enoch, Elijah, and Moses: Some Observations," *Journal of Biblical Literature* 109 (1990): 691–93. He refers to G. Lohfink, *Die Himmelfahrt Jesu*, SANT 26 (Munich, 1971) 41 n. 58, 61. Begg

has pointed out, ἀφανίζομαι is used in an almost technical sense by Hellenistic authors when they speak of "Entrückung." The verb is not used in this sense by the New Testament writers, but ἄφαντος ἐγένετο is said of Jesus (Luke 24:31) when he disappeared from the sight of his disciples after the Resurrection.

The cloud that descended on Moses is a symbol for God's presence for Josephus (*Ant.* 3.12.5 § 290, 14.4 § 310) as well as for the New Testament writers—in the Transfiguration episode and also in Acts 1:9 (Christ ascends in a cloud) and Mark 13:26 (cf. Matth. 24:30, 26:64; Luke 21:26: clouds will be his vehicle at his second coming).

The dramatic Old Testament account of Elijah's ascension or assumption is hardly recognizable in Josephus' version (*Ant.* 9.2.2 § 28): "About that time Elijah disappeared from among men, and to this day no one knows his end." Here, the concept of the "return to the divinity" seems conspicuously absent, even though the story, as told in the Old Testament, suggests it as strongly as in the case of Enoch and Moses. Tabor offers several possible reasons for what seems to him a change of approach. But Josephus uses the verb ἀφανίζομαι, as he does when he deals with Moses (in the second passage), in the technical sense of "Entrückung." In other words, even though he leaves out the chariot of fire and the whirlwind, Elijah's departure from this earth is, in fact, a "return to the divinity," and he receives, essentially, the same treatment as Enoch and Moses. It is only a difference in language, I think. Josephus' readers would naturally supply from memory the dramatic details that he omits.

Before we return to the transfiguration of Jesus, it seems worthwhile

---

makes another point which also seems excellent to me: "Josephus's presentation can be understood to mean that, although Moses actually did undergo an *Entrückung,* he chose to describe what happened to him simply as his dying." Why would he do such a thing? Because of his modesty, Begg says, and this must be the right answer. The theme of Moses' modesty runs through Josephus' whole account. Begg refers to Ant. 3.8.8 § 212 and other passages (p. 629 n. 6). If we keep in mind that Moses was, at the same time, the author and the subject of the account found in Deuteronomy, it makes sense that his own modesty would prevent him from "upgrading" his disappearance. Since, as Josephus puts it, Moses "desired in nothing to appear different from the crowd," he also wished to describe himself as sharing the common lot of dying, as Begg remarks. This could be applied to Jesus: he chose to share the common lot of humanity and "taste death," and he did not want people to realize the full meaning of the experience on the mountaintop until after the Resurrection.

to look at the "translation" of Enoch, as interpreted in Hebrews 11:5: "By faith Enoch was placed somewhere else, so that he would not see death.[11] He was not found, because God had placed him somewhere else. Before his being placed somewhere else, there was a testimony that he had pleased God. Without faith, it is impossible to please [him]."

The author of Hebrews uses μετατίθημι, which is sometimes rendered as "to transfer" or "to carry away" or "to take (from this life)." This must be an allusion to Genesis 5:24 (Septuagint) where μετέθηκεν αὐτὸν ὁ θεός translates "God took him." The rendering "to place somewhere else" is a little awkward, I admit, but then the Greek itself is rather awkward or ambiguous, perhaps on purpose. It seems hardly necessary to point out that μετατίθημι here takes the place of Josephus' ἀφανίζομαι as well as his ἀναχωρεῖν πρὸς τό θεῖον. Enoch has disappeared, but he has not died; therefore he must be "somewhere else." But where? And how did he get there? These were things that could not easily be put into words and were better left to speculation; and there was a good deal of speculation, as Tabor (226 n. 3) shows.

There is, however, another aspect to μετάθεσις. Not only does it signify the "removal" or "transfer" or "taking up" of someone like Enoch (cf. Philo *Praem. et poen.* 3.17 on Gen. 5:24), but it may also signify "change," "transformation" (cf. Josephus *Ant.* 15.1 § 9). The verb μετατίθημι is therefore related to the verb μεταμορφόω, used by Mark and Matthew to describe the transfiguration of Jesus, but it would have been less appropriate there, since Jesus was not actually "removed" or "placed elsewhere" at this time. His time had not yet come, and yet the language strongly suggests the possibility of such a "transfer" before the Crucifixion.

It is curious what an important part language, or terminology, plays in these narratives, once they approach the supernatural. The fact that μετατίθημι has two fairly distinct meanings and that μεταμορφόω covers one, but only one, of these meanings, made the latter verb, but not the former, suitable in the context of the Transfiguration. This is an unmistakable clue that, for the Gospel writers, it was natural not only to speak and write but to think in Greek, just as it was for Josephus and Philo.[12]

---

11. The expression "to taste death" occurs in the synoptic Gospels (Mark 9:1; Matth. 16:28; Luke 9:27) in close proximity of the Transfiguration context.

12. On "Jewish Greek" and bilingualism in the first century A.D. see the excellent article of G.H.R. Horsley, in *New Documents Illustrating Early Christianity*, vol. 5 (Macquarie, 1989), 5–40.

We can take it for granted that Jesus and his disciples were familiar with the traditional accounts of the departures of Enoch, Moses, and Elijah. To convey the symbolism, one or two or all three of them might have appeared to Jesus and the three disciples on the mountaintop. Considering the special role that Enoch had for the author of Hebrews, one might wonder why the synoptic Gospels did not include him in the vision. Perhaps a "divine triad"—Moses, Elijah, Jesus—was needed to counterbalance a "human triad"—Peter, John, and James. Or, perhaps, in a sense, Enoch was present in his descendant Jesus (cf. Luke 3:37), just as Elijah was present in John the Baptist. The Book of Enoch is certainly present in the whole narrative. From the material collected by Strack-Billerbeck (on Matth. 16:28–17, 12) I will only mention Jesus' shiny face (Enoch 38:4, after Exod. 34:39ff.; cf. 2 Cor. 3:7), his shiny clothes (Enoch 62:15f.),[13] and Elijah as a symbol of life eternal (Enoch 89:52).[14]

The story of Enoch's "translation," as told in the Septuagint (Gen. 5:24) and as interpreted by the author of Hebrews, foreshadows the transfiguration of Jesus in a striking way. Both Enoch and Jesus were "well pleasing to God." In both instances, "translation" or "transformation" was involved. Jesus is a descendant of Enoch. The Gospel narratives weave allusions to the Book of Enoch into their texture. The implication of the symbolism, the parallels, and the allusions seems to be that Jesus, at this point, is offered a "way out," ἔξοδος, through μετάθεσις or ἀναχώρησις, but he declines, because he must accomplish the other ἔξοδος, the one in Jerusalem, as Luke writes; that is, he must undergo the Passion first, in order to fulfill the prophecies. Moses and Elijah are the emissaries who bring Jesus the offer, and as he turns it down, the voice from the cloud approves.

---

13. D. Hillers refers to Dan. 10:6.

14. There is a list of over sixty possible or probable New Testament allusions to the Book of Enoch in Nestle and Aland, *Novum Testamentum Graece et Latine,* 26th ed. (Stuttgart, 1979), 773–74. It is not as long as the list of allusions to the Book of Daniel, but it is longer than the list s.v. "Malachi." The recent critical editions of the New Testament seem to acknowledge only one direct quotation (Jude 14), but Bowyer's conjecture in 1 Peter 3:19 is virtually certain; the paradosis ἐν ᾧ καὶ τοῖς ἐν φυλακῇ πνεύμασιν πορευθεὶς ἐκήρυξεν makes no sense, and ΕΝΩΚΑΙ for ΕΝΩΧΚΑΙ is a case of haplography. "Enoch went and preached to the spirits in prison" is a clear reference to Enoch 9:10; 10:11–15; 12:4–5. (Harris' ἐν ᾧ καί Ἐνώχ may be an improvement on Bowyer's proposal.) It has been objected that the transition from Jesus to Enoch is forced or abrupt, but this is not true, if we keep in mind, that Jesus was a descendant of Enoch.

It has become clear, I hope, with what extraordinary care the Trans-figuration narratives have been composed. They point backward to the great figures of the Old Testament who "returned to the divinity" with-out having to "taste death"; they point forward to Jesus' own ascension; they skillfully weave the relevant prophecies into their texture. But they also point backward to Jesus' baptism through the theme of the voice from heaven (cf. Matth. 3:17). As the Baptism was the beginning of Jesus' ministry, the Transfiguration might have been its end, had he consented.

The Gospel writers were in a peculiar situation. Unlike Josephus, for example, who dealt with the heros of a golden age or a remote past, they dealt with a historical figure. Jesus' death at the cross was a matter of record, witnessed by Jews, Greeks, and Romans. A full-fledged apotheo-sis at this point would have been a blatant piece of propaganda, quite out of the question. But the offer of another "way out" was a different matter. Not only is Jesus offered this privilege, but he turns it down, confident of his ultimate resurrection and ascension. In having him de-cline this opportunity, the synoptic Gospels rank Jesus with Enoch, Moses, and Elijah in terms of divine favor, without abandoning the historical fact of his death on the cross. If we read the episode in this way, we can only admire the complexity and depth of the idea and the powerful symbolism by which it is conveyed.

The Literary Form of Suetonius' Biographies and the Early Lives of Saints

Of all of Suetonius' works, the *Caesares* were most widely read in late antiquity. In spite of the not very approachable manner of presentation, in spite of the reserve of the author, these portraits are magnificent, and the very mass of facts digested in them is impressive. The private life of Augustus, the last moments of Nero—these are and always will be exciting topics. Suetonius knew how to make the history of the first Roman emperors "interesting."

Unquestionably, Suetonius had a great influence on pagan historiography, and after F. Leo[1] many scholars seem to take the influence of "the Suetonian format" on Christian vitae for granted. In his excellent article on Suetonius in Pauly-Wissowa (*RE* 4A:637) Funaioli says: "So ward zunächst in der Biographie Sueton das Vorbild; bald übernahm diese literarische Gattung direkt oder indirekt von ihm die Form bei Heiden und Christen, bis herab zu Petrarca." This is also the view of W. Steidle[2]: "Dass Suetons Form, die heute als völlig unangemessen für biographische Darstellung angesehen wird, bei Heiden und Christen und bis tief ins Mittelalter hinein grossen Einfluss ausgeübt hat, ist längst festgestellt."

Of certain Christian biographies the handbooks say that they depend on Suetonius. Thus we read in Schanz-Hosius-Krüger[3] that Paulinus' vita of Ambrosius is composed like one of Suetonius' lives of the Caesars. Similarly, Kappelmacher, in his article "Sulpicius Severus" (*RE* 4A:869), declares: "Bei genauer Untersuchung zeigt sich, dass, da überall in den äusseren Werdegang die Wundertaten des Heiligen eingeschaltet werden, sich endlich nur jener Aufbau findet, wie er unter

From *Mullus: Festschrift Theodor Klauser,* ed. Alfred Stuiber and Alfred Hermann, Jahrbuch für Antike und Christentum, Ergänzungsband 1 (Muenster, 1964), 230–41.

1. *Die griechisch-römische Biographie* (1901).
2. *Sueton und die antike Biographie,* Zetemata 1 (1951), 9.
3. *Geschichte der römischen Literatur,* 3d ed., vol. 3 (1922), 65.

anderem auch bei Sueton uns entgegentritt und wie er durch die antike Tradition der Biographie gegeben war."

These statements sound very confident, but they can be disproved by a close examination. The problem of the form of the early lives of saints is not unimportant. Does it really depend on Suetonius?

But first we have to agree on a definition of the "form" of Suetonius biographies. No one will deny that there is such a form. One could also call it a pattern which is not stereotyped but varies considerably from one biography to another. Primarily, it is nothing else but a kind of blueprint designed to collect information, a depository, a system of drawers into which facts can be stored conveniently. The difference between Suetonius and Tacitus is that Suetonius barely makes an effort to hide this pattern while Tacitus' artistic conscience protests against such a convenience. Suetonius may have believed that the information he had collected was so interesting that no reorganization was needed, while for Tacitus, the historian's job began when all the facts were well arranged.

The pattern reveals itself most distinctly in the vita of Augustus, which may be considered typical for all of Suetonius' biographies. Here, he has digested an unusual amount of primary sources and secondary material; in the other vitae he has not always worked quite so hard.

Once we understand the structure of the vita of Augustus, we know what the "Suetonian form" is. The structure itself is simple enough, but it is obliterated, to some extent, by the standard division into chapters which is based on Erasmus' Basel edition of 1518. Therefore, it has never been described accurately in all details. We can only understand certain contexts if we disregard the division into chapters and paragraphs found in both older and more recent editions. Since Leo followed W.L. Schmidt,[4] who, in turn, based his conclusions on the traditional arrangement, Leo's theories must be examined critically. Any scholar who would be willing to revise, following certain clues in the *Codex Memmianus*, the main witness of the *Caesares*, the conventional arrangement into chapters and paragraphs, would deserve our gratitude. What he should keep in mind is the fact that Suetonius very often—as observed by Schmidt—hints at a section's main content in the first word or the first few words of the section.

In the vita of Augustus, chapters 1–4 *(gentem Octaviam)* deal with the family of the future emperor. His birth is told in chapters 5–6 *(natus est Augustus)*; his early childhood, in chapter 7 *(infanti)*; his early manhood

---

4. "De Romanorum imprimis Suetonii arte biographica" (Diss., Marburg, 1891).

until Caesar's assassination, in chapter 8. What follows is a kind of preview of his long reign. In a programmatic statement frequently discussed (*proposita vitae eius velut summa partes singillatim neque per tempora sed per species exequar, quo distinctius demonstrari cognoscique possint*), Suetonius announces the transition of his text from a chronological narrative to a presentation *per species*, that is, according to categories. For him, these are two different but equally valid methods of writing a biography. What he means by *singillatim* can be seen from *Tiberius* 42.1, where he first speaks of the ruler's vices in general and adds *de quibus singillatim ab exordio referam*; we also may compare 61.2: *singillatim crudeliter facta eius exequi longum est: genera, velut exemplaria saevitiae, enumerare sat erit.* Another example is *Claudius* 29.1: *ne singillatim minora quoque enumerem.* Thus, while he chooses for Augustus a presentation *per species* (κατ᾽εἴδη)—that is, he proceeds *singillatim*—he prefers for Tiberius' monstrosities an account *per genera* (κατὰ γένη), avoiding too many details. Of course, it is the presentation *per species* in the vita of Augustus which allows the author to display an abundance of material, a wealth of concrete detail. Perhaps there is no criterion which would allow us to distinguish, in the biographic tradition, between *species* and *genera*; the distinction itself probably derives from the school of Aristotle.

In the following section of the vita of Augustus, we find the *species* into which Suetonius divides Augustus' deeds.[5] Chapters 9–19 (*bella civilia*) deal with the Roman civil wars; chapters 20–23, with wars against foreign powers (*externa bella*). Chapters 24–25 (*in re militari*) give a sketch of military organization. Chapters 26–28.2 (*magistratus atque honores*) deal with offices and honors;[6] 18.3–34 (*urbem*), with the administration of Rome in a broader sense; 34 (*leges*), with the laws he enacted; 35–38.2 (*senatorum*), with measures concerning the Senate; 38.3–40.1 (*equitum*), with measures concerning the knights;[7] 40.2–45 (*populi*), with measures concerning the people[8]—this includes games in the theaters and the circus. After this, in chapters 46–50, Suetonius turns to measures concerning Italy and the provinces, but they are introduced not in the keyword

---

5. The first sentence of chap. 9, the transition mentioned earlier, is actually a kind of *praefatio*; a new chapter should begin with *bella civilia*.

6. A new chapter should begin with 28.3.

7. This is the beginning of a new section; after the Senate, the knights are dealt with as another power group.

8. The same principle as in n. 7 applies here: after the Senate and the knights, Suetonius deals with the people. Chap. 40.2 (*populi*) forms a caesura; the new section extends as far as chap. 45.

style but by a kind of recapitulation: *ad hunc modum urbe urbanisque rebus administratis Italiam duodetriginta coloniarum numero deductarum a se frequentavit.* What follows (chap. 47) is, once more, introduced by a keyword *(provincias).* Clearly, Suetonius' structure reflects the political structure of the empire.

Suetonius now describes Augustus' character and personality; he emphasizes two qualities, *clementia* and *civilitas*,[9] thus explaining the ruler's great popularity.

A new section is prefaced in a slightly cumbersome manner: *quoniam qualis in imperiis ac magistratibus regendaque per terrarum orbem pace belloque re publica fuerit, exposui, referam nunc interiorem ac familiarem eius vitam quibusque moribus atque fortuna domi et inter suos egerit a iuventa usque ad supremum vitae diem.* Here, we learn details of Augustus' private life. His father is no longer mentioned; his mother and sister are mentioned only briefly (chap. 61.2), followed by his wives, his daughter, his step-son (chap. 62.3), the grandchildren (chap. 64). Then there is a brief diatribe on the topic *sed laetum eum atque fidentem et subole et disciplina domus Fortuna destituit* (chap. 65), which culminates in a deeply moving quotation from the *Iliad* and reveals the tragic personal life of the emperor. After the members of his family, his friends are introduced (chap. 66, *amicitias*), then the slaves, freedmen, and clients (chap. 67, *patronus dominusque*). Thus, the structure of Suetonius' presentation here reflects the social structure of the commonwealth, just as chapters 35–50 reflected its political structure.

The following sections could be furnished with the heading *vitia*. The real or supposed transgressions of Augustus are partly told in the form of rumor, to be withdrawn halfheartedly almost at once. Suetonius does not take a firm stand, but, personally, he seems to believe at least some of the rumors,[10] for instance, rumors involving Augustus' sexual relationships with men and women (chaps. 68–69), certain secret banquets which the emperor sponsored, and gambling, for which Augustus had a passion (chap. 70). At the end of the section (chap. 71), Suetonius leaves open the question whether all of this should be called *crimina* or *maledicta;* the emperor is said to have led an impeccable life in later years,

---

9. This pair of qualities is important for the imperial ideology; see the excellent remarks of Steidle (66) and those of L. Wickert in his outstanding article "Princeps," *RE* 22: 2231–48.

10. His attitude as far as Titus is concerned is equally vague; see my article in *Rhein. Mus.* 107 (1964) 203–15.

though he never gave up gambling and in fact openly admitted to this addiction.

After a few concluding remarks—*in ceteris partibus vitae continentis-simum constat ac sine suspicione ullius vitii*—Suetonius deals with the various houses which Augustus inhabited over the years, their furniture, his clothes (chaps. 72–73, organized according to the keywords *habitavit* and *suppellectilis*, then *veste*).[11] Sections on meals and invitations on normal days and on festivals follow (chaps. 74–77, *convivabatur*); then we hear about his looks, appearance, and health (chaps. 79–80, *forma* and *corpore*), then about his illnesses (chaps. 81–82, *graves et periculosas valetudines*), sports (chap. 83, *exercitationes*), education and intellectual pursuits (chaps. 84–89, *eloquentiam studiaque liberalia*), and attitude toward religion and popular beliefs (chaps. 90–93, *circa religiones talem accepimus*).

As a kind of appendix to this section *(et quoniam ad haec ventum est, non ab re fuerit subtexere)*, Suetonius devotes some space to a topic that is of particular interest to him, the supernatural signs which predicted the greatness and the success of the future emperor before his birth, on the day of his birth, and since then (chaps. 94–96). He found the individual events in various authors, which means that he had opened up, as he did his research, a file entitled *omina et portenta;* but the arrangement and interpretation are his own work.

The words *mors quoque eius, de qua dehinc dicam, divinitasque post mortem evidentissimis ostentis praecognita est* look like a somewhat forced transition, but the biographer had to pick up the chronological thread which goes through chapters 97–101 at a certain point. There are two subsections, it would seem: *supremo die* and *testamentum.*

This, I think, is the skeleton of this most important and probably most widely read Suetonian biography. In view of the many facts and events which had to be told in order to produce a portrait of Augustus' personality, the author has subdivided both the official and the private sphere of the ruler into a number of subsections and has filed his material under the appropriate headings.

A similar principle is found in all the other biographies, even when there is much less material to digest, as, for instance, in the vita of Titus.[12] The biography of Titus, who ruled only for a short time, is not very rich in details; thus it was relatively easy to survey and organize the

---

11. Here I would within the chapter, even though it is so brief, begin a new section and treat 72 and 73 as one chapter.

12. See my article in *Rhein. Mus.,* cited in n. 10.

material, and the main categories offered themselves, so to speak. The order adopted is mainly chronological until Titus' accession to the throne, with the exception of the list of his physical and intellectual qualities in chapter 3. This sequence is followed by the headings *vitia* (chaps. 6–7.1), *virtutes* (chaps. 7.2–8.2), *fortuna, tristia, adversa* (chaps. 8.3–9.3); then comes the account of his death. A rapid examination of the structure shows once more how misleading the division in chapters in our editions is.[13]

We now have an idea of the typical form or format of Suetonius' biographies. Is it really true that the Christian hagiographers were strongly influenced by it?

Following F. Leo, F. Kemper ("De vitarum Cypriani, Martini Turonensis, Ambrosii, Augustini rationibus" [Diss., Münster, 1904]) has discussed this problem and has found the answers which were accepted by the handbooks, as mentioned earlier. As often happens, a few good observations and valid insights were generalized and exaggerated.

A few years later, H. Mertel, also following Leo, devoted his dissertation, "Die biographische Form der griechischen Heiligenlegenden" (Diss., Munich, 1909), to the same problems. He concluded that the Greek hagiographers had taken Plutarch as their model, and his opinion found its way into the handbooks and was accepted or at least considered seriously by scholars such as Krüger and Norden. It was K. Holl who protested, in an outstanding article entitled "Die schriftstellerische Form des griechischen Heiligenlebens,"[14] against this oversimplified and slightly biased view of things. Following Holl, S. Cavallin, in his important monograph *Literarhistorische und textkritische Studien zur "Vita S. Caesarii Arelatensis"* (1936), warned (6) against the careless use of convenient terms such as "peripatetisch-plutarchisch" and "alexandrinisch-suetonisch." He was right when he wrote, "Es sollte doch selbstverständlich sein, dass nur Sondermerkmale der suetonischen oder plutarchischen Form uns das Recht geben könnten, Plutarch oder Sueton als die Vorbilder der christlichen Biographie aufzustellen." On the other hand, Cavallin himself seems to admit (26) a "literary form" which was created for purposes such as those of some hagiographies, a form which began to "dissolve" at a relatively late stage, that is, with the vita of Caesarius of Arles. Thus, Cavallin does not deny the

---

13. Ibid.

14. First published in *Neue Jahrbücher Klass. Altert.* 15 (1912), 406ff.; reprinted in *Gesammelte Aufsätze zur Kirchengeschichte,* 3d ed. (1927), 249ff.

existence of this form *before* the Caesarius vita. Most of the biographies that we are concerned with in this context were composed before the form was "dissolved." These are Pontius' *Life of Cyprian*, the *Life of Martin* by Sulpicius Severus, the *Life of Ambrosius* by Paulinus, and Possidius' *Life of Augustine*. Only Eugippius' *Life of Severinus* belongs in the period of "dissolution." We shall see that it fits the description, but Cavallin does not deal with it.

Thanks to the work done by M. Pellegrino,[15] the structure of the vitae just mentioned is much better understood today. In *Studies in Honor of Funaioli* (1955), he formulated a number of problems and indicated various possibilities of dealing with them (354–59). He also edited several biographies, with Italian translations, notes, and substantial introductions. In his edition of Pontius' *Life of Cyprian* (Edizioni Paoline, 1955), he gives a useful survey of the development of Christian biographies (7–33), but he only deals marginally with our problem.

Let us begin with the *Vita S. Cypriani*, the oldest Christian biography preserved.[16] Does it have a structure comparable to one of Suetonius' biographies? As noted by Jerome (*De vir. ill.* 68)—he addresses the work as *egregium volumen*—it has two main parts: (1) *vita;* (2) *passio*.[17] These two sections can be further divided as follows: (1) *vita* (chaps. 1–10), (a) preface (chap. 1), (b) beginning of his life as a Christian (chaps. 2–4), (c) election as bishop (chap. 5), (d) pastoral office, justification of his flight (chaps. 6–10); (2) *passio* (chaps. 11–19), (a) exile (chaps. 11–14), (b) arrest (chap. 15), (c) confession and conviction (chaps. 16–17), (d) execution and epilogue (chaps. 18–19).[18]

The structure is practical and, in its symmetry, not without elegance. But it is not the structure of a Suetonian biography. On the whole, Pontius follows the chronological order, but he does not begin with the actual birth of Cyprian: *hominis facta non debent aliunde numerari nisi ex quo Deo natus est* (2.1). What counts for the biographer is the *secunda genitura,* also called *caelestis nativitas;* he is not interested in the time before the conversion. This is why we know practically nothing about this period in the life of Cyprian.

---

15. For the references to Pellegrino I am indebted to the kindness of my colleague, Wolfgang Schmid.

16. A. Harnack, *Texte und Untersuchungen* 39, no. 3 (1913): 33.

17. A. Harnack, *Geschichte der altchristlichen Literatur bis Eusebius,* 2d ed., vol. 2, pt. 2 (repr., 1958), 367.

18. Harnack, *Texte und Untersuchungen,* 57.

Eugippius, on the other hand, would like to know something about the origins, the birthplace, of St. Severinus (see *Commemoratorium Vitae S. Severini* praef. 7: *sane patria de qua fuerit oriundus, fortasse necessario a nobis inquiritur, unde, sicut moris est, texendae cuiuspiam vitae sumatur exordium*), but he is unable to find out any details, for Severinus used to avoid such questions amiably, sometimes jokingly, but always firmly (8–10), and there was no one else who knew anything definite. There were no memoirs, no records, no archives for a biographer to do his research.

Without such archives, without large libraries, Suetonius could not have written his *Caesares*. The Christian biographers mainly report what they heard and saw themselves or what they heard from others. They are witnesses, or they had spoken to other witnesses. Their work is, in an essential sense, a testimony.

In the records Suetonius uses—that is, in the memoirs, histories, monographs, and political pamphlets of a past age—he finds many points of view, many interests which have to be balanced against each other. For the Christian biographers, there was only one point of view. Under certain circumstances, he might look at official documents or similar records; thus, Pontius, even though he was an eyewitness of Cyprianus' *passio*, had an opportunity to see the *Acta Proconsularia*, that is, the interrogation records which are preserved.[19]

Unlike Suetonius, the Christian biographer, as a rule, is barely interested in the secular παιδεία of his saint. In other words, a rubric typical for Suetonius is omitted or only referred to very briefly. Pontius has something to say concerning this, almost as if he wanted to stress the difference between his hagiography and the standards of pagan biography: *fuerint licet studia et bonae artes devotum pectus imbuerint, tamen illa praetereo: nondum enim ad utilitatem nisi saeculi pertinebant*. Thus he seems to recognize this particular biographical rubric as such, although he says, at the same time, that it does not concern him. It would be paradoxical to say that this remark proves influence of the "Suetonian form." He obviously thinks of readers who might be interested in this aspect, but to him this is not a legitimate interest. Even to Cyprian's spiritual παιδεία he grants little space, pleading the limits of his own knowledge: *postquam et sacras litteras didicit et mundi nube discussa in lucem sapientiae spiritalis emersit, si quibus eius interfui <vel> si qua de antiquioribus comperi, dicam.*[20]

---

19. H. v. Soden, *Texte und Untersuchungen* 25, no. 3 (1904): 232.

20. Something is missing in the text; Harnack assumed a lacuna after *emersit*; perhaps all we need is *vel* before the second *si*.

Clearly, two categories important to Suetonius, γένος and παιδεία, are treated as secondary and their role in proportion to the whole biography is entirely different. There are some remarks concerning Cyprian's ἦϑος in chapter 6, after he has been elected bishop, but they are very brief and not as concrete as what Suetonius has to say on appearance and clothing.

Our analysis of this—to us—oldest Christian biography seems to confirm the verdict of K. Holl (*Neue Jahrbücher,* 412): "Plutarch unterbaut seine Lebensbeschreibung mit einer eingehenden Schilderung des Charakters und der Umstände, unter denen sein Held geboren wurde. Er sammelt diesen Stoff so vollständig wie irgend möglich. Auch kleine Züge sind ihm bedeutsam, wenn sie nur auf die Persönlichkeit ein Licht werfen. Denn für ihn ist der Lebenslauf nur die Entfaltung desjenigen, was von Anfang an in dem Menschen liegt. Er hat seine künstlerische Aufgabe um so besser gelöst, je restloser er den fertigen Mann und sein Schicksal aus den gegebenen Bedingungen ableiten kann."

What is true for Plutarch is not necessarily true for Suetonius or is true only in a limited way. Suetonius may have an artistic temperament—this would be difficult to deny—but he reveals few artistic ambitions. Perhaps it was more difficult for a Roman to paint a portrait rich in details and nuances yet forming a unit. An effort in this direction may be detected in the vita of Julius Caesar, although the differences are striking if one contrasts his biography with the one by Plutarch. Both authors actually have the same goal: they want to present a person as he really was, no matter whether he was good or evil. The Christian biographer, on the other hand, whether his name be Pontius or Athanasius, omits in the portrait of his hero, as Holl (loc. cit.) put it, all features which make him an individual; they are, for him, accidental, irrelevant. He wants to draw an ideal life, an ideal development, as a model for others.

No doubt Pontius knows the categories of Suetonian biographies, but he has no use for them. One should not be deceived by apparent analogies. An example follows: Pontius reports a dream of Cyprian which foreshadows his imminent death (chap. 12.3–9); this is something Suetonius would report too. Cyprian dreams that a youth of superhuman size comes to him and leads him before the chair of the proconsul in the Praetorium. The Roman official writes the judgment on a tablet, without saying a word. The youth who now stands behind the proconsul reads the judgment and silently makes the gesture of cutting off one's head. Cyprian told this dream to his companions when they went into exile. The narrative itself and the circumstances leave not the slightest doubt that this is exactly what happened. Under the pressure of constant dangers and threats, Cyprian must have had a precognition of his martyrdom. He desires it, yet he cannot abandon his congregation. No one will deny that this emotional conflict could take shape in a dream. Therefore we may exclude the possibility that this is a literary motif treated in the manner of Suetonius. Moreover, in a Christian biography, a dream like this does not have the meaning it would have in a pagan author. For Pontius and the whole congregation, this dream was sent by God, because he wanted to prepare Cyprian for martyrdom. Thus, the reader knows at once that Cyprian went to heaven.[21]

Suetonius, on the other hand, personally believed in the validity of certain dreams and used them in his biographies. He himself and many of his pagan readers were familiar with the idea of a great cosmic συμπάθεια which coordinates, so to speak, dreams and other premonitions with the events that follow. This συμπάθεια makes dreams and other relevant signs possible. The idea is characteristic for Middle and Late Stoicism.

The vita of Cyprian has been called an encomium, for example, by Kemper ("De vitarum Cypriani") and by R. Reitzenstein.[22] I am not sure that much is to be gained by deriving a Christian biography from other literary genres before its peculiarities are described exactly. It is true that Pontius' work here and there resembles an encomium, especially at the beginning; but it is more than that. Even Harnack,[23] in his rather harsh verdict, seems to admit this: "Die Schrift, obgleich ein Panegyricus im schlechten Stil des Zeitalters, ist für die Biographie Cyprians von höchstem Wert und überall in historischen Dingen, soweit wir sie zu kontrollieren vermögen, zuverlässig." If it were only a panegyric and nothing else, historical truth would not be its main concern. Edward Gibbon (Decline and Fall of the Roman Empire [1776–88], chap. 16) considered it a kind of apology: "Pontius labours with the greatest care and diligence to justify his master against the general censure." This applies to chaps. 7–8, where the biographer explains why Cyprian postponed his martyrdom by his escape. But it would be a mistake to consider this explanation the main motif of the whole work. Pontius simply states the less obvious reasons for this decision, as Cyprian may have told them himself.

---

21. On the vita of Antonius see Holl 410.
22. Sitzungsberichte Heidelberg (1913), 52f.
23. Geschichte der altchristlichen Literatur, 367.

More than a century after the vita of Cyprian, the lives of Martin, Ambrosius, and Augustine are written in fairly rapid sequence. Let us look first at Sulpicius Severus, the biographer of the bishop of Tours. Because of his elegant style, he has always received good grades as a writer, ever since Scaliger called him *ecclesiasticorum purissimus scriptor.* Gibbon (*ibid.*), on the other hand, felt that an author who was such a good stylist had no right to be so uncritical: "The Life of St. Martin, and the Dialogues concerning his miracles, contain facts adapted to the grossest barbarism, in a style not unworthy of the Augustan age. So natural is the alliance between good taste and good sense, that I am always astonished by the contrast." The verdict of Adolf von Harnack[24] is essentially the same: "Die Biographie ist ein Heiligenbild, entworfen in dem massiven Wunderglauben der Zeit; es fehlen ihr aber doch sehr charakteristische historische Züge nicht ganz." In his view, this biography is comparable to one of *Vitae Patrum,* if one discounts the elegance of the language and the style.

What seems dangerous to me is to take the miracles out of the context and look, in what remains, for the outlines of a Suetonian biography. But the miraculous stories are, in the Christian biographical tradition, not just an appendix. Holl (410) has shown this in the case of Athanasius. Through these stories, the biographer affirms that he is telling the life of a genuine saint: ". . . der Legendenschreiber will durch sein Werk nicht müssige Stunden des Lesers ausfüllen, sondern ihn dazu ermuntern, den betreffenden Heiligen als Fürsprecher anzugehen." The kind of superficial approach against which this criticism is directed may find in any biography, ancient or modern, a "Suetonian structure."

Sulpicius almost certainly knew the *Caesares.* In his important monograph *Ueber die Chronik des Sulpicius Severus* (1861; reprinted in *Gesammelte Abhandlungen,* ed. H. Usener [1885], 2; 81ff.), Jacob Bernays has shown that Sulpicius knew Sallust and Tacitus and that in fourth-century Gaul such authors as Velleius Paterculus were read in schools.[25] Even so, an analysis of the *Vita S. Martini* shows that the *Caesares* are irrelevant for its structure and format. It is of no use to cite chap. 1.7, *igitur Sancti Martini vitam scribere exordiar, ut se vel ante episcopatum vel in*

---

24. *Realencycl. protest. Theol. und Kirche,* 3d ed., vol. 19 (1907), 158.

25. It is generally recognized that Bernays (*Ueber die Chronik,* 53ff. = *Ges. Abh.,* 2: 167ff.) was able to prove—brilliantly, I think—that Sulpicius used Tacitus' lost account of the sack of Jerusalem.

episcopatu gesserit, for this programmatic statement does not reveal the structure of the work. The author informs us of Martin's birth, his education, and his military career (chap. 2.1ff.) and then describes the character of the young man, but what he says toward the end (chap. 27) on Martin's ἦθος in later years is more relevant.

In his note on chapter 27 of Suetonius' *Augustus,* Casaubonus (1595) observed that the well-known transition from public life to *interior ac familiaris vita* has a parallel in Sulpicius (chap. 26.2: *interiorem vitam illius et conversationem cotidianam et animum caelo semper intentum nulla umquam—vere profiteor—nulla explicabit oratio*). Later on, we find this transition once again in Eginhard's *Vita Caroli Magni.* Actually, Sulpicius' attitude is the same as Pontius': he acknowledges the existence of this distinction in the pagan biographical tradition but does not adopt it himself; he says, in fact, that it would be impossible to do justice to this particular aspect of Martin's life. Suetonius, too, faced an overabundance of things to tell, but it was his particular skill not to give up altogether but to make a judicious selection, and he succeeded again and again in bringing a person to life in a few words.

It is sufficient to look at the connection between certain sections in Sulpicius work to realize how its structure differs from that of Suetonius' *Caesares.* Miracles, for instance, are sometimes introduced by *eodem tempore* (chap. 17.1) or *per id tempus* (chap. 17.5) or *sub idem fere tempus* (chap. 9.1) or *nec multo post* (chap. 8.1). Sometimes the name of a person or a place serves as the keyword for another section (chaps. 18.3, 19.1, 19.3). No attempt is made to organize Martin's activities as bishop, whereas Suetonius characterizes Augustus' administration brilliantly with a few broad strokes. Individual episodes are juxtaposed without any plausible connection or transition, and a theme that emerges somehow from the narrative serves as an introduction to the next pericope. Chapter 22.6 is a good example: *et quia de diabolo eiusdemque artibus sermo exortus est, non ab re videtur, licet extrinsecus, referre quod gestum est, quia et quaedam in eo Martini virtutum portio est et res digna miraculo recte memoriae mandabitur, in exemplum cavendi, si quid deinceps uspiam tale contigerit.*

Paulinus, the biographer of Ambrosius, acknowledges as his models the vita of Antonius by Athanasius, the *Vita Pauli* by Jerome (which also shows the influence of the Greek text just mentioned)[26] and

---

26. See R. Reitzenstein, *Hellenistische Wundererzählungen* (1906), 62f. and 8off.; but he emphasizes too much one side of the problem, I feel.

Sulpicius' biography of Martin. Paulinus composed this work[27] at the request of Augustine. Cavallin's careful analysis (*Studien*) shows that the author was actually guided by the models he mentions and that Suetonius' influence is negligible.[28] Paulinus calls his work a *narratio* (chap. 2). Suetonius uses the verb *narrare* for his own work as a biographer, for example, at *Caligula* 22.1: *hactenus quasi de principe, reliqua ut de monstro narranda sunt.*

As far as chronology is concerned, Paulinus is "almost pedantic," according to Cavallin (16). But Cavallin seems to base his judgment on stereotypic introductions, such as *per idem tempus* (e.g., chaps. 14, 17, 21, 24, 25, 39, etc.), or he uses an ablative absolute as a connecting device. Here, I disagree with Cavallin. Such a way of dating an event always remains a little vague.

Cavallin has observed that the chronological account of Ambrosius' life (chapter 2 relates his γένος; chapter 5, his παιδεία) is interrupted by chapter 38, the description of his ἦθος which continues until chapter 41; with chapter 42 the chronological narrative resumes. This is essentially correct, but Paulinus anticipates, in chapter 36, an event which happened after Ambrosius' death. Chapter 37 follows, introduced by the phrase *temporibus vero Gratiani, ut retro redeam,* then, as already mentioned, we are told about his ἦθος in chaps. 38ff. Here, Paulinus also has something to say about Ambrosius as an author, but mainly in connection with the *diligentia* which Ambrosius devoted to ecclesiastical affairs.

The same reserve may be noticed in the vita of Augustine. Both saints are represented primarily as churchmen, not as authors. They used the written word as one vehicle among others to reach the largest possible number of faithful. Paulinus reports in great detail the funeral of the bishop of Milan and the miracles that happened after his death, such as the whining demons who complained that they were tortured by the proximity of Ambrosius' mortal remains and could not stand it any more.

At the very beginning of his work, Augustine's favorite disciple, who died after 437, defines his task, and in doing so, he borrows from a passage of *de civitate Dei* (as documented by Pellegrino, in his commentary, ad loc.): *de praedicti venerabilis viri et exortu et procursu et debito fine,*

---

27. Incidentally, this is not Paulinus' only work, as H. v. Campenhausen, *Die Religion in Ge   'e und Gegenwart*, 3d ed., vol. 5 [1961], 165) says; see the same author, *RE* 18, no. 2 (1958): 2331.

28. Campenhausen (loc. cit.) does not think Suetonius' influence very likely.

quae per eum didici et expertus sum, quam plurimis annis eius inhaerens caritati, ut Dominus donaverit explicandum suscepi (preface 3). His narrative proceeds at first *per tempora*, and Augustine's παιδεία is taken care of right at the beginning (chap. 1.1–2). In the first part of the biography (chaps. 1–17) the emphasis is definitely on Augustine's fight against the heretics. He must have talked about this many times to his disciple. At the end of this part, there is a recapitulation of his activities as bishop and author; but here, too, his literary work is seen as a kind of extension of his ecclesiastical office: *et erat ille memorabilis vir praecipuum dominici corporis membrum, circa universalis ecclesiae utilitates sollicitus semper ac pervigil.* He adds that Augustine wrote so many works that it was almost impossible to read them all.[29]

In the second part (chaps. 19–27.5), Possidius deals with the *interior ac familiaris vita.* Here, one senses, perhaps, the influence of Suetonius. The individual features are so telling that they seem to anticipate the curiosity of a large reading public—just like certain details in the *Caesares.* We are told what clothes Augustine wore; that wine was always served at his table, meat only occasionally; and that during meals it was strictly forbidden to say anything negative about persons who were absent.[30] We

---

29. At the end of the first part of his vita of Augustine, Possidius tells the reader how to obtain the writings of the church father. It seems worthwhile to look at this passage, because it is an important testimony for the dissemination of texts in late antiquity. I understand it as follows: If one wished to read a particular work of Augustine's, one had to get in touch with the library of the church in Hippo, which had an *exemplar emendatius.* This was sent to the petitioner, who then had it copied. For this he had to pay a fee; Possidius says pointedly, *qui magis Dei veritatem quam temporales amant divitias.* Moreover, he was under obligation to lend his own copy to others. This had the advantage for the library in Hippo that it did not always have to send out its own copy; instead, it could give an address where a copy of the work in question was available; this would have been someone who already had his own copy and did not live too far from the new petitioner. Hence, the library must have kept a list of all those who owned copies of individual works of Augustine. Based on this list, the librarians were able to decide whether it was necessary to send out their own copy. As time went by, the library had to send out fewer and fewer copies of its own, which helped limit the risks. Augustine was very anxious—as Pellegrino, with a reference to *Epist.* 147, has shown—that all copies were made from an archetype that he himself had authorized; see H.-I. Marrou, *Vigiliae Christianae,* vol. 3 (1949), 220f.

30. This was prohibited *expressis verbis* by an inscription in the dining room. If someone ignored it, Augustine became cross and said that the inscription would have to be deleted or he would have to leave the room.

are also told that no persons of the female sex were allowed to live in the house, that Augustine never was alone in a room with a woman, and that he visited convents only when there was an urgent reason. These bits of information are quite remarkable, considering the rather stiff, almost official character of the rest of the biography.

As in Suetonius' vita of Augustus, the *vita domestica* of Augustine is followed by an account of his last years and his death. We may, therefore, speak of an arrangement *per species* (Kemper 49; cf. Pellegrino, Einleitung 24), but the attempt to divide the whole work into two sections, *vita publica* and *vita privata*, as Kemper (38ff.) has done, referring to Suetonius (46), seems questionable. The division into three parts suggested by Pellegrino (21) makes much more sense. The middle section, however, shows the influence of Suetonius.

Finally, there is Eugippius' vita of Severinus, sent in 611 to Paschasius, the Roman deacon. No one would doubt its value as a historical document: it is an eyewitness account from a period which has left practically no other written records. In it we relive the years following Attila's last campaign in Italy; we see the weakening of the Roman defenses along the Danube and the gradual crumbling of the Roman administration. In this period of anxiety, a strong personality such as Severinus assumes the role of leadership, in the secular, as well as in the spiritual, domain. In the midst of the dissolution of the old order, he seems to be the only one who has a clear picture of the situation, anticipates future developments, and calmly makes decisions.

Eugippius had at least two literary models: Sulpicius Severus (chap. 36.3) and Paulinus (chap. 36.2). Of the "Suetonian form," there is very little left, as the connections between certain sections show. There is the temporal connection, as in Sulpicius Severus: *per idem tempus* (chaps. 4, 20, 28, etc.), *eodem tempore* or *isdem temporibus* (chaps. 3, 27, 32, etc.), or *post haec* or simply *alio rursus tempore*. This type of format seems natural for someone who writes from memory, not for an author who has done research in archives and libraries. There are also local connections, (e.g., *accidit etiam eiusdem loci*), and sometimes the name of a person who came into contact with Severinus appears rather abruptly at the beginning of a section. This, too, seems characteristic for a work based on recollections: a name or a face emerges in the author's memory, and this name or face suggests a story. This is the way it happens in conversations, and these Christian biographies are essentially the continuation, in writing, of conversations in which the faithful wished to hear more about the life of a person they revered.

Notes on the *Vita Macrinae* of Gregory of Nyssa

Gregory's *Letter Concerning the Life of St. Macrina*[1]—this is the title which the work has in the manuscript tradition—seems a rather unusual biography from various points of view. To explain its unusual character, it is necessary first to consider some other Christian biographies. The fact that a brother—a brother who is a saint—records the life of his saintly sister has parallels in the funeral oration of Gregory of Nazianzus in honor of his sister, Gorgonia,[2] and in the funeral orations of Ambrosius on his brother Satyrus.[3]

It is noteworthy that Gregory of Nazianzus finds it necessary to begin his speech with an elaborate apology.[4] He is fully aware that he is honoring his own family by praising his sister, but the truth (so he says) must be told, and the fact that he was related to this remarkable woman should not present an obstacle.

Gregory of Nyssa does not feel the need for an apology of this kind. One feels throughout his letter that he is proud of his sister and that he is enjoying this opportunity to write about her and about his family.

In a sense, the *Vita Macrinae* can be considered a piece of propaganda, but other vitae of saints serve the purposes of polemic and propaganda in the best sense of the word. Thus Possidius, in his *Life of St. Augustine*,[5] attacks the Manichaeans, the Arians, the Pelagians, the

---

From *The Biographical Works of Gregory of Nyssa*, ed. Andreas Spira, 21–32 (1984).

1. Throughout this essay I am quoting from the edition of P. Maraval, *SC* 178 (Paris, 1971).

2. Greg. Naz., *PG* 35.790–814. Cf. *Funeral Orations by St. Gregory Nazianzen and St. Ambrose*, trans. Roy J. Deferrari and others, in *Fathers of the Church*, vol. 22 (New York, 1935).

3. S. Ambrosii *De obitu Satyri fratris*, ed. B. Albers (Bonn, 1921 = *Florileg. Patrist.* 15); *Funeral Orations*, 159ff.

4. *V. Gorg.* 1f.

5. Possidius, *PL* 32.33–66, esp. 40, 46. Cf. *Early Christian Biographies*, trans.

Donatists; and Athanasius, in his *Life of Antony*,[6] attacks Arians and pagans.

Generally speaking, the biographers have been close to the men and women whose memories they preserve. A disciple writes about the life of his teacher—Pontius on Cyprianus, Paulinus on Ambrosius, Possidius on Augustine, Hilarius on Honoratus, who was also a relative. Gregory emphasizes the fact that Macrina was not only his sister but his teacher as well.[7]

This personal contact may be the reason why many of the lives of saints have a quality of immediacy which one does not find in other ancient biographies, for instance, Suetonius' *Caesares*, whose structure has been discussed so often. Christian vitae are very often based on personal knowledge, and they are usually composed very soon after the death of the person they honor. This is almost certain for the *Vita Macrinae*, which was composed in 380, the very year of Macrina's death, it seems.[8] Hilarius' sermon on Honoratus was probably delivered on the first anniversary of his death.[9] The first of Ambrosius' two funeral orations on his brother was delivered at his funeral; the second, a week later.[10] The first is more personal; the second, rather formal, reminiscent of the style of a *consolatio*.

Here, I think, we have an essential difference between hagiography and pagan biographies. Suetonius draws from historical works, from memoirs, letters; he writes his *Life of Julius Caesar* long after Caesar's death. Gregory, on the other hand, knew the subject of his biography personally and wrote soon after her death. Jerome could not write about Hilarion from his own experience, but at least he was able to use the work of Epiphanius, who had known Hilarion well.[11] On the other hand, Jerome makes it quite clear that he had learned Malchus' life story from Malchus himself and introduces as the speaker an old monk whom he had visited in Syria.[12] Formally, this is unique, I think: a fictitious

---

Roy J. Deferrari and others, in *Fathers of the Church*, vol. 15 (New York, 1952).

6. Athanasius *V. Antonii*, PG 26.835–976, esp. chaps. 33, 69; *Early Christian Biographies*, 69ff.

7. *V. Macr.* 19; cf. p. 272, n. 1, in Maraval's edition.

8. See Maraval's preface, pp. 57ff.

9. PL 50.1249–72; *Early Christian Biographies*, 355ff.

10. Cf. n. 3; *Early Christian Biographies*, 355ff.

11. Jerome's *Vitae Patrum* are to be found in PL 23.18–62; *Early Christian Biographies*, 241ff.

12. *V. Malchi* 1f.

autobiography with a brief introduction and an even briefer epilogue; there seem to be no parallels in pagan biography, as far as I know.[13]

It goes without saying that Gregory's *Vita Macrinae* contains a good deal of autobiographical material, but it is not allowed to dominate the account of his sister's life.

Generally speaking, the early biographers of saints were specially qualified, because of their personal relationship with their subject, to write a vita, and this vita had an authority, an immediate recognition which was hardly ever contested. These hagiographers were, in fact, specialists because they were in a position to record events, anecdotes, sayings which nobody else could know. In this respect, Jerome, once more, is an exception: In the preface to his vita of Hilarion,[14] he complains bitterly that his biography of the hermit Paul was attacked by some critics. It appears that this genus appealed to Jerome and that he turned it, so to speak, into a literary cottage industry. The fact that he produced all these lives of saints, almost like a series, turning hagiography into a minor literary industry, may have created some enemies, because the individual vita could no longer claim to be a unique testimony. Readers, perhaps, thought that nobody should write more than one biography of a saint. This would explain the hostility that Jerome complains about, but, of course, it is only a hypothesis.

The parallels between the *Vita Macrinae* and the oration in honor of Gorgonia mentioned earlier might be pursued a little further, since little has been said about them so far.

First there is the simplicity of the lifestyle of these saintly women. It must have been quite different from that of the society ladies of that period. Gregory of Nyssa records[15] that his sister had only an old cloak, a veil, a pair of worn-out shoes, a cross which she wore around her neck, and a ring. Her bed was a long wooden board with a bag on top of it, and her pillow was a smaller wooden board.

This corresponds to the lifestyle of Gorgonia. Gregory of Nazianzus writes[16] about his sister: "She never adorned herself with gold jewelry made by artists; she never showed her locks either as a whole or in part: her hairdo was not fashionable, not designed to impress the ordinary

---

13. *V. Hilarionis* 4, 10 (second part).
14. *V. Hilarionis* 1.
15. *V. Macr.* 29f.
16. *V. Gorg.* 10.

person. She wore no expensive pleated and transparent robes, no beautiful gleaming jewelry which emit their colorful shine into all directions and surround the human figure with light. Cosmetic illusions meant nothing to her, and the cheap kind of beauty which is produced on earth and competes with the art of the Creator by hiding God's image under deceitful layers of color, diminishing it through so-called beautification, thus representing the divine image as a meretricious idol and disfiguring by a false charm the natural face that we ought to preserve for God and the next world—all this meant nothing to her . . ."

Both Macrina and Gorgonia are charitable. During the famine which visited Cappadocia in 368/9, Macrina fed the people,[17] and Gorgonia was always ready to help the needy and the afflicted.[18] The idea that a saint has the ministry of teaching can also be found in both vitae.

During an illness or a period of intense suffering, both Gorgonia and Macrina acted very much alike. Once Gorgonia had a serious accident. She lost control over the mules that drew her carriage; apparently she fell from it, was dragged along on the ground, and suffered multiple injuries. Even so, she wanted no other physician but God, who let the accident happen. She also refused to undress in front of a human physician.[19] At another time she was critically ill; the symptoms were alarming: high fever, rapid pulse, weariness that turned into coma, physical and mental paralysis. This time the physicians were summoned, but their efforts were in vain.[20]

Once again, Gorgonia prayed to the "greatest of all physicians" for recovery, imitating the woman whose hemorrhage was healed when she touched the hem of Jesus' garment. Gorgonia begged him to help her, touched the altar with her head, and wept and wept. Holding in her hand the host and the consecrated wine, she rubbed her whole body with her tears, and she felt at once that her health was restored. But she did not tell her brother about this miracle until shortly before her death.

The miracle has a parallel in the *Vita Macrinae*. Only after his sister's death did Gregory learn that many years ago, she suffered from a breast cancer declared incurable by the physicians. Although her mother urged her to seek more medical advice, she declined.

---

17. *V. Macr.* 39.

18. *V. Gorg.* 12f.

19. Ibid. 15.

20. Ibid. 17ff.; cf. 31: τὸ γυμνῶσαί τι τοῦ σώματος ὀφθαλμοῖς ἀλλοτρίοις τοῦ πάθους χαλεπώτερον κρίνασα . . .

But one evening she entered the παναγιστήριον and prostrated herself all night before the God of all healing. Tears streamed from her eyes, tears which mingled with the soil on which she lay, and this mixture Macrina applied as a kind of salve. When her mother urged her once more to see a doctor, Macrina simply said it would be sufficient if she— the mother—would make the sign of the cross, τὴν ἁγίαν σφραγῖδα, over the tumor. She did it, and the tumor disappeared; only a small mark remained.[21]

A related theme—death—is treated similarly in both texts. Macrina is happy to die, because she is—as Gregory puts it—full of that divine, pure love for the invisible bridegroom, a love that nourishes her "deep inside and hidden in her heart." She longs, indeed, to be delivered as soon as possible from the bonds of her body and to hurry into her lover's embrace. Gregory uses the terms ἔρως and ἐραστής.[22] In a similar vein Gregory of Nazianzus writes on Gorgonia, "She longed to be dissolved . . . and no lustful, sensuous person loves the body as much as she strove to be freed of these shackles and to rise from the mud in which we live and to give herself purely to the most beautiful being and to wholly embrace her beloved—yes, I may say her lover . . ."[23] Pierre Maraval, the learned editor of the *Vita Macrinae*, cites (98 n. 1) parallels to illustrate the use of ἐράω, ἔρως in contexts where one would expect ἀγαπάω, ἀγάπη.

Gregory's last conversations with Macrina, her last prayer, her death and burial are fundamental for the vita.[24] The preliminary material— recollections of her youth, the whole family, and so on—all serves to lead up to this climax, as it were. Now Gregory himself, who has not seen his sister for years, introduces himself, and now Macrina becomes real for the reader. We get to know her when she is already suffering from her illness, without hope of getting well. We have been prepared for the worst by Gregory's prophetic dream.

Most of these features are alien to the pagan biographies, it seems to me. Prophetic dreams and other anticipations of future events are, of course, common enough.

Gregory's narrative of her dying[25] is very moving, a literary work of

---

21. *V. Macr.* 31ff.
22. Ibid. 22.
23. *V. Gorg.* 19.
24. *V. Macr.* 15ff.
25. Ibid. 22ff.

art. At this point, the biography turns into a novel, if I may say so. I do not want to suggest that we are dealing with fiction; it just seems to me that the author uses the technique of a novelist to dramatize a very real event. Labriolle[26] and others have used similar terms to describe Jerome's lives of saints, among other writings.

Another example is Gregory's encounter with a high army officer,[27] the commander of the garrison of Sebastopolis. This meeting gives him the opportunity of relating a further story illustrating Macrina's miraculous healing powers, a story which he had not heard before. The officer tells how Macrina was able to heal his little daughter during a visit to her convent. His report differs stylistically from the rest of the vita, I think, and I should like to make the point because it seems to have been overlooked so far. Here, Gregory writes what must be a kind of colloquial Greek, not the elegant, cultivated Greek (*Kunstprosa*) that he normally writes. This is only a suggestion which I cannot follow up and document, but it seems to show how deliberately Gregory has shaped the vita as a literary work of art. One would certainly not expect to find such a stylistic change in Suetonius.

In Gregory's biography there seems to be a constant fluctuation between detailed narratives, impressions of the narrator, and eyewitness and literary reminiscences. Macrina's last prayer,[28] for example, is a very impressive fabric made of biblical passages which Macrina no doubt knew well, but her brother probably composed the prayer when he wrote the vita, because he felt that this tissue represented best the emotions of a devout soul waiting for death. The dirges of the nuns after her death remind one of a choral ode in a Greek tragedy. Everywhere we see evidence of Gregory's consummate skills. This vita is not a memorandum in the sense that Abbot Maurus Berve defined so admirably in his lecture but a literary production which reflects great care and experience. Compared to such a work, Suetonius, with his captions, seems rather dry and awkward.

In the *Vita Macrinae* we are told a good deal about her periods of illness. We hear about her breast cancer,[29] healed miraculously by her intensive prayer. We also hear about the eye disease of the little girl that she healed.[30] Strangely enough, her last illness is barely alluded to; no

---

26. P. de Labriolle, *Histoire de la littérature latine chrétienne* (Paris, 1921), 456.
27. *V. Macr.* 37f.
28. Ibid. 24.
29. Ibid. 31.
30. Ibid. 38.

doctor was consulted, and no diagnosis is mentioned. Other vitae are just as reticent in this respect. The situation is different from the one in Muriel Spark's novel *Memento Mori*, which Father Cummings has discussed. There, the characters all die of specific conditions which can be understood in medical terms, while the medicine of this earth plays no great role in hagiography.

Though doctors are consulted during Epiphanius' last illness, their efforts are in vain, as Ennodius says.[31] Honoratus dies peacefully in his sleep.[32] Antony apparently was in good health almost to the end but then died fairly soon of an illness which is not specified.[33] Augustine was able, shortly before his death, to heal a patient who was brought to him, and he is supposed to have said,[34] half jokingly, that he was sorry he could not heal himself; but even here no diagnosis is given, although no doubt good physicians were available. Hilarion is ill and suddenly dies.[35] In his funeral oration on Basil, Gregory of Nazianzus describes his death mainly in terms of biblical quotations: "He had fought the good fight, he had finished the race, he had kept the faith" (2 Timothy 4:7); "his desire was to depart" (Philippians 1:23); "the time to be crowned had come" (2 Timothy 4:8).[36] On the other hand, Gregory[37] describes the fatal illness of his father with all the symptoms; he also acknowledges the efforts of the doctors, but he makes it clear that his father was ready to die.

In general, the physical aspects of being ill and dying are given less attention than this readiness to die, this longing for death, this urge to be united with Christ. For the Christian reader this was clearly much more important than anything else. He did not want to know more; he need not know more. The death of a saint provided a kind of model which he could imitate when his own death was imminent, when medical science would fail, as it inevitably would someday. This, I think, is the essential message of the *Vita Macrinae* and other hagiographies.

What formal criteria apply to this particular vita? It is in the form of a very long letter, as Gregory says, a document which could be read everywhere and on every occasion, whenever there was a need for it. It was

---

31. *PL* 63.238B; *Early Christian Biographies*, 349.
32. Hilarius *V. Honorati* 34.
33. Athanasius *V. Antonii* 34.
34. Possidius, 29.
35. Ennodius, 45.
36. Gregory of Nazianzus 77.
37. Ibid. 28.

meant to be an edifying document. Many hagiographies are more like tracts than biographies.

For the epistolary form there are parallels, Paulinus' *Vita Ambrosii*, Athanasius' *Vita Antonii*, for instance, but the latter is also a drama or a dramatic agon between the saint and Satan, who tempts him again and again in so many disguises. A sermon preached by Antony forms the central part of the work.[38]

Sermons, tracts, funeral orations are closely related genres. They all have their "place in life"; they are *Gebrauchsliteratur*, if I may use the word, but of course they can deal with the same topics as biographies. In Gregory's time, the funeral oration—ἐπιτάφιος λόγος—had already a long history. In Athens, Byzantium, Antiochia, and many other great cities, students of rhetoric were introduced into the theory and practice of this species of the ἐγκώμιον.

But the rules which the student learned from the professor of rhetoric could be applied to letters, biographies, and other genres as well, and certain issues almost inevitably are touched on. We see, for instance, how some early biographies of saints became classics, models, and were imitated. Paulinus acknowledges the *Life of St. Antony* by Athanasius, Jerome's biography of Paul the hermit, and Sulpicius Severus' vita of St. Martin of Tours. The classics of the genre had already been established.

On the one hand, these vitae served as literary models for later vitae; on the other hand, the saints themselves became models for later saints. The relationship between life and literature has many aspects, but it seems to me that life is like a stream that nourishes literature, while literature, on the other hand, nourishes life.

Something ought to be said about the quotations from the Bible in the *Vita Macrinae*, because the Bible is the prime example of literature that nourishes life. Most of them are identified in Maraval's edition (the reference to Job[39] ought to be added; Gregory sees in his dying sister a parallel figure to Job. Maraval offers parallels in Gregory of Nazianzus and Basilius but omits the Old Testament source). The last conversation between brother and sister is full of biblical quotations, and so is—as I observed earlier—Macrina's last prayer.

In the whole vita there is not a single certain quotation from a pagan author, though there are a few possible allusions to Plato. Gregory must have known Plato and other pagan authors well, but here he seems to

---

38. Athanasius *V. Antonii* 17–43.
39. *V. Macr.* 18.

exclude any kind of non-Christian traditions. This is not unusual. In Athanasius' vita of St. Antony we find numerous quotations from the Bible but not one certain reference to a pagan author, it seems. One does not exclude the other: thus in Jerome and in Ambrose biblical quotations alternate with quotations from Cicero, Virgil, and Ovid, and in his funeral oration in honor of Basilius, Gregory of Nazianzus quotes from Homer and Pindar. Gregory's restraint in the vita of his sister may reflect the way she felt; perhaps she lived so completely in the world of the Bible that she did not want to share in pagan παιδεία. Thus we may solve the problem which Jean Daniélou poses in the introduction to his edition of Gregory's vita of Moses:[40] on the one hand, Gregory recommends pagan culture (ἡ ἔξωθεν παιδεία); on the other hand, he practically urges the reader to avoid it. He himself has read the classical authors. In some ways he is a Platonist, and he has learned from Libanius the "modern" prose style which characterizes the Second Sophistic Age. But what suited him and helped him was not for everybody. I think that he quoted only from the Bible in the vita of his sister because the Bible was her world.

Twenty years ago I wrote for *Mullus*, the Festschrift in honor of Theodor Klauser, an article entitled "Die Form der suetonischen Biographie und die frühen Heiligenviten."[41] In this article I tried to show that a statement which has been repeated in handbooks and monographs for many decades simply is not true. According to this theory, Suetonius' *Caesares* influenced in a very significant way the Christian biographies that we have. It is a theory that seems to have appeared for the first time in F. Leo's book *Die griechisch-römische Biographie* (1901) and that was then elaborated on in a dissertation by F. Kemper (1904); from there it found its way into the handbooks and is still accepted by many. In the essay just mentioned, I examined this thesis, using the biographies written by Pontius, Sulpicius Severus, Paulinus, Possidius, and Eugippius as examples. My conclusion was that the Christian biographers have created their own literary form which owes practically nothing to Suetonius and his Greek and Roman predecessors but almost everything to the gospels and the early Christian tradition, as it developed through the mission of the church and its self-assertion in times of persecution.

Even a highly educated man such as Gregory, a man who had absorbed the great philosophical and rhetorical traditions of the pagan

---

40. *La Vie de Moïse*, in *SC* 1 bis (Paris, 1955), XXIVff.
41. (1964), 230–41.

world, refused to use the Suetonian type of outline, refused to quote from the classical authors, even though he could easily have done so, and limited himself to his personal experience, his recollections of a θεία γυνή who happened to be his sister, and to the biblical passages which directed her life and gave meaning to it.

I hope that I have been able to make a few observations which may help us to understand a little better this biographical portrait which is so full of love and yet so carefully formed as a literary work of art. Let me conclude with the words which Gregory uses in the last chapter of the vita:[42] "The radiations of her grace happened according to her faith; this may seem little to those of little faith, but to those who possess the great world of faith, great" [ἡ τῶν χαρισμάτων διανομὴ παραγίνεται μικρὰ μὲν τοῖς ὀλιγοπιστοῦσιν, μεγάλη δὲ τοῖς πολλὴν ἔχουσιν ἐν ἑαυτοῖς τὴν εὐρυχωρίαν τῆς πίστεως].

---

42. *V. Macr.* 39.

The Doctrine of Salvation in the Hermetic Writings

The invocation of Hermes Trismegistos represents an appeal to "Thoth the Very Great," Thoth being the Egyptian equivalent of the Greek Hermes. A number of treatises known as *Hermetica* and collected in the *Corpus Hermeticum* were revealed to mankind by this Greco-Egyptian deity. Most of them are philosophical and theological in nature, but there are Hermetic works on magic, astrology, and alchemy as well.

No one knows when and where these texts were written. They may be the work of several authors, composed over a long period of time. The *Asclepius* is preserved among the philosophical works of Apuleius (second century A.D.), although he cannot possibly be the author or translator; and St. Augustine was acquainted with Hermetic thought. Since it is a form of Gnosticism, it may have been contemporary with this movement, and its Egyptian origin is not improbable.

During the later Hellenistic period Alexandria had become a great intellectual center comparable to the Athens of Plato and Aristotle. It attracted scholars, scientists, philosophers, and poets from the whole Greek world. At the same time, the ancient mysteries were still celebrated in the temples of Egypt, and there was a large modern library and other facilities for research. It is easy to imagine an atmosphere in which a blend of Platonism, Stoicism, Judaism, and Gnosticism could be associated with a Greco-Egyptian deity and gain prestige through such an association. That the substantial philosophical legacy of Philo of Alexandria influenced the Hermetic movement can hardly be doubted. Philo, who was both a Jew and a Platonist, may have founded a school along the lines of the Academy and the Peripatos in Alexandria. Nothing is known of such a school, but the author (or authors) of the Hermetic

From *Second Century* 8 (1991): 31–41.

This is the revised version of an essay that was delivered at the annual meeting of the Society of Biblical Literature (Greco-Roman Religions Group), Anaheim, California, 23–26 November 1985. I am very grateful to Everett Ferguson and the anonymous readers for a number of valuable suggestions.

corpus could be understood as disciples of it who had possibly already heard of the new doctrine of Jesus, as interpreted by St. Paul or St. John, and tried to adapt it to their own pagan syncretism and astral mysticism. Nowhere else but in Alexandria does such a blend of ideas and doctrines seem possible at this time. Hermeticism is based on revelation, but it is really a popularizing version of older philosophies and theologies, much easier to grasp than Philo.

The main texts which we have are written in Greek and Latin, but some Coptic and Armenian versions are known. Greek was then an international language used by Egyptians, Syrians, Jews, and Romans. The one treatise preserved in Latin, the *Asclepius,* is the translation of a lost Greek original.[1] Curiously, one of the Hermetic authors (assuming that there were several) acts as if he were writing in Egyptian: "The Greeks have only empty words, good enough for demonstrations, and that is exactly what Greek philosophy is like—a mere verbal noise [λόγων ψόφος]. But we [i.e., the Egyptians] do not use mere words: we use sounds that are full of action" (*Corp. Herm.* XIV.2). No doubt he has in mind the magical power which he ascribes to the Egyptian language, but not to Greek. Does this remark mean that all Hermetic treatises were originally written in Egyptian, which, in that period, would probably mean Coptic? The question remains open, but the Hermetic Writings clearly perserve a good deal of native Egyptian lore.[2]

Before we approach the main topic of this paper, it seems necessary to think about the meaning of "salvation" (σωτηρία) in the ancient world. The word itself does not always have a religious connotation. A human being may be saved from sickness, from an accident, from shipwreck, from any other kind of misfortune or trouble. A human benefactor as well as a god could be called "savior" (σωτήρ), and the word became part of the official title of the Ptolemies as kings of Egypt.[3] In a strictly religious sense,

---

1. The Greek original was entitled τέλειος λόγος, "accomplished discourse." The Latin title suggests, perhaps, the idea of healing, which can be considered an aspect of salvation. Asclepius, the god of healing, was considered a savior god; cf. A.D. Nock, *Essays on Religion and the Ancient World* (Oxford, 1972), 1:78, 2:723.

2. Cf. K.-W. Tröger, "On Investigating the Hermetic Documents Contained in Nag Hammadi Codex VI: The Present State of Research," in *Nag Hammadi and Gnosis,* ed. R. McL. Wilson, NHS 14 (Leiden: Brill, 1978), 120; and see now E. Iversen, *Egyptian and Hermetic Doctrine* (Copenhagen, 1984), 50.

3. R. McL. Wilson, "Soteriology in the Christian-Gnostic Syncretism," *La soteriologia dei culti orientali nell'Impero romano: Atti del colloquio internazionale su la*

σωτηρία means salvation from death at a given point in time, or the assurance of life eternal through a god, with a god, or by assimilation with a god.[4] Often, salvation implies a previous fall from grace and a sinful condition; to avoid the consequences of this state, a spiritual regeneration or a ritual of purification was considered necessary.[5]

The doctrine of salvation in the Hermetic treaties can be studied from a linguistic point of view. Thanks to the *Index Verborum* compiled by L. Delatte and others,[6] the uses of σώζω, σωστικός, σωτήρ, σωτήριος, σωτηρία in the Greek treatises and those of *salvo, servo, conservo* in the *Asclepius* can now be compared. The results, however, are not very significant, it would seem.[7] The word σωτήρ, "savior," appears only once, in XVI.12, connected with τροφεύς, "nourisher," and both nouns are applied to the sun. Σωτηρία, "salvation," appears twice at the very beginning of VII.[8] The neuter plural of the adjective σωτήριος, used as a noun, may be translated as "means of salvation" (II.12, VI.11, X.15).[9] The verb σώζω, "to save" (through the intervention of a divine being) or "to endow with everlasting life," appears nine times (I.26, 29; VII.5 bis; IX.5; XII.14; XIII.1, 19; XXIII.68). The verbal adjective σωστικός is found once, in XX.1. The Latin vocabulary is even more limited than the Greek: *salvo* is used only once in the *Asclepius* (XLI.25.5), *servo* nine times (IV.23.1; VIII.35.6; XI.17.2, 23.3, 36.4; XXIV.16.4; XXX.18.4; XL.11.2; XLI.36.3), *conservo* twice (XXXI.9.5, XXXVII.38.3). There is no evidence for *salvatio, salvator, servator,* and *conservator.*[10]

---

soteriologia dei culti orientali nell'Impero romano, ed. U. Bianchi and M.J. Vermaseren, EPRO 92 (Leiden: Brill, 1982), 848f.

4. F. Cumont, *Lux Perpetua* (Paris, 1949), 309ff.; R. Turcan, "Salut Mithriaque et sotériologie Néoplatonicienne," in *La soteriologia,* 174.

5. R. Turcan, in *La soteriologia,* loc. cit. The questions that may be asked in order to understand the phenomenon more fully are, according to R. McL. Wilson (*La soteriologia,* 848), the following: (1) from what does the believer hope to be saved? (2) by what means? (3) toward what goal?

6. L. Delatte, S. Govaerts, and J. Denooz, *Index du Corpus Hermeticum* (Rome: Ateneo e Bizzarri, 1977).

7. G. van Moorsel, *The Mysteries of Hermes Trismegistus* (Utrecht, 1955), 22ff.

8. There are parallels to this use in the Septuagint, in Aelius Aristides, Apuleius, and Firmicus Maternus.

9. This meaning is attested in classical and neoclassical Greek, in the Septuagint, Philo, Josephus, and the New Testament.

10. Apuleius uses *sospitator* and *sospitatrix,* nouns apparently not attested before his time; he does not use *salvator* and *servator; servatrix* appears only in a figurative sense (Apuleius *Plat.* 2.6).

We shall see that the doctrine of salvation is much more important to the Hermeticist than the linguistic evidence might suggest. This should serve as a warning: the linguistic approach alone, by means of computers or otherwise, is insufficient in itself, and a close reading of the texts remains indispensable.

Having read the texts and consulted the main scholarly contributions concerning the *Corpus Hermeticum*, I would suggest, following Festugière,[11] two main aspects of salvation in these treaties: (1) the spiritual life (I.20–23, IV, VII, XII.1–14), and (2) "becoming like God" (ὁμοίωσις τῷ θεῷ, XIII).[12]

For the disciple of Hermes, salvation does not come about as the result, at a given point in time, of the sudden arrival of a divine being who lives among men for a while, formulates a doctrine, institutes certain sacraments, then dies and returns to heaven. For the Hermetics, salvation essentially consists in knowing oneself, in recognizing within oneself the share of Light, the Divine Intellect (νοῦς), which one possesses as a natural gift. To recognize this gift is to love it and, at the same time, to hate the material, earthly side of one's nature.

Salvation through γνῶσις, "knowledge" or "understanding," therefore, has a double purpose: to know oneself and to know God (I.18–19). Self-knowledge can be only one form of γνῶσις;[13] the contemplation and study of God and the universe represent the other.[14] Since salvation comes through γνῶσις, it follows that ἄγνοια, "ignorance," is the worst sin.[15] It also follows that there are two categories of human beings: those who know, and those who live in ignorance. The latter deserve nothing better than to die; in fact, they are already dead (I.20). Only he who has recognized himself as what he is will make progress toward his real self

---

11. *Hermétisme et mystique païenne* (Paris, 1967), 58ff.

12. Cf. W.C. Grese, *Corpus Hermeticum XIII and Early Christian Literature,* Studia ad Corpus Hellenisticum Novi Testamenti 13 (Leiden: Brill, 1979), 71f., 89f., 97f.

13. Van Moorsel 25.

14. On the ability to see God (θεοπτικὴ δύναμις) see VI.18 and VII.3, with Festugière's note. One does not find the term in the New Testament. The word θεόπτης is attested in Philo, and the Neoplatonists were familiar with the concept.

15. Cf. Grese 111, 121ff.; he refers to H.D. Betz in *HThR* 63 (1970): 465ff. and others. Cf. also D.M. Parrott, ed., *Nag Hammadi Codices V.2–5 with Papyrus Berolinensis 8502.1 and 4,* NHS 11 (Leiden: Brill, 1979), 404, 409. There is a striking parallel in Seneca *Epist.* 31.6: *quid ergo est bonum? rerum scientia. quid malum est? rerum imperitia.*

(I.21). God knows us and wants us to know him; through γνῶσις man can identify himself with God; this is the path to salvation (X.15).

All of this seems reasonably straightforward, but it involves a problem (I.21; IV.3–5; XII.6–7, 12–13, 22). Do not all human beings share a common Intellect, thanks to their common ancestor, Divine Man? How can they differ from one another in this respect? Can it be true that only some achieve salvation through γνῶσις, while others never will?

The Hermetic theologians worked out an answer to the problem. All men have potentially received the νοῦς, but they do not use it in the same way; in fact, every individual uses it according to his own character and way of life. Those who are good, holy, and compassionate not only have the νοῦς as a potential; they fully realize it, and it becomes, for them, their guardian angel.[16] All men share the νοῦς, but it is not the same for all men (*Asclepius* VII). If someone is senseless, evil, greedy, vicious, or criminal, the divine νοῦς withdraws from him and yields its place to an avenging demon which tortures the sick soul by the very appetites and urges that haunt it and cause the sickness from which it suffers.

In IV the image of the "Mixing Bowl" offers a different solution to the same basic problem. The interlocutor asks (para. 3), "Why has God not given an [equal] share of νοῦς to all people?" And Great Hermes answers, "Because he wanted to give away the νοῦς to the souls, as if it were a prize to be won [by them]." Therefore God filled a huge mixing bowl full of νοῦς and sent it down to earth with a herald who had to proclaim this message: "Every soul that is able, every soul that believes that it can ascend to him who sent the bowl, every soul that knows why it has come into existence, ought to plunge into the bowl." The image implies that the soul actually possesses part of the νοῦς already—or else it could not realize the importance of the gift—and that it ought to acquire as much extra νοῦς as possible from the vast supply that God has made available. The soul has a choice: it may choose the life of the νοῦς—or it may reject it (XII.5–9). If the soul makes the right decision, it will avoid the evil influence of the body, the passions, and—most importantly—of fate. Through our bodies we are all subject to fate, but the soul does, at the same time, have a free choice. It is clear, then, that evil, guilt, and fate are closely connected.

At this point a curious exercise enters the process of salvation. In my view, its peculiar nature has not been recognized by the modern scholars

---

16. What we call "guardian angel" seems to be a combination of the Socratic δαιμόνιον, the Roman *genius,* and, possibly, the Gnostic νοῦς.

who have dealt with these problems, probably because there is only a brief reference to it in *Corpus Hermeticum* XII. Perhaps it was explained in more detail in a treatise which is no longer extant. What we have is, after all, only part of a larger body of hermetic writings; the number of isolated fragments and the recent discoveries of previously unknown texts establish this point beyond a doubt. In the absence of more explicit statements, my attempt at a reconstruction of this particular doctrine must remain hypothetical. It might be called the "doctrine of voluntary suffering."

The true Hermetic ought to remain guiltless, but he should suffer, as if he had committed a crime, adultery, for example, and it is this voluntary suffering without any basis in fact which will eventually free him from evil and fate. The key formula seems to be: Not having committed adultery, I shall suffer (in this world) the punishment for adultery in my mind. One can only guess that this involved some kind of spiritual exercise or ascetic discipline. Let us assume that I pretend to myself that I have committed adultery, although I have not done anything wrong. Yet I force myself somehow to imagine the circumstances of the act of adultery. I would then imagine that I was caught and punished. This imaginary punishment, painful and humiliating, if dramatized properly, will cause me real anguish, like some horrible nightmare, and henceforth I will never be tempted to commit the crime for which I have already been punished in my mind. And since I have not committed any real crime, fate will not catch up with me. I am saved (XII.7).

To commit a crime in one's imagination and suffer for it may seem bizarre, but it could be seen as a kind of psychotherapy that worked for many. The performance of a tragedy on the stage had a similar effect. Once the spectator identified himself with the tragic protagonist who suffered, sometimes horribly, for a crime that had been committed—not necessarily by himself, but often by someone else, an ancestor, for example— he felt the pain as if it were his own and left the theater, as Aristotle thinks, purged and perhaps a better human being.

I realize that this hypothesis may not appear convincing at first sight, although the context strongly suggests a kind of spiritual καθοδηγία, as it was practiced in philosophical schools of later antiquity, as well as in some mystery religions.[17] Similar techniques have been described by

---

17. Cf. K.-W. Tröger, *Mysterienglaube und Gnosis in Corp. Herm. XIII*, TUGAL 10 (Berlin: Akademie-Verlag, 1971), 63f.

P. Rabbow.[18] Perhaps it is not surprising that our texts are sometimes reticent, since it is not easy to describe methods that had to be learned from a teacher or spiritual guide (καθοδηγός, καθηγητής). The philosophers were more articulate. They seem to have encouraged their disciples to create in their imagination certain situations as a challenge, so to speak, or as an opportunity to test their self-control, their inner resources. Sin and the temptation to commit it are evils, but they also happen to be realities of life, and no one should pretend that they do not exist; on the contrary, one should be prepared for them.[19]

The mystery religions recognized a "cathartic" type of psychotherapy which relied on mystic experiences, ecstasy, drama, music, dance, and symbols.[20] It has been shown, I think, by J. Gwyn Griffiths that an anticipated divine judgment could become, under certain circumstances, a very real experience in the life of the believer, followed by an imagined or symbolic punishment which led to the assurance of salvation.[21] Ascetic practices were part of Egyptian mystery cults and could, therefore, have influenced Hermetic doctrine.[22] To think about adultery in this way would not necessarily go against the teaching of Jesus (Mt. 5:27–28), because one clearly dramatized the painful, not the pleasant, aspects of that sin.

The Hermetic texts are often tantalizing. They offer clues that were probably developed in oral teaching. One may view these treatises as propaganda, designed to attract people who were looking for a new creed, a different path to salvation. Once they had joined the Hermetic community, they were probably initiated into higher mysteries. The texts which we have appear to lead up to a crucial point and then break off. Outsiders obviously learned only part of the truth; more was in store for them once they had joined. Even the Platonic dialogues, the literary models of the Hermetic treatises, could be (and have been) described as propaganda in this sense. They are often frustrating because they formulate problems and offer no solutions. These solutions were reserved for oral teaching by the master himself, after years of study, one assumes, when the disciples were ready for the "unwritten doctrine."

---

18. P. Rabbow, *Seelenführung* (Munich, 1954), 188f., 224ff., 289ff., 330ff.; cf. G. Luck, *Gnomon* 28 (1956): 268ff (in this volume, pp. 35–38).

19. Cf. Seneca *Epist.* 24.2: *si vis omnem sollicitudinem exuere, quicquid vereris, ne eveniat, eventurum utique propone;* Rabbow, *Seelenführung,* 239f.

20. Rabbow 289ff.

21. J. Gwyn Griffiths, in *La soteriologia,* 195, 211f.

22. Cf. Parrott 343 on the technique of dramatic dialogue as used in *Corp. Herm.* XIII and elsewhere.

After this admittedly hypothetical treatment of "voluntary suffering" as part of the Hermetic scheme of salvation,[23] it is time to return to the main concept. No matter what path to salvation the disciple had chosen, once he was saved himself, he acquired the authority and inherited the duty, as it were, to save others (VIII.5). Thus, salvation was seen as a progressive and collective process, and its final goal must be the redemption of all mankind. In order to save as many souls as possible, the true Hermetic had to work as a preacher and missionary.

A specific way toward salvation is outlined in XIII, the "most original treatise of the *Corpus Hermeticum*," as Festugière has called it. According to this doctrine, salvation is possible through a sudden inner regeneration, a spiritual rebirth (παλιγγενεσία) in God. "No one can be saved before rebirth" is the opening statement of this treatise.[24] Rebirth (or regeneration) is possible only after the death of the former self:[25] "Having had a spiritual vision inside myself, thanks to God's compassion, I have left my own self and entered an immortal body, and I am no longer what I was before" (XIII.3).[26]

The *Poimandres* also stresses the necessity of regeneration. The human body is composed of the four material elements—earth, water, fire, and air—and is, therefore, evil. But it also contains the astral substances which it inherited from First Man. He received them as he descended through the planetary spheres, when the evil powers of the planets rubbed off on him as he passed through their spheres. All of us have inherited this bad admixture, and it is our duty to replace all the evil powers in us by the ten good powers, such as joy, truthfulness, and self-discipline, which came from God. Therefore the disciple is urged to

---

23. See also Festugière's note, *Corpus Hermeticum*, 1:194.

24. Cf. R. Reitzenstein, *Hellenistische Mysterienreligionen* (Leipzig, 1927; Eng. trans., Pittsburgh: Pickwick 1978), 262ff.; idem, *Poimandres* (Leipzig, 1922), 231, 368ff.; C.H. Dodd, *The Bible and the Greeks* (Oxford, 1935), 240; Grese 70ff., 132, 134.

25. See *Romans* 6:6 and cf. Festugière, *Corpus Hermeticum*, 2:210.

26. Cf. XIII.7ff. Παλιγγενεσία is translated as "regeneration" rather than "rebirth" by Grese (3, passim). Thus he translates XII.4, "Who is the producer of regeneration? HERMES: The Son of God, the one Man, by the will of God" (11; cf. n. 6). According to Hermetic doctrine, regeneration is a miracle (ἀρετή in the Hellenistic sense of the word) and must be kept secret (Grese 33, 196). That salvation without regeneration is impossible seems to be the central theme of XIII (Grese 70f.), but the concept itself is different from that of the New Testament (Grese 132ff.). Immortality is to be had through regeneration, according to XIII (Grese 151; Grese compares the corresponding New Testament concepts).

enter a program of self-renewal by firmly resisting all the bad tendencies within him and by acquiring certain well-defined virtues.[27]

Actually, the two paths of salvation, γνῶσις and ὁμοίωσις τῷ θεῷ, can be seen as two aspects of one and the same experience, as we learn from XI.20: "If you do not make yourself like God, you cannot know God, for like can only be known by like." Since we can only know God through the νοῦς, and since the νοῦς in us is divine, to use its full power in order to know God is becoming like God.

There is actually some evidence of a curious Hermetic doctrine that man is even greater than the gods, at least potentially, but there seems to be a distinction between *the gods* and the one *God*. According to *Asclepius* XXII, man has been created good and potentially immortal *(qui posset immortalis esse)*, and the one God wanted him to be better than the gods *(esse meliorem diis)*. This might be derived from a Stoic interpretation of the myth of Heracles, who, being only semidivine in his mortal life, showed himself greater in many ways than his divine enemy, Hera, and was rewarded by fully divine status after his life on earth had ended.[28]

From what we have considered so far, it appears that salvation, according to Great Hermes, does not enter human life at any given point. It is more like the gradual awakening of the divine soul which is in all of us, though more or less dormant. It could be compared to the rekindling of a divine flame which is in danger of being extinguished within us from our neglect.

There is, however, as Wilhelm Bousset[29] has been able to show, another aspect of salvation through γνῶσις, if we understand γνῶσις not just as a rediscovery of the divine νοῦς in us but as a mystic experience, an ecstatic vision, a revelation, a consecration. To achieve this goal, even the most willing and most advanced disciple of Hermes needs help from outside in the form of a teacher, a mystagogue, and, above all, a redeemer.

This redeemer has not entered our world at some given point in history; he represents the eternal struggle that has been going on ever since light and darkness were blended in the human soul, with just

---

27. The tractate VI.6 of the Nag Hammadi codex transmits the doctrine that the spheres can be gone through in a spiritual sense during the present life; cf. Parrott 342.

28. Cf. *Asclepius* IX; *Corp. Herm.* X.24; F. Cumont, *Recherches sur le symbolisme funéraire des Romains* (Paris, 1942), 507. On the idea of immortality cf. Grese 66, 151; on the belief that redeemed man is God cf. Parrott 412n.

29. W. Bousset, *Kyrios Christos* (Göttingen, 1921; Eng. trans., Nashville: Abingdon, 1970), 201ff.

enough light to feed the soul's longing for the eternal home, the source of light.

To explain this longing for salvation, the Hermetics told a number of myths, but I shall limit myself to the one told in the *Poimandres* as interpreted by Bousset.[30] At the beginning of the world the "Urmensch," prototypical man, descended through the planetary spheres, whose evil powers rubbed off on him as he passed through one after another. Why did he leave heaven? He either was cast out or left of his own will, irresistibly attracted by the beauty of the world as we know it. Once he became immersed in matter, he could only free himself with great difficulty, but in the end he succeeded and ascended to heaven, giving back, as he passed through them, their evil powers to the planetary spheres. Then he took his rightful place in the heavenly realm.[31]

Through this action the "Urmensch," whose descendants we all are, became our redeemer and shares his own knowledge with those who are ready to be saved, so that they, after their physical death, will also be able to pass through the planetary spheres as they ascend to heaven, to enter the world of everlasting light.[32]

The only passage in which the word σωτήρ, "savior" or "preserver," is discussed (XVI.12) deserves a brief comment. Here the sun is called "preserver" and "nourisher," σωτήρ καὶ τροφεύς, of all forms of life in the universe. The sun is then compared to the "intelligible world," νοητὸς κόσμος, which preserves the visible world because it embraces, fills, and loads it with an infinite diversity of forms and shapes. To "embrace" is to "save"; to "fill" is to "nourish." How can the sun be said to "embrace" (περιέχειν) the world? Because it envelops the world with

---

30. Bousset 203ff.

31. On this idea cf. XXIII.3.

32. The figure of the Heavenly or Primal Man appears in many Gnostic and Manichean texts, but in the Hermetic *Poimandres* it is almost exclusively anthropological; i.e., only other men, not the whole of the world, are derived from it. The myth was traced back to an Iranian "Salvation Mystery" by R. Reitzenstein, but his interpretation of the source material is open to objections, and the alternative explanation offered, among others, by T.H. Tobin (*The Creation of Man: Philo and the History of Interpretation*, CBQMS 14 [Washington: Catholic Biblical Association, 1983], 102ff.) is more plausible. It can, indeed, be shown that the texts in which the figure of Primal Man appears are all more or less Jewish (possibly heterodox) interpretations of Genesis 1–3, especially 1:27 versus 2:7. Philo's own exegesis, in spite of his fundamentally Platonist point of view, is a good example (Tobin 108ff.).

light and creative power. He who embraces is a savior, and the act of embracing is, indeed, an act of salvation. This interpretation can be confirmed by VIII.5, "God causes and embraces all things and keeps them together," and II.12, "The νοῦς saves, because it wholly embraces itself and contains all things."

Repentance and spiritual rebirth are the conditions for salvation, as we have seen. What else does salvation involve? The *Poimandres* answers this way: After having received the whole doctrine (the emphasis seems to be on "whole"), the one who has been initiated must become the guide (καθοδηγός) of those who are worthy.[33] Ultimately, through God, all of mankind (ἀνθρωπότης) should be saved. The first step is repentance (μετάνοια); it prepares those who repent for the message about the ways and means of salvation (σωτηρία). The guide then plants in their minds the seeds of wisdom (σοφία), and these seeds are nourished with the water of ambrosia. Finally, the disciples give thanks to God and retire to go to sleep, each in his own bed, as the author is careful to observe (I.29).

Thus, the *Poimandres* seems to record, if not a complete ritual, at least a kind of framework, an organized spiritual environment in which the individual could be assured of salvation.[34] Bits and pieces of the doctrine shared on such occasions can be supplied from other treatises, but even with these supplements we cannot reconstruct the complete liturgy of a Hermetic community, if such a liturgy ever existed. One symbol which was no doubt offered in this context is the beautiful image of the "port of salvation," as we find it in XVII.1–2: "Do not get carried away by the strong current [i.e., ignorance or temptation], but take advantage of the countercurrent, you who are able to reach the port of salvation, and drop your anchor there, and look for the guide who will direct you to the door of knowledge where there is a shining light, free of darkness, where no one is drunk. . . ."[35]

The prayer of thanks with which the ceremony outlined in the

---

33. Καθοδηγός seems to be equivalent to μυσταγωγός. On the term ἐξοδιακός cf. Parrott 371; K.-W. Tröger, *Mysterienglaube und Gnosis in Corpus Hermeticum XIII,* TUGAL 110 (Berlin: Akademie-Verlag, 1971), 63.

34. On cultic elements in the new Hermetic documents see K.-W. Tröger, in *Nag Hammadi and Gnosis* 121.

35. "Save that which is in us, and grant us the immortal wisdom" (*Nag Hammadi Codex VI.6,* 58.22–24; Parrott 359). According to *Corp. Herm.* XIII, man has not fallen; hence, he is saved by God's undoing the body which the Zodiac had made (Grese 71f., 89f., 131).

Poimandres concluded[36] can possibly be recovered, at least in part, from the conclusion of the *Asclepius* (XLI), where the faithful are told that γνῶσις is the highest gift that God has bestowed on mankind and that men duly rejoice because they are saved by God's divine power and because he showed "all of himself" to them: *numine salvati tuo gaudemus, quod te nobis ostenderis totum.*[37]

---

36. On Hermetic hymns of thanksgiving see Grese 180, 183, 187f.: Parrott 375ff., (*Nag Hammadi Codex VI.7* as a parallel to *Asclepius* XLIb and *P. Mimaut* cols. 591–611); see also M.J. Vermaseren, in *La soteriologia*, 21f.; K.-W. Tröger, in *Nag Hammadi and Gnosis*, 121.

37. For the "total vision" see Festugière (ad loc.), who compares 1 Corinthians 13:10.

Recent Work on Ancient Magic

In a sense, ancient magic, is the forerunner of modern science and technology. If, as according to James Frazer, humankind has lived through three stages—magic, religion, and science—we may conclude that magic and science have something in common. Both formulate laws, laws that happen to be true in the case of science, largely false—from our point of view—in the case of magic.[1] It has been pointed out that, psychologically, there is a kinship between modern technology and ancient magic.[2] Most people today use the technology available to them without really knowing how and why it works. In their trust, they are like the people of ancient times who relied on magic that was supposed to be working.

In his article "In Search of the Occult: An Annotated Anthology," C.R. Phillips III offers a number of valuable remarks on the English edition of "Arcana Mundi."[3] As a starting point, he uses the view of magic held by the British anthropologists of the nineteenth century. For Edward Tylor, for example, magic was either bad religion or bad science—bad religion because it had not evolved to Christianity, bad science, because it had not evolved to modern technology. And evolved it should have, as Phillips points out, because Darwin's theories, transferred from zoology to the history of civilization, demanded it.

Phillips quotes E. Leach:[4] "First *science* was distinguished as knowledge and action which depends upon the 'correct' evaluation of cause and

Published for the first time in Spanish, in Georg Luck, *Arcana Mundi*, translated by Elena Gallego Moya and Miguel E. Pérez Molina (Madrid, Gredos, 1995), 9–28.

1. See now O. Costa de Beauregard, *La physique moderne et les pouvoirs de l'esprit* (Paris, 1981).

2. J. Gwyn Griffiths, in *Classical Mediterranean Spirituality*, ed. A.H. Armstrong (New York, 1986), 15.

3. C.R. Phillips, III, *Helios* 15 (1988), 151–70.

4. In *Nineteenth-Century Religious Thought in the West*, ed. N. Smart et al. (Cambridge, 1985), 243.

effect, the specification of what is correct being determined by the syllo-gisms of Aristotelian logic and the mechanical determinism of Newtonian physics. The residue was *superstition*. From superstition was then dis-criminated *religion*. The minimal definition of religion varied from author to author . . . ; the residue was then *magic*. Magic was then refined by some into white magic (good) and black magic (bad). Black magic, re-named *sorcery*, was then discriminated from *witchcraft*, and so on."

It is fairly clear that such statements could only be made from a secure vantage point. If we know what true religion is, we can also define magic. If we know what true science can do, we are also able to define pseudoscience. This subjective knowledge, as Phillips points out, is not enough; we also need to know that we are a solid majority and that we can enforce our convictions, if necessary. In antiquity, of course, the vast majority believed in magic.

It is more difficult to say what distinguishes magic from religion.[5] For one thing, ancient magic borrowed extensively from religion and possibly also from cults and rituals that are no longer attested. Magic seems to have grown on a substratum of religion, like a fungus: it used religious ceremonies, divine names, liturgical elements. Magic has al-ways been a master of disguises, because it can operate in a twilight zone, deliberately exploiting religious traditions while claiming that it achieves better results.

Some criteria that have been suggested to separate magic from reli-gion may be considered as guidelines:[6] magic is manipulative, while religion is supplicative; magic applies means to specific ends, while reli-gion stresses ends in themselves; magic concentrates on individual needs, while religion concentrates on the needs of the community; magi-cal operations tend to be private, secret (they often take place at night), while religious rites take place in the open, normally during the day, visible for all; magic is characterized by the relationship between a practi-tioner and his client, while the relationship characterizing religion is that between a founder, leader, or prophet and his followers. Prayers to the heavenly gods are normally offered aloud, while magical incantations to a demon or a deity of the underworld were apparently either said si-lently or with a hissing sound, the *susurrus magicus*.

---

5. See, e.g., C.H. Ratschow, *Magie und Religion* (1955); J.Z. Smith, *ANRW* 2.16.1 (1978): 430f.

6. These guidelines have been suggested by W.J. Goode, *Ethnos* 14 (1949): 172–82.

A well-balanced assessment is offered by R. Arbesmann:[7] "While in prayer man tries by persuasion to move a higher being to gratify his wishes, the reciter of a magic formula attempts to constrain that being or to force the effect to his own ends by the very words of his formula to which he ascribes an unfailing, immanent power. In the first instance, the answer to man's invocation lies within the will of the higher being; in the second, the binding of the higher being effected by the formula is considered to be absolute, automatically producing the result desired." But he adds a word of caution: "In many ritual acts, it is true, the two attitudes exist side by side and often blend one into the other so completely that it is difficult, if not impossible, to decide which of the two attitudes is present or dominant. It is also true that of the two attitudes the one taken by the reciter of the magic formula is cruder. But this does not warrant the conclusion that the magic formula is older than the prayer and that the latter grew out of the former . . ."

According to Philostratus (*Vita Apoll.* 5.12) some magicians thought they could change fate by torturing the statues of the gods. Since the statues are, to some extent, identical with the gods themselves, the gods would feel the pain inflicted on their statues. On the other hand, we know that in a crisis, when the people felt that their gods had failed them, they would punish their statues. It is doubtful that they felt that this would change the course of destiny.

It has also been said that magic and logic are two radically different ways of understanding reality, magic representing a prelogical or paralogical mentality. This is obviously true to a certain extent, but one should not forget that there is a kind of logic in magic. No matter how primitive its basic assumptions may appear to us, it did pass through a philosophical stage in the late Hellenistic period and, again, in Neoplatonist circles. Magicians did not only think in terms of cosmic sympathy or mystic participation; they were aware of cause and effect, space and time.[8]

This is one reason why it can be such a frustrating experience to read a work like Iamblichus' *On the Mysteries of Egypt.* Essentially, this is a defense of theurgy, a higher form of magic, but on the surface it is a philosophical work, using the terminology developed by generations of Platonists. Both Iamblichus and Proclus, another Neoplatonist, had

---

7. In *New Catholic Encyclopedia,* vol. 11 (1967), 667.
8. On the question whether magic may be considered a universal idea see E. Evans Pritchard, *Theories of Primitive Religion* (Oxford, 1965), 111.

inherited the magic lore and the philosophical discipline of past centuries. They thought that the two could be reconciled and used to explain or justify each other.[9]

Of a θεολόγος, who mainly talked about the gods, no miracles or magical feats were expected, but a θεουργός, who claimed to have a certain power over the gods, had to prove his supernatural abilities now and then. This is an area where we cannot exclude the possibility of elaborate fraud. When someone like Julian the Apostate was about to be initiated into the higher mysteries, nothing was left to chance, one would assume.

Magic uses symbols rather than concepts. Thanks to some anthropologists,[10] symbols are better understood today than at the time of Tylor. Symbols help people think, associate, and remember; they are a shorthand for ideas too complicated to be put into words, and because of that they seem to help decipher reality. No matter how abstruse the drawings in the Magical Papyri may seem to us, they are symbols and preserve, as "psychograms," certain types of experience.

The concept of cosmic sympathy was formulated in philosophical terms by the Stoic philosopher Posidonius of Apamea (ca. 135–ca. 50 B.C.), called "the Rhodian" after the island where he taught. This concept implies that anything that happens in any part of the universe will affect something else in the universe, no matter how distant it may be. This concept is fundamental for magic, alchemy, and astrology.[11]

What is called "sympathetic" magic is based on the following principles: (1) similarity (like calls forth like); (2) contact (things that touch each other will act on each other for a long time or retain each other's

---

9. See G. Luck, in *Religion, Science, and Magic,* ed. J. Neusner et al. (New York and Oxford, 1989), 185–225 (in this volume, pp. 110–52).

10. See C. Lévi-Strauss, *Anthropologie structurale* (Paris, 1958), chaps. 9 and 10; F. Isambert, *Rite et efficacité symbolique* (Paris, 1979), chap. 2.

11. The best treatment is probably still that of J. Frazer, *The Golden Bough,* 2d ed., vol. 1 (New York, 1935), 52–219; but see also M. Mauss, *A General Theory of Magic* (London, 1972). In an important sense, Swedenborg rediscovered this principle and based his own occult philosophy on it; see his *Clavis Hieroglyphica Arcanorum per Viam Repraesentationum et Correspondentiarum* (1784). According to Swedenborg, the universe consists of a number of analogous realms whose elements interact, serve as each others' symbols, and are permeated by Divine Light in different degrees of intensity, thereby revealing their properties. Among later authors who explored analogy as a cosmic principle, one should mention E. Geoffroy Saint-Hilaire (*Principes de philosophie zoologique* [Paris, 1830], esp. 97).

proprieties); (3) contrariety (to affect one thing, one can use its opposite, for antipathy works like sympathy). Hence the processes of association, imitation, and reaction were constantly exploited by magicians and alchemists.

It should also be said that some scholars distinguish between sympathetic and contagious magic. Sympathetic magic works because similar causes produce similar effects. If a man is in love with a woman and wants her to love him too, he may fashion an image of her in wax or clay and melt the image in fire, hoping that the person represented will also melt. This is what happens in Theocritus' second *Idyl* and in Virgil's eighth *Eclogue*. On the other hand, if you hate someone and wish to harm that person, you also fashion an image of that person and pierce it with nails or bind it or break it into pieces. Such figurines, nowadays called "voodoo dolls," have been found in Athens and elsewhere, and ways of fabricating them are described in the Magical Papyri. When you burn the image of your enemy or throw something that belongs to him—a piece of clothing, for instance—into the fire, you hurt him indirectly. This may be called "contagious" magic, and it is also mentioned by Theocritus.

Other ways to describe the workings of cosmic sympathy are: "Inside is like outside"; "what is above is like what is below." The concept involves a constant exchange of energies between the outside world, the macrocosm, and the inside world, the microcosm. Everything around us can be used to our advantage, either as a source of energy or as a message which we should not neglect. There is a saying in the Talmud: "A dream not interpreted is like a letter not read"; this applies to all "cosmic" messages.

It would be worthwhile to compare the ancient concept of cosmic sympathy with C.G. Jung's theory of synchronicity. Jung used this term to designate a coincidence which, in reality, is no coincidence at all. The belief in magic excludes, strictly speaking, coincidence: in anything that happens, a supernatural force is at work, even if we do not understand what it is.

This force which can either help or hurt us was called δύναμις by the ancient Greeks and is called *mana* by the modern anthropologists. It is the power that works miracles, and it is the miracle itself.[12] It is there to be exploited by "plugging in," like electricity. There is a subjective

---

12. Cf. Bauer, Arndt, and Gingrich, *A Greek-English Lexicon of the New Testament*, 5th ed. (Chicago, 1979), s.v. δύναμις; J. Röhr, *Der okkulte Kraftbegriff im Altertum* (1923), 1ff.

element in all of this: people believe that magic works for them; therefore it works. It is, in a sense, a placebo effect.

Δύναμις resides in certain things and in certain types of knowledge, for instance, in the name of a deity, as we may see from the use of the Semitic names for God, such as *Adonai* or *Iao*.[13] There is also special power in a formula, like "God is One"[14] or "Alpha and Omega."[15] In addition to pronouncing the name or the formula, the practitioner sometimes absorbed it physically by licking or eating it: thus, at the end of the "Mithras Liturgy" (*PGM* 4.785–9), the devotee is told to write the "eight-letter name" on a leaf and lick the leaf while showing it to the god.[16]

The story of Simon Magus, as told in the Book of Acts (8:9–21), illustrates the meaning of δύναμις. This man, who apparently had great influence in Samaria in the first century A.D., was called by his supporters, according to the commonly accepted textual form, ἡ δύναμις τοῦ θεοῦ ἡ καλουμένη μεγάλη, but τοῦ θεοῦ and καλουμένη seem to be *glossae* which found their way into the text.[17] What his followers actually called him was ἡ δύναμις ἡ μεγάλη, "the great power." This man, impressed by the δύναμις of the apostles, which was clearly superior to his own, wanted to join them and asked them to sell their special magic to him, whereupon he was sternly rebuked.[18]

In recent scholarship, a distinction between "direct" and "indirect" magic has been advocated. The protection offered by rings or amulets or by the medical charms described, for instance, in Marcellus' work *De medicamentis;* various concoctions, incantations, invocations of the "great name" of a deity or a demon—all this may be called "direct" magic. "Indirect" magic might be illustrated by the summoning of the dead in book 11 of the *Odyssey:* Here Homer describes a kind of magic that leads to another kind. The hero uses a certain ritual to conjure up the ghosts, but he needs one particular ghost, that of the seer Tiresias, who, even in Hades, has kept his prophetic powers. Normally, necromancers use any ghost that appears, but for Odysseus, no ghost but Tiresias will do.

---

13. Cf. G.H.R. Horsley, *New Documents Illustrating Early Christianity* (Macquarie 1981–), 1:35.

14. Ibid., no. 69.

15. Ibid., no. 22.

16. See F. Eckstein, in *Handwörterbuch des deutschen Aberglaubens*, ed. Bächtold and Stäubli, vol. 8 (1936–37), 1156–57.

17. See Horsley, *New Documents*, 1:107.

18. See Hippolytus *Refutatio* 6.2.14d; Ps.-Clement. *Recogn.* 1.72; J.M. de Salles-Dabadie, *Recherches sur Simon le Mage*, vol. 1 (Paris, 1969).

The distinction between "private" and "official" magic has the disadvantage that most magic, as we understand it, was practiced privately, while "official" magic is very close to religion; it may involve rainmaking or fertility rites (the "Sacred Marriage," e.g.), purifications of a community, formal cursing of a foreign country, and so on.

The old distinction between "ritual" and "natural" magic has been revived in recent years, but it is not really helpful. In a sense, all magic is ritual.[19] It has been asserted that specific rites are essential in certain societies:[20] (1) rites that reinforce the mana (success in hunting, fishing, fighting wars); (2) rites that reduce the mana (black magic); (3) apotropaic measures (protection from the evil eye, from demons—e.g., by means of amulets); (4) purification rites; (5) healing rites (ablutions, lustrations).

So much for "ritual" magic. "Natural" magic, on the other hand, is a kind of applied science, involving relatively simple experiments or demonstrations that are miraculous only for the naïve and the ignorant. Giambattista della Porta first published his *Magia naturalis* in 1558; the work was reprinted many times. Its influence can be seen in the *Disquisitiones magicae* by Martin del Rio, first published in 1599 and also reprinted several times. There, magic is defined (1.2) as *ars seu facultas vi creata et non supernaturalis quaedam mira et insolita efficiens quorum ratio sensum et communem hominum captum superat. . . . Vim creatam et non supernaturalem nominavi, ut excludam vera miracula.* When del Rio adds that *magica naturalis seu physica nihil aliud est quam exactior quaedam arcanorum naturae cognitio,* he clearly goes back to Apuleius, who, in his *Apologia sive de magia* declared himself to be a harmless scientist, definitely not a magician, and insisted that the seemingly strange experiments he carried out were done in the interest of research. But this involved *curiositas* (another popular name for magic) and did not make him any less suspicious.

Magika Hiera, a volume published in 1991, illustrates very well some trends in contemporary research on ancient magic.[21] It assembles ten essays on various aspects of ancient magic. C.A. Faraone deals with early Greek "binding spells" *(katadesmoi)*; J.H.M. Stubbe ("Cursed Be He That Moves My Bones"), with funerary imprecations; H.S. Versnel ("Beyond

---

19. See L. de Heusch, in *L'unité de l'homme* (Paris, 1974); Isambert, op. cit.; N. Habel, *Powers, Plumes, and Piglets* (London, 1980).

20. E.g., by Habel, in *Powers, Plumes, and Piglets*.

21. Ed. C.A. Faraone and D. Obink (New York and Oxford, 1991). I am quoting, with permission, from my review in *Classical Outlook* 69 (1992): 140f.

Cursing"), with prayers for justice and confessions of guilt; J. Scarborough, with the pharmacology of plants, herbs, and roots. From an unfinished work by Sam Eitrem (1872–1966) there is a chapter on dreams and divination in magic and religious ritual, translated by D. Obink and prefaced by F. Graf, who also contributes an essay on prayer in magic and religious ritual. J. Winkler's "The Constraints of Eros" is followed by H.D. Betz' "Magic and Mystery in the Greek Magical Papyri," and C.R. Phillips III concludes the volume with a substantial treatment of sanctions, *"Nullum crimen sine lege:* Socioreligious Sanctions on Magic."

A wealth of material is presented, and intriguing new ideas emerge. What is evident everywhere is the impact of the English translation, with notes, of the Greek Magical Papyri by H.D. Betz and a team of other scholars (see discussion later in this essay).

Versnel's essay is especially impressive because, with flawless scholarship, he sheds light on an area that was largely neglected so far. It seems that there was an alternative to taking an enemy to court or putting a curse on him: it was possible to appeal to a deity.

Scarborough shows in detail that real "scientific" knowledge of the properties of plants existed in antiquity; this kind of knowledge—especially if kept secret—represented a very powerful kind of magic. This is fully confirmed now by J. Mann's *Murder, Magic, and Medicine.* Graf argues that one commonly used criterion to distinguish religion from magic—that the religious person approaches his or her gods respectfully and humbly, while the magician attempts to force them—is not really valid. However, he seems to carry his case too far, and Betz presents a more balanced view.

One of the main problems is the fact, well stated by Phillips (269), that neither the lawgivers nor the priests nor the philosophers had an interest in clearly defining "unsanctioned religious activities." This places us at a serious disadvantage. If the average Athenian or Roman was not sure where the boundaries between religion and magic—between normal, acceptable practices and weird, possibly illegal activities—were, how can we be sure today?

After all, we are dealing with the interaction between different spheres. It would be nice if we could label them properly as "religion," "magic," "medicine," and so on, but in reality they overlap. In our world—and already in ancient Rome, to a certain extent—everything is compartmentalized. For one type of problem, we consult a physician; for another one, a lawyer; and so on. In ancient Athens, you consulted your sorcerer as well as your lawyer if you wanted to win in court. Magic is still a reality today in West Africa, in Haiti, and elsewhere, very much in the sense in which it was a reality in Europe long ago, but it is no longer that kind of reality for academics who write books about it.

In remote antiquity, magic was essentially a method of dealing with all problems of life. But we have to go back very far in time before we find the magus, the great figure of authority in a society where people talked freely about supernatural experiences and took them for granted. In our society, people who hear voices are locked up in institutions, but there have been and still are cultures in which people who do not hear voices and have never seen a ghost are considered abnormal.

Just as Greco-Roman magic borrowed from various religions, it borrowed from the magic of other cultures. It may be useful to consider briefly some possible influences.

The Hittites considered magic a technique that had been invented by their gods.[22] A Hittite practitioner of magic therefore belonged to a privileged group, a caste (like the Persian magi), entrusted with secrets faithfully transmitted from generation to generation, ever since they were first revealed by a god. In fact, the practitioner could pretend to be a god.

This kind of attitude is familiar to anyone who has studied Greco-Roman magic. Pretending that one is not a mere human being but a demon or a god is a common type of masquerading, evident in the Magical Papyri and the Hermetic writings. The magician acquires another identity, adopts another image: he or she is the person with two or more images.

Sumero-Accadian magic, as far as it is known, exhibits some familiar features.[23] Gems and shiny stones were used as amulets; people wore them around the neck, waist, wrists, and ankles. Colors were important. Magicians relied on demons, and they visualized them as follows: they are invisible; they are innumerable (remember the demon in the Gospel according to Mark [5:9, 15] who says that his name is "Legion"); they have no compassion, no understanding; they are evil, yet share in the nature of the divine, and their names are preceded by the divine ideogram; they move fast; they can penetrate walls and control the elements. Human beings—mostly women and mostly foreigners—are the helpers of the demons; that is, they are the sorcerers and witches.

Thanks to an abundance of written texts and monuments, Egyptian

---

22. See M. Vieyra, *Les religions de Proche-Orient* (Paris, 1977), 533ff.
23. See R. Largement, in *Dictionnaire de la Bible,* supp. 5 (Paris, 1953), 706–21.

magic is fairly well known.[24] Its Egyptian name was *heka*, and it was considered an attribute of Re, sometimes represented as a male anthropomorphic deity, grasping a serpent in each hand. Magicians were called "prophets of *heka*" or "those who know." This reminds one of the voodoo term for the *bokor*, that is, the enchanter: "un qui a connaissance."

Magic per se was apparently not illegal in ancient Egypt. Only one criminal case, the "Harem Conspiracy" under Ramses III, is documented (from the Papyrus Lee); in this particular case, wax images of gods and men were made to serve as voodoo dolls. The sorcerer behind this was put to death for conspiring against the life of the king.

The deities of the Egyptians, like those of the Hittites, practiced magic. It was by magical means that Thoth and Isis were able to heal young Horus. On the other hand, even the gods were sometimes powerless against magic aimed at them by the living and the dead.

In Egyptian magic, the dead had special powers. They could predict the future, like the ghosts conjured up by Greek and Roman necromancers; they could also be held responsible, as the Egyptian "Letters to the Dead" show, for some of the evils that befall the living. The dead were able to put pressure on the gods themselves by reciting secret names, by chanting elaborate spells, and by the use of amulets. This can only mean that Egyptian magicians had a "working relationship" with the dead, much like Lucan's Erictho. The mummies of the dead were often buried in the houses of the living, presumably to exploit their power, a custom shocking to Greeks and Romans.

The Egyptians also practiced the ritual of the "Opening of the Mouth." A priest (or a magician) was able to open, through particular spells the lips of a statue representing a god or a dead person. The Greek theurgists claimed to make statutes of the gods smile. Egyptian magicians used spells to protect their powers and make sure that they would keep them in the next world. Some of them were apparently buried with their books, so they could practice their profession in the next world; this is probably why the Magical Papyri were preserved.

On the whole, Egyptian spells are very similar to the ones found in the papyri, and they reflect the same way of thinking, although, perhaps, on an earlier level. Curse tablets and "voodoo dolls" have been

---

24. See J. Pirenne, *Histoire de la civilization Egyptienne*, 3 vols. (Neuchâtel and Paris, 1961–63); A. Massart, in *Dictionnaire de la Bible*, 721–32. On Coptic magic see A. Kropp, *Ausgewählte koptische Zaubertexte*, 3 vols. (Brussels, 1930–31).

found in large quantities. In the texts, the ritual gestures to be executed are often described.

In Egypt, magic and medicine were twin sisters: trying to cure an illness is sometimes represented as a struggle between the magician/ physician and the forces of evil. An Egyptian specialty not found in Greco-Roman culture are the "healing statues." The best-known example is the Statue of Djedher in the Cairo Museum. It represents a kneeling person, arms crossed on the knees, the body covered with pictures and written texts. In front of the statue there is a stele of Horus on crocodiles. The statue is surrounded by a basin which communicates, through a channel, with another, deeper, basin. A liquid which was poured over the statue absorbed the magical power of texts and images. The patient then bathed in the larger basin or drank from the smaller one.

Magic and other occult arts are mentioned in the Bible many times.[25] The author of Wisdom, a hellenized Jew who wrote around the middle of the first century B.C., condemns the ἔργα φαρμακειῶν (12:4) and ridicules the μαγικὴ τέχνη of the Egyptians. In the Old Testament, magic is often practiced by foreigners, and foreign religions are considered a kind of magic. (The attitude of the Greeks was similar: their misunderstanding of Persian religion gave a new meaning to the word μάγος). The prophet Ezekiel (8:17) describes an embassy sent to Jerusalem by King Nebuchadnezar II in 586 B.C. These Persians, among them an ἀρχίμαγος, turned their back to the temple, held branches to their faces, and worshiped the sun. All this was clearly an abomination in the sight of the Jewish onlookers. The Book of Daniel, composed in the second century B.C., tells the story of a young Jewish hostage at the court of the king of Babylon and makes it clear that he was more powerful than all the Babylonian magicians and diviners.

The theme of confrontation—"*my* kind of magic" versus "*their* kind of magic," or "*my* religion" versus "*their* magic"—actually runs through the Old and the New Testaments. Time and again, true religion overcomes foreign magic. A few well-known examples are: Joseph versus the Egyptian diviners (Genesis 41), Moses versus the magicians of Pharaoh

---

25. See A. Lefèvre, in *Dictionnaire de la Bible*, 732–39. Other articles to be consulted in the *Dictionnaire* are the following: "Magie dans la Bible," "Malédiction," "Médécine," "Miracle," "Ordalie," "Parole," "Prière," "Prophétisme," "Psaumes," "Purifications," "Rites," "Sacrements," "Sacrifice," "Sang," "Serment," "Sorts," "Symboles."

(Exodus 7:10–13, 19–23, 8:1–3), and the story of Balaam (Numbers 22–24). In the New Testament we have the confrontation of the apostles with Simon Magus, mentioned earlier; the conflict with Elymas, the Jewish consultant to the Roman proconsul; the prophetess of Philippi (Acts 16:16–18); the Jewish exorcists of Ephesus (Acts 19:13–20). Some Apocrypha exploit this theme even further.

Magic was practiced occasionally in ancient Israel, but there are sanctions against this in the Mosaic Code (Exodus 22:17; Leviticus 22:2–7; Deuteronomy 18:9–14), and these were upheld by the Prophets, who also attack the magic of foreign nations (Isaiah 9:1–3, 11–13 [against Egypt] and 44:25 [against Babylon]). Magic is often associated in the Old Testament with idolatry and the worship of demons.

On later Jewish magic we are now better informed, thanks to the reconstruction of the *Sepher Ha-Razim* by M. Margalioth. This is a magical handbook from the early Talmudic period.[26]

Hellenistic magic is a syncretistic, multinational conglomerate that took shape in Egypt. The term *syncretism* is normally used in the history of religion or philosophy, but it characterizes also the peculiar blend of Egyptian, Jewish, Greek, and Babylonian elements which interacted in Alexandria, the great melting pot of the ancient world. Even though the Magical Papyri date from a later period, the system they reflect is older and probably changed little over the centuries. The papyri are still the most important source for our knowledge of Hellenistic magic.[27]

Until recently, these texts were mainly studied by papyrologists and historians interested in the religious ideas and the social life of Greco-Roman Egypt. Along with the curse tablets *(defixionum tabellae)*, amulets, and so on, they provide a mine of information. The early studies devoted to them by scholars such as A. Dieterich, R. Wünsch, F. Pfister, Th. Hopfner, A.-J. Festugière, and A.D. Nock are still valuable.

The texts published by K. Preisendanz and A. Henrichs are now available in English translations, with excellent introductions, notes, illustrations, and a glossary, thanks to H.D. Betz and a group of other scholars

---

26. Ed. M. Margalioth (Jerusalem, 1966). There is an English translation by M.A. Morgan (Atlanta, 1983). See also S. Liebermann, *Greeks in Jewish Palestine* (Philadelphia, 1942), 91–114; J. Goldin, in *Aspects of Religious Propaganda in Judaism and Early Christianity* (Notre Dame, Ind., 1976), 115–47; J. Neusner, in *Studies in Judaism* (Lanham, Md., 1987), 46–70.

27. See, e.g., A.F. Segal, in *Studies in Gnosticism and Hellenistic Religions*, ed. R. van den Broek and M.J. Vermaseren (Leiden, 1981), 349–75.

(vol. 1, Chicago, 1986). No less than fifty newly discovered or newly published papyri are included in the first volume, and the demotic portions of the bilingual Greek-demotic papyri are also translated. The second volume will include an index of Greek words, a subject index based on the translations, a collection of parallels between the Magical Papyri and early Christian literature, and a comprehensive bibliography.[28]

The series *New Documents Illustrating Early Christianity*, edited by G.H.R. Horsley and others (vols. 1–6 Macquarie, 1981–91), includes many magical texts and is very useful because of the comments it offers.

What remains to be done is, among other things, an interpretation of the theology, the kind of religious mood that reveals itself in the papyri. There has been considerable disagreement among scholars so far. E.R. Dodds, for instance, said that these texts "constantly operate with the débris of other people's religions,"[29] while A.-J. Festugière felt that some texts could be called religious in nature.[30] This was also the view of M.P. Nilsson, who wrote, "Several invocations are quite beautiful and marked by a genuine religious spirit."[31]

The prescriptions given in these "working copies of practical magicians" (A.D. Nock) could easily be copied onto other materials. A recently discovered love charm on a lead tablet shows this process. It was

---

28. For more recent work, see, e.g., D. Wortmann, *Bonner Jahrbücher* 168 (1968): 56–111; R. Daniel, *ZPE* 19 (1975): 249–64; Christine Harrauer, *Meliouchos: Studien zur Entwicklung religiöser Vorstellungen in griechischen synkretistischen Zaubertexten* (Vienna, 1987); M. Fantuzzi, *RFIC* 119 (1991): 79–86. Fantuzzi reviews, among other works, R. Merkelbach and M. Totti, *Abrasax: Ausgewählte Papyri religiösen und magischen Inhalts*, vol. 1, *Gebete* (Opladen, 1990), and R.W. Daniel and F. Maltomini, *Supplementum Magicum*, 2 vols. (Opladen, 1990–92). These two volumes also include texts inscribed on earthenware vessels, lead and silver tablets, linen cloth, etc. There is now a Spanish translation of selected texts, thanks to J.L. Calvo Martínez and Dolores Sánchez Romero (Madrid, 1987). Incidentally, the material presented in *Supplementum Magicum* is conveniently divided into six categories: (1) φυλακτήρια, (2) ἀγωγαί, "love spells"; (3) ἀραί, "curses"; (4) θυμοκάτοχα, "restrainers of wrath"; (5) χαριτήσια, "spells to win someone's favor"; (6) μαντεῖα, "predictions." In some categories, we find pagan and Christian texts (yes, "Curses, Christian" is an entry!), but in categories 2 and 6, only pagan ones.

29. E.R. Dodds, *Pagan and Christian in an Age of Anxiety* (Cambridge, 1965), 73.

30. A.-J. Festugière, *L'idéal religieux des Grecs et de l'Evangile*, 2d ed. (Paris, 1981), 282.

31. M.P. Nilsson, *Die Religion in den griechischen Zauberpapyri* (Lund, 1949), 155. See also H.G. Gundel, in *Proceedings of the 12th International Congress of Papyrologists at Michigan* (Toronto, 1970), 185.

probably written by a professional magician in the third or fourth century A.D. on the basis of *PGM* 4.296–434 or a closely related text.[32] This rolled-up lead tablet, roughly eleven square centimeters in size, was found inside a clay vase, together with a clay statuette of a kneeling woman, with her hands bound behind her back and her body pierced with needles, a set of objects which combines the curse tablet with the voodoo doll. Sometimes, the curse appears on the doll, and occasionally the doll is broken.[33] It is clear that the magical recipes not only could be put to practical use right away but also might be copied, and some instructions actually call for transcriptions to be made.

Several studies of amulets, talismans, and magical gems have been made in recent years.[34] The Byzantine tradition that preserves stories about Apollonius of Tyana tells of an unusual talisman:[35] The miracle worker set up τελέσματα (talismans) in many cities. These were sacred objects designed to protect people from all kinds of plagues and diseases. A large scorpion, for instance, would protect a whole city from scorpions. What was the idea behind this? Probably that one single monumental amulet was sufficient to protect a large number of people from scorpions, thus making it unnecessary for them to carry individual amulets at all times.

It is easy to imagine all the fears and all the obsessions that tortured the superstitious (see Theophrastus' *Portrait* of the type). If one constantly worried about lurking dangers—snakes, scorpions, the evil eye—one would have to wear many amulets, one for each specific danger. The more superstitious a person was, the more he or she would be loaded down by the sheer weight of the amulets carried around the neck or worn on the fingers in the form of rings with gemstones. (Incidentally, all jewelry may have its origin in magic.)

There were, at all times, more perishable magical tools, such as aromatic fragrances, girdles, and little stones mentioned in the papyri.

---

32. Horsley, *New Documents,* vol. 1, no. 8.

33. On curse tablets see S. Eitrem and H. Herter, *RAC* 2 (1954): 380–85; K. Preisendanz, *RAC* 8 (1972): 1–19; D.R. Jordan, *ZPE* 19 (1975): 254–58; idem., "Contributions to the Study of Greek Defixiones" (Ph.D. diss., University of Michigan, 1985).

34. See F. Eckstein and J.H. Waszink, *RAC* 1 (1950): 397–411; A. Delatte and Ph. Derchain, *Les intailles magiques Gréco-Egyptiennes* (Paris, 1964); D. Wortmann, *Bonner Jahrbücher* 175 (1975): 63–82.

35. G. Petzke, *Die Traditionen über Apollonios von Tyana und das Neue Testament,* Studia ad Corpus Hellenisticum Novum Testamenti 1 (Leiden, 1970), 24ff.

These were supposed to concentrate the occult forces of the earth, the moon, and the stars and make them useful. Apollonius of Tyana (Philostratus, *Vita Apoll.* 7.39) implicitly acknowledges such realizations. And if jewels had, originally, a magical function, why not perfume? Alchemists manufactured perfumes in Egypt, and strong fragrances were used in theurgical rites.[36]

The Hellenistic conglomerate spread from Egypt to Italy, where it associated itself with native traditions. This could happen anywhere, even in countries which had, long ago, furnished ingredients to the melting pot of Alexandria.

In Italy, the situation is different. The Romans preserved some very ancient beliefs and rituals which probably never reached Alexandria. Hellenistic magic, on the other hand, may have reached Italy at a time when the Hellenistic system had already taken shape. Nigidius Figulus no doubt played an important role: he was a Roman senator, a friend of Cicero's, a scholar (like Pliny the Elder), an astrologer, and a clairvoyant— a very unusual type of Roman, in other words.[37]

Through the Law of the Twelve Tables (fifth century B.C.) we are informed of some very ancient forms of magic practiced in Italy and prosecuted as criminal offenses. One of them is the practice of *fruges excantare*, by which one farmer could attempt to ruin another farmer's harvest by chanting certain spells or to transfer a neighbor's abundant harvest onto his own property.[38] It must have happened now and then that, in the same year, in the same area, one farmer did exceedingly well, while the others were disappointed. Presumably, all the farmers had offered the same prayers and sacrifices to the same gods; hence the farmer who did conspicuously better than the rest must have, in their opinion, done something in secret, and this additional something could only be black magic.

The Law of the Twelve Tables also made it a criminal offense to recite a *malum carmen*. A *malum carmen* is any magical spell designed to hurt another person; the Law of the Twelve Tables uses the verb *incantare*, from which came the noun *incantamentum* and the verbs *enchanter* in French and "to enchant" in English. The earliest Roman law distinguishes *malum*

---

36. For new perspectives see Jacqueline de Romilly, *Magic and Rhetoric in the Ancient World* (Cambridge, Mass., 1975). On magic and art see, e.g., J. Vidal, in *Dictionnaire des religions* (Paris, 1984), 993f.

37. See the excellent treatment of D.P. Harmon, *ANRW* 2.16.3 (1986): 1909–73.

38. See Anne-Marie Tupet, *ANRW* 2.16.3 (1986): 2610–17.

carmen from *famosum carmen*, which means "libel," but libel, or defama-
tion, was also a kind of magic.[39]

Some new curses have been found in recent years, for example, a
bilingual inscription on a gold tablet from Dacia, from the late imperial
period (Horsley, *New Documents*, vol. 2, no. 12). In the Greek part,
Ἀδωναί and θεοὶ ὕψιστοι are invoked, while the Latin part reads as
follows: *Demon immunditiae te agitet, Aeli Firme. Stet supra caput Iuliae
Surillae* [may the demon of impurity pursue you, Aelius Firmus. May it
stand over the head of Iulia Surilla]. The letter *F* of the first name is
pierced with a needle, and a small cross stands beside the letter *S* of the
second name. The oldest specimen of this kind of *defixio* found in Greece
dates from the fifth century B.C.; the oldest one found in Italy dates from
the fourth century B.C.[40]

In Italy, the belief in the evil eye seems to be very old. *Fascinum,* the
word which designates a spell caused by an enemy who has the evil eye,
seems to be related to Greek βασκανία, "envy, jealousy." One of the
reasons why people would cast spells on other people is clearly the envy
and jealousy they felt. To protect oneself against the evil eye, it was
necessary to wear an amulet, a talisman. Such objects, called φυλακτήρια,
have been found in large numbers: they consist sometimes of animal
figurines, especially horned beasts ("casting out the devil with the devil");
sometimes of parts of the human body, for instance, an eye pierced with
an arrow, an open hand, a phallus (also called *fascinum* in Latin).[41]

It is impossible to say which features of Italic magic are typical or
unique. The magic of all periods and cultures has much in common, but
there are striking local variations of universal practices and beliefs. There
are too many gaps in our sources, but the following practices seem to be
characteristic of Italic witchcraft: the "breaking of snakes" *(angues ruptae)*
through spells; the werewolf phenomenon *(versipellis,* "one who can
change his skin"); *striges* or *strigae,* that is, women who could transform
themselves into birds and were feared as vampires; the use of dead bodies
or their parts for witchcraft (e.g., by Erictho in Lucan's *Pharsalia* 6).[42]

There are some curious customs or rites that cannot easily be labeled

---

39. Ibid., 2595.

40. A well-known example, *CIL* 1.2.2520, has been discussed by W.S. Fox
(*AJP* 33, supp. 1 [1912]) and by Tupet (*ANRW*, 2602f.). This curse is designed to
destroy a woman by the name of Avonia and is addressed to Proserpina Salvia.
The style is similar to that of curses in the Magical Papyri.

41. Tupet, *ANRW*, 2606–10.

42. Tupet, *ANRW*, 2617–26, 2647–53, 2657–68.

as "magical" or "religious." An example is the rite of Tacita, "the Silent One," the mother of the Lares, who was worshiped during the Feralia, the period of nine days in February which was sacred to the family dead. Young girls of a family gathered around an old woman from outside the family, who, with three fingers, placed three grains of incense on the threshold of their house, as an offering to the Manes. She then tied a lead doll with threads, recited some formulas, and chewed seven black beans. After that, she cooked the head of a sardine that had been pierced by a bronze needle. After having poured out a few drops of wine, she drank a large share, divided the rest among the girls, and said, "We have tied the hostile tongues, the mouths of our enemies." As she spoke these words, the old woman left the house, probably not too sober.

This is the ritual as described by Ovid (*Fasti* 2.569–82), and much has been written about it.[43] It may be understood as an apotropaic ritual, more magical than religious in nature. The old woman, who was not part of the family but summoned from outside for this specific purpose, looks very much like a witch. The family had to be protected against the "evil tongue," which could be just as harmful as the evil eye. But what is the connection with the cult of the Manes?

A good deal of work has been done recently on some of the magicians, miracle workers, and "pseudoprophets" of the first and second centuries A.D. Apollonius of Tyana, often presented as a pagan imitator of Christ, still fascinates historians.[44] New evidence for his cult has been found,[45] and there is a new edition of his letters.[46] A theologian who has studied his feats comes to the conclusion that they are not essentially different from those reported in the Gospels;[47] but it would not be difficult to maintain the opposite thesis, for Apollonius, unlike Jesus, managed to manipulate people by suggesting to them that they were

---

43. S. Eitrem, *Hermes und die Toten* (Christiania, 1909), 10, 18; R. Wünsch, *RhM* 56 (1901):402ff.; H.J. Rose, *JRS* 23 (1933): 60; L. Deubner, *ARW* 33 (1936): 103f.; etc.

44. Among more recent studies, one should mention K. Gross, *RAC* 1 (1950): 529–32; G. Petzke, *Die Traditionen über Apollonios*; J.L. Bernard, *Apollonius de Tyane et Jésus* (Paris, 1977). There is a new translation by C.P. Jones, with an introduction by G. Bowersock (Baltimore, 1970).

45. Horsley, *New Documents*, 3:49f.; cf. C.P. Jones, *JHS* 100 (1980): 190ff.

46. By R.J. Penella, in *Mnemosyne* supp. 56 (Leiden, 1979). Of the 115 letters preserved as a corpus, together with 16 preserved in Philostratus' vita, Penella rejects or suspects roughly one-third. On no. 53 see C.P. Jones, *Chiron* 12 (1983): 137–44.

47. G. Petzke, *Die Traditionen über Apollonios*.

possessed and needed to be exorcised by him. Another scholar points out that there is a curious inconsistency in Philostratus' vita of Apollonius: on the one hand, he presents his hero as a "Wise Man," along the lines of Pythagoras or Empedocles; on the other hand, he enriches this tradition with a substantial amount of folklore.[48]

Simon Magus has already been mentioned. It would be useful to compare him with Alexander of Abonuteichus,[49] the "False Prophet," and the kind of magician that Apuleius, at one time, apparently wanted to become.

All these figures are quite different, and yet they seem to have something in common: they were trying to revive and embody the old tradition of the shaman. What makes it so difficult to compare them with each other is the nature of the evidence. In the case of Apollonius of Tyana, we have practically only the testimony of an uncritical admirer, Philostratus. In the case of Simon Magus and Alexander of Abonuteichus, we have mainly a hostile tradition. In the case of Apuleius of Madaura, we have his own testimony, but it must be used with caution, because part of it (the *Apologia*) is self-serving, and because the other part (the *Metamorphoses*) is fiction.

It is easy to understand that a brilliant young man like Apuleius, a Platonist, wished to become a magus, just as some Neoplatonists, like Iamblichus, were attracted later by the possibilities of theurgy. Apuleius was motivated by *curiositas*, which is, like its Greek equivalent, περιουργία, almost a synonym for "magical knowledge." Apuleius learned the hard way (πάθει μάθος!) the lesson that religion is superior to magic, and he found salvation in the religion of Isis. His novel is the story of a spiritual pilgrimage which led the hero from Platonism via the magical arts to mystery religion.[50]

In conclusion, it might be worthwhile to review the opposition to magic and the occult arts in antiquity. We have seen so far that magic is

---

48. F.E. Brenk, *ANRW* 2.16.3 (1986): 2136; cf. E.L. Bowie, *ANRW* 2.16.2 (1978): 1652–99.

49. One still needs to consult O. Weinreich, *NJbb* 24 (1921): 129–51; but see now Phillips, *Helios*, 158 nn. 52–53.

50. See A.-J. Festugière, *Personal Religion among the Greeks* (Berkeley, 1954), chap. 5; F. Solmsen, *Isis among the Greeks and Romans* (Cambridge, Mass., 1979); J. Gwyn Griffiths, *Classical Mediterranean Spirituality*, 52–64. On the two *lamiae* see Brenk, *ANRW*, 2132f.; on the relationship between Lucius and the charming, but treacherous, Photis see R. de Smet, *Latomus* 46 (1987): 612–23. On Apuleius' "Conversion" see this volume, pp. 223–38.

often represented as a caricature of religion, something strange and foreign, difficult to control. In Greece as well as in Italy there was a powerful religious establishment, and esoteric, nonconformist groups were eo ipso suspicious and could be denounced as heretical. These suspicions are well attested in the Bible and throughout the Middle Ages. In ancient Egypt, on the other hand, magic was more or less tolerated, unless it threatened the sacred person of the pharaoh.

In book 11 of the *Odyssey*, the hero conjures up the souls of the dead and seeks a prophecy from the seer Tiresias. This is essentially a magical ritual, and his instructions came from Circe, who is usually called a sorceress, although she might be a minor deity left over from a pre-Greek culture. In the Homeric *Hymn to Demeter* (228–30), witchcraft, called ἐπηλυσίη, is rejected, but the text is corrupt, and the very word ἐπηλυσίη has been restored on the basis of another uncertain passage in the *Hymn to Hermes* (37).

Plato attacks the abuses of φαρμακεία but seems to consider them a fact of life. Some philosophers representing Middle Platonism and quite a few Neoplatonists were interested in magic, theurgy, or demonology. The Stoics, with few exceptions, believed in divination. It was Posidonius who formulated the principle of cosmic sympathy, furnishing a philosophical basis for magic, astrology, and other occult practices.

The oldest Roman legislation known to us, the Law of the Twelve Tables, condemned various forms of witchcraft. Later, under the emperors, magic was illegal, even though the laws were not always rigorously enforced.[51]

An edict on an Egyptian papyrus dated 198/9 A.D. (Horsley, *New Documents*, vol. 1, no. 49) is particularly intriguing. It was sent out during the reign of Septimius Severus, notorious before his accession to the throne for his habit of consulting astrologers, and notorious afterward for his determination not to allow anyone to do this. He was afraid someone might ask the same question he used to ask: When will the emperor die? Just to ask this question was a serious offense—as we know from Ammianus Marcellinus (29.1.25ff.)[52]—because it would indicate a conspiracy.

---

51. See F.H. Cramer, *Astrology in Roman Law and Politics* (Philadelphia, 1954); R. MacMullen, *Enemies of the Roman Order* (Cambridge, Mass., 1960), 95ff., 125ff.; Phillips, in *Magika Hiera* (see n. 21), 260ff.

52. On Ammianus Marcellinus as a source for religious beliefs and magical practices see Phillips, in *Magika Hiera*, 260, 263, 264.

What was the attitude of the church? It seems that, for the early church, magic, demonology, and divination were facts of life. It would have been difficult for the new faith to sweep away deeply ingrained beliefs and habits overnight. The new converts were still somehow in awe of the power of the ancient idols all around them, and they obviously worried about the presence of spirits and evil demons in this world. Therefore, they wore amulets and practiced some sort of magic to be on the safe side.[53] The earliest Christian amulets are from the fourth century, the latest from the eighth.

But the fourth century witnessed the stiffening of the resistance of the church against all forms of magic. We see this from the writings of St. John Chrysostom and St. Augustine and from canon 36 of the Council of Laodicea, held sometime between 341 and 381. Canon 36 specifies that "priests and clergy may not be sorcerers (μάγοι), enchanters (ἐπαοιδοί), or astrologers (μαθηματικοί) and must not make so-called amulets (φυλακτήρια), which are poisons of their souls." Those who still wore such amulets were to be cast out of the church.[54] If these practices were condemned so strongly, they must have been fairly common until, say, 381, and the archaeological evidence suggests that they did not cease for a long time. Magical books were burned at various times: at the order of pagan authorities; under Augustus, and, again, under Diocletian; and also by the new converts at Ephesus, guided by St. Paul.

---

53. See J. Engemann, *Jahrbuch für Antike und Christentum* 18 (1975): 22–48; D.E. Aune, *ANRW* 2.33.2 (1980): 1507–57.

54. See B.M. Metzger, in *Historical and Literary Studies, Pagan, Jewish, and Christian,* New Testament Tools and Studies 8 (Grand Rapids, 1968), 106f.; Horsley, *New Documents,* 3:116.

Magic, Miracle, and Salvation: The Spiritual Journey of Apuleius

Lucius Apuleius was born in Madaura in North Africa about 125 A.D. He received an excellent education, mostly in rhetoric and literature in Carthage, and went on to Athens to study philosophy with various teachers. Apuleius traveled widely both in Greece and in the Near East, and during these travels he was apparently initiated into several mystery religions. Some of his experiences probably serve as background to his great novel *Metamorphoses,* or *The Golden Ass,* which culminates, in book 11, in the initiation of the hero, Lucius, into the mysteries of Isis.

For a while, the author seems to have practiced law in Rome, but then he returned to North Africa. On a trip to Alexandria, he fell sick at Oea (today Tripoli) and had to stay there for a while. He met a rich widow, Pudentilla, and married her. For reasons that are obvious, members of her family disapproved of this marriage and accused Apuleius of being a sorcerer. As a well-trained lawyer and orator, he defended himself before the proconsul Claudius Maximus, and the speech he delivered in court—or, more likely, a revised version—has survived and is a very valuable source for our knowledge of ancient magical beliefs and practices. It is also a very entertaining literary production, because Apuleius elegantly shows off his own intellectual superiority to his accusers. Of course, he was in real danger, for a conviction of sorcery led to a mandatory death sentence. Apuleius, however, was acquitted and spent the rest of his life comfortably in Carthage, as a celebrated writer, lecturer, and philosopher. Among the honors he received was his election as priest of the imperial cult.

We have some of his more technical philosophical works—for example, an introduction to Platonism, *De Platone et eius dogmate,* and an essay on Socrates' δαιμόνιον, *De Deo Socratis* (discussed later in this essay)—but the novel was his most popular work. It is partly based on an earlier Greek novel by Lucius of Patrai, known in antiquity as *Lucius, or the Donkey,* which was also used by the Greek satirist Lucian of Samosata, roughly Apuleius' contemporary, for one of his works. To some extent, however, Apuleius' novel must be autobiographical. We know that Apuleius was interested in magic, and it was this that put his life at risk. *Curiositas* is the key word Apuleius uses, and, like its Greek equivalent, περιουργία, it is almost a synonym of *magia*.[1] Intellectual curiosity, to us, is a good thing, but there was—and is—a school of thought which maintains that certain things ought not to be explored. The hero of Apuleius' novel had to learn this the hard way—πάθει μάθος. The novel, taken together with the unpleasant experience of the author who was accused of witchcraft, could reflect the author's own experiences. This, at least, seems to be the consensus of scholars. I would like to suggest that this view overlooks a certain irony which is built into the novel and which fits its style very well.

The anonymous scholar who contributed the article "Apuleius" for the famous eleventh edition of the *Encyclopaedia Britannica* (1911) describes the *Metamorphoses* as follows: "The dignified, the ludicrous, the voluptuous, the horrible, succeed each other with bewildering rapidity; fancy and feeling are everywhere apparent, but no less so affectation, meretricious ornament and that effort to say everything finely which prevents anything from being said well." Part of this assessment has been carried over, still anonymous, into the more recent editions of this work of reference.

What happens in this bewildering novel? The events are interesting enough in themselves, and even though some of them may seem trivial or ludicrous or sensational to us, they lead up to a kind of spiritual rebirth of the author, almost a conversion. It is a novel that can be enjoyed for its own sake, because it has all the necessary ingredients of grand entertainment: suspense, sex, a variety of colorful characters, funny episodes, dramatic adventures, and so on. In addition, it has a moral or spiritual message for readers who are looking beyond these ingredients. This essay is mainly concerned with the message, but it will also deal with some of the events leading up to it.

Lucius, a personable young man from a good family, well educated

---

1. See H.-J. Mette, "Curiositas," in *Festschrift Bruno Snell* (Munich, 1956), 227–35; A. Labhardt, "Curiositas," *Mus. Helv.* 17 (1960): 206–24; H. Blumenberg, "Curiositas," *Revue Des Etudes Augustiniennes* 7 (1961): 35–70; E. des Places, introd. to *Oracles chaldaïques*, (Paris, 1971), 20–21. Des Places comments on a pun in St. Augustine *Civ. Dei* 10.16: θεουργός, περιουργός. See also A. Scobie on *Met.* 1.2, in *Commentary on Apuleius'* Metamorphoses, Beitr. z. Klass. Philol. 54 (Meisenheim, 1975).

and well connected, is traveling on business in Greece and arrives at a city named Hypata in Thessaly, a part of the world reputed for its accomplished witches and sorceresses. He decides to take advantage of this opportunity and find out all he can on the subject of magic. He stays at the house of a guest-friend whose wife, Pamphile, happens to be a famous witch. Lucius promptly seduces Pamphile's beautiful young maidservant, Photis, or is seduced by her. He asks her to provide a magical ointment which would transform him into a bird, any kind of bird, just so he could fly through the air. Photis seems to be more than willing to help him, but she gets the wrong ointment, and poor Lucius is transformed into not a bird but a donkey. It is not clear whether the wily Photis tricked her lover or made an honest mistake. In any event, she seems devastated and tries to comfort Lucius by telling him that there is a very simple remedy: all he has to do is eat roses, and then he will regain his human shape at once. Simple as it seems—and the remedy will be within reach several times—the irony of fate demands that Lucius remain a donkey for a long time and suffer, in this condition, all sorts of humiliations, frustrations, and miseries. Because he is now an animal, though he still thinks and feels like a human being, his fate is worse than that of the lowest slave.

This is, in fact, the beginning of a long series of tragicomical adventures for Lucius. He falls into the hands of robbers, who take him to their hideout. There he meets another captive, a beautiful young woman. In order to cheer her up, the old woman who keeps house for the robbers tells her the enchanting fairy tale of Cupid and Psyche, one of the best-known episodes of the work (4.28–6.24), which can be interpreted on different levels, like the whole novel.

Psyche, a beautiful young princess, has offended the goddess Venus, who sends out her son, Cupid, to punish her. But Cupid falls in love with Psyche and makes her his wife—under one condition: she may never look at him to find out who he really is. She agrees and is allowed to dwell in a marvelous palace and enjoy the most pleasant life; but her lover only visits her at night, shrouded in darkness.

Out of jealousy, her sisters poison her mind and make her believe that she is married to a horrible monster and must kill him. She gets a sharp knife and a lamp, but when she actually sees Cupid lying asleep beside her, she is overcome by his beauty and loves him more than ever. Of course she is unable to harm him, but she manages to wake him up, because a drop of hot oil from her lamp falls on his body. In his anger he leaves her at once, and as a punishment she must wander through the world, trying to find his forgiveness.

She submits to Venus, who treats her harshly, like a runaway slave, and inflicts cruel tasks and trials on her. One of them involves a descent to the underworld, from where she must bring back a jar without trying to find out what is inside. Of course, she is tempted by *curiositas*, lifts the cover and is in trouble again. But Cupid, who has been looking for her and still loves her, is able to save her. He obtains Jupiter's permission to marry his beloved Psyche; Venus agrees and even dances at the wedding. Finally, Psyche is admitted to the rank of the immortals.

Much has been written about the meaning of this sophisticated fairy tale. It may have more than one meaning. Here are some of the possible interpretations.

1. Psyche—that is, the human soul—becomes immortal through the love of a higher being and through trials and sufferings undergone in the search for the beloved.
2. The tale is a "modern" interpretation of Plato's doctrine of the pilgrimage of the soul in the *Phaedrus.*
3. Ill-directed *curiositas* is dangerous. The tale reinforces this particular theme of the novel.
4. As Psyche finally submits to the will of Venus and accepts her conditions, she prefigures Lucius' submission to the goddess Isis and his initiation into her religion.[2]

Now the main story continues. Along with the young woman for whose benefit the tale was told, Lucius, in his donkey shape, is freed from his captivity. But there are still no roses within reach, and fortune hands him over to new tribulations. He is bought by a group of priests of the "Syrian goddess" (books 8–9, a grotesque interlude), a miller, a market gardener, and then a soldier; the soldier sells him to two slaves, a cook and a baker, and he is well fed for a while at least, for he has kept his human appetites. He is even exhibited as a freak, an animal behaving uncannily like a human being. On the whole, this period in Lucius' life is not too unpleasant, but then a new owner involves him in sexual intercourse with a woman sentenced to be thrown to the beasts in the arena. The idea thoroughly disgusts Lucius, and he flees to Cenchreae, one of

2. See T. Hägg, *The Novel in Antiquity* (Berkeley, Calif., 1983), 183.

the two ports of Corinth. His successful escape eventually leads to his deliverance (book 11).

First, he finds a secluded beach where he can get some rest. Night falls; the sea is perfectly calm; nature seems peaceful. But suddenly he wakes up and sees the full moon rising from the sea, and he knows that fate, finally, offers him the hope of deliverance by placing him in the presence of a benevolent divine power. He gets up, purifies himself by plunging his head seven times into the waves and then addresses a prayer to the moon. He invokes the Queen of Heaven under various names—as Ceres, Venus, Diana, Hecate—and in his prayer he implores the "goddess with many names" (πολυώνυμος), that is, Isis, to bring an end to his misery and restore him to human shape. He begs that if his restoration is impossible, he be allowed to die.

At this point, something ought to be said about Apuleius' use of the transformation theme. Unlike the many figures in Ovid's *Metamorphoses*, Lucius, the one and only "hero" of Apuleius' novel, is promised a chance to return to human shape. Ovid's characters, after their transformation, forever remain the flowers or animals or stars they have become, even though the principle of continuing change is granted in book 15, where Pythagoras himself proposes his doctrine of the transmigration of the soul, which includes the possibility of a return to human shape after one has been a bird or a dog or a donkey for a certain time. For Apuleius, Plato was "to a large extent a Pythagorean" (*Florida* 15), and it must have been natural for him to read the idea of transformation into Plato's thought. Apuleius' own interpretation of the doctrine seems fairly obvious: It is not difficult to become an animal in this life, a donkey, for instance, and lead the life of a donkey, with all its misery and degradation. But it is very difficult to become a human being, that is, a true human being, *homo vere humanus*, as Cicero would say. This kind of transformation, a very gradual one, is only possible with the help of philosophy or religion or, preferably, both.

Lucius, still in the shape of a donkey, once more falls asleep and has a vision of Isis, in which she emerges from the sea. We should remember that Isis had become, by this time, a kind of cosmic goddess who combined, in her person, the powers and qualities (ἀρεταί) of all the deities Lucius had addressed before. The propaganda of the missionaries of Isis skillfully exploited her universal appeal.

Isis could also be invoked by magicians. Apuleius does not mention this, but I will deal with this aspect a little later. What he delivers here, in book 11, is her ἀρεταλογία, that is, a liturgical catalogue of her qualities and powers. It follows a certain pattern.[3] One of them is the universal appeal mentioned before: she is worshiped all over the world under different names. She is the "day of salvation," *dies salutaris,* and promises a new life to those who believe in her. Isis comforts Lucius and tells him not to worry. She now is his true mother.

The next day, she announces, will be the festival of the "ship of Isis," *Isidis navigium,* for, among many other things, she is also the goddess of navigation. This festival is celebrated on the fifth of March every year by a solemn procession from the city to the shore. The priest of Isis, walking at the very end of the procession, will be holding a wreath of roses; Lucius must eat the roses and will then become a human being again. After this miraculous event, Lucius will have to devote the rest of his life to Isis. Strict obedience and self-discipline will be required of him, but the reward is great: life in the world to come!

On the following day, everything happens as predicted by the goddess. Her priest has already been instructed in a dream that a donkey is in need of the roses which he will be carrying, and he offers them to him. Lucius is also given a garment to cover his nakedness, and the priest, in a state of trance, has a vision of the kind of life that Lucius, after his rebirth, will lead. He now has reached "the harbor of calm, the altar of mercy." Everyone congratulates him, as he joins the procession and takes part in the festivities, until the faithful come to the temple of Isis at Cenchreae.

Lucius then rents lodgings within the sacred precinct, so he can remain close to the goddess for some time. As a layman, he shares the life of the priests and spends long hours every day in contemplation before the statue of Isis, experiencing a state of perfect bliss. Almost every night, Isis appears to him in a dream and urges him to let himself be initiated into her mysteries. Clearly, this is the kind of healing incubation customary at Epidaurus: Lucius is still a patient and needs to be shown the way to salvation. Incidentally, we know that Asclepius, the god of healing, was associated with Isis (and Serapis) in the sanctuary of Aegira in Achaea.[4]

But Lucius still hesitates, partly because of his awe of the deity, partly because of the austerities demanded by his new way of life. One day, however, after a new dream vision (11.20), he makes up his mind

---

3. See, e.g., *P. Oxy.* 1380 and A.-J. Festugière, *Harv. Theol. Rev.* 42 (1949): 209ff.

4. See Pausanias 7.26.7; L. Edelstein, *Asclepius,* 672.

and goes to see the high priest *(primarius sacerdos)*, only to be told that no one may be initiated unless Isis herself has approved of the candidate, chosen the day, and indicated how much the whole ceremony will cost, a matter of some importance.

Through Lucius' experience, presented as fiction, mixed with autobiographical experiences, we realize that an initiation into the mysteries of Isis had to be approached with proper reverence. It was seen as a kind of voluntary death, a self-sacrifice, followed by a new life, a better life. To approach this ritual without actually being called or chosen would be sacrilege. The candidate must prepare himself or herself by a rigorous diet (11.27.7–8), among other things.

At long last, the great moment comes. Isis declares her will, and the initiation can take place (11.22–24).

Overjoyed after his initiation, Lucius remains in the sacred precinct for a few more days. Then, after having addressed a prayer to the goddess and embraced her priest, whom he now loves like a father, he returns to his native land.

A few days later, Isis sends him to Rome, where he leads the same kind of life he knew at Cenchreae. He prays frequently and earnestly in the temple of Isis on the Campus Martius. After a year has passed, he is told in a dream that the time has come for him to be initiated into the mysteries of Osiris.

One would imagine that, having become a worshiper of Isis, he would already be a worshiper of Osiris, but perhaps this new initiation represented a higher degree. Or is Apuleius telling us that, once one joins a religion of this type, initiations and other rituals never end? As we have seen, they were not free of charge. The "hero" submits once more, although his savings have dwindled by now; he has spent a good deal of money on his first initiation, on the trip to Rome—which was not really part of the deal—and for the outrageous living costs in the capital.

All these details are apt to remind us of the earlier part of the novel and of Lucius as he was before. He has not really changed that much. He realizes that even religion is a kind of business and that salvation is not entirely free. He accepts this as a fact of life, though with some misgivings, and spends his money once more, because it seems a good investment. He is a little annoyed when, in another dream, he is ordered to undergo a third initiation, which means further expense. Nevertheless, he obeys and is assured by Osiris himself that he will have a successful career as a lawyer. Lucius is a loyal supporter of Isis, but he is not entirely uncritical. This is part of his self-irony.

He now enters the order of the *pastophori* (11.29–30), and things work out for him professionally. His money was well spent. His trials and tribulations had not been in vain. Life treats him well in this world, and he is assured of eternal life in the next world.

In his book *Conversion* (Oxford, 1933), A.D. Nock offers a persuasive analysis of the religious experience described in Apuleius' novel. He calls this an "approximation" to a true conversion (14–15), as we may observe it in Judaism and early Christianity. Due to special circumstances (Nock 138), Lucius' new loyalty to the cult of Isis has the "emotional value" of a true conversion. It is the result of a whole series of initiations (Nock 114–15). Today, one might call this a program of conditioning: Lucius is being "programmed," "brainwashed," and part of him knows it; but he accepts it, and it works out for the best, for his professional success proves that he has chosen the right path. Part of ancient religion was, in a sense, a business deal, a bargain you made with the deity: you do something for Isis, and she may be expected to do something for you. This is not a matter of pure faith or deep sentiment: it is a practical arrangement. Paganism is different from Judaism and Christianity in many ways and especially in this respect. As Nock (14–15) has pointed out, Jews and Christians demanded from converts a complete renunciation of the old and a completely new start; they demanded a strong faith and a new way of life within a new group, not just the formal acceptance of new rites. It was essential to belong to the new faith, body and soul.

As a Platonist, Apuleius was familiar with the concept of two kinds of life, a higher and a lower. In the philosophical sense, conversion is the turning from the lower to the higher. This may happen under the impact of a dream or a vision. It may be, more likely, the result of years of intense study and meditation.

Nock was certainly right when he called Lucius' religious experience an "approximation" to conversion. Referring to *Metamorphoses* 9.14, Nock wrote (63; cf. 283): "A normal pagan might well feel that there was something of value and use in customs so strenuously maintained, without being prepared to go to the drastic length of becoming a proselyte, which meant a complete renunciation of his past, an acceptance of heavy obligations, previously not incumbent upon him, and not a little social disapproval or ostracism."

This may not directly apply to Lucius; at least Apuleius says nothing about it. Lucius seems a little annoyed by the pressure put on him to undergo still further initiations and spend even more money, but he cooperates. Does this mean that he is now a completely new human being? Not if we weigh his own testimony. Basically, he is still a shrewd, realistic, practical-minded observer of the human scene. He reasons as follows: "I provided what was wanted for the initiation liberally, contributing everything according to the zeal of my piety rather than the measure of my resources. . . . I did not at all regret my toil or my expenditure, for through the liberal providence of the gods I was now enriched with legal fees" (11.30).

He did accept the idea of personal sacrifice. He spent money for Isis that he would have liked to save. He did humiliate himself by shaving his head; he would have preferred to keep his hair and look attractive. But these were temporary inconveniences, considering the rewards in this life and in the next.

Like the main characters in Petronius' *Satyricon,* the other great Latin novel that has survived (in fragments), Lucius moves in a world that values sensuous pleasures, ἡδονή, such as food, wine, sex, perfumes, music, elegant clothes, luxuries of all kinds. But Lucius also desires knowledge, from the beginning: he is an intellectual, like the seedy protagonists of Petronius' novel, and his *curiositas* is genuine, not merely motivated by the desire for power or money. When the time comes, he understands that a religion which demands a sober lifestyle, abstinence, and self-discipline is what he needs, and he conforms.[5]

To become a devotee of Isis (or Mithras) was, in some ways, like becoming a soldier in the Roman army. It was necessary to promise "diligent obedience, faithful devotion, steadfast self-discipline" (11.15). The word *sacrament,* which may be defined as a "visible sign of an inward grace," is derived from *sacramentum,* the Latin word for the oath of loyalty required of the Roman soldier, but it also renders μυστήριον. To be a good soldier of your god—that was the challenge people accepted once they were ready for it.

The salvation that Isis promised in return was not free of charge, but ultimately it led to freedom. Lucius agrees to undergo the obligatory apprenticeship (see Nock 142) and become, as it were, a lay brother in a monastery.

There is an unmistakable religious element in Lucius' "conversion." It is the message he receives from Isis' priest, the promise of the "harbor of calm and the altar of mercy," if he agrees to become a "holy soldier" of

---

5. Cf. Plutarch *Dio* 2.

Isis and to take on himself the voluntary yoke of service, for only through devoted service will he ever gain freedom.

This goal may seem totally different from the goals of magic. Witchcraft and magic rely on conscious manipulation in view of instant success, not on devotion, submission, and self-sacrifice. By agreeing to serve a higher power, Lucius will give up the practice of magic. The two things are simply not compatible, it would seem. But is he really ready to abandon magic for good? This is not clear. One might argue that he would like to have it both ways. He will never abandon Isis, but magic still may have a certain appeal for him.

What Isis has done for him is important. She has released him—through voluntary servitude—from the whims of Τύχη, who is a blind, often seemingly malicious goddess, and who has tortured our "hero" more than enough. Τύχη plays, in a sense, the role of Poseidon in the *Odyssey* or the role of Priapus in the *Satyricon*. Actually, she is not evil: it turns out that she is a manifestation of Isis herself, who has guided the "hero" mysteriously through toils and troubles toward initiation and salvation. Isis is so many deities wrapped in one—why should she not be Τύχη? Was she not behind everything that happened to Lucius, even though he had no idea that his misadventures were blessings in disguise?

The symbolism in Apuleius' novel is rather complex. We have seen that the story of Psyche and Cupid is an allegory. The whole novel is an allegory. What Apuleius is trying to tell his readers is this: All of us share an animal nature, and witchcraft brings it out, as we know from the Circe episode in the *Odyssey*. In the face of all the temptations and dangers of human life, we must attempt to become fully human, to realize the full potential of our humanity to come closer to the deity, be like the deity.

Lucius' pilgrimage is a conversion to *humanitas* thanks to a miraculous intervention. In his *Apologia sive de magia* (55–56), Apuleius also attests his devotion to Isis. He declares that he had learned many religious rites, because he was always guided by "an enthusiasm for truth and a duty toward the gods" [*studio veri et officio erga deos*]. These are two different things: the truth of philosophy is one thing; the revelation through religion is something else. And magic is something else again. Miracles may belong to all these spheres.

It is tempting to view Lucius' experience, as told by Apuleius, as a kind of pilgrim's progress, a journey from the low level of magic to the higher level of religion through an act of conversion. Pilgrimage and conversion are part of the human experience. The yearning for higher things, the desire to refine what is our lower nature, the pursuit of ideals—these characteristics are ingrained in us. The questions to be answered are only: What is higher? What is more desirable? Where should our path lead us? Can we safely return to our old ways without abandoning our new ones?

The power of magic runs as a theme through some other ancient novels. Iamblichus describes in his *Babyloniaca* various kinds of magic practiced in Babylonia. In Heliodorus' *Aethiopica*, the heroine is saved because she carries a magical stone with her onto the pyre on which she is supposed to be burned. An extraordinary episode is told in the "Alexander Romance," attributed to Callisthenes, but probably written in the fourth century A.D. There the pharaoh Nectanebus, who is, according to this particular story, the real father of Alexander the Great, is also a formidable magician and astrologer. To seduce Olympias, the wife of King Philip of Macedonia, he picks certain plants and extracts their dream-inducing juices. Then he shapes a wax figure of a woman and writes the name "Olympias" on it.[6] He also lights lamps and pours into them the juices he made. With secret "oaths" he invokes the "spirits appointed to perform this function, so that Olympias may have a vision of the god Ammon embracing her." This whole magical operation, which is reminiscent of rituals described in the Greek Magical Papyri, enable the pharaoh-magician to pose as the god Ammon and take his place in Olympias' royal bed, thus becoming the real father of Alexander the Great.

It would be wrong to assume that, after his conversion, Lucius gave up the pursuit of magic altogether. In fact, this is one of the ironies of the novel. There are indications that Isis has a special appeal to him because she plays such an important role in late Hellenistic magic. It is well known that her name as well as certain rituals and sacred objects from her cult were used by professional magicians.[7] The "Isis band" of *PGM* 1.59; 7.227, 231; 8.67 is just one example; this was a piece of the black cloth worn by statues of the goddess (cf. Plut. *De Is. et Osir.* p. 366; Griffiths in his comm., pp. 90, 451, 462). Sometimes, the magician is dressed like a priest of Isis (*PGM* 4.3089ff.; cf. Plut. *De Is. et Osir.* p. 352C).[8] Isis herself is invoked in *PGM* 7.490ff.

---

6. See S. Eitrem, in *Magika Hiera*, ed. C.A. Faraone and D. Obink (New York and Oxford, 1991), 181; J.J. Winkler, in *Magika Hiera*, 230.

7. See F. Sbordone, "Iside maga," *Aegyptus* 28 (1946): 31ff.

8. See J. Griffith's commentary on Plutarch, *De Iside et Osiride* (Cardiff, 1970), 270; S. Sauneron, *The Priests of Ancient Egypt* (New York, 1960), 40.

Of course, the magicians invoked the names of deities of different cultures and exploited them for their purposes. They also borrowed freely from other cults and experimented with foreign rituals. Still, it seems that Isis and Osiris had a peculiar appeal for the practitioners of magic of the late Hellenistic period, mainly because Egypt was one of the countries reputed for its magical lore.[9]

As J.J. Griffiths suggests in his commentary on *De Iside et Osiride* (p. 565), the religion of Isis could be seen as making salvation possible by purely magical means, such as the recitation of spells similar to those found in the Magical Papyri. But Plutarch makes it clear that high moral standards were essential. And from Apuleius we know that self-discipline bordering on asceticism was required. Thus, a genuine conversion was a total commitment.

In the treatise devoted to Isis, Plutarch sees in her mysteries a journey toward philosophy and truth. For him, Isis is the repository of ancient wisdom which makes this journey possible and meaningful. Nevertheless, it is a religion with magical, rather than philosophical, characteristics.[10]

In his book *Ich bin Isis*,[11] Jan Bergman has dealt convincingly with the magical aspects of the religion of Isis. This is not just a Hellenistic misunderstanding. The secret force which can produce supernatural effects has a special name in Egyptian, *heka*. This force can be personified as a separate deity, with a body of priests attached to it. On the other hand, *heka* is a frequent attribute of Isis—"she who is rich in *heka*." The Greek equivalent would be δύναμις, which often means "magical power." On the Metternich stele, Isis proclaims: "I am Isis, the divine, the mistress of magical power who exercises the magical power, who is magnificent in her spells." These are the specific powers that protect the faithful from accidents and make them stronger than fate and fortune.

Apuleius' novel is an illustration of this. In his *Apologia* (26) he

---

9. R.E. Witt, *Isis in the Graeco-Roman World* (Ithaca, N.Y., 1971) writes, "The medico-magical tradition in Egypt with which the name of Isis is inseparably linked, goes back more than fifty centuries. . ." Egypt was considered by many the real home of all the occult sciences, of theosophy and thaumaturgy. Isis, in particular, represents the divine power, δύναμις *(mana)*, which is often understood as magical power. When Lucius was restored to human shape, the amazed witnesses saw in the miracle a manifestation of the δύναμις of Isis. See Witt 187ff.

10. See Festugière, *Révélation* (Paris, 1948) 1:88; Griffiths Commentary, 70–71.

11. Acta Univ. Upsal., Hist. Rel. 3 (Upsala, 1968).

defines the magus as *(is) qui communione loquendi cum deis immortalibus ad omnia quae velit incredibili quadam vi cantaminum polleat*. Therefore, the magus stands above fate and is comparable, in this respect, to the devotees of Isis, according to *Metamorphoses* 11.5: *nam in eos quorum sibi vitas in servitium deae nostrae maiestas vindicavit, non habet locum casus infestus*. Of course, this is also true of the philosopher, according to the *Asclepius* (12), a Hermetic treatise preserved among Apuleius' works but probably someone else's translation of a lost Greek original.

Richard Reitzenstein analyzes Apuleius' account of the initiation rites and compares them to those known to us from magical texts.[12] A candidate to whom a vision of his god was granted offers a sacrifice of thanksgiving because he feels endowed by ἰσόθεος φύσις. Another prays to Hermes, "Enter me, as children enter their mother's womb," and adds, "You are I, and I am you; . . . I am your image," and again, "Enter the soul of your child, so that it takes shape according to your immortal shape."

Since Isis has many names, it is important for both the worshiper and the magician to know them all and be able to recite them. This is, of course, impossible, hence the need to know at least the goddess' "true name" (αὐθεντικὸν ὄνομα), which most people do not know.[13]

Lucius was transformed into a donkey by an act of magic. Had he been able to eat roses without divine intervention, this would not have been a miracle, but as it happened thanks to Isis, it will add to her glory and will gain her new devotees.

Apuleius' profile appears on a Roman contorniate medallion of the second half of the fourth century, now in Paris.[14] It is both as a philosopher and as a magician that he is honored, probably not as a novelist. On a contorniate medallion of the same period, also in Paris,[15] Apollonius of Tyana is represented. The stamping of these medallions was, as Hägg, following A. Alföldi, points out,[16] a means of pagan propaganda directed against Christianity. Both Philostratus and Apuleius (one a Neo-Pythagorean, the other a Platonist; both regarded as magicians by many)

---

12. *Die hellenistischen Mysterienreligionen*, 3d ed. (Leipzig, 1927), 38–46, 185–91, 220–34.

13. Sbordone ("Iside maga," 141ff.) documents this from the papyri and from literary texts, such as Lucan 6.744–46; Statius *Theb.* 4.516.

14. Hägg, *Novel in Antiquity*, fig. 46.

15. Ibid., fig. 31.

16. Ibid., p. 116.

seem to have become the spiritual heroes, the θεῖοι ἄνδρες, of the last resistance against the successful church. Just as Apuleius defended himself against the charge of being a sorcerer, Philostratus defends Apollonius against the same suspicion. In both cases, the distinction between a lower kind of magic (γοητεία) and a higher kind (θεουργία), akin to philosophy and theology, is involved.[17]

It may not be unnecessary to observe that Apuleius' Platonism had room not only for the moral perfection which the "hero" of the novel achieves through his initiation at the end but also for the practice of magic which attracted him so powerfully at the beginning. A brief look at Apuleius' philosophical writings will show this.

In his treatise *De Deo Socratis*, called by J. Dillon "the most complete connected version of Middle Platonic daemonology extant,"[18] Apuleius states (13) that "demons are being of genus animate, of mind rational, of spirit passionate, of body airy, of duration eternal"—that they are subject to passions, can be roused to anger and pity, can be placated by gifts and prayers, and are enraged by abuse. Needless to say, this class of higher powers is ideally suited for manipulation by magicians.

Plutarch's demonology is not identical with that of Apuleius, but they seem to agree on several points. In *De Iside et Osiride* (p. 361B), Plutarch surveys the forms of worship demons enjoy: "Hence we may be confident that there are some among this number of divinities who like to be honored by night or by day, openly or in secret, and with joyful or gloomy victims, ceremonies, and rites." This seems to include ritual magic as well as religious laments in the Near Eastern style. Dillon (319) is right when he points out the "weird variety of religious observances" directed at satisfying the appetites of countless demonic forces. Middle Platonism certainly accounts for the possibility of magic, just as Neoplatonism does, and anyone who studies Apuleius' demonology carefully is astonished by the hints and clues between the lines.

According to Apuleius, some demons are souls which have left human bodies, and some of those are good, while others are evil. He identifies some of the good demons with the Roman Lares or with certain heroes of foreign cults, such as Osiris. The evil ones wander over the world, as if they were in permanent exile, and cause whatever damage they can. Apuleius identifies them with the *larvae*, that is, with malicious ghosts (*De Deo Socr.* 153). People had believed in ghosts for

---

17. See *Vita Apollonii* 3.29.7–8.
18. *The Middle Platonists* (London, 1977), 317–20.

thousands of years before Apuleius, but with him a piece of folklore became part of a respectable philosophical system.

Apuleius recognizes another class of demons (*De Deo Socr.* 154), those who never enter bodies. They are the most exalted type. As examples, he mentions Eros (cf. Plato *Symp.* 202E) and Hypnos. The most important demons of this type are the guardian spirits who accompany us through life, know our innermost thoughts and all the actions we try to keep secret, and, after our death, act as our accusers or advocates before the throne of judgment. Incidentally, this is also the role that Isis plays for Lucius, her "convert."

God's Providence, according to Apuleius (see Dillon 325), is superior to fate, although fate rules almost everything here below, including the lower element of the human soul. As far as Apuleius is concerned, one could easily substitute "Isis" for "God" in the preceding statement. For someone else, it could be "Mithras." It is almost like filling in a form: where the form leaves space for "God," the practitioner fills in the name of his or her main deity.

The outline of ethics which Apuleius offers in *De Platone* (3) is remarkably consistent with the story of Lucius. Human beings are born neither good nor evil: they have a nature which may incline either way (Dillon 329). It is the role of education to foster the seeds of virtue sown into the human soul, so that virtue and vice eventually come to coincide with pleasure and pain. It should be painful to be bad and pleasant to be good. Here we have the moral of the novel in a nutshell.

Even some specific points in Apuleius' summary of ethics can be applied to his novel. He condemns *fatuitas* (a translation of χαυνότης, as Dillon [330] observes). This describes Lucius' state at the beginning of the novel, and it is connected with his unhealthy *curiositas*. After his "conversion," Lucius gains the virtues of his rational soul, such as "prudence" (φρόνησις) and "wisdom" (σοφία). The rational part of his soul has now become "perfect" or "self-sufficient" (τέλειος). Apuleius actually distinguishes (*De Plat.* 6) between "perfect" and "imperfect" virtues and assigns them to the triad φύσις, ἦθος, λόγος, which, (according to Dillon 331) is not found in this form anywhere else, though it seems to correspond to the triad φύσις, ἄσκησις, διδασκαλία found in Albinus' handbook of Platonism, which is practically contemporary. In terms of Lucius' personal experience, his "nature," φύσις, is obviously not all bad, but it needs "discipline," ἄσκησις, and "teaching," διδασκαλία, and all this is provided by Isis and her "holy ones."

For the sage, the τέλος is "likeness to the god," ὁμοίωσις τῷ θεῷ. By the assiduous practice of justice, piety, and wisdom, he will attain this goal. The hero of Apuleius' novel found this kind of perfection in a religious experience which filled his Platonism with new meaning and showed him the way to a higher kind of magic, θεουργία rather than γοητεία.

Palladas: Christian or Pagan?

In 1929, in his lecture on "Die geistige Gegenwart der Antike,"[1] Werner Jaeger said: "Niemals ist die Dauer der antiken Kultur im Wandel der Zeiten und Völker sichtbarer hervorgetreten, als zu der Zeit, wo das römische Weltreich dem Ansturm der Germanen erlag und das Christentum wie eine Sturmflut über die Antike hereinbrauste. . . . Zwar die Hoffnung . . . [Kaiser Julians] erfüllte sich nicht: der Traum einer nationalen Wiedergeburt Roms aus der Besinnung auf die höchsten Werte der klassischen Kultur erwies sich als ein Phantom. Aber unter der führenden Schicht erwuchs in dieser Zeit des Zusammenbruchs aus dem unzerstörbaren Glauben an die Roma aeterna eine Renaissance der klassischen Bildung, und sie wurde zur Geburtsstunde der christlich-abendländischen Kultur."

It would be difficult to characterize more concisely the turbulent period in which Palladas of Alexandria lived. In a few sentences, Werner Jaeger has laid down the program, as it were, for a whole monograph on the struggle between Christianity and paganism. Such a monograph might possibly include a chapter on that strange and controversial figure to whose thought the following pages are devoted.

Although a very large number of his epigrams have been preserved, Palladas is still one of the least known poets of the Greek Anthology. Too little has been done for the text of his poems, especially for those included in books 10 and 11, neither of which is available in a modern critical edition. Stadtmüller's Teubneriana ends at *Anth. Pal.* 9.563, and Waltz' edition in the Budé series has not gone beyond book 8. For many of the Palladas' epigrams, the readings of Planudes' autograph, *Marcianus 481*, are still unpublished.[2] As a result of this, the text is admittedly doubtful in many instances. The only commentary is that of Friedrich

From *Studies in Honor of Werner Jaeger,* Harvard Studies in Classical Philology 63 (1958), 455–71.

1. *Humanistische Reden und Vorträge* (1937), 169ff.

2. They are now embodied in H. Beckby's edition of the *Anthologia Graeca,* esp. vol. 3 (Tusculum series).

Jacobs,[3] published in 1801, still an admirable achievement, but not help-ful in many crucial passages.

This uncertainty may be one of the reasons why critics have not yet agreed on Palladas' stature as a poet. Casaubonus' preemptory statement—*versificator insulsissimus*—is still repeated by many. The most congenial modern translator of the Anthology,[4] an American poet and critic, expresses his dislike for the "dyspeptic didacticisms of Palladas." Others, from Opsopoeus to Gilbert Highet,[5] have compared him to Martial. Their feeling is by no means unfounded; Palladas might have been a Greek Martial or Juvenal had he lived in another century. Perhaps the controversy can be summed up as follows: Palladas' per-sonality may not appeal to us; we may find his pessimism shallow, his invective excentric; but he still deserves our respect as a literary crafts-man. He was no great poet, but he handled the epigrammatic form very competently, he was imaginative, and he had a feeling for felici-tous sound values.[6]

There is enough evidence to show that, at one time, he enjoyed great popularity. The surprisingly large number of his epigrams in the Greek Anthology seems to suggest that his outlook and manner ap-pealed to the Byzantine scholars who compiled this collection. An un-known admirer, presumably a contemporary of his, has paid this humble tribute to him: "If a lark can sing like a swan, and if owls dare compete with nightingales; if the cuckoo claims he is more sweet-voiced than the cicada—then I too can write like Palladios."[7] He was read by the

---

3. Vol. 10 of his edition = vol. 2, part 3 of his commentary.
4. Dudley Fitts, *Poems from the Greek Anthology* (1938; repr., 1956), XIV.
5. *Juvenal the Satirist* (1954), 142.
6. Cf. *Anth. Pal.* 10.84.

Δακρυχέων γενόμην, καὶ δακρύσας ἀποθνήσκω,
    δάκρυσι δ' ἐν πολλοῖς τὸν βίον εὗρον ὅλον.
ὦ γένος ἀνθρώπων πολυδάκρυτον, ἀσθενές, οἰκτρόν,
    συρόμενον κατὰ γῆς καὶ διαλυόμενον.

In the last line, συρόμενον (Plan.; φερόμενον P., φαινόμενον Boissonade) is the correct reading; cf. *Anth. Pal.* 10.62.2; Euteknios on Oppian. *Cyneg.*, ed. Tuesel-mann, *Abh. Gött.*, n.s., 4, no. 1 (1906), p. 41.33, a text which Stadtmüller did not know when he called it "eine verunglückte Konjektur," *Ilb. Jbb.* 137 (1888): 359.

7. *Anth. Pal.* 9.380. The identity of this Palladios with our Palladas is generally accepted, since Salmasius noticed that the corrector C of the *Palatinus* refers it to Palladas. The form Palladios stands in relation to Palladas as Lukios to Lukas.

people as well as by the educated; witness the quotation that has been found on a wall in Ephesus, far from his native Alexandria.[8]

In view of this, the traditional portrait of Palladas as the gloomy outsider who nurses a grudge against everyone and everything needs a few corrections. The *communis opinio* is stated eloquently by T.R. Glover:[9] "In the unhappy Palladas we have one who saw the old order pass away giving place to none, and his bitter hopelessness is the last dark mood of dying heathenism." This statement is slightly exaggerated. The term "hopelessness" cannot be applied to Palladas in a meaningful way. One who wrote,[10]

> Ἐλπίδος οὐδὲ Τύχης ἔτι μοι μέλει, οὐδ᾽ ἀλεγίζω
>   λοιπὸν τῆς ἀπάτης· ἤλυθον εἰς λιμένα.
> εἰμὶ πένης ἄνθρωπος, ἐλευθερίῃ δὲ συνοικῶ·
>   ὑβριστὴν πενίης πλοῦτον ἀποστρέφομαι,

has clearly reached a point where he considers "hopelessness" (i.e., the absence of hope) as a positive achievement. Because he has given up hope, Palladas is able to live for the day. More than once, he praises the enjoyment of life in concrete terms.[11] Does this make him an Epicurean? But the dominant mood of his poems is, indeed, a brooding and obstinate pessimism. Was he a Neoplatonist? a Cynic? All these views have been defended, none of them convincingly.[12] As the evidence is contradictory, it may seem safe to consider him an eclectic,[13] but even this compromise has little in its favor. Eclecticism implies a conscious effort, a synthesis, of which there is no trace in Palladas' verse. Fragments of different philosophies follow each other abruptly. He adopts them for the moment, whenever they happen to bring out the point of one particular epigram, and abandons them if they do not suit his purpose any

---

Here, the longer form is used *metri causa*. Style, manner (cf. the colloquialism ἴσα ποεῖν in v. 4), and versification seem to suggest a disciple of Palladas.

8. *Anth. Pal.* 10.87; cf. E. Kalinka, *Wiener Studien* 24 (1902): 292ff.

9. *Life and Letters in the Fourth Century* (1910), 309.

10. *Anth. Pal.* 9.172; cf. anon. 9.49, 134, and 135 (in Palladas' manner). On the imagery see Kamerbeek's note on Soph. *Ajax* 682f.; F. Cumont, *Recherches sur le Symbolisme funéraire des Romains* (1942), 168 n. 2; *Lux Perpetua* (1949), 123 n. 1.

11. Cf. *Anth. Pal.* 10.34, 59, 77, 78; 11.54, 55, 62.

12. Schmid-Stählin, *Gesch. d. griech. Lit.* (in Müller's *Handbuch*) vol. 2, pt. 2 (1924), 979.

13. W. Peek, "Palladas," *RE* 18²:159.

longer. Today, he may be a Cynic, tomorrow an Epicurean, without transition. To Palladas, philosophy is no longer a βίος; it is a φάρμακον,[14] a specific drug which he tries out and discards at once if it does not work. It is important to note that in the case of "the unhappy Palladas," philosophy, any philosophy, has failed.[15] He would have been the last to protest when Justinian, in 529, closed the philosophical schools.

Hence, the recent assertion that Palladas, far from being the last protagonist of dying paganism, was actually a Christian should not come as a surprise. In 1899, A. Franke concluded a section of his valuable monograph on Palladas with these words:[16] *Quibus rebus cognitis Palladam non fuisse Christianum nobis putandum est.* In 1901, T.R. Glover wrote:[17] "He had ceased to take joy in the old, he hated the new." Less than fifty years later, P. Waltz, the French editor of the Anthology, summed up the evidence as follows:[18] "Il est donc, non pas établi d'une manière irréfutable, mais infiniment probable que Palladas était Chrétien."

These statements seem to exclude one another, but they could be reconciled. If we were better informed about the relative chronology of Palladas' epigrams, we might be able to distinguish different phases in his life, tracing his way through various philosophies which he found all equally unsatisfactory, following him on his search for truth which led ultimately to his conversion. Unfortunately, no such construction can be upheld. Only very few of Palladas' poems can be dated on external grounds;[19] the rest show no trace of any stylistic or metrical development. For all we know, most of them could have been written within a year or two.

Waltz was aware that none of his arguments was really convincing, but he considered them highly probable. First, he points out that Palladas speaks almost always of one God. But so do numerous pagan writers from Homer onward.[20] Second, he treats the pagan gods ironically. But so

---

14. *Anth. Pal.* 10.46 (cf. 10.50.10). The "remedy" may be a Cynic concept; cf. Crates *Anth. Pal.* 9.497; on its role in late Greek philosophy see G. Luck, *Gnomon* 28 (1956): 268ff. (in this volume, pp. 35–38).

15. Cf. *Anth. Pal.* 9.170 and 10.62 and 96 on the ἀδηλία and ἀνωμαλία of life, as he sees it.

16. "De Pallada epigrammatographo" (Diss., Leipz., 1899), 47.

17. *Wiener Studien* 24 (1902): 319.

18. "Palladas était-il Chrétien?" *Rev. d'Ét. Grecques* 59/60 (1946/47): 209.

19. There is a useful discussion of Palladas' chronology in L.A. Stella, *Cinque poeti dell' Antologia* (1951), 377–83, by far the best part of her chapter on this poet.

20. Kleinknecht in Kittel's *Theol. Wb. z. NT* (1938), 3:66ff.

does Lucian, without being a Christian. Third, he uses the names of the old gods allegorically; Aphrodite signifies love, Bacchus wine, the Muses poetic inspiration. But this is a literary device which neither Palladas nor any Christian invented. Fourth, he speaks of Constantinople as φιλόχριστος πόλις, but most editors read φιλόχρηστος,[21] and the epigram, if it is genuine, may well be ironical. Fifth, Waltz lends to the term Ἕλληνες, as used by Palladas,[22] a meaning which is not acceptable.

None of these arguments carries any weight at all, and yet Waltz' thesis may possibly be right. There is some evidence that Palladas was familiar with Christian writings. This, I think, would be a very important point, although hardly anyone has paid much attention to it so far. Palladas was read by the Christians—did he read the Christians?

Before we turn to this question, we should consider two additional arguments which Waltz has ignored. First, there is the possibility that Palladas' epigrams were included, less than a century after his death, in the *Kyklos* of the Christian Agathias. This is an assumption, held by some,[23] but never proved conclusively. In the introduction to the Greek Anthology,[24] Waltz rejected it, but his premature death prevented him from stating the specific reasons, which he had announced for the introductions to books 10 and 11 of the Anthology. If we knew that Palladas was represented in Agathias' *Kyklos*, we might argue that the Byzantine editor, at least, considered him as a Christian. For the time being, this argument should be disregarded, since it rests on a hypothesis.

---

21. *Anth. Plan.* 282. The adj. φιλόχριστος does not appear, it seems, until a century or two after Palladas (*IG* 4.205, *saec.* VI, of Justinian; *Suppl. Epigr.* 8, 230, *saec.* VI/VII, from Palestine).

22. *Anth. Pal.* 10.82, 89, 90. According to Waltz (205ff.), these poems refer to a "great national disaster." This may be true, but the context is clearly religious (cf. 10.91). A.D. Nock (*Sallustius concerning the Gods* [1926], xlvii, n. 43) has shown that in Palladas' time, Ἕλληνες is the common term for "pagan" and "heathen." Since Waltz has chosen this group of epigrams, he should have mentioned the attractive hypothesis of L. Sternbach (*Festschrift Th. Gomperz* [1902] 398 n. 8), who has seen in *Anth. Pal.* 10.90.4 (and 91.1f.), μωρίᾳ δουλεύομεν. Ἕλληνές ἐσμεν ἄνδρες, a reference to 1 Cor. 1:23, of Christ as Ἰουδαίοις μὲν σκάνδαλον, Ἕλλησι δὲ μωρίαν. I might add that the expression ὃν (τὸν) θεὸς φιλεῖ (90.2, 91.1 and 5) has a Christian connotation. See the passages in R. Bultmann, *Das Evangelium des Johannes* (Meyer's Comm. üb. d. N.T., z. Abt., 11. Aufl., 1950), 419 n. 3; he points out that the term "Friend of God" plays an important role in the writings of the Alexandrian Christians (it is usually applied to martyrs and ascetes).

23. R. Weisshäupl, *Die Grabgedichte der griech. Anth.* (1889), 21ff.

24. *Anth. Gr.* (Budé series), vol. 1 (1928), xxiii n. 1.

Second, there is the fact that Palladas addressed himself primarily and purposely to the lower classes. Although he has earned his living as a schoolteacher,[25] he sneers at education. He quotes from the classics now and then, but he is ready to sell his books, notably the school authors[26]—

Καλλίμαχον πωλῶ καὶ Πίνδαρον . . .

—unless he receives financial assistance from a friend. He admits that without his books, ὄργανα Μουσάων, he can no longer write poetry,[27] but he bids farewell to the Muses as soon as a new profession seems to be open to him. Actually, he would not need them. If we examine the bulk of his verse, we find that he relies extensively on puns, proverbs, and similar devices of popular poetry.[28] Among all his epigrams there is only one which praises the true σοφία, but it is probably not genuine, as we shall see below. Again, Palladas' contempt for education is not necessarily a Christian theme; he might have inherited it from the Cynic-Stoic diatribe. Palladas distrusts all speculation because it endangers his peace of mind, ἡσυχία.[29] Similarly, Epicurus and his followers ignored παιδεία which did not lead to ἀταραξία. Palladas hates his own profession; he rejoices at the downfall of one who is λόγιος,[30] eruditus; he ridicules a fellow grammarian who poses as a Platonist.[31] All this may sound genuine enough but is, perhaps, dictated by specific situations and personal animosity.

To solve our problem, we should have to prove that Palladas is familiar with Christian texts and that he quotes or adapts them in their original meaning, not polemically, but as the truth or part of the truth in which he personally believes. In doing this, we should exclude all doctrines, isolated phrases, and purely formal reminiscences that are not specifically Christian. The dangers of this method may be illustrated by the one example which Waltz happened to choose.[32]

---

25. *Anth. Pal.* 10.97.

26. On Callimachus see R. Reitzenstein, *DLZ* 1898, p. 225.

27. *Anth. Pal.* 9.171.

28. Peek 166f.

29. *Anth. Pal.* 11.349; cf. 7.687.

30. *Anth. Pal.* 7.683.3.

31. *Anth. Pal.* 11.305; on the text see C. Dilthey, *Rh. Mus.* 27 (1872): 305f. K. Preisendanz, *Rh. Mus.* 70 (1915): 329.

32. *Anth. Pal.* 10.88.

Σῶμα πάθος ψυχῆς, ᾅδης, μοῖρ᾽, ἄχθος, ἀνάγκη,
    καὶ δεσμὸς κρατερός, καὶ κόλασις βασάνων.
ἀλλ᾽ ὅταν ἐξέλθῃ τοῦ σώματος, ὡς ἀπὸ δεσμῶν
    τοῦ θανάτου, φεύγει πρὸς θεὸν ἀθάνατον.

It is true that the last line reminds one somewhat of Christian epitaphs, such as *Anth. Pal.* 8.131.1–2, by Gregory the Theologian.

Ἤλυθε κ᾽ Ἀμφιλόχοιο φίλον δέμας ἐς μέγα σῆμα,
    ψυχὴ δ᾽ ἐς μακάρων ᾤχετ᾽ ἀποπταμένη.

But here, needless to say, a real tomb is mentioned, not the body as the tomb of the soul. Waltz himself admits that pagan epitaphs, such as *Anth. Pal.* 7.61, on Plato's tomb,

Γαῖα μὲν ἐν κόλποις κρύπτει τόδε σῶμα Πλάτωνος,
    ψυχὴ δ᾽ ἀθάνατον τάξιν ἔχει μακάρων,

and many others, offer close parallels to thought and expression. Such formulas are much too conventional[33] to imply any religious commitment. Furthermore, the main thought of *Anth. Pal.* 10.88 is clearly Platonic; these four lines might have been written on the title page of the *Phaedo*. Incidentally, this is one of the reasons why Palladas' authorship has been questioned.[34]

So far, our evidence is still inconclusive. There are, however, two or three epigrams of Palladas' whose authenticity is incontested and which could have been written by a Christian. There is the curious poem *Anth. Pal.* 9.441, on a statue of Heracles cast down at the crossroads.

Τὸν Διὸς ἐν τριόδοισιν ἐθαύμασα χάλκεον υἷα,
    τὸν πρὶν ἐν εὐχωλαῖς, νῦν παραριπτόμενον.
ὀχθήσας δ᾽ ἄρ᾽ ἔειπον· "Ἀλεξίκακε τρισέληνε,
    μηδέποθ᾽ ἡττηθείς σήμερον ἐξετάθης;"[35]
νυκτὶ δὲ μειδιόων με θεὸς προσέειπε παραστάς·
    "Καιρῷ δουλεύειν καὶ θεὸς ὢν ἔμαθον."

---

33. Even in epitaphs for animals, e.g., *Anth. App.* 2.295 (Headlam's restitution); in Plato *Phaedo* 85a2, the swans sing because they go away to their god, Apollo.

34. Franke 9; but Sternbach (398) thinks it may be sarcastic.

35. This punctuation was suggested to me by A.D. Nock.

The poet is indignant (ὀχθήσας) at this humiliation of Heracles, but the god does not seem to mind (μειδιόων). His explanation, "Even though I am a god, I have learned to accommodate myself to the occasion," or "I have learned to be an opportunist," has often been compared with the textus receptus of Epistle to the Romans 12:11. There, the expression τῷ καιρῷ δουλεύοντες is symmetrical to τῇ ἐλπίδι χαίροντες, one participle referring to the present, the other to the future.[36] It could be argued that Palladas' sympathy with Heracles is not sincere, that he is actually gloating over his downfall, and that the whole point of the epigram consists in the admission of the son of Zeus that he himself had to experience the truth of St. Paul's words. It could also be argued that Palladas, if indeed, he has the passage from Romans in mind, invites his readers to supply the corresponding member quoted earlier. In this case, Heracles would yield to the present circumstances but look forward to a comforting change—hence his smile. Consequently, the poet's sympathy is with the fallen idol of paganism. He would regretfully acknowledge, in the god's own words, that the first part of St. Paul's statement even applies, for the time being, to the once powerful (μηδέποθ' ἡττηθείς) god, hoping tacitly that the events will justify the second part as well. But Palladas is such a pessimist at heart that we could hardly expect him to share the confidence of Julian; the change that has taken place is irrevocable (*Anth. Pal.* 10.90.7).

ἀνεστράφη γὰρ πάντα νῦν τὰ πράγματα.

The expression καιρῷ δουλεύειν and its equivalents are by no means infrequent in pagan texts.[37] The phrase καιρῷ ἄμ' ἕπεσθαι, for example, seems to be almost proverbial. Kairos is often visualized as a god[38] who had an altar at Olympia and in whose honor Ion of Chios composed a hymn. Palladas agrees with Menander on this point (*Anth. Pal.* 10.52.1)—

Εὖγε λέγων τὸν Καιρὸν ἔφης θεόν, εὖγε, Μένανδρε

---

36. O. Michel, *Der Brief an die Römer übersetzt und erklärt* (Meyer's Commentar, 10th ed., 1955), 271.

37. Many examples are collected by the Swiss theologian J.J. Wettstein, in his commentary to the New Testament, vol. 2 (1752), ad loc., and by W.G. Headlam, *Journ. of Philol.* 30 (1907): 300.

38. Cf. W. Vollgraff, *L'Oraison Funèbre de Gorgias*, Philos. Ant. 5 (1952), 22ff.

—and adds that an opportune thought or event is often more desirable than the result of careful preparation. Hence, the unfavorable connotation which many church writers detected in the textus receptus cannot have been foremost in Palladas' mind, and it is conspicuously absent from many of the ancient contexts in which the expression occurs. According to Palladas, all men are slaves to the lot that fell to them at their birth.[39]

Τίπτε μάτην, ἄνθρωπε, πονεῖς καὶ πάντα ταράσσεις
κλήρῳ δουλεύ ων τῷ κα τὰ τὴν γένεσιν;

But he adds significantly that it is possible to enjoy life, even παρὰ μοίρην. It would be only human to be a slave to Kairos. Does this excuse Heracles? The pagan god does not play a very heroic role in Palladas' poem; but Palladas has little respect for the ancient gods in general. Zeus is actually a murderer,[40] and he and all the other Olympians would be threatened by extinction if they had not found an unexpected asylum in the house of an art-loving Byzantine princess.[41] While Pindar once protected his gods against certain myths, Palladas uses myths in order to prove that they are malicious.[42] His aversion against the ancient religion in general provides the framework into which this particular poem fits. The possibility that he might add to his invective a specifically Christian thought—which is doubtful in this instance—is independent of his personal belief.

Palladas is a very elusive writer. As soon as we try to commit him to a specific point of doctrine or even opinion, he seems to wrestle free from our grip. The following epigram provides an example of the Protean versatility which enables him to hold a precarious balance between the schools and religions, in this case between Christianity and Epicureanism.[43]

Γῆς ἐπέβην γυμνός, γυμνὸς δ'ὑπὸ γαῖαν ἄπειμι·
καὶ τί μάτην μοχθῶ, γυμνὸν ὁρῶν τὸ τέλος;

---

39. *Anth. Pal.* 10.77.

40. *Anth. Pal.* 10.53, "On the House of Marina," the daughter of Arcadius.

41. *Anth. Pal.* 9.528.

42. Cf. his use of the Pandora myth, *Anth. Pal.* 9.165 and 167. A Christian, the consul Macedonius, deals with the same theme in Palladas' manner (*Anth. Pal.* 10.71).

43. *Anth. Pal.* 10.58. The relationship between the following texts has been outlined briefly by Wolfgang Schmid, *Gnomon* 27 (1955): 409 n. 1. Professor Schmid indicated that he was about to publish a full discussion of this problem.

Epicurus had said (*Gnom. Vat.* 60), πᾶς ὥσπερ ἄρτι γεγονὼς ἐκ τοῦ ζῆν ἀπέρχεται, and Seneca translated or paraphrased this thought in two slightly different versions: *nemo non ita exit e vita, tamquam modo intraverit* (*Epist.* 22.13); *nemo aliter quam qui modo natus est, exit e vita* (*Epist.* 22.15). It is precisely the small divergence in the two Latin versions that seems to confirm that Seneca had this particular fragment of Epicurus in mind. While one is slightly more hypothetical and the other more direct and descriptive, the Greek, in its conciseness, admits of both translations. Having proposed one, Seneca returns to the same thought, offering another alternative. In either version, Epicurus' statement is more general than that of Palladas, but even in its more general form it is acceptable to the poet who complains elsewhere[44] that the past is lost forever and that we have no part in our former selves. If the sum of the years (ἔτη ἀπελθόντα) counts for nothing, we are indeed, as Palladas says, "born day by day."

There is no mention in Epicurus of man's γυμνότης at his birth and his death. What is its meaning in Palladas? The dead are often called γυμνοί, *nudi*, in ancient literature, but usually *after* their burial (Propert. 3.5.14: *nudus in inferna, stulte, vehere rate*; Lygdamus 3.10: *nudus Lethaea cogerer ire rate*; Sil. Ital. 5.267: *nudum Tartareo portabit navita cymba*; Lucian *Mort. dial.* 10.1: γυμνοὺς ἐπιβαίνειν χρή). I do not think that we should stress this point and substitute in Palladas' epigram the Platonic meaning of "nakedness," that is, "being without a body," as in *Cratylus* 403: ἡ ψυχὴ γυμνὴ τοῦ σώματος. Palladas' advice "Do not toil in vain; the end is nakedness" would hardly be acceptable to a Platonist. From the same premises, Philo (*De spec. leg.* 1.294–95) comes to a totally different conclusion: he speaks of man as having brought nothing into this world, not even himself, for "naked you came, naked you leave again"; but for this very reason, one's life should be dedicated to φιλανθρωπία.

There is no trace of Platonic idealism in Palladas' distich. He understands the "nakedness" of man in its most obvious sense, and the "toil," as he understands it, includes no intellectual pursuits, no ethical discipline; it is merely concerned with material things. A very similar version of this thought occurs in 1 Tim 6:7: ". . . for we brought nothing into the world, nor can we carry anything out; if we have food and covering, these should satisfy us." This is a close parallel, but it contains nothing specifically Christian,[45] just as Palladas' epigram contains nothing specifi-

---

44. *Anth. Pal.* 10.79.
45. Sir R. Falconer, *The Pastoral Epistles* (1937), 153.

cally anti-Christian. With a little goodwill, it might have been interpreted favorably by the Byzantine scholars who compiled the Anthology. None of their scholia registers any criticism of Palladas, while the epigrams of admittedly pagan poets often provoke them to venomous comments. Only once is Palladas called μετέωρος, but even this epithet—which has been strangely misinterpreted by modern critics[46]—is not deprecatory. Its ordinary meaning in late Greek, "hovering between hope and fear, anxious, restless,"[47] applies very well to Palladas.

I have not mentioned one important text because it suggests a number of problems that have been ignored so far. It is the often quoted epigram *Anth. Pal.* 9.400, addressed, as the lemmata tells us, "to Hypatia, the daughter of Theon."

Ὅταν βλέπω σε, προσκυνῶ, καὶ τοὺς λόγους,
τῆς παρθένου τὸν οἶκον ἀστρῷον βλέπων·
εἰς οὐρανὸν γάρ ἐστι σοῦ τὰ πράγματα,
Ὑπατία σεμνή, τῶν λόγων εὐμορφία,
ἄχραντον ἄστρον τῆς σοφῆς παιδεύσεως.

This is an extraordinary tribute to a learned woman, from a man who hates women[48] and distrusts learning. It has very little of Palladas' usual fluency and glibness; on the contrary, it sounds rather solemn and self-conscious. A youthful poem? According to the traditional chronology, partly based on this very poem, Palladas was in his fifties when Hypatia was assassinated, in 415, by a mob of Christian fanatics. He would have known her for a number of years. It is hard to imagine that anyone who admired Hypatia as fervently as did the author of this epigram could have felt much sympathy for those who represented the new religion in her city, Cyril and Theophilus.

Since the discovery of the *Codex Palatinus*, no one has had any doubts[49] that Palladas is the author of these lines, but they are anonymous in Planudes and in another part of the *Palatinus*, where they are

---

46. Lemma to *Anth. Pal.* 9.528; cf. lemma to *Anth. Pal.* 9.481, Julian. Scholast.; Franke 41; Stadtmüller ad loc.; Waltz 209.

47. Cf. Polyb. 3.107.6; it is contrasted to ἀμέριμνος in a letter from Egypt: *Aeg. Urk. Mus. Berl.* 417.4 and 6.

48. Cf. *Anth. Pal.* 9.165–68 and Highet, *Juvenal* (1960), 264 on the theme in general.

49. Stella (379) is wrong: even Franke (12) considers it as genuine.

repeated, after *Anth. Pal.* 15.17. The only place where the epigram is attributed to Palladas is between *Anth. Pal.* 9.399 and 401. The lemma of the former, written by A*, reads as follows:

εἰσ γνωστικ° πα

Part of the last word (παλλαδᾶ?) has been erased by the corrector, C. The lemma of 9.400, written by A*, read originally as follows:

εἰς τὴν φιλοσοφ° ὑπατίαν
Θέωνος θυγατέρα παλλαδᾶ.

This was corrected by C in different ways. He added Παλλαδᾶ after ὑπατίαν. Then he deleted his own addition[50] and wrote over the lemma of A*,τοῦ αὐτοῦ Παλλαδᾶ, without noticing that he himself had denied Palladas' authorship of 399. He seems to have maintained it for 400 and 401; to the lemma of the latter, ἄδηλον εἰς ἐπιστολήν, written by A*, he adds καὶ τοῦτο Παλλαδᾶ.

This last poem, a sentimental little piece, is anonymous in Planudes and so different from anything that Palladas has written[51] that we must assume another oversight of C. It is, perhaps, significant that soon after this group of epigrams, C puts down his pen; his last remark concerns 9.460.

I think it can be shown that Palladas is not the author of 9.400 and that the epigram has nothing to do with Hypatia, the daughter of Theon. When it reappears in the *Palatinus*, after 15.17, it stands in the middle of a heterogeneous little group of poems: 15.17, by Constantinus of Rhodes, "On the Image of the Mother of God"; 15.17A = 1.122, by Michael Chartophylax, "On the Mother of God Carrying Christ"; 15.17B = 9.400, anonymous, "On the Philosopher Hypatia"; 15.17C = 9.180 + 181, anonymous. The first two poems were written by Christian authors on a religious subject; the last two poems are apparently[52] by Palladas;

---

50. Not the whole lemma, as Franke (12) maintains; see the photograph of p. 426 in *Anth. Pal., cod. Pal. et cod. Paris. phototyp. ed.* (by K. Preisendanz, 1911).

51. Franke 12.

52. 180 is closely related to 183, 181 to 182. All four epigrams are attributed to Palladas in P₁ and Plan., but 180 + 181 are anonymous in P₂. They are clearly different in style from 182 and 183. Without going into a detailed analysis, I should like to suggest that they are actually Byzantine imitations (cf. n. 68); 181.1 is an almost literal quotation from Palladas 10.90.7.

who wrote the one in the middle? To which group does it belong, to the
former or the latter? Its position between the Mother of God and the
pagan Tyche (the subject of 15.17C = 9.180 + 181) is almost symbolical;
but a close textual analysis will establish that it is a Christian poem,
written in honor of a saintly Christian woman whose name may or may
not have been Hypatia. Its attribution to Palladas and the identification
of this woman with the Neoplatonist philosopher is pure guesswork,
one error probably leading to the other. All editors of the Anthology
agree that lemmata and scholia are generally of doubtful value, because
they tend to derive their information from the poem itself, as they
understand it. Very often, their information is based on good independent sources. Naturally, the question must be decided for each individual case.

The second line of the poem is crucial for its interpretation.

τῆς παρθένου τὸν οἶκον ἀστρῷον βλέπων.

Stadtmüller explains this as follows: *Poeta cum Hypatiae sedem velut side-*
ream praedicat, animum eius sublime ferri dicit ad contemplanda caelestia. If I
understand his note correctly, he implies that the παρθένος is Hypatia
herself and that οἶκος refers to her house or, perhaps, lecture room. He
does not explain the awkward syntactic change from the personal pro-
noun σέ (v. 1), addressing Hypatia directly, to the genitive, speaking of
her in the third person. All the other critics who have dealt with this
epigram (unless they evade the issue), explain παρθένος as distinct from
Hypatia.

Another interpretation, now generally accepted, was first suggested
by Jacobs in his commentary: ὁ οἶκος ἀστρῷος τῆς παρθένου, *si recte*
intelligo, est domicilium signi, quod virgo appellatur. Cum hoc igitur signo . . .
Hypatiam comparat, hanc quasi vivam illius imaginem veneratur. Dübner repeats this note verbatim, without omitting the doubtful *si recte intelligo.*
As it often happens, others have ignored the qualification and adopted
Jacobs' statement, unsubstantiated as it is, as the literal truth. Even such
authorities on ancient astronomy and astrology as F. Boll[53] and W.

---

53. *Kl. Schr. zur Sternkunde des Altertums* (1950), 147 n. 4 (repr. from *Sokrates* 9
[1921], 2ff.). He quotes the epigram from Halma's edition of Ptolemaeus'
Procheiroi Kanones (1822), pt. 1, p. 166, as "ein spätes schlechtes Epigramm auf
Hypatia," without mentioning Palladas. Boll compares it to Hor. C. 1.28.5, *aerias*
temptasse domos, adding "die himmlischen οἶκοι im technisch-astrologischen

Gundel[54] seem to take this meaning for granted. The latter is inclined to believe that the constellation Virgo played an important role in Hypatia's horoscope. According to tradition, scholars were born under this sign.

This is an attractive suggestion—but impossible. Οἶκος is never used by the ancient astrologers for any sign of the zodiac as such. The correct term is τόπος, Latin *locus* or *pars*. Salmasius[55] has clarified these terms in a short note: *Antiqui astrologi Loca numquam nomine* οἴκων *donaverunt, sed* τόπους *semper appellaverunt. Singulis planetis* [for Virgo this would be Mercury] *sua signa attribuerunt, in quibus domicilia quasi haberent constituta,* οἴκους *appellant.* It is true that this terminology is not always applied correctly in nontechnical contexts, by poets, for example, by Nonnus (*Dionys.* 3.222ff.), but even Nonnus calls the constellation Virgo Παρθένος ἀστερόεσσα (12.94, 41.335); similarly, Synesius,[56] a contemporary of Hypatia, speaks of ἡ παρθένος ἡ . . . ἀστρῷα. Virgo might be called "the house of Mercury," but not "the house of Virgo." Nor is it possible to take βλέπω in its astrological sense;[57] no matter how we translate the first two lines of our epigrams, it is always a human being looking at the "house," not two heavenly bodies "looking at each other" or looking down at the person whose character and life they influence.

As soon as we place the epigram in a Christian context, the meaning of the "starry house of the Parthenos" is clear. As we have seen already, it is preceded on p. 668 of the *Codex Palatinus,* after 15.17, by three lines on the Mother of God. These lines appear at the very end of book 1, written by the same scribe, J, and attributed to Michael Chartophylax, as *Anth. Pal.* 1.122. There they are preceded by a poem on a Byzantine church, *Anth. Pal.* 1.121, the famous Church of the Mother of God in the

---

Sinne bedürfen keines Belegs"—not, perhaps, if one places, as Boll does, a comma after παρθένου, but even if this punctuation would offer a satisfactory sense, the technical connotation of "house" is by no means as obvious as Boll suggests; cf. *Anth. Pal.* 7.62.2, ἀστερόεντα θεῶν οἶκον. Boll's reference to his own p. 149, n. 2, is wrong, for Marc. Aurel. 7.47 has ἄστρων δρόμους not δόμους.

54. "Parthenos," RE 18². 1948 and 1956.

55. *De ann. climact.* p. 181f., quoted by V. Stegemann, *Astrologie und Universalgeschichte,* Stoicheia 9 (1930), 29. To his references, I should like to add the horoscope, *P. Oxy.* 235.

56. Synesius p. 124 D. = col. 1272 Migne; cf. *Anecd. Bekk.* 688, ἀστρῷος κύων; *Anth. Pal.* 11.158.6, οὐράνιος κύων; Cercidas fr. 6.6 Di.; E. Norden, *Fleck. Jbb. Supp.* 19, no. 2 (1893): 380 n. 1.

57. Manil. 2.466ff. and (in a different sense) Hor. *C.* 2.17.1; see Boll 121 (repr. from *Sokrates* 5 [1917]).

Blachernae Quarter. The first half of its second line is identical to the first half of the second line in our epigram.

Ἔδει γενέσθαι δευτέραν Θεοῦ πύλην
τῆς παρθένου τὸν οἶκον ὡς καὶ τὸν τόκον . . .

The "house of the Virgin"[58] is a standing phrase in Byzantine poetry and designates always a church of the Mother of God. It is called "starry" (*astrigera,* as Hugo Grotius translated correctly) because its walls or vaults are decorated with stars. To list examples for this well-known feature of Byzantine art hardly seems necessary. Time and again, the authors of *ekphraseis* marvel at the mosaics of stars, sun, and moon in the churches they describe and speculate on their symbolic meaning. It appears from the context that the church referred to in our epigram contains a portrait of the woman (Hypatia?) to whom these lines are addressed, perhaps the founder of the church.

Every single line of the poem could be paralleled from such *ekphraseis.* I shall limit myself to a few examples. Constantine of Rhodes, the author of the epigram which precedes ours in book 15 of the Anthology, has also written a description of the Church of the Holy Apostles in Constantinople.[59] It is sufficient to quote the following passage[60] in order to point out the similarities of style and diction.

ὅταν δ᾽ ἀπίδω πρὸς Θεοῦ δόμον μέγαν,
τὸν τῆς Σοφίας οἶκον οὐρανοδρόμον,
ἐκ γῆς ἀναθρώσκοντα πρὸς τὸν αἰθέρα,
καὶ τοὺς χόρους φθάνοντα τοὺς τῶν ἀστέρων . . .
. . . τὸν ἀστρολαμπῆ τῶν Ἀποστόλων δόμον . . .

In both poems, the visual description leads to a spiritual vision; rhetorical *ekphrasis* and symbolical interpretation are closely interwoven. The concrete reality of the portrait, the person whom it represents, and the ornaments by which it is surrounded are less important than the spiritual meaning, fixed and predetermined by tradition which the observer projects into the work of art. In our epigram, the central concepts are the following: heaven, Logos, wisdom. Heaven is represented by the stars

58. Cf. *Anth. Pal.* 1.120.2, 109.1, etc.
59. Ed. by E. Legrand and Th. Reinach (1896).
60. Vv. 358ff. (cf. 84ff., 501ff.; *Anth. Pal.* 1.15.4).

(vv. 2 and 5) and by the phrase εἰς οὐρανόν[61] (v. 3). Logos is represented twice, by the λόγοι through which he reveals himself (vv. 1 and 4). The whole epigram culminates in the praise of wisdom. These concepts follow each other in this order, in an anonymous Christian epigram, *Anth. Pal.* 1.22.1.

Πατρὸς ἐπουρανίου λόγε πάνσοφε, κοίρανε κόσμου . . .

These parallels could be multiplied.[62] The whole poem conforms to the style of the Christian encomium represented by such epigrams as *Anth. Pal.* 1.105 on Eudokia and 106 and 107 on the emperor Michael and by the epitaph which Arethas wrote for his sister Anna, *Anth. Pal.* 15.33.

It is very unlikely that Hypatia, the daughter of Theon, would have been buried in a Christian church.[63] The name itself is not too frequent; we know of another Hypatia and of a poem composed in her honor by Panolbios.[64] Is this the poem or part of it, and was Πανολβίου corrupted to Παλλαδίου (-ᾶ) by someone who identified this obscure Hypatia with the famous Alexandrian Neoplatonist and wanted to establish a connection between her and the widely read Alexandrian epigrammatist? Or is the attribution to Palladas the πρῶτον ψεῦδος, resulting from a mechanical error, leading to the corruption of another name (but which?) to the metrically awkward Ὑπατία? This alternative opens a wide field for speculation, but it does not affect the main part of our argument.

We have seen that the only epigram which would prove conclusively that Palladas was a Christian cannot be authentic. We also know, at last, that Palladas' dislike of Platonism[65] is genuine; for there is no longer any evidence for his friendship with Hypatia. At the same time, the only redeeming feature of his personality—his devotion to that noble woman, his admiration for her mind—has vanished altogether. If we take this epigram away from him, his invectives seem even more venomous, because they are not balanced by a sense of values which recognizes the

---

61. Which is not quite the same as οὐράνια (Jacobs) but rather = οὐρανοδρόμα; cf. Georg. Pisid. *De van. vit.* 238; *Hexaem.* 3; *Ad Heracl.* (ed. Sternbach, *Wiener Stud.* 13 [1891]: 8ff.) 25f.

62. Cf., e.g., *Anth. Pal.* 9.687.1, 817.1, 818.4.

63. A Latin letter to Cyril in which Hypatia professes to be a Christian is a forgery; Hoche, *Philol.* 15 (1860): 452.

64. *Suda*, s. v. "Panolbios." He lived in the fifth century; J.B. Bury, *Hist. of the Lat. Rom. Emp.*, vol. 1 (1889), 320 n. 2.

65. *Anth. Pal.* 11.305 (cf. 355), 10.45.

good and the beautiful next to the corrupt and the ridiculous in human life. We can only agree with his own statement that his satirical temper is a "disease,"[66] perhaps we should say, a form of neurosis.

In a sense, the alternative Christianism versus Paganism does not apply to a writer like Palladas. He may have paid lip service to the new religion, because it was convenient, not because he held any strong convictions. If it is true that every satirist is a frustrated moralist, Palladas must be the exception to the rule.[67] Living in an age of transition, unable to commit himself to any philosophy or creed, unless it be a colorless blend of Epicureanism and skepticism, he plays the role of the unsympathetic observer who "tears the coverings from human frailty and holds it up in its meanness and misery."[68] His satire resembles those mirrors at a carnival which distort the face of anyone who comes too close; but he shows us only the distortions,[69] not the ideal, because he has no ideal. His eloquence is, indeed, the eloquence of the manager of a freak show;[70] he does not have to appeal to moral standards in order to attract his public. We have seen that he succeeded in attracting his public; he was widely read in his own time and later, during the time when the Anthology was compiled. Whatever his Byzantine readers found in Palladas' epigrams, it was neither the ethos of dying paganism nor the enthusiasm of the new religion; they must have appreciated his literary qualities, as slight as they may seem to many of us.[71]

---

66. Cf. *Anth. Pal.* 11.340.4, which has often been compared to Persius *Sat.* 1.12; Juvenal *Sat.* 1.30, 79; 7.52 (cf. Mayor's notes and the pamphlet of J.C.F. Meister, *Letzte Studien über A. Persius Flaccus* [1812], which offers a remarkably full discussion of this concept).

67. Highet (173) misses in Palladas a strong sense of moral purpose.

68. J.W. Mackail, *Sel. Epp. fr. the Gr. Anth.,* 3d ed. (1911), 330.

69. Cf. *Anth. Pal.* 7.681ff., 11.285.4f., 11.357, etc.

70. Cf. *Anth. Pal.* 11.353.

71. One of Palladas' best-known distichs, *Anth. Pal.* 10.73 (cf. Jebb on Soph. *Oed. Col.* 1693f.; Pease on Verg. *Aen.* 4.376) is variously attributed to St. Basil the Great (Boissonade, *Anecd. Gr.* 2.475) and the emperor Julian (*Cod. Barocc.* 133; cf. F. Cumont, *Rev. Phil.* 16 [1892]: 163f.). I have discovered another version of it among the poems of the Byzantine nun Kasia (or Ikasia), published by K. Krumbacher, SB München, Phil.-Hist. Kl. (1897), 359.71ff. She lived under Theophilus and his son Michael (842–67). Many of her other epigrams are obviously inspired by Palladas, for example, her "Hassgedichte," all beginning with μισῶ (p. 363f. Kr.: cf. *Anth. Pal.* 10.96.7), and her invective against a pseudo-philosopher (p. 363.4 Kr.; cf. *Anth. Pal.* 11.305); she even attacks her own sex in Palladas' manner (p. 367 Kr.; cf. *Anth. Pal.* 11.287 and my n. 46). But she also defends the

monastic life against such jests as Palladas *Anth. Pal.* 11.384, explaining why they are justly called μόναχοι (p. 368.94 Kr.). Among the poems of Kasia, published by Krumbacher from *Cod. Brit. Mus. Addit.* 10072, there are several epigrams by another Byzantine poet, Michael, who is named *in margine* three times. He, too, is familiar with Palladas (cf. p. 361.120ff. Kr. and *Anth. Pal.* 9.379). Krumbacher (p. 329) and others have been unable to identify this poet. But we know of another epigrammatist, Michael Chartophylax, author of *Anth. Pal.* 1.122 = 15.17A, preceding "Palladas" 9.400 = 15.17 B. He is also described as the editor of an abridged anthology on which the corrector, C, relied for his revision of the *Cod. Palatinus;* cf. his marginal note on 7.428 and 432. I should like to suggest that this anthology contained 15.17 A and B, as written by J, whereas the notes of C on 9.400 are derived from another source; he was unable, as he tells us himself (on 7.432), to use the collection of Michael for the second part of the manuscript. We have seen how strongly Palladas influenced the Byzantine epigrammatists; is it conceivable that 9.400 is a Christian adaptation of a (lost) original by Palladas and that original and imitation were placed next to each other, as it is often done in the Anthology? This hypothesis would help to explain the erroneous attribution.

I am very grateful to Arthur Darby Nock for help and friendly advice.

Two Predictions of the End of Paganism

The Hermetic dialogue *Asclepius*[1] contains near the end (chaps. 24–26) a prediction of doom for the pagan religions practiced in Egypt. This prediction, entitled "The Apocalypse" in Festugière's French translation, grows out of a brief discussion of theurgical operations concerning the gods.[2] The gods have always been worshiped properly in Egypt, but soon they will leave that country and return to heaven. Strangers will settle in Egypt and make it a crime to practice the ancient rituals. Hermes Trismegistus continues, *tunc terra ista sanctissima, sedes delubrorum atque templorum, sepulcrorum erit mortuorumque plenissima* (chap. 24, p. 327, 11–14 Festugière). He adds that "evil angels" [*nocentes angeli*] will remain and by "mixing with men" [*humanitate commixti*] instigate them to commit all sorts of crimes. We shall see later in this essay what this last phrase probably means.

Following J. Kroll and others, Festugière (n. 201 on p. 379) says that this prediction does not refer to any historical event in particular but develops certain topoi of apocalyptic literature. It can be argued, however, that the author of the *Asclepius*, or the author of its Greek original, the τέλειος λόγος, is predicting, that is, describing *ex eventu*, the destruction of the Serapeum in Alexandria and other pagan sanctuaries, by the Christians.

There is a remarkable parallel to this vision in Eunapius' *Lives of the Sophists* (pp. 471–73 Boissonade). The parallel was pointed out first by J. Geffcken, discussed in a brief article by A.D. Nock and S.C. Neill, and treated at greater length by P. de Labriolle.[3] Eunapius' anti-Christian

---

From *Euphrosyne*, n.s., 14 (1986): 153–56.

1. *Corpus Hermeticum*, ed. A.-J. Festugière and A.D. Nock 2: 259–401.

2. On this type of theurgy, known as the "Opening of the Mouth," see E. Otto, *Das ägyptische Mundöffnungsritual: Aegyptologische Abhandlungen* (Wiesbaden, 1960); E. Iversen, *Egyptian and Hermetic Doctrine* (Copenhagen, 1938), 37–38, 65; to his reference add *Asclepius* chap. 36, p. 347 F.-N.

3. J. Geffcken, *Der Ausgang des griechisch-römischen Heidentums* (Heidelberg, 1920), 83, 158, 172, 276 (n. 76). P. de Labriolle, *La réaction païenne* (Paris, 1934), 365–67, points out a similar prediction in Eunapius p. 476 Boiss.

tendency is obvious and helps us to understand the meaning of the prophecy in the *Asclepius.*

Eunapius records the impressive career of Antoninus "the anchorite," a priest, a philosopher, and—or so it would appear—a theurgist, who seems to have inherited the "psychic" gifts of his famous mother, Sosipatra. Mother and son clearly represent the leading intellects of paganism opposed to the growing power of Christianity.

Antoninus becomes a priest in the temple at the Canobic mouth of the Nile and trains candidates for the priesthood. The rites of the gods worshiped there were secret, as Eunapius implies; he says nothing about the famous incubation oracle. Antoninus was clearly a great teacher, and we can assume that he was also a theurgist, but not openly. According to Eunapius, when Antoninus lectured on Plato, he avoided any "theological" (which here means no doubt "theurgical") discussions. Eunapius uses a picturesque phrase worth quoting: "Whoever proposed one of the more divine problems encountered a statue"; that is, the teacher froze and pretended that he had heard nothing. Eunapius stresses this point, because it must have been unusual for a Platonist who also served as a priest in an Egyptian temple not to be a theurgist. He suspects that Antoninus was afraid of the imperial legislation which prosecuted all kinds of magic (and theurgy was essentially a higher form of magic). E.R. Dodds writes:[4] "Julian's patronage made theurgy temporarily fashionable. When as emperor he set about reforming the pagan clergy, the theurgist Chrysanthius found himself *archiereus* of Lydia while Maximus, as theurgic consultant to the imperial court, became a wealthy and influential *éminence grise. . . .* But Maximus paid for this in the subsequent Christian reaction, when he was fined, tortured and eventually, in 317, executed on a charge of conspiracy against the emperors. . . . For some time after this event theurgists deemed it prudent to lie low." There can be little doubt (see Dodds' n. 48) that Antoninus was a theurgist and did possess the occult faculties which he refused to claim.

One day, Antoninus had a prophetic vision which came true. This alone would prove to his admirer Eunapius that he was a son worthy of his clairvoyant mother, Sosipatra. Antoninus told his disciples that soon after his death the temple would cease to be the great sanctuary it was and that the magnificent temple of Serapis would be transformed into "the dark and shapeless" [τὸ σκοτοειδὲς καὶ ἄμορφον] and that "some-

---

4. E.R. Dodds, *The Greeks and the Irrational* (Berkeley, 1951), 93.

thing fabulous and formless" [μυθῶδες καὶ ἀειδές] would rule over the most beautiful things on earth.

Eunapius describes in some detail the ways in which the prediction was fulfilled: the temple of Serapis was demolished; the temples of Canobus were too. The statues of the gods and the votive offerings were stolen. Only the vast floor of the temple of Serapis was left intact for some time, because the stones were too heavy to be carried. Monks took over the ancient sacred sites, and the "bones and skulls of criminals" were buried inside the former pagan sanctuaries and worshiped under the names of "witnesses, ministers of some kind, and ambassadors from the gods to carry prayers" [μάρτυρες γοῦν ἐκαλοῦντο καὶ διάκονοί τινες καὶ πρέσβεις τῶν αἰτήσεων παρὰ τῶν θεῶν].

The Serapeion was destroyed in 391 A.D., probably less than a year after Antoninus' death, and the temples of Canobus were ransacked at the time when Theophilus was bishop of Alexandria, that is, between 385 and 412.

In his *City of God*, written between 413 and 426, St. Augustine[5] quotes part of the Hermetic "Apocalypse" (8.26) and deals with what he recognizes as a reference to the Christian cult of the martyrs. The presence of dead bodies in temples or even near temples[6] was an abomination to the pagans, and their indignation shows that they still considered these temples their own and had not given up all hope.

St. Augustine does not seem to know Eunapius, but in the prediction of Antoninus we find the same allusions to the martyrs, whose cult replaced not only that of the ancient heroes (for, in a sense, the martyrs and the saints of Christianity took the place of the ancient heroes) but even that of the pagan gods. They were thought to act as messengers or ambassadors between the highest divine powers and mankind. The testimonies collected by H. Delehaye[7] illustrate the terms which Eunapius uses. A messenger of God with whom the faithful will be united after their death is called ἄγγελος (Barnabas 18.1; Hermas *Vision* 2.2.7; *Similitude* 9.27.3). Gregory Nazianzen (*Oratio funebr. in patrem, PG* 35.990) uses the word πρεσβεία to describe the role that his dead father plays, and Basil the Great (*Homilia in XL martyras, PG* 31.523) calls the martyrs πρεσβευταὶ δυνατώτατοι. It is clear that the pagan propagandists are familiar with Christian theology, especially the doctrine concerning the

5. See M.-J. Lagrange, *Revue Biblique* 34 (1925): 386; de Labriolle, *La réaction païenne*, 359.

6. G. Bowersock, *Julian the Apostate* (Cambridge, Mass., 1978), 93.

7. H. Delehaye, *Les origines du culte des Martyrs* (Brussels, 1933), 100ff.

martyrs. What was shocking to the pagans—the presence of dead bodies, the worship of relics in former temples—was a special act of *pietas* for the Christians. This is, perhaps, one of the most dramatic differences between the two worlds.

The events predicted by Antoninus and the *Asclepius* are reported from the Christian point of view in Sozomen's *Church History* (7.17.2). In a passage reminiscent of both pagan texts, Sozomen first praises the beauty and the size of the Serapeion. He then mentions a philosopher, Olympius,[8] who comforted the pagans when he saw how distressed they were at the disappearance of the statues of their gods. He urged them to continue their worship, as if nothing had happened, adding: "The statues are [made of] perishable material, [mere] forms and, therefore, may suffer destruction, but certain powers dwell in them, and these have flown away to heaven." This is exactly the theory developed in the *Asclepius* (chap. 24): *statuas animatas sensu et spiritu plenas. . . . E terris enim et ad caelum recursura divinitas.*

In his treatise *De divinatione daemonum* (1.1 = PL 40.581) St. Augustine seems to refer to this passage of the *Asclepius*. In this treatise he discusses the possibility that the pagan gods (i.e., their statues) can actually predict the future, especially as far as it affects them. He writes, *cum . . . de divinatione daemonum quaereretur et affirmaretur praedixisse nescio quem eversionem templi Serapis quae in Alexandria facta est, respondi non esse mirandum, si istam eversionem templi et simulacri sui imminere daemones et scire et praedicere potuerunt.* Hence, even a Christian could credit the statues of the pagan gods with certain magical faculties. The treatise was written in 406 A.D., fifteen years after the destruction of the Serapeion. The *nescio quis* is almost certainly the speaker of the *Asclepius*, a work with which St. Augustine was familiar.

Although St. Augustine treats the prophecy of doom as a genuine prediction, scholars today are inclined to consider it a *vaticinium ex eventu*. If they are right, it must have been added to the *Asclepius* or its Greek original between 391 and 406 A.D.[9]

---

8. On Olympius (n. 19) see W. Ensslin, *RE* 18 (1939): 249. According to Sozomen (loc. cit.) the philosopher left Egypt in a great hurry. One night he heard the voice of one singing "Halleluiah" in the empty Serapeum. The doors were shut, and he could see no one. He understood at once the meaning of this *ostentum* and embarked for Italy.

9. On the attempts of dating the *Asclepius* see the addenda in S. MacCormach's English translation of Geffcken's book *Der Ausgang,* based on the 1929 edition (Amsterdam, 1978), 322; de Labriolle, *La réaction païenne,* 359; Nock, *Corp. Herm.,* 2:288.

The two prophecies add up to a remarkable piece of anti-Christian propaganda of Egyptian provenience. The destruction of the temples, the removal of the statues of the ancient gods, the cult of relics, the worship of a new deity and his "evil angels"—all this is clearly part of the pagan polemic against the Christians, as we encounter it in Celsus, the emperor Julian, and Porphyry. In this context the "evil angels" who "mix with men" acquire a special meaning. How do they mix with men? Festugière (n. 217, with a reference to chap. 22, p. 324, 1f.) has given what I think is the right explanation: "en s'introduisant en eux avec la nourriture." But then this can only be an allusion to the Eucharist, viewed by the pagans as a way of communicating with higher powers through food and drink, that is, bread and wine.

Humor in Pagan Culture and in the Early Church

General Remarks

Concepts and Definitions

Humor is a species of the comic genre and represents, together with jokes and play, a contrast to seriousness and dignity (W. Förster, *Theol. Wörterbuch z. NT* 7 [1964]: 190–95; K. Gross, "Gravitas," *RAC* 12:758). Anything that provokes laughter or a smile is humorous. Some scholars distinguish between humor properly speaking, joke, jest, and ridicule (satire), and all these forms are attested in pagan antiquity, but not in Christianity, it seems, or at least not as clearly. Linguistically, neither Greek nor Latin has an exact synonym for *humor,* and the etymology is not very helpful, though it is of historical interest: *(h)umor,* literally "moisture, a liquid," translates, in the medical terminology of the Middle Ages, the Greek term χυμός, "body juice," used by Hippocrates. The mixture of the four body juices—blood, phlegm, gall, and black gall—determines, according to a theory which also goes back to Hippocrates (W. Müri, *Gymnasium* 57 [1950]: 191) the temperament of a human being. The literal meaning of "temperament" (= mixture), incidentally, is already attested in Pliny the Elder. Hence, *humor* all by itself was too vague an expression and had to be modified as "grim temperament" or "friendly temperament." Only later did it lose its negative connotation and come to mean "happy mood" or "inclination to joke." This semantic development had reached its final point in seventeenth-century Britain and influenced, via the French language (where there is *humour* besides

From *Reallexikon für Antike und Christentum,* vol. 16 (Stuttgart, 1992), cols. 753–73.

For help and advice I am very grateful to the following: A. Dihle, J. Engemann, R. Geesmann, Ch. Gnilka, H. Goedicke, R. Luck, J.H. Waszink, and the other editors of the *Reallexikon für Antike und Christentum.*

humeur), the German usage. In German, "Humor" is related to "Heiter-keit" (i.e., serenity), which is derived from an Indo-European root *kai-*, "shining, luminous." In Middle High German, "Heiterkeit" still means "clarity." From external observations, such as "bright, cloudless," may be derived psychological statements, such as "happy, cheerful, in a good mood." "Heiterkeit" is further related to "Freude" (i.e., "joy"; cf. O. Michel, *RAC* 8:348–418, esp. 350 on the etymological experiments in Plato *Cratyl.* 419b/d).

Terminology and Nuances

Since no Greek or Latin words correspond in every respect to *humor*, we cannot avoid a look at the lexica. The wealth of synonyms or near synonyms in both Greek and Latin shows what an important role wit and humor played in pagan society, while the vocabulary attested in Christian contexts appears to be more limited; this, in itself, points to a change in values.

Greek
The term ἅλς or ἅλας, meaning "wit, joke," does not seem to be attested before Plutarch (*Comp. Aristoph. et Men.* 854C, where we ought to read ἅλες ἱλαροί with Emperius). Latin *sal* seems to be a direct loan from the Greek. In the New Testament this meaning is controversial (see the commentary on Col. 4:6). Ἀστειότης signifies "politeness, polish," but also "wit." Ἀστεῖος is originally "urban," and the qualities implied in this attribute could be expected of the inhabitants of Athens, while the Attic peasant might be ἄγροικος in more than one sense of the word, like Menander's Cnemon (see Schol. Aristoph. *Pax* 370). In Acts 7:2 ἀστεῖος probably means "pleasant." Βωμολοχία means the coarse, grotesque humor of the clown, the buffoon, and is definitely not part of the ideal of the Athenian gentleman (see Plato *Rep.* 606C; Aristot. *Nic. Eth.* 2.7.1108a24; Isocr. *Or.* 7.49; Lammermann 16f.). Τὸ γελοῖον can be anything that we would call "funny" or "comical," not just what seems "ridiculous." According to Aristotle (*Poet.* 5.1449a34), it is the τέλος of comedy. It corresponds to Latin *ridiculum*. Γέλως stands in non-Christian authors not only for "laughter," specifically "scornful, insulting laughter" (also in the Septuagint), but also for the target, the object of scorn or derision (Hdt. 7.209). Xenophon (*Conv.* 4.50) refers to coarse jokes. In the New Testament (Luke 6:21, 25; Jac. 4:9) laughter in this life has a negative connotation. Εἰρωνεία may be rendered literally as "dissimulation" (Lat. *dissimulatio*). For Plato,

it is a kind of playful understatement, a mock modesty that pretends ignorance rather than authority in order to show, in a debate, the real ignorance of the adversary. For Plato (*Rep.* 337A), Aristotle (*Nic. eth.* 4.3.1124b30) and Cicero (*Ac.* 2.5.15) the term designates not only Socrates' own, very personal kind of humor but his characteristic method of teaching. Aristotle considered ἀλαζονεία, "false pretension," as the extreme opposite to εἰρωνεία and saw the right attitude in the middle between the two (*Nic. eth.* 4.12.1127a14). Εὐτραπελία is, before the Christian era (and even in Philo *Leg. ad Gai.* 361, where it is associated with χάρις), a desirable attribute; it may sometimes be rendered with "esprit." Generally, it seems to imply adaptability and pleasant manners. According to Aristotle (*Nic. eth.* 2.7.1108a24) it is a virtue that lies in the middle between two extremes, βωμολοχία and ἀγροικία (mentioned earlier). It implies a certain attitude of "laissez-faire" and suggests "easy familiarity," for example, with younger people (Plato *Rep.* 563A). In the New Testament (though it is only attested at Eph. 5:4) εὐτραπελία is placed on the same level as μωρολογία and αἰσχρότης (here equivalent to αἰσχρολογία). What has happened? One of the social ideals of paganism has become a taboo, for Christians to avoid. Ἱλαρότης is "cheerfulness, gaiety" (see Rom. 12:8; in Plut. *Vit. Ages.* 2 it is parallel to τὸ εὔθυμον and τὸ παιγνιῶδες). Καχασμός is an onomatopoetic expression for "laughter," for example, "scornful, insulting laughter" (Soph. *Ajax* 198), as opposed to κιχλισμός, "giggling." Clemens Alexandrinus (*Paed.* 2.5.46) condemns the giggling of women as a form of shameless flirtation. Παιδιά is "fun, play, pleasure, entertainment," as opposed to σπουδή, "earnestness" (Plato *Leg.* 647D; Aristot. *Pol.* 8.5.1339a16). Plato attributes to παιδιά an important educational function (see G. Reale, *Storia della filosofia antica* [1979], 2:179f.). We might add the adjectives γηθόσυνος and φαιδρός; both imply brightness and serenity, and both can be used metaphorically.

Latin

Acetum is "sharp wit, biting satire," since Plautus (*Truc.* 179; cf. Hor. *Sat.* 1.7.32: *Italo perfusus aceto*). *Argutiae* may be translated as "jesting, pleasantries, wit" (cf. Phaedr. *App. Epil.* 4: *temperatae suaves sunt argutiae/ immodicae offendunt*). The opposite would be *contumeliae* (cf. Seneca *Dial.* 2.11.13: *pueros quidam mercantur procaces . . . qui probra meditate effundunt; nec has contumelias vocamus, sed argutias*). *Dicacitas* signifies, as the *Oxford Latin Dictionary* informs us, "mordant or caustic raillery" and is considered a rather valuable asset by Cicero (*Ad Att.* 1.13.2), while Seneca

(*Dial.* 7.10.2) associates it with *superbia* and *contumelia.* According to Cicero at *De oratore* 2.218, *facetiae* would be the generic term which includes both *dicacitas* and *cavillatio,* "railery, banter, badinage." A different classification is offered at *Orator* 87: here, *sales* is the generic term which includes both *facetiae* and *dicacitates.* According to some critics quoted by Quintilian (*Inst.* 6.31.21), Demosthenes was *urbanus,* but not *dicax;* obviously these are two different kinds of humor. Similarly, Dionysius of Halicarnassus (*Demosth.* 54) asserts that the great orator lacked εὐτραπελία. *Facetiae* denotes both the "gift of being witty" and a "witty remark," a "joke." Cicero (*De or.* 2.218) distinguishes this from *dicacitas* (cf. *De or.* 87); in his opinion, this kind of humor is entirely compatible with *gravitas* (*De or.* 3.30). Catullus (12.9) combines *facetiae* and *lepos.* *Festivitas* is "gaiety, charm, wit" (it is combined with *iocus* in Plaut. *Capt.* 770, with *lepos* in *Rhet. Her.* 4.32). *Hilaritas,* "cheerfulness, gaiety," is not attested before Varro, who calls the wine *hilaritatis dulce seminarium* (*Men.* 11); the adjective appears already in Plautus. *Hilaritas* is combined with *iocus* in Cicero (*De or.* 2.221), with *risus* in Cornelius Nepos (*Epam.* 8.5; Epaminondas was able to make his judges laugh, and they acquitted him). It is the opposite of *severitas* (Cic. *Brut.* 197; cf. 322). *Humanitas,* one of the social ideals of the Ciceronian Age, includes, among other things, a sense of humor (cf. Cic. *De or.* 1.27; Plin. *Epist.* 4.34; O. Hiltbrunner, "iocus," *Thes. Linguae Lat.* 7.2.287.3–289.36; F. Klingner, in *Römische Geisteswelt,* 4th ed. [1961], 690–732; Rieks 229). *Iocus,* "joke, jest," designates, like *ridiculum,* anything that provokes laughter (cf. Laevius *Carm.* fr. 14: *cachinnos ioca dicta risitantes;* Ovid *Fast.* 3.695; W. Ehlers, "Humanitas," *Thes. Linguae Lat.* 6.3.3078.7–28). *Lepos* can mean "charm, grace, humor, wit, witticism" (cf. Plaut. *Asin.* 13: *inest lepos ludusque in hac comoedia;* Cic. *De or.* 2.270: *Socraten opinor in hac ironia . . . longe lepore et humanitate omnibus praestitisse*). The term is used in conjunction with *facetiae* by Catullus (12.18) and is not incompatible with *gravitas* (Cic. *Rep.* 2.1 on Cato Maior; see Gross, *RAC* 12:758). *Ludus* denotes "sport, play, entertainment, fun, merriment" and may be compared to Greek παιδιά. It is combined with *risus* by Gellius (13.3.1). The phrase *per ludum,* "in jest (and not in earnest)," is analogous to *per iocum.* There is no clear distinction between *ludus* and *lusus;* the latter is sometimes translated as "joke" but can also mean "mockery" (Quintil. *Inst.* 5.13.46); the opposite is *seria* (Pliny *Epist.* 7.9.10). *Ridiculum* is anything that provokes laughter, but we ought to remember that not all *ridicula* are necessarily also *faceta.* A jester (*sannio,* Greek γελωτοποιός) who makes his audience laugh may be *salsus* but not *facetus* (Cic. *De or.* 2.251). It all depends on the level of the humor. Ultimately, this is a question of good taste. *Risus* can be, like Greek γέλως, the object of laughter (cf. Hor. *Sat.* 1.5.98, where *risus* is combined with *iocus*). *Sal* is "wit," *sales* "witticisms" (cf. Cic. *Orator* 87). *Sal* is combined with *lepos* in Catullus (16.7) and Martial (3.20.9: *lepore tinctos Attico sales*), and Horace says of Lucilius, his predecessor in the satire, *sale multo / urbem defricuit* (*Sat.* 1.10.3). *Serenus* and *serenitas* correspond to Greek ἱλαρός and ἱλαρότης. *Urbanitas* was probably formed after ἀστειότης and includes a sense of humor, a specific elegance of wit. As a quality, it is detected not in one particular joke but rather in the whole *color dicendi*, according to Quintilian (*Inst.* 6.3.104–7). According to Seneca (*Dial.* 9.6.2) it can be exaggerated (see Rieks 118f., 154–58).

Non-Christian Contexts

Egypt

Laughter as part of worship is attested in ancient Egypt as well as in Asia Minor. It is an expression of joy over the return, the resurrection, of a deity, such as Osiris, Adonis, Tammuz (see Hvidberg 11–16; Hvidberg's learning is impressive, though much of his material seems irrelevant). The third day of the festival in honor of Osiris found again was called Hilaria, because of the wild jubilation of the faithful (*CIL* 1, 2d ed., 334). When a deity of light, a lord of the universe, a redeemer is born, all of nature rejoices (see W. Speyer, "Religiös-sittliches und frevelhaftes Verhalten in seiner Auswirkung auf die Naturgewalten," (*Jahrbb. f. Antike und Christentum* 22 [1979]: 39 n. 67). We may wonder whether there is any relationship between this phenomenon and the *risus paschalis*. In ancient Egypt, humor was considered, in the human sphere, an ingredient of common sense or even part of the kind of wisdom which places everything into the right perspective. The humor of the Egyptian gods reminds one of Homer (van de Walle 15). There are epic parodies comparable to the Batrachomyomachia (ibid. 19). There are satires (E. Brugsch, *Zeitschr. ägypt. Sprache* 35 [1897]: 140; S. Curto, *La satire nell'antico Egitto* [1965]) and animal fables reminiscent of Aesopus (E. Brunner-Traut, *Altägyptische Tiergeschichten und -fabeln*, 3d ed. [1970]). Witty proverbs were passed around such as "better to have lived half a life than to be wholly dead" (see van de Walle 8). Puns comparable to those found in the Old Testament were popular. It is possible that they have their origin in magic beliefs (see S. Morenz, "Wortspiele in Aegypten," in *Festschr. J. Jahn* [1957], 32).

The Greek World

Religion, Mythology, Folklore
In his novel *Ardinghello* (1787) Wilhelm Heinse coined the phrase "die heiteren Griechen," and in his poem "Die Götter Griechenlands" (1788) Friedrich Schiller emphasized the role of merriment, laughter, and play in Hellenic religion. His aphorism "Der Mensch ist nur da ganz Mensch, wo er spielt" contains the same message. The Greek gods were able to laugh at others and at themselves (Pfeiffer); this is, in fact, one of their privileges (Friedländer). They are, as Plato (*Crat.* 406C) puts it, φιλοπαίγμονες, that is, "in a playful mood," and Greek religion has been described (Sikes 126) as a jolly or at least comfortable agreement with the gods. You could hardly say this about the Etruscans and the Romans. Greek myth is rich in comic and even grotesque motives. Thus, Heracles is at the same time a saviour figure and a buffoon; although this may already be a travesty of a more respectable myth (W. Nestle, *Vom Mythos zum Logos*, 2d ed. [1942], 120; M.P. Nilsson, *Gesch. d. griech. Rel.*, 3d ed. [1955] 2: 192f.). Mockery and laughter have a role in ritual and folklore; thus, the γεφυρισμός, the ritual mockery directed at the participants in the Eleusinian procession, is well attested (O. Kern, s.v. γεφυρισμοί, *RE* 7.1 [1910]: 1229). At Greek funerals, mourning was followed by merriment, it seems, and H. Usener (*Kl. Schr.* 4 [1914]: 469f.) saw a connection between the Sardinian "buffona" and the laughter of Iambe in the Homeric *Hymn to Demeter* (189–211); there seems to be an analogy in the Roman world (Marquardt, *Privatalt.*, 2d ed. [1886], 1:342). Apuleius (*Met.* 2.31–3.11) probably did not invent the deity of Laughter for the purposes of his novel, for Plutarch (*Vita Cleom.* 9) knows such a god. A magical papyrus (*PGM*, 2d ed., 13.161f., 472f.) attests a cosmogony which postulates the creation of the planetary gods by a primeval god through laughter (see R. Reitzenstein, *Die Vorgeschichte der christlichen Taufe* [1929], 134). Parodied prayers are a curious phenomenon, too (see H. Kleinknecht, *Die Gebetsparodie in der Antike*, Tüb. Beitr. z. Altertumswissensch. 28 [1937]); we can observe it in Christian contexts in the sixth century and later (see P. Lehmann, *Die Parodie im Mittelalter*, 2d ed. [1963]); E. Pax, "Epiphanie," *RAC* 5:847f.).

Literature
In General. We find comic features here and there in archaic epic poetry which could be parodied itself, as the *Batrachomyomachia* and the tragedy (B. Seidensticker, *Palintonos Harmonia: Studien zu den komischen Elementen in der griech. Tragödie* [1982]) show. But there are autonomous literary

genres which are predominantly playful and whose main purpose is to entertain and amuse. Such genres are comedy, satyr play, mime, iambic poetry, animal fable (Radermacher 33), epigram, satire, joke (a collection of jokes, the *Philogelos,* compiled in late antiquity, is preserved; see Thierfelder), gnome (F. Wehrli, *Museum Helvet.* 30 [1937]: 193–208), apophthegm, proverb, riddle.

Homer. The Homeric gods live on the far side of guilt and punishment. What is tragic from the human point of view may seem comical to them. Their laughter at the sight of Hephaestus limping by (*Il.* 1.599f.) is typical. The misfortune of Ares and Aphrodite caught in adultery makes the other gods and goddesses laugh (*Od.* 8.266–366). This spontaneous, seemingly uncontrollable merriment (ἄσβεστος γέλως) is sometimes called "Homeric laughter." This kind of humor sometimes borders on "gloating" (for which the Greeks had a word, ἐπιχαιρεκακία). Sometimes, the essential horror of a scene is relieved by comic elements, as in the Polyphemus episode (*Od.* 9.105–542; see Radermacher 14–17). Homer also knows the "Sardonic smile" (*Od.* 20.302; after this, Plato *Rep.* 337A; Cic. *Fam.* 7.25.1): the hero whose true identity is still unknown laughs, because he is already planning his revenge on the pretenders. The adjective *sardonic* is, perhaps, connected with σεσηρώς, "grinning," though it was derived, in antiquity, from a plant found on Sardinia, *Ranunculus Sardous;* people who ate it were supposed to die from convulsive spasms of laughter.

Other Poets. For Hesiod (*Theog.* 40–43), laughter is an expression of joy over the singing of the Muses. According to Theognis (5–10), all of nature rejoices at the birth of Phoebus (cf. Hom. *Hymn to Demeter* 11–14). One would expect wit and humor in the iambic poets, more so than in lyric poetry, although it is not absent. There is no "loud laughter" in Pindar, but there is wit, raillery, and a kind of well-bred esprit (see G. Kurz, "Humor bei Pindar," in *Musa iocosa* [1974] 3–25; B.A. van Groningen, *Pindare au banquet* [1960]). It cannot be denied that tragedy deliberately employs humorous features, for instance, in order to characterize lower-class types (see Seidensticker, cited earlier, under "Literature: In General"). Euripides' *Alcestis,* which borders on the ludicrous here and there, is, technically speaking, not a tragedy but takes the place of a satyr play. The Old Comedy pulls all the stops of the comical and the grotesque—persiflage, farce, buffoonery, satire, caricature, obscenity, and so on—but not only to provoke laughter and merriment. The comic playwrights aimed at creating a mood of relaxation which relieved political and social tensions and reconciled various groups within the audience.

Aristophanes was a jokester of genius and a wonderful lyrical poet, but he was also a keen observer of Athenian society. Some of his best comical effects result from the clash between ideal and reality. The Middle Comedy, practically only known from fragments, seems to have specialized in cooks, bons vivants, and clever parasites; but there is also evidence of the travesty of myths and of farcical interaction between deities. The humor of the New Comedy, one of whose masters was Menander, is more refined than that of Aristophanes, and its dialogues reflect the "laissez-faire," the amused, broad-minded tolerance typical of polite Attic society. The Alexandrian poets discover the humorous aspects of myth as well as of everyday life (see, e.g., A.E.-A. Horstmann, *Ironie und Humor bei Theokrit*, Beitr. z. Klass. Philol. 67 [1976]). This is even true for Callimachus' *Hymns* to gods (see G. Giangrande, *L'humour des Alexandrins*, Class. -Byzant. Monogr. 2 [1976]). The satiric epigram as a genus probably existed before the Hellenistic period (Theocritus of Chius) reached its zenith under the emperors (see F.J. Brecht, *Motiv- und Typengeschichte des griechischen Spottepigramms*, Philol. Suppl. 22, no. 2 [1930]; G. Luck, "Witz und Sentiment im griech. Epigramm," *Entretiens Fondation Hardt* 14 [1968], 387–411). Lucian's delightful wit spares neither philosophy nor religion.

Orators. Demosthenes (*Or.* 23.206) complains that, in Athens, a defendant whose guilt was practically certain might get acquitted because the judges liked his jokes or because he had important connections. Strangely enough, there are almost no jokes in the speeches as they have come down to us; Demosthenes' own joke about the donkey's shadow is preserved in the indirect tradition (Schol. Aristoph. *Vesp.* 191). This could mean that the orators inserted jokes into the speeches they actually delivered in court—whether improvised or carefully prepared—but left them out when they revised their texts for publication (Bonner 99–101).

Philosophy

In the fragments of the pre-Socratics, we find the elements, so to speak, of a theory of wit (see the testimonies collected by Grant [17]). Thus, they assert that people need to relax from time to time and then devote themselves to serious pursuits again. Or we hear that laughter is good for you but only in moderation (cf. Plato *Leg.* 732C; Radermacher 53, 90–93). Gloating, we are told, is unbecoming. Democritus lives on as the "laughing philosopher" (see A. Buck, "Democritus ridens et Heraclitus flens," in *Festschrift F. Schalk* [1963], 167–83), perhaps because he ridiculed the proverbial stupidity of the Abderites, his fellow citizens (Thierfelder 16). But he also wrote a famous treatise *On Cheerfulness*,

Περὶ εὐθυμίης (see R. Hirzel, *Hermes* 14 [1879]: 354–407). Cheerfulness or serenity as an ideal has been described as an expression of inner freedom and independence, and it may be compared to Socrates' behavior as he was facing death; the banter with his friends may be called a kind of "Galgenhumor" (H. v. Campenhausen, in *Tradition und Leben* [1960], 431–40). It would be difficult to characterize Socrates' accomplished self-irony better than Xenophon did (*Conv.* 1.1.5; Radermacher 107). Plato calls one of his greatest dialogues a παίγνιον, a "toy," for, as he says, of the most important subjects one can only talk in a mixture of jest and earnest. Plato also believes in the educational value of play, παιδιά: P. Boyancé, *Le culte des Muses chez les philosophes grecs* [1936]; Dihle 41. In the *Philebus* (47D–52), Plato presents a kind of theory of wit and humor (see R. Hackforth, *Plato's Examination of Pleasure* [1945]; Duckworth 306f.; H.D. Rankin, "Laughter, Humor, and Related Topics in Plato," *Class. et Mediaev.* 27 [1966]: 186–213). According to Aelian (*Var. hist.* 3.35) laughter was not allowed in the Academy; but this rule, if it really existed, may have applied only to the hours of formal teaching. Aristotle observes (*Part. an.* 3.10.673a; cf. Clem. Alex. *Strom.* 8.21.1, 5) that of all living creatures only human beings have the ability to laugh. Cheerfulness is therefore the characteristic of the Highest Being (*Met.* 12.7.1072a23f.). There is a clear reference to these thoughts in the Peripatetic author quoted by Strabo (10.3.9) who suggests that people can approach the status of deities by joking, by being merry, and through relaxation (ἄνεσις). We all need to rest and relax now and then, Aristotle says (*Rhet.* 1371b34; cf. Cicero *Off.* 1.103), and this we can achieve through jokes, play, and entertainment. Aristotle's positive view of εὐτραπελία has been mentioned already; cf. further *Nic. eth.* 4.13.1127b21, 4.14.1128b9. The Attic "gentleman" ought to be clever and witty and be able to joke, but he must not always provoke others to laugh, otherwise he might be considered a "buffoon," βωμολόχος; obscene jokes must be avoided at all costs (*Pol.* 7.17.1336b3). Aristotle distinguishes between harmless, playful jokes and stinging insults (Grant 39). The elements of a theory of the comical may be found in the *Poetics* (5.1449a32; cf. H. Herter, *Gnomon* 3 [1927]: 721–27; W. Kroll, s.v. "Rhetorik," *RE* supp. 7 [1940], 1076f.; Duckworth 305–14, 321–28, 332–69; R. Janko, *Aristotle on Comedy* [1984]). This theory is treated in later handbooks of poetics under the heading περὶ κωμῳδίας, in the rhetorical handbooks under the heading περὶ γελοίου or *de ridiculo*. Following Plato and Aristotle (and, possibly, also Theophrastus; cf. his character sketch of the Ἀλάζων), the *Tractatus Coislinianus* (G. Kaibel, *Comicorum Graecorum Fragmenta* chap. 1, para. 1 [1899], 50–39) stresses the liberating force of laughter, in analogy to the cathartic effect of πάθος in tragedy. The ancient Cynics created, it seems, the literary genre of the diatribe for their popular discourses which were characterized by a blend of seriousness and humor, the σπουδογέλοιον (see Horace *Sat.* 1.1.32–36; *Epist.* 2.2.60). In Stoicism, serenity is propagated as an ideal in life: for the wise man, all of life is one great festival, an occasion to rejoice constantly (ἑορτή, παιδιά, πανηγυρίς; cf. Dihle 44). This idea is alien to the New Testament (Bonhöffer, *Epiktet*, 293–98; idem, *Epiktet und das NT* [1911], 254f.).

Art. Ancient art does not contribute very much to our topic. E. Simon (*Gnomon* 33 [1961]: 644–50) points out, in a criticism of H. Kenner, *Weinen und Lachen in der griechischen Kunst* (Sitzungsberichte Wien 234, no. 2 [1960]) that ultimately neither tears nor laughter can be represented in art, only grief or smiling. On the other hand, our texts clearly distinguish between "to laugh," γελάω, and "to smile," μειδιάω. The typical smile of archaic statues may be understood as a "Miene erstarrter Heiterkeit" (ibid. 64); any interpretation in terms of magic beliefs or animism should probably be rejected (Simon 648). The smile could be understood as an expression of vitality, exuberance, "joie de vivre."

The Roman World

Roman Comedy experienced a first great period with Plautus, whose humor is often coarse and appealed to the people, while Terence later entertained the upper classes. Lucilius was Rome's first great satirist. He cultivated successfully a genre which the Romans considered their very own creation (Quintil. *Inst.* 10.1.93), although Lucilius had Greek models (early iambic poetry, Callimachus' *Iambs,* comedy, Stoic-Cynic diatribes; cf. J.W. Duff, *Roman Satire* [1964], 126). Both Cicero and Caesar were famous for their ready wit, and their *facete dicta* circulated and were collected (see H. Peter, *Jahrbücher f. Klass. Philol.* 43 [1897]: 853–66). In *De oratore* 2.216–90, Cicero puts into the mouth of C. Julius Caesar Strabo a theory of humor which is later developed by Quintilian (*Inst.* 6.3; see F. Kühnert, *Philol.* 106 [1962]: 29–59, 306–14). It should be noted that, for Cicero as for Quintilian, a sense of humor is part of the social ideal of *humanitas.* In Catullus' book of poems, we find next to ambitious, learned pieces satirical and humorous verse in a light vein. Horace uses his *Satires* as a vehicle for "telling the truth while laughing" [*ridentem dicere verum*]. This is essentially the technique of the Hellenistic diatribe (*Sat.* 1.1.24f.), whose influence on the Christian diatribe has been noticed by Th. Haecker (*Satire und Polemik* [1922], 137) and others. *Satires* 1.4 is important for our understanding of the whole genus (cf. G.L.

Hendrickson, *American Journal of Philology* 21 [1900]: 121–42). Humor is not absent from the *Epodes,* the *Epistles* (cf. *Carm.* 2.16.25–28), and the *Ars poetica* with its whimsical beginning and its scurrilous ending. Horace himself calls the particular mood of Virgil's pastoral poems *molle atque facetum* (*Sat.* 1.10.44), but here *facetum* may mean "graceful" rather than "witty" (see Zinn, "Elemente," 47f.). There is humor in the *Georgica* (see W. Richter's commentary [1957] on 1.370; 3.123, 289) and even in the *Aeneid* (e.g., 4.128; 5.182, 358)—reflecting *Il.* 23.555, 784). The laughter of the newborn baby in the "Messianic Eclogue" (Virg. *Ecl.* 4.51) has always fascinated scholars. As a rule, babies do not smile before they are six weeks old (Plin. *Nat. hist.* praef. 7.2); only children of the gods smile earlier (Lucian *Dial. Deor.* 11.1). E. Norden (*Die Geburt des Kindes* [1924] 58) compares a Sibylline dictum of Christian origin: "when the little boy was born, the earth jumped for joy, the throne of heaven laughed, and the world was jubilating" (see F.J.H. Letters, *Virgil* [1946], 87f.). Ovid's humor is reminiscent of the Alexandrian poets. With the exception of the poetry written in exile, his work is dominated by playful irony (on the *Metamorphoses* see Zinn, "Elemente," 53). Seneca's *Apocolocyntosis,* a Menippean satire, does not spare the gods. For Seneca, humor is a combination of *sal, lepos,* and *facetiae* (see Rieks 116). He praises the ancient lawgivers who ordered festivals and holidays, *ut ad hilaritatem homines cogantur* (*Dial.* 9.17.7; cf. Rieks 116). It is a remarkable idea that people have to be forced by law to make merry, for their own good, so to speak. The most diverse elements of humor enliven the novels of Petronius (Duff, *Roman Satire,* pp. 98–101) and Apuleius (see J. Tatum, *Apuleius and "The Golden Ass,"* [1979], 62–68). In Apuleius' narrative (*Met.* 3.5–11) we have a description of the festival of Risus, the god of laughter. In his epigrams, Martial displays his life and everyday life in Rome, especially in its scurrilous, all-too-human aspects (cf. 10.4.10: *hominem pagina nostra sapit*). For the younger Pliny, humor is the essential condiment of life. Thanks to the comedies he writes, thanks to the frivolous verse he composes, thanks to his ability to relax at fun and games, he is able to realize his own true humanity (*Epist.* 5.3.2). Here, we admire once more the social ideal which gave Attic culture in the classical and postclassical ages its incomparable charm.

Judaism

Scholars (e.g., I.M. Casanovicz, *Paronomasia in the Old Testament* [1894], and Voeltzel 14–20) have found almost five hundred puns and plays on words in the Old Testament, many of them quite witty. The story of creation preserves some humorous features (e.g., the woman made from a rib, the mutual recriminations of Adam and Eve after they have sinned, the fig leaves). Sarah's laughter after the divine announcement that she will be pregnant (Gen. 18:5–9) serves, perhaps, to strengthen the impact of the wonder (although Ambrosius [*Isaac* 1.1] interprets her laughter as an expression of joy, not skepticism; cf. Voeltzel 26f.). The story of Samson, the strong man, reminds one of folktales and has humorous undertones. Some scholars (e.g., B. Sarrazin, *Recherches Sciences Religieuses* 76 [1988]: 39–56) have understood the theophany in the Book of Job as a kind of parody. God laughs more than once in the Old Testament (Ps. 2:4, 36:13, 58:9, etc.), for instance, to show his contempt of the high and mighty of this world (see W. Vischer, "Der im Himmel Thronende lacht," *Beiträge zur Evang. Theol.* 44 [1966]: 129–35; in general: Rengstorf 656–60; Voeltzel 47f.). Raucous laughter is unbecoming (Eccl. 2:2; cf. 7:3f.). The Song of Songs is dominated by a festive mood, and the joy which it celebrates would be unthinkable without singing, dancing, and jesting. Satire and irony figure prominently among the tools of prophetic preaching, and Amos and Micah are the masters of these particular techniques; another master is Isaiah, who comments with gleeful sarcasm on the arrival of the king of Babylon in hell. His tale of the man who fells a tree, burns part of the wood, and carves a statue of a god from the rest (Isaiah 44:14–16; cf. Horace *Sat.* 1.8.1–3) is clearly satirical. After the destruction of the Temple of Jerusalem, God is no longer able to laugh (H.J. Schoeps, *Aus frühchristlicher Zeit* [1950], 152), but Jewish humor lives on (E. Edel, *Der Witz der Juden* [1909]; S. Landmann, *Der jüdische Witz: Soziologie und Sammlung* [1960]). The didactic methods of the rabbis, who make fun of themselves, involve God in a variety of comical situations, and even discover the devil's humorous side, produce pointed remarks and paradoxical statements (Jónsson 51–89).

Christianity

The New Testament

In this area opinions vary widely. Many scholars discover merriment, jests, and cordiality in the New Testament (e.g., Campenhausen, "Witz," 324, partly contradicting Grönbech). There are also laborious, but uncritical, compilations (Jónsson, e.g.) which suspect discreet jokes or hidden ironies almost everywhere. Perhaps it will be possible to reach an agreement, as far as play on words is concerned (there are supposed to be about two hundred examples; see E. Russell, "Paronomasia and Kindred Phenomena in the New Testament" [Ph.D. diss., University of Chicago, 1920]), but not all such play is necessarily humorous. Clavier certainly goes too far in his search for subtle irony, and even Voeltzel is not fully convincing, though many of his observations seem sensible. (I was unable to find F. Paulsen, "Das Ironische in Jesu Stellung und Rede," in *Schopenhauer, Hamlet und Mephistopheles*, 3d ed. [1911], 259–84). At any rate, it would seem dangerous to apply the ancient theories περὶ γελοίου to the New Testament. With all due caution I shall list a few passages that might be understood in a humorous, satirical, or ironic sense. This might include exaggerated images, like the plank in the eye of the person who sees the speck of sawdust in his brother's eye (Matth. 7:3; cf. Kretz, *Witz, Humor*, 19–44), the hypocrites who strain out a gnat and swallow a camel (Matth. 23:23f.), the camel that goes through the eye of a needle (Mark 10:20–27), and the "persistent friend" (Luke 11:5–8; see the useful remarks of Jónsson [117f., 171, 182, 187f.], following Clavier; see also Grönbech 103; less convincing is J. Jeremias, *Die Gleichnisse Jesu*, 6th ed. [1962], 157f.). We might also consider the children who playfully act out weddings and funerals (Matth. 11:16–19; see Voeltzel 12); the confrontation between the man who was blind from birth and the Pharisees, after Jesus had healed him (John 9); and the beginning of the Zacchaeus pericope (Luke 19:1–6). We find features that are familiar to us from folktales, with their subdued irony. That Jesus had a sense of humor can hardly be doubted: as K. Marti (*Lachen-Weinen-Lieben* [1985], 37) said, "wem's ernst ist, kann lachen." The jokes made by Jesus' antagonists and detractors should also be considered (although the story of Jesus being mocked [Matth. 27:27–44] is strongly influenced by Psalm 22; see Voeltzel 39–41). We detect Paul's irony in the story of the seven sons of Sceva, the Jewish chief priest (Acts 19:13–18; see Campenhausen, "Witz," 324f.); and in his speech before Agrippa (Acts 26:25–29), at least one scholar (P. Harlé, *New Testament Studies* 24 [1977/78]: 527–33) has seen a "private joke": Paul wishes that all those who listen to his words should become like him— with the exception, that is, of the chains he wears. There is sarcasm in the comparison of the apostles with the self-satisfied Corinthians (1. Cor. 4:6–13). Paul sometimes uses dramatic exaggerations: the woman who refuses to wear the veil might as well have her head shaved (1. Cor. 11:5f.); the Jewish convert who insists on circumcision might as well have himself castrated (Gal. 5:12; see Campenhausen, "Witz," 104f.). In a catalogue of undesirable types of behavior (Ephes. 5:4), Paul also mentions εὐτραπελία, a quality much appreciated by the Athenians (see Origenes *Fragm. in Ephes.* 5.4; J.A.F. Gregg, *Journ. Theol. Studies* 3 [1902]: 559). On the other hand, he recommends (Col. 4:6) a style of speaking adorned with χάρις and ἅλας; this can hardly refer to the "religiös-sittliche Wert" (F. Hauck, *Theol. Wörterbuch z. Neuen Testament* [1933], 1:220, without any arguments), although it should not be interpreted in a neoclassical sense, either (as M. Dibelius does, in his commentary, *Handbuch z. Neuen Testament,* 3d ed. [1953], 12:50f.).

The Church Fathers

The "laughter on Easter Day" *(risus paschalis)* after the proclamation of the priest that Christ is risen indeed is attested for the Eastern church in late antiquity and in the Western church in the early Middle Ages. It can be understood as an apotropaic rite (Dölger 85) but also as a pagan rite surviving in a Christian form (J. Grimm, *Deutsche Mythologie,* 4th ed. [1876], 65; another interpretation is given by Fluck, "*Risus*," 207f.; see also E. Fehrle, *Zeitschrift für Volkskunde,* n.s., 2 [1930]: 1–7). We know of other Christian rituals involving laughter and merriment (see Basil. *Serm.* 14 = *PG* 31.445). Derision, sarcasm, and satire are used as weapons not only in the polemic between Christianity and paganism but also within the Christian context against heretics (Irenaeus *Haer.* 1.11.4, 1.13.2, etc.). The jokes of the church fathers (which ought to be collected; cf. Campenhausen, "Witz," 189; Tsananas 258–79) almost always have a polemic point. They attack all forms of games and entertainments in the pagan tradition, especially the mime, the pantomime, the theater, even instrumental music. Only for Terence's comedies is an exception made, because of their educational value (H. Marti, "Zeugnisse zur Nachwirkung des Dichters Terenz im Altertum," in *Musa iocosa* 170). The exuberant merrymaking of pagan festivals is frowned on (see Chr. Gnilka, *Rhein. Mus.* 109 [1966]: 84 n. 1) but not strictly avoided (Dihle 39–54). Sarcasm and irony are the main forms of humor in Tertullian's writings (see K. Holl, *Gesammelte Aufsätze zur Kirchengeschichte* 1 [1928]: 32–38; W. Süss, *Der hl. Hieronymus und die Formen seiner Polemik,* Giessener Beiträge z. Deutschen Philol. 60 [1938], 214f., 230f.; Fredouille 143–58). In *De Monogamia* 16 he ridicules the sensualists who recommend a second marriage because the flesh is so weak. He recognizes the value of humor in polemic confrontations (*Adv. Val.* 2): "When you laugh here and there, you only do justice to your cause; there are some things that deserve no other refutation." Even play on words may serve a polemical purpose; thus, Justin (*Apol.* 2.3) calls the Cynic Crescens a φιλόψοφος and φιλόκομψος, since he was not worthy of being called φιλόσοφος. A specimen of rather coarse humor is cited by O. Kresten ("Die 'Häretikerin' Simplikia: Ep. 115 des Basileios von Kaisareia in Wiener Handschriften," *Cod. Manuscr.* 6 [1980]: 41–58). In the *Shepherd of Hermas* there is a praise of "serenity," ἱλαρότης (*Mand.* 10.2.6–31), a theme which has been derived from paganism (M. Dibelius, in *Die Apostolischen Väter*, vol. 4 = Handbuch z. Neuen Testament, Ergänzungs-Bd. [1923], 534). On the other hand, pseudo-Cyprian (*Singul. Cler.* 26) declares that laughter is akin to sensuality and that the apostles never laughed. A specific system of ethics related to humor is designed by Clement of Alexandria (*Paedag.* 2.5.45–48; see Campenhausen, "Heiterkeit," 435; Steidle, 271–78; M. Pohlenz, "Klemens von Alexandria und sein hellenisches Christentum," in *Nachrichten Götting. Gel. Ges.* [1943], no. 3, p. 130). Clement's whole chapter must be seen within the context of the whole work: it offers instructions for the young Christian from a good family on how to behave properly in society. The Hellenistic philosophers had established such rules. In the Bible, as one might expect, there are only hints here and there. Clement wishes to fill this gap by borrowing mainly from Musonius Rufus, the Stoic, and from Philo, the Platonist, but also from Plato and Aristotle. Some points of view are especially important, for example, τὸ ἀστεῖον, τὸ εὔσχημον, ἡ σεμνότης. In book 2 he deals with eating and drinking, dishes and furniture, symposia, laughter, obscene talk, social life in general, sleep, reproduction, extravagance in clothes, shoes, jewelry; topics treated in book 3 include bathing, cosmetics, and sport. This more or less covers the areas in which proper behavior and a civilized lifestyle counted. As the background, we must imagine a major city of the Roman Empire in which pagan culture is still alive, although many prominent citizens were Christians. As far as humor is concerned, Clement gives the following guidelines: Professional jesters should be banished; to imitate them is reprehensible. People who tend to laugh and joke too much cannot be respected and trusted, because they dishonor the λόγος. It is all right to be χαρίεις, but not to be γελωτοποιός. Laughter must be restrained in order to reflect the inner κοσμιότης. What is natural to human beings—and laughter is something natural (cf. *Strom.* 8.21.1, following Aristot. *Part. an.* 3.10.673a8)—should be not completely suppressed but kept under control and always adjusted to the καιρός. Just because man is able to laugh does not mean that he should laugh all the time; after all, a horse does not neigh continuously. It is important to relax, but relaxation should be moderate and proportionate (κόσμιος ἄνεσις). A smile is the laughter of the philosopher; harlots giggle (κιχλισμός), and the pretenders guffaw raucously (an allusion to Hom. *Od.* 18.100). The smart man smiles silently; the fool laughs heartily (an allusion to Sir. 21:20). One's face should not be gloomy, but one should not smile at the wrong moment or laugh in the presence of elderly gentlemen, unless they jest themselves, in order to "create a relaxed atmosphere." For women and young men, laughter is ὄλισθος εἰς διαβολάς. A serious face discourages tempters. One should be especially careful when drinking wine. Obscene talk (jokes) must be avoided under all circumstances (*Paed.* 2.6.49–52). The same is true for mockery and derision (*Paed.* 2.6.53). A Christian ideal of merriment with moderation is formulated by Minucius Felix (*Oct.* 31.5): *nec indulgemus epulis aut convivium mero ducimus, sed gravitate hilaritatem temperamus casto sermone, corpore castiore* (see O. Hiltbrunner, "Vir gravis; Sprachgeschichte und Wortbedeutung," in *Festschr. A. Debrunner,* [1954], 207). In his polemic, Jerome makes use of jokes, irony, and play on words (see Wiesen; I. Opelt, *Hieronymus' Streitschriften* [1973]). He talks affectionately of Nepotian, a priest who died young, whom he praises for the way in which he combined humor and gravity (*Epist.* 60.10): *gravitatem morum hilaritate frontis temperabat; gaudium risu, non cachinno intellegeres.* There are testimonies of ecstatic devotion in the monastic life (Michel 412): it found its expression in *laetitia, gaudium, exultatio* (perhaps in the spirit of the Song of Songs), but it might also happen that demons provoked monks to laughter in order to control them (*Vita Pachom.* G¹19 Halkin; A.J. Festugière, *Moines d'orient,* chap. 4, para. 2 [1965], 168). Frivolous laughter is not appropriate for nuns (*Vita Melan.* 23 = *Sources Chrétiennes* 90:176; cf. also A. Guillaumont, "Le rire, les larmes et l'humour chez les moines d'Egypte," in *Hommages à F. Daumas* [1986], 2:373–80; P. Devos, "De 'légers sourires' chez les Pères du désert de Pallade," *Analecta Bollandiana* 105 [1987]: 279). Palladius trades jokes with John of Lycopolis, the ascete (*Hist. Laus.* 35 Butler); and in the *Collationes Patrum* we find precepts for the conduct of life that are full of irony and wisdom and a deep understanding, tinged with humor, for human weaknesses (see H. Waddell, *The Desert Fathers* [1936], 21). Augustine's sense of humor expresses itself in the letters written in his youth (one must distinguish, with Campenhausen ["Heiterkeit," 435], between the young and the old Augustine) and in his sermons, for example, in the homilies on the Gospel according to John (F. van der Meer, *Augustinus der Seelsorger* [1958], 435–56; P. Brown, *Augustine of Hippo* [1967], 253f.). He advises the catechetes to tell a funny story when they see that their students are yawning (*Catech. Rud.* 13.19), and occasionally he uses the expression *ioco dictum* (e.g., *Retract.* 1.1.2, 1.3.2, etc.). Martyrs sometimes laugh (see *Passio Cassiani* 345 Ruinart; Euseb. *Hist. eccl.* 8.9.5; *Passio Philippi* 13 (163 Franchi de' Cavalieri). John Chrysostom (*Hom. in Hebr.* 15.4 = *PG* 63.121f.) condemns laughter in church: "Whenever someone makes a witty remark, the people who sit there at once begin to laugh, and—what is astonishing— many do not stop laughing even during the prayer" (see F. van der Paverd, "Zur Geschichte der Messliturgie in Antiocheia und Konstantinopel gegen Ende des 4. Jahrh.," *Or. Chr. Anal.* 187 [1970]: 445). (On Gnosis and Manichaeism see *Act. Joh.* 102 [*Acta Apostolorum Apocrypha* 2.1.102], and for the "Great Greek Formula of Forswearing," see A. Adam, *Texte zum Manichäismus,* 2d ed. [1969], 99, 73–76.)

Conclusion

The role of humor and merriment in Christianity is not too obvious. It seems that there is a break between the new and the old. The fairly coherent and uniform pagan lifestyle is discontinued. On the one hand, the gospel of Jesus Christ is the "good news"; on the other hand, the new religion demands from the faithful a seriousness which is alien to the "heitere Götterglauben" of paganism. It would be wrong to say that Christianity took a hostile attitude toward humor from the beginning; it would be more appropriate to say that it confined humor within certain limits. The difference between smiling and laughing became important. Wit and humor had their place in popular sermons and in Christian education; they were used as weapons in the fight against pagans and heretics, just as they were the weapons in the conflicts between the various philosophical schools, for example, the Stoics and the Epicureans. Ultimately, humor can mean for Christians not to take themselves too seriously. It is also a way of recognizing one's neighbors and appreciating them. In a sense, humor can even be called an aspect of humility, and it is related to a kind of cheerfulness and inner joy that has its roots in faith.

Bibliography

Albrecht, M. v. "Ovids Humor." *Der altsprachliche Unterricht* 6, no. 2 (1962): 47–72.

Antony, H. *Humor in der augusteischen Dichtung.* 1976.

Apelt, O. "Ueber Platons Humor." *Neue Jahrbücher* 10 (1907): 247–66. Reprinted in *Platonische Aufsätze* (1912), 72–95.

Arndt, E. "De ridiculi doctrina rhetorica." Diss., Bonn, 1904.

Bergson, H. *Das Lachen.* 2d ed. 1920.

Bonhöffer, A. *Epiktet und die Stoa.* 1890.

———. *Die Ethik des Stoikers Epiktet.* 1894.

Bonner, R.J. "Wit and Humor in Athenian Courts." *Class. Philol.* 17 (1922): 97–103.

Braun, H.S. "Humor." In *Lexikon für Theologie und Kirche,* 2d ed., 5: 536. 1960.

Campenhausen, H. v. "Die Heiterkeit der Christen." *Zeitwende/Die neue Furche* 27 (1956): 239–46. Reprinted in *Tradition und Leben* (1960), 431–40.

———. "Ein Witz des Apostels Paulus und die Anfänge des christlichen Humors." In *Neutestamentliche Studien: Festschrift für R. Bultmann, Zeitschrift für Neutestamentliche Wissenschaft* 21, 2d ed. 189–93. 1957. Reprinted in *Aus der Frühzeit des Christentums* (1963), 102–8.

———. "Christentum und Humor." *Theologische Rundschau* 27 (1961): 65–82. Reprinted in *Aus der Frühzeit des Christentums* (1963), 308–30.

Clavier, H. "L'ironie dans l'enseignement de Jésus." *Novum Testamentum* 1 (1956): 3–20.

Curtius, E.R. "Die Kirche und das Lachen." *Romanische Forschungen* 53 (1939): 1–17.

———. *Europäische Literatur und lateinisches Mittelalter.* 6th ed. 1967.

Dihle, A. "Zur spätantiken Kultfrömmigkeit." In *Pietas: Festschrift B. Kötting,* Jahrbücher für Antike und Christentum Erg. Bd. 8, 39–54. 1980.

Dölger, F. "Lachen wider den Tod." In *Pisciculi: Festschrift F.J. Dölger,* 80–85. 1939.

Dover, K.J. *Aristophanic Comedy.* 1972.

Duckworth, G.E. *The Nature of Roman Comedy.* 1962.

Fiske, J.C. *Lucilius and Horace.* 1920.

Fluck, H. "Skurrile Riten in griechischen Kulten." Diss., Freiburg i. Br., 1931.

———. "Der *risus paschalis.*" *Archiv für Religionswissenschaft* 31 (1934): 188–212.

Fraccaroli, G. *Per gli umoristi dell'antichità.* 1885.

Fredouille, J.C. *Tertullien et la conversion de la culture antique.* 1972.

Friedländer, P. "Lachende Götter." *Antike* 10 (1934): 209–26.

———. *Studien zur antiken Literatur und Kunst.* 1969.

Goldmann, M.D. "Humour in the Hebrew Bible." *Austral. Bibl. Review* 2 (1952): 2–11.

Grant, M.A. *The Ancient Rhetorical Theories of the Laughable.* University of Wisconsin Studies 21. 1924.

Grönbech, W. *Zeitwende I. Jesus, der Menschensohn.* 1941.

Hewitt, J.W. "Homeric Laughter." *Class. Weekly* 23 (1928): 436–47.

Highet, G. *The Anatomy of Satire.* 1962.

Hoffding, H. *Humor als Lebensgefühl.* 1928.

Horstmann, E.-A. *Ironie und Lebensgefühl bei Theokrit.* Beiträge zur Klass. Philol. 67. 1976.

Hvidberg, F.H. *Weeping and Laughter in the Old Testament.* 1962.

Joepgen, U. "Wortspiele bei Martial." Diss., Bonn, 1967.

Jónsson, J. *Humour and Irony in the New Testament Illuminated by Parallels in Talmud and Midrash.* 1965.

Kretz, L. *Witz, Humor und Ironie bei Jesus.* 1981.

———. *Der Reiz des Paradoxen bei Jesus.* 1983.

Kroll, W. "Der Witz bei Quintilian." *Philologus* 89 (1934): 341–48.

Kuppe, E. "Sachwitz bei Martial." Diss., Bonn, 1972.

Lammermann, K. "Von der attischen Urbanität und ihrer Auswirkung in der Sprache." Diss., Göttingen, 1935.

Leclercq, J. "Humour." In *Dictionary of Christian Spirituality*, 201f. 1982.

Lesky, A. "Griechen lachen über ihre Götter." *Wiener humanistische Blätter* 4 (1961): 30–40.

Lützeler, H. *Ueber den Humor.* 1966.

Mader, M. *Das Problem des Lachens und der Komödie bei Platon.* Tübinger Beiträge zur Altertumswissenschaft 47. 1977.

Meltzer, G. "Dark Wit and Black Humor in Seneca's 'Thystes.' " *Transactions and Proceedings of the American Philol. Ass.* 118 (1988): 309–30.

Michel, O. "Freude." In *Reallexikon für Antike und Christentum*, 8: 348–418. 1975.

Morreal, J., ed. *The Philosophy of Laughter and Humor.* 1978.

Musa iocosa—Arbeiten über Humor und Witz, Komik und Komödie der Antike: Festschrift A. Thierfelder 1974.

Ong, W.J. *The Barbarian Within.* 1962.

Pascal, B. *Oeuvres complètes.* 1954.

Quispel, G. "De humor van Tertullianus." *Nederl. Theol. Tijdschr.* 2 (1948): 280–90.

Radday, Y.T., and A. Brenner, eds. *On Humour and the Comic in the Hebrew Bible.* *Journ. Studies Old Testament* supp. 92. 1990.

Radermacher, L. *Weinen und Lachen.* 2d ed. 1947. Reviewed by H. Herter in *Theologische Zeitschrift* 75 (1950): 600f.

Rapp, A. "The Dawn of Humor." *Classical Journal* 43 (1948): 275–80.

Rengstorf, K.H. "γελάω," "καταγελάω," and "γέλως." In *Theologisches Wörterbuch zum Neuen Testament*, 1: 656–60. 1933.

Rieks, R. "Homo, humanus, humanitas." Diss., Münster, 1967.

Roi, J. *L'humour des Saints.* 1980.

Rosenfeld, F. *Humor in the Early Islam.* 1965.

Saint-Denis, E. de. *Essai sur le rire et le sourire des Latins.* 1965.

Sikes, E.E. "The humour of Homer." *Class. Review* 54 (1940): 121–27.

Soyter, G. *Griechischer Humor von Homer bis heute.* 2d ed. 1961.

Steidle, B. "Das Lachen im alten Mönchtum." *Benediktinische Monatsschrift* 30 (1939): 271–80.

Steiger, L. "Humor." In *Theol. Realenzyklopädie*, 15: 696–701. 1986.

Stinespring, W.F. "Humor." In *Interpreter's Dictionary of the Bible*, 2: 660–62. 1962.

Stoecker, Ch. "Humor bei Petron." Diss., Erlangen, 1969.

Süss, S. "Das Problem des Komischen im Altertum." *Neue Jahrbücher* 45 (1920): 29–45.

———. *Lachen, Komik und Witz in der Antike.* 1969.

Szelest, H. "Humor bei Martial." *Eos* 69 (1981): 293–301.

Thielicke, H. *Das Lachen der Heiligen und der Narren: Nachdenkliches über Witz und Humor.* 1975.

Thierfelder, A., ed. *Philogelos.* Greek text with German trans., introd., and comm. 1968.

Tsananas, G. "Humor bei Basilius dem Grossen." In *Philoxenia: Festschrift B. Kötting*, 258–79. 1980.

Voeltzel, R. *Le rire du Seigneur.* 1955. Translated into German under the title *Das Lachen des Herrn* (1961).

Vries, G.J. de *Spel bij Plato.* 1949.

Vulgarakis, E. *Das spöttische Duell zwischen Heiden und Christen.* 1972.

Walle, B. van de. *L'humour dans la littérature et dans l'art de l'ancienne Egypte.* 1969.

Wiesen, D. *St. Jerome as a Satirist.* Cornell Studies in Class. Philology 34. 1964.

Zinn, E. "Elemente des Humors in augusteischer Dichtung." *Gymnasium* 67 (1960): 41–56, 152–55.

———. "Humor." In *Artemis Lexikon der Alten Welt,* 1337–39. 1965.

Index of Greek Words

Index of Latin Words

Index of Ancient Texts and Passages

III. Hebrew and Others

Index of Names and Subjects